More praise for *This Is an Uprising*

"Building a truly mass, nonviolent resistance movement is key to solving the twin crises of climate change and gaping inequality. Thankfully, the dynamics of past uprisings are not some inscrutable mystery—and as Mark and Paul Engler so vividly show here, today's organizers are building on a deep and rich political tradition. As absorbing as it is ambitious, this indispensable book is studded with memorable stories and sharp arguments."
—**Naomi Klein, author of *This Changes Everything* and *The Shock Doctrine***

"Simply outstanding. The success or failure of future campaigns for peace and justice could depend on how many people read this book. Yes, it's that good." —**Stephen Zunes, University of San Francisco**

"If you want to understand the social movements that are erupting all around us, you should be reading the Englers. Their writing is a revelation."
—**Andy Bichlbaum, The Yes Men**

"This is truly an important work. The moments and movements that drive societal change have remained elusive and misunderstood by most, whether pundits, activists, or everyday people consuming the news. In *This Is an Uprising*, Mark and Paul Engler brilliantly unearth, explain, and contextualize the dynamics of breakout mobilizations—both dispelling the popular notion that transformational progress simply arises from historical circumstance, and pushing back on long-held dogma that hinders more successful engineering of people-driven campaigns. For all those who seek to play an effective role in creating social or political change in the modern era, the Englers' book is a must-read."
—**James Rucker, cofounder, ColorOfChange.org and Citizen Engagement Lab**

"This book tells the stories of the mass movements that have made our world and continue to change it, and it tells them with excitement, insight, and hope like few have told them before."
—**Maria Elena Durazo, international union vice president for civil rights, diversity, and immigration, UNITE HERE**

"I love this book. The Englers have written a fresh and exciting addition to the literature of social movements, a page-turner that is both hopeful and practical. . . . We all need to read this now."
—**George Lakey, author, activist, and founder of Training for Change**

"This incredible book gives us the tools we need both to understand this watershed moment in history and to chart a course toward a transformed future. Movement wildfires are starting all around the world. This work connects them in a way that is both inspirational and informational. I believe that we will win, and this book told me how we have before."
—**Umi Selah (formerly known as Phillip Agnew), mission director, Dream Defenders**

"This book could not have arrived at a more critical time. We are at a pivotal moment in history as climate justice, economic justice, racial justice, and immigrant justice movements are building people power with the ability to win. . . . I encourage movement builders to not only read this book, but to read it over and over. The relevance of its lessons in today's world cannot be overstated."
—**Paulina Gonzalez, organizer and executive director, California Reinvestment Coalition**

"This book is the *Rules for Radicals* for a new generation. Mark and Paul Engler have written a defining work on the science of popular movements. It brings clarity and insight to many of major debates that I have experienced firsthand as an organizer in the immigrant rights movement and beyond. A must-read for everyone fighting the battle for justice in this world."
—**Carlos Saavedra, lead trainer, Ayni Institute, and former national coordinator, United We Dream**

THIS
IS AN
UPRISING

THIS IS AN UPRISING

How Nonviolent Revolt Is Shaping the Twenty-first Century

MARK ENGLER

—— AND ——

PAUL ENGLER

NATION
BOOKS
New York

Nation Books is a co-publishing venture of the Nation Institute and the Perseus Books Group.

Books published by Nation Books are available at special discounts for bulk purchases in the United States by corporations, institutions, and other organizations. For more information, please contact the Special Markets Department at the Perseus Books Group, 2300 Chestnut Street, Suite 200, Philadelphia, PA 19103, or call (800) 810-4145, ext. 5000, or e-mail special.markets@perseusbooks.com.

Designed by Jeff Williams

A CIP catalog record for this book is available from the Library of Congress.

ISBN: 978-1-56858-733-2 (HC)
ISBN: 978-1-56858-514-7 (EB)

10 9 8 7 6 5 4 3 2 1

CONTENTS

INTRODUCTION

When Martin Luther King Jr. and a dozen of his top advisors arrived at the Dorchester retreat center near Savannah, Georgia, in early January 1963, the mood of the group was somber. The organizers had just suffered one of their greatest defeats, and they could not afford to fail again. They were about to risk their lives by launching a major series of protests against segregation in one of the most foreboding cities in the American South: Birmingham, Alabama. They resolved that this time they would have a plan to win.[1]

Over the previous year, King's Southern Christian Leadership Conference (SCLC) had been involved in a civil rights campaign in Albany, Georgia—a small city in the southwestern part of the state. There, months of demonstrations resulted in the arrest of more than two thousand participants. Yet, in the end, the national press focused on the reserve and good judgment shown by segregationist city officials. The *New York Times* noted "the deft handling by the police of racial protests" in Albany, while another publication remarked that "not a single racial barrier fell."[2]

At Dorchester, King gathered his inner circle to regroup, reflect, and strategize. Among those in attendance were Ralph Abernathy, King's best friend and spiritual counsel, and Wyatt Tee Walker, the SCLC's thirty-three-year-old executive director. Dorothy Cotton and Andrew Young were also present. Although they were still considered junior staffers in the organization, their influence was rising. Cotton, already a powerful force in the organization's training programs, was one of few women to break into the organization's male-dominated command. For his part, Young served for King as a moderate voice—a counterweight to the leader's more radical advisors. These radicals included James Bevel, a veteran of the militant Student Nonviolent Coordinating Committee (SNCC), who had gained a reputation as an expert in mobilizing students for sit-ins and other high-stakes acts of resistance.[3]

Together, the group reviewed their failure in Albany and mapped their next move. To this end, they began laying the foundation for an audacious scheme that would be implemented over the following months. Today, their strategy is sometimes referred to as the "Birmingham model." But early on, when preparations were known to only a few, the plan was referred to as "Project X," and later "Project C."

The *C* in Project C stood for confrontation.

~

In 1963, Birmingham possessed a well-earned reputation as a bastion of reactionary racism. The homes and offices of local civil rights leaders were so regularly bombed that one prominent black neighborhood was known as "Dynamite Hill." Just a few years before, African American singer Nat King Cole had been attacked during a public performance at the city's Municipal Auditorium, with several members of the white-supremacist North Alabama Citizens' Council rushing the stage and knocking him from his piano bench before security could pull Cole from the melee. The musician pledged that he would never perform in the South again. More recently, after a court order decreed that, as of January 15, 1962, the city's sixty-seven parks and eight public swimming pools would have to be open to persons of all races, public safety commissioner Eugene "Bull" Connor announced that he would simply close the facilities rather than allow black residents to use them.[4]

Aware of the hazardous terrain they were about to enter, King addressed his advisors during one solemn moment of their retreat: "I think everybody here should consider very carefully and decide if he wants to be with this campaign," he said. "I have to tell you that in my judgment, some of the people sitting here today will not come back alive from this campaign. And I want you to think about it."[5]

Despite the dangers, the organizers believed their campaign could produce a major media event that would tap the conscience of the country. Their intent, as King would later write from the confines of Birmingham's city jail, was to "create a situation so crisis-packed" that the too-often-ignored boil of segregation would be opened and all of its "pus-flowing ugliness" exposed "to the light of human conscience and the air of national opinion."[6]

The idea of creating a public crisis was not merely a rhetorical goal for those in the retreat. Nor was the pursuit of nonviolent conflict simply a matter of having the proper moral conviction or spiritual resolve. Project C, as it was conceived at Dorchester and then developed through subsequent months of nuts-and-bolts planning, included detailed calculations. In order to force store owners and city officials to desegregate Birmingham's downtown business district, the campaign would create an ambitious combination of several tactics that had been employed before: the economic pressure leveled against merchants during the Montgomery Bus Boycott, the dramatic lunch-counter sit-ins that had exploded in cities such as Nashville in 1960, the pack-the-jails arrest strategy of Albany. This time, organizers would bring together these tactics to form a multistaged assault that sociologist and civil rights historian Aldon Morris would later dub "a carefully planned exercise in mass disruption."[7]

King assigned Wyatt Walker, a cunning strategist and demanding administrator, to lead the preparations. Mapping the battlefield, Walker timed precisely how long it would take participants to walk from the movement's 16th Street Baptist Church headquarters to the various stores and public facilities selected as the campaign's primary, secondary, and tertiary targets. Likewise, SCLC organizers anticipated the probable legal moves of their opponents, weighing the costs of violating any court injunctions that might be handed down. They calculated the costs of city bail fees and made plans for how long arrested activists should stay in custody before being bailed out—their stay and release timed to best keep the jail cells filled. Walker and others projected the value of the business that would be lost to Birmingham store owners at different levels of boycott effectiveness, and they debated what losses would be convincing enough to make the business leaders remove the "Whites Only" signs from the fitting rooms and drinking fountains in their stores.[8]

The civil rights activists imagined that, with mass protest in Birmingham, they could crack the segregationists' stoutest fortress—and thus open the floodgates for change nationally. If successful, King argued, the campaign "might well set the forces in motion to change the entire course of the drive for freedom and justice."[9]

Before the fact, most people would have considered SCLC's blueprint for confrontation in Birmingham to be outlandish. In January 1963, Martin Luther King Jr. had just turned thirty-four. It had been seven years since the success of the 1956 Montgomery Bus Boycott thrust him onto the national stage. In the time since, both conservative opponents and competing civil rights organizations had raised questions about the efficacy of his leadership. Some foundations that had funded the SCLC were dissatisfied, and the public did not have a clear sense of the organization's direction.

Among those close to King, an awareness of their leader's precarious standing was pervasive. Some undertook measures to compensate. Whereas SCLC staff members typically interacted with one another on a first-name basis, Walker insisted that they call their president "Dr. King" at all times. "This was important because he was so young—and looked younger," writes Andrew Young. "If we didn't show him an exaggerated respect, the concern was that others would not show it to him either."[10]

Beyond the questions about King's leadership, the very idea that a mass public "crisis" could be engineered—that a major uprising could emerge not as an unstructured product of an era's zeitgeist but as a planned effort—was a suspect notion. Social movements in general were not held in high regard, and scholars of the time doubted nonviolent resistance in particular. They considered Gandhi's example in India to have little application in a country like the United States, and they did not expect the success of the Montgomery Bus Boycott to be replicated. In May 1963, Wyatt Walker explained in a speech in San Francisco:

> It was interesting to note that sociologists and some prophets of doom said of Montgomery, "Well, this is just one of those sociological freaks, a phenomenon that will never happen again. Nonviolence can't have its effect in America because we're too Westernized. Our chromium-plated push button society won't take it." Or, "This discipline comes out of an Eastern culture where people are meditative and reflective and we're too busy ripping and running, trying to make a living."[11]

In the wake of the Albany debacle, members of the national media were "pronouncing that the direct-action phase of the civil rights movement was over," Andrew Young notes.[12]

And yet, when the Birmingham campaign was finally launched on April 3, 1963, the careful calculations of Project C were proven sound. Within just six weeks, the tensions simmering in Birmingham had exploded into an event that made headlines across the country. As historian Michael Kazin argues, the scenes of police dogs snapping at unarmed demonstrators and water cannons being opened on student marchers "convinced a plurality of whites, for the first time, to support the cause of black freedom."[13]

Popular versions of the Birmingham story, which tend to focus only on the campaign's climax, often skip over the preparations that began at Dorchester. But the implications of such planning are very important. The landmark civil rights uprising that took so much of the country by surprise was no sociological freak. Nor was it happenstance that a clash with segregationists put the normally hidden injustices of racism on stark public display, prompting a stunned Northern media to spread outrage nationally. To the contrary, these were the consequence of a premeditated strategy of conflict.

And it was not the last time that a strategy of this kind would be put to use.

～

"Spontaneous." "Unplanned." "Uncontrolled." "Emotional."

Whether it is a rush of resistance to dictatorship throughout the Middle East, the explosion of protests against corporate power in cities such as Seattle, a province-wide student revolt in Quebec, a million people spilling into the streets of Los Angeles to demand immigrant rights, a call for new elections in a former Soviet republic, an encampment on Wall Street that gives rise to hundreds of tent cities across the United States and beyond, or an insistent cry that #BlackLivesMatter, the perception is the same: when mass movements burst onto our television screens, the media portrays them as being as sudden and unmanageable as a viral epidemic or a prairie thunderstorm.

In 2011—a year that featured the Arab Spring, mass antiausterity demonstrations throughout Europe, and the emergence of the Occupy movement—*Time* magazine described those uprisings as "leaderless, amorphous, and spontaneous." The *Washington Post* wrote of the wave of Middle Eastern protest as something that "spread like a virus" and "hits each country in a different and uncontrollable way." And, according to the *New York Times*, the surge of citizen resistance was "beyond the scope of any intelligence services to predict."[14]

Such characterizations, as it turns out, are not unusual. In 1999, when students and labor unions in Serbia challenged the regime of Slobodan Milosevic, the press commented on work stoppages "accompanied by spontaneous acts of civil disobedience across the country." The *Moscow Times* wrote that the 2004 Orange Revolution in the Ukraine, a reaction to corruption and electoral fraud, "was, at its core, a spontaneous, emotional outburst by the Ukrainian people." In 2006, when immigrant-led marches brought hundreds of thousands of people onto the streets of American cities, the *Washington Post* described it as "a spontaneous groundswell of activism."[15]

Regarding the civil rights movement, Aldon Morris has pointed to the commonly held view that protesters were "reacting blindly to uncontrollable forces" and that the lunch-counter sit-ins "were a spontaneous collegiate phenomenon." Indeed, the historical record is full of such depictions.[16]

But what if periods of mass, spontaneous uprising are neither as spontaneous nor as unbridled as they might at first appear? What if the fits of social change that burst into our headlines like flash storms can actually be forecast? What if one can read the clouds and understand their signs?

Or what if, in fact, it is possible to influence the weather?

∾

For Martin Luther King Jr. and the SCLC organizers, the confrontation in Birmingham proved to be a tremendous boon—a validation of their belief that widespread, purposeful, nonviolent disruption could change the course of national politics. Victory in that city sent ripples throughout the country: in the two and a half months after they announced a settlement with Birmingham storeowners to begin desegregation, more than 750 civil rights protests took place in 186 American cities, leading to almost fifteen thousand arrests.[17] And less than a year and a half after the SCLC's campaign had commenced, President Lyndon Johnson signed into law the landmark Civil Rights Act of 1964.

But this reversal of fortune leaves unanswered a crucial question: Why did Birmingham succeed while the attempted effort to end Jim Crow discrimination in Albany had so badly, so tragically, and so recently failed?

The problem in the thwarted Albany drive was not a lack of creative tactics. Like the Birmingham campaign, the movement took an innovative approach to combining sit-ins, boycotts, marches, mass arrests, and legal action. Albany was, in fact, notable for being the first time the civil rights movement deployed the full range of weapons in its arsenal of civil resistance. King would dub Albany "the most creative utilization" of nonviolent protest to date.[18]

And yet, despite this level of tactical sophistication, few could deny that the effort fell short. Even King—who publicly tried to put a positive spin on the Albany movement—acknowledged that, after more than a year of protest, "the people were left very depressed and in despair." A regional director for the National Association for the Advancement of

Colored People (NAACP) was more blunt: "Albany was successful," the staffer quipped, "only if the objective was to go to jail."[19]

Many factors played a part in the failure. In Albany, the SCLC had been drawn into a conflict it did not create. Local activists had already begun a diffuse, broad-based attack on the segregationist power structure without adequately analyzing their opponents' weaknesses. As the NAACP's backbiting comments suggest, there was rampant rivalry among civil rights organizations, with groups, including SNCC, allowing their disagreements with King and his staff to go public. Savvy city authorities, led by the personable and restrained police chief Laurie Pritchett, were able to make just enough arrests to quell dissent without overflowing their jails or overwhelming their police forces.

All of these factors contributed to a catastrophe. But together they pointed to a more fundamental problem: in Albany there was no clear plan for how to use the steady escalation of nonviolent conflict to make the pressure on racist structures unbearable. Missing was an overarching framework through which acts of personal sacrifice could be channeled into a concerted effort to increase tension and break the back of segregation at its weakest point. With Birmingham, that had changed.

~

"There is no tactical theory so neat that a revolutionary struggle for a share of power can be won merely by pressing a row of buttons," King wrote in a perceptive reflection after Albany. "Human beings with all their faults and strengths constitute the mechanism of a social movement. They must make mistakes and learn from them, make more mistakes and learn anew."[20]

No magic formula exists for ousting Jim Crow or overthrowing a dictator. The dynamics of nonviolent conflict are subtle and complex. And, certainly, there is an element of unpredictability in any given mass mobilization. Yet Project C is part of a tradition that has sought to study, map, and apply the principles of an underappreciated art that is becoming one of the most influential forces in the world today—the art of unarmed uprising.

This book is the story of that art. It is about the type of strategizing that went into creating Project C and about why the architects of nonviolent upheaval in Birmingham thought their plan for escalation could work. It is about the decades-long tradition of experimentation that led up to Project C and about how the lessons from that tradition have continued to be refined in the years since, contributing to landmark social justice victories. Finally, it is about why the tradition of nonviolent action may yet reshape political life in the coming century.

This book is concerned with a specific phenomenon: momentum-driven mass mobilization. It contends that those who have most carefully studied these mobilizations—examining how to construct and sustain scenarios of widespread protest—come out of a tradition of strategic nonviolence. It argues that political observers watching the democratic upheavals of the twenty-first century should incorporate this tradition's insights into their understanding of how social transformation happens. Those wishing to bring such upheavals into existence, meanwhile, do well to marry these insights with their existing approaches to leveraging change.

Nonviolence is often written off as obsolete, an idea that has been mostly forgotten and is largely irrelevant in global affairs. Yet, every time it is cast aside, strategic nonviolent action seems to reassert itself as a historic force. Without taking up weapons, and with little money and few traditional resources, people forming nonviolent movements succeed in upending the terms of public debate and shifting the direction of their countries' politics. Nonviolence in this form is not passive. It is a strategy for confrontation.

Decade after decade, unarmed mobilizations have created defining moments. In the United States, these include the sit-down strikes in Michigan auto plants in the 1930s, the antiwar and campus free-speech movements of the 1960s, the welfare and women's rights protests of the 1970s, the nuclear freeze campaigns and AIDS activism of the 1980s, direct action to protect old-growth forests and oppose corporate globalization in the 1990s, and demonstrations against the Iraq War in the early years of the new century. Internationally, strategic nonviolent conflict has been critical in helping to overthrow undemocratic rulers in a litany of countries, from Chile and Poland, to the Philippines and Serbia, to Benin and Tunisia.

When such outbreaks occur, they sometimes feel like whirlwinds of activity—rare and exceptional intrusions upon the norms of daily politics. They seem to be once-in-a-lifetime events. But, curiously, once you start looking for them, these once-in-a-lifetime uprisings start to appear constantly, in diverse forms and unexpected places. The year 2011, which saw the Arab Spring and the rise of the Occupy movement, was a time of peak activity. But the pace has only somewhat relented. Since then, eruptions of mass resistance have burst forth in Mexico, Turkey, Brazil, and Hong Kong, to cite just a few of the most prominent international cases. Within the United States, major demonstrations around climate change have taken place, and bold protests against racism and police brutality coalesced under the banner of #BlackLivesMatter.

The principles of momentum-based organizing sometimes seep into electoral politics. This was the case with the drive that coalesced in 2008 around a young senator, Barack Obama—an effort that borrowed grassroots mobilizing techniques from social movements and ended up astonishing those familiar with the typical practices of presidential races. On a smaller scale, momentum-driven campaigns have been used to make living wages for service workers a defining issue on college campuses and to fill state capitols with demonstrators demanding resignations from disgraced public officials. In instances where countless reports, exposés, and congressional speeches have failed, nonviolent conflict has succeeded in taking disregarded injustices and bringing them to the fore of popular consciousness.

∽

That most pundits have little to say about social movement eruptions, no matter how often they seize the spotlight, reflects a bias in their thinking about how social change happens. The same analysts who invariably describe waves of unarmed revolt as spontaneous and uncontrolled spend endless hours speculating on which candidates might enter into elections that are still years away. They closely track developments in Congress, in the courts, and in the White House. They carefully study the arts of electioneering, lobbying, and legislative deal making—processes that dominate public understanding of US politics and that are shaped by elite values and practices. In doing so, they appeal to realism. This is how the system works, they tell us. This is how the sausage gets made.

But is this really how change happens? Many of the critical advances of the last century and a half—the end of slavery, women's suffrage, the restriction of child labor and implementation of workplace safety standards, and the outlawing of many forms of discrimination—owe less to the legislative endgame that formalized acceptance of these causes and much more to the social movements that put them on the map. Likewise, on the international scene, an increasing number of unelected leaders have ceded power not as a result of traditional diplomacy or military maneuvering. Instead, they were ousted through the demands of unarmed mass mobilizations.

As important as it has proven itself, the strategic application of nonviolent force is poorly understood. Nonviolence is usually regarded as a philosophy or moral code. Much less frequently is it studied as a method of political conflict, disruption, and escalation. This is a missed opportunity. If we are perpetually surprised by unarmed uprising, if we decline to incorporate it into our view of how societies progress, then we pass up the chance to understand a critical phenomenon—and to harness its power.

∾

For King, Birmingham was a revelation. Although the Montgomery Bus Boycott had been his baptism into mass action, he would write that it was only in watching marchers defy Bull Connor's menacing troops that he felt, "for the first time, the pride and power of nonviolence." Project C provided him with an epiphany about doing politics differently—for acting outside the bounds of traditional elections and lobbying and also outside the methodologies of conventional community or church-based organizing. It altered King's life as a public figure, and it changed the way he saw the possibilities for social transformation within his lifetime.[21]

Over the past century, many others have had similar revelations. Experiencing the disruptive power of a major mobilization, they have decided to stop being surprised by waves of mass protest—to stop re-garding these uprisings as uncontrollable sociological curiosities—and to start paying closer attention to their dynamics. These activists and scholars have become interested in examining how nonviolence works, and not simply as a moral philosophy. Some of them have sought to use strategies of nonviolent confrontation to provoke and guide moments of widespread citizen action.

As King cautioned, there is no neat row of buttons that can be pushed to oust Jim Crow or overthrow a dictator; the dynamics of non-violent conflict are subtle and complex. Yet it is possible, as organizers in Birmingham insisted, to create situations so crisis-packed that long-ignored injustices are forced into the public spotlight. It is possible, as Aldon Morris asserted, to create planned exercises in mass disruption.

The course of strategic nonviolence's development runs through many biographies. In part, it is a story of personal epiphanies. It con-cerns how a young Mohandas Gandhi, inspired by Tolstoy, put aside the training he had received as a lawyer to embrace a different type of action, a form of collective resistance that he saw as more powerful than the filing of petitions. It involves a scholar, Gene Sharp, initially im-mersed in the pacifist tradition, who discovered that nonviolence need not merely be a personal credo followed by a small community of peo-ple who reject all war but rather is something that can be adopted much more widely as a pragmatic weapon of struggle. And it is about Judi Bari, a feminist and union veteran, who reshaped the struggle to save California's redwoods—bringing a new set of tactics to a radical envi-ronmental movement whose culture had been defined by an ethic of cowboy machismo.

Whether mass mobilizations are spearheaded by high-profile lead-ers or are propelled by people who go unheralded and unnamed in the history books, they can have a transformative impact on those who ex-perience them. When people discover momentum-driven organizing as a new mode of action, it can fundamentally change how they ap-proach some of the most basic questions of politics: How do you start a campaign, and how do you frame a demand for change? How do you respond to repression by the state, and how do you interact with the media? How can groups exploit the energy of an event that unexpectedly triggers a wave of interest in their cause, and when must they buckle down and institutionalize past gains? When is the right time for movements to declare victory, and what are the lasting changes that can result from their efforts?

The body of knowledge about strategic nonviolence that exists today has been passed between generations and honed over decades of trial and error. At times, this process has been disjointed and unruly. Activists on different continents and in different decades have independently reinvented key principles for guiding mass action, drawing on diverse political traditions and sources of inspiration. Many have acted with limited planning, and too rarely have they documented their learning. The creation of Project C was one occasion when those experimenting in nonviolence took time to map out key aspects of their strategy. Other instances of codification and reflection have occurred independently in movements throughout the world. Although haphazard, each represents a step forward in the collective accumulation of knowledge about the art of unarmed uprising.

Yet even as this slow accretion of knowledge has progressed informally for more than a century, it has recently been supplemented by a much more deliberate type of training and study. In an intriguing turn, a group of scholars and activists has decided that the development of strategic nonviolent conflict is vital enough that it should not be left to circumstance. And they have mobilized to do something about it.

Their story starts with a figure known as the Machiavelli of nonviolence.

CHAPTER ONE

THE STRATEGIC TURN

IN THE STRANGE world of Internet bookmakers, it is possible to bet on almost anything—and that includes the question of who will next win the Nobel Peace Prize. Given the arcane and secretive politics surrounding the prize, predicting a winner is always chancy. However, over the past several years, one of the odds-makers' favorite picks has not been a head of state, a major nongovernmental organization, nor a charismatic resistance leader but rather a soft-spoken Boston academic in his eighties. His name is Gene Sharp.

In 1953, when Gene Sharp was a twenty-five-year-old war resister, one of his proudest possessions was a letter from Albert Einstein. At the time, Sharp, the son of an itinerant Protestant minister in Ohio, had recently finished a master's degree in sociology at Ohio State University. He moved to New York City with a plan to write a book about Mohandas Gandhi. However, he soon found himself in a federal detention center, arrested for refusing to cooperate with the Korean War draft.

Before going to trial, Sharp struck up a correspondence with Einstein, who had gained renown as a peace activist in his later years. Einstein wrote to the young pacifist: "I earnestly admire you for your moral strength and can only hope, although I really do not know, that I would have acted as you did had I found myself in your situation." Sharp ultimately served nine months and ten days in prison in Danbury,

Connecticut, for draft resistance, a stint he regarded at the time as an important political stand.[1]

Decades later, he had a very different view of his solitary act of defiance. "I don't think it did a damned thing to get rid of the war system," Sharp told one interviewer. In 2010, he stated that his stand had been utterly ineffectual, except "in keeping my sense of personal integrity together."[2]

Over the years, Sharp had not given up on the idea of nonviolent action. But he had gone through a sort of conversion—one that would shape his career and ultimately reverberate through social movements in dozens of countries. His understanding of nonviolence had become anything but ineffectual.

Today, Sharp is known as a theorist and author of seminal works on the dynamics of nonviolent conflict. In addition to the "Machiavelli of nonviolence," he has been called the "dictator slayer" and the Clausewitz of unarmed revolution. His circumstances are humble: he runs his research outfit, known as the Albert Einstein Institution, out of the ground floor of his row house in East Boston, and the organization has just one other staffer. For the most part, Sharp has labored for decades in quiet obscurity—well respected within a small field of study but virtually unknown outside of it.

At the same time, Sharp's work has had an unusually broad impact. His pamphlet *From Dictatorship to Democracy*, a ninety-three-page distillation of his core teachings and a handbook for overthrowing autocrats, has been translated into more than thirty languages. The slim volume has a habit of turning up in hot spots of global resistance. Originally written in 1993 to help dissidents in Burma use nonviolent action against the ruling military junta, the book became a valued possession of Serbian students seeking to overthrow the regime of Slobodan Milosevic. It circulated among activists during uprisings in Georgia and the Ukraine in 2003 and 2004. And it was downloaded in Arabic amid mass protests in Tunisia and Egypt in 2011.

The Iranian government has denounced the book and its author by name. In the summer of 2005, two independent bookshops in Russia were burned down after stocking the newly available Russian translation of Sharp's pamphlet on their shelves. ("I still keep a half-burned copy on a shelf in my office," one opposition leader told the *Wall Street Journal*.)[3] Particularly after the Arab Spring, Sharp's renown has grown. He was the subject of a feature documentary, entitled *How to Start a Revolution*, released just as the Occupy movement was taking shape in 2011.

The conversion that Sharp underwent not long after his stint as a draft resister—the epiphany that would guide his later research and teaching—revolved around a simple idea: that nonviolence should not be simply a moral code for a small group of true believers to live by. Rather, Sharp came to argue that nonviolent conflict should be understood as a political approach that can be employed strategically, something that social movements can choose because it provides an effective avenue for leveraging change. Out of this principle has emerged the modern study of "civil resistance," devoted to understanding how unarmed social movements are able to stage uprisings of dramatic consequence.

The conversion experienced by Sharp was a consequential one. Yet it is not altogether uncommon within the history of nonviolent social movements. Over the past century, many great innovators have arrived at the same conclusion: nonviolence must be wedded to strategic mass action if it is to have true force in the world. Martin Luther King Jr., born within a year of Sharp in the late 1920s, was one of those innovators. In King's case, it would take years of political evolution to fully appreciate the use of nonviolent conflict as a means of political struggle and to commit to schemes such as Project C. But, in the end, it was his mastery of this technique—not merely his personal courage or spiritual conviction—that would secure his place in American history.

∽

Gene Sharp spent the first years of his political life immersed in a mainstream current of the pacifist tradition, and he has spent much of the rest of his career declaring independence from it. Upon his release from prison in 1954, Sharp worked briefly as an assistant to prominent radical pacifist A. J. Muste. He then contributed to the weekly publication *Peace News* in England before moving to Oslo and researching how teachers during World War II successfully used nonviolent tactics to resist the imposition of fascist schooling in Norway. His investigations into nonviolence would ultimately lead to a doctorate at Oxford and to a nine-hundred-page treatise called *The Politics of Nonviolent Action*, published in 1973. Widely regarded as a classic, the work remains in print and is available in a three-volume edition.

By the time he had published this work, Sharp had begun to distance himself from the peace groups with which he used to associate. Pacifism—moral opposition to war and violence—has existed for hundreds if not thousands of years and can trace its roots to the core texts of major world religions. These roots continued to show in Sharp's time as a young researcher. Proponents of nonviolence regularly emphasized its moral and spiritual dimensions.[4]

In the 1950s and 1960s, Sharp found himself veering in a different direction. Reading through old newspaper coverage of Gandhi's 1930 resistance campaign in India, he made a troubling discovery, one that he considered omitting from his writing. He found evidence that most participants in that *satyagraha,* as Gandhi called the campaign of defiance, did not embrace nonviolence out of a sense of moral commitment. Instead, they chose to employ nonviolent struggle because they believed it worked. The discovery was troubling for Sharp because it contradicted the cherished convictions of many people he knew—adherents to what is now known as "principled nonviolence"—who believed that the practice requires deep ethical resolve. As Sharp explained in a 2003 interview, he puzzled over what to do:

> I wondered: Should I put that down? Better just leave it out!
>
> But I put it down. And later it dawned on me that, rather than that being a threat, it was a great opportunity, because it meant that large numbers of people who would *never* believe in ethical or religious nonviolence could use nonviolent struggle for pragmatic reasons.[5]

Sharp's decision to record his discovery altered the trajectory of his research. Ultimately, he would become a leading proponent of the position sometimes known as "strategic nonviolence." While he continued to personally believe in nonviolence as a "philosophy of life," he grew increasingly unconcerned about whether others did. He began arguing to his pacifist colleagues that people turn to war and violence not because they are wicked or hateful. They resort to violence because they do not see any other option for resolving intractable conflicts. It made little sense, he reasoned, to try to win these people over with "moral injunctions against violence and exhortations in favor of love." It was far more fruitful to show how a strategy of nonviolent conflict could be an effective alternative to armed struggle—perhaps even a superior alternative.[6]

In books such as *Gandhi as a Political Strategist*, a collection of essays written between 1959 and 1970, Sharp sought to establish the independence leader not as an otherworldly *mahatma*, but as a shrewd and calculating tactician. He similarly battled the common beliefs that strategic nonviolence somehow involves avoiding conflict and that it can only be used in democracies. Instead, he set out to show that, far from being passive, nonviolent action could be "a technique of struggle involving the use of psychological, social, economic, and political power" and that it can be used even against viciously repressive regimes.[7]

Just like armed struggle, Sharp argued, nonviolent conflict involves the "waging of 'battles,' requires wise strategy and tactics, and demands of its 'soldiers' courage, discipline, and sacrifice." Perhaps for this reason, he has claimed, those with military backgrounds have sometimes been quicker than peace activists to catch on to his ideas. In later years, one of his closest collaborators has been a retired US Army colonel, Robert Helvey, who became fascinated with the inner workings of nonviolent uprisings after seeing Sharp lecture at Harvard.[8]

Sharp's analysis of nonviolent struggle could be notably unflinching. He recognized that if the target of a campaign is a tyrannical regime, repression can be severe. "There must be no illusions," he wrote. "In some cases nonviolent people have not only been beaten and cruelly treated but killed . . . in deliberate massacres." Nor did Sharp promise success: "The simple choice of nonviolent action as the technique of struggle," he explained, "does not and cannot guarantee victory, especially on a short-term basis."[9]

That said, Sharp documented how unarmed uprisings could produce remarkable and sometimes counterintuitive results. Whereas violent rebellions play to the strengths of dictatorships—which are deft at suppressing armed attacks and using security challenges to justify the creation of a police state—nonviolent action often catches these regimes off guard. Through what Sharp calls "political jiu-jitsu," social movements can turn repression into a weakness for those in power. Violent crackdowns against unarmed protests end up exposing the brutality of a ruling force, undermining its legitimacy, and, in many cases, creating wider public unwillingness to cooperate with its mandates. Niccolò Machiavelli recognized this dynamic as early as the 1500s. Of the leader who seeks to impose his rule on a mass of hostile people, he wrote: "the greater his cruelty, the weaker does his regime become."[10]

For Sharp, nonviolent efforts could not be limited to acts of noble sacrifice. They needed to have real political impact if they were to be worthwhile. And this insistence on effectiveness was another way in which he broke with previous traditions of pacifism and principled nonviolence.

Earlier strains of peace activism regularly involved small groups of individuals "bearing witness" or "speaking truth to power." Typical tactics included conscientious objection, war tax resistance, and refusal to participate in air raid drills. Although participants in these actions acknowledged that they might appear isolated or quixotic, they prided themselves on setting a positive example for others. Since the Vietnam era, some in this lineage have undertaken more extreme acts of moral witness. Advocates in the Ploughshares Movement and members of the Catholic Worker Movement—founded by Christian pacifists Dorothy Day and Peter Maurin—have attempted to enact the biblical injunction to "beat swords into plowshares." In their opposition to war and nuclear arms, these religious activists have burned draft files, poured blood on the decks of battleships, and crossed onto military facilities with the intent of crippling nuclear missiles by hammering on their nosecones.

Such protests have been imbued with a spirit of moral righteousness, and they have been averse to political calculation. Although participants sometimes faced long jail sentences, they put little emphasis on conceiving of how their bold acts of defiance might advance a concrete strategy for change. A saying popular in Catholic Worker circles summed up the approach: "Jesus never told us to be successful," movement participants would say, "only to be faithful."[11]

If the twenty-five-year-old Gene Sharp, who was willing to spend time in jail as an act of personal conscience against war, might have been sympathetic to such thinking, the Sharp who published *The Politics of Nonviolent Action* two decades later wanted nothing to do with it. In such writing, Sharp repeatedly challenged the notion that good intentions were sufficient to create change. As he wrote in one of his later books, "Feeling good, not engaging in violence, or being willing to die, when you have not achieved the goals of your struggle, does not change the fact that you have failed."[12]

What was remarkable, from Sharp's point of view, was the number of times nonviolent struggle had in fact prevailed, sometimes against hardened opposition. Advocates of principled nonviolence often talked of the goal of "conversion," or winning over the heart of the enemy. Sharp contended that, although such changes of conscience may be desirable, they were not necessary. To win, activists did not need to express love for their adversaries or make hated opponents see the errors of their ways. In fact, insistence on converting the enemy could be counterproductive, Sharp believed. He argued that "the demand for 'love' for people who have done cruel things may turn people who are justifiably bitter and unable to love their opponents towards violence."[13]

Once again, Sharp's perspective would be far more practical. If a dictator can be made to resign through popular protest, the question of how this undemocratic ruler feels about losing his grip on power need not be a main concern of the social movements that compel his ouster. Sharp approvingly quoted civil rights leader James Farmer: "Where we cannot influence the heart of the evil-doer, we can force an end to the evil practice."[14]

Sharp's disagreements with pacifist groups did not end well. The arguments they produced, he reports, were "long and frustrating." When he was unable to make headway, Sharp resolved to chart his own path. As he gained influence as a theorist, he came to eschew the term "nonviolence" altogether, believing that it was too ambiguous and too loaded with connotations of passivity and religious belief. Instead of using the word as a noun, Sharp began employing it only as an adjective, referring to "nonviolent action" or "nonviolent conflict." This would prove an influential move. Recently, some academic researchers studying strategic nonviolence, influenced by Sharp, have made a further break in terminology. They now discuss campaigns of unarmed popular action simply as "civil resistance," a formulation that is notably free of pacifist associations.[15]

～

Unlike Gene Sharp, Martin Luther King Jr. was not shaped early on in the pacifist tradition. King's introduction to nonviolence—both principled and strategic—would be a gradual one.

Few are aware that, as a young preacher, King once sought official license to carry a concealed handgun. In his 2011 book *Gunfight*, UCLA law professor Adam Winkler notes that, after King's house was bombed in 1956, the clergyman applied in Alabama for a concealed carry permit. Local police, loath to grant such permits to African Americans, deemed him "unsuitable" and denied his application. Consequently, King would end up leaving the firearms at home.[16]

The lesson from this incident is not, as some members of the National Rifle Association (NRA) have tried to suggest, that the Nobel Peace Prize winner should be remembered as a gun-toting opponent of firearms regulation. Rather, the fact that King would request license to wear a gun in 1956, just as he was being catapulted onto the national stage, illustrates the profundity of the transformation that he underwent over the course of his public career.[17]

Although this transformation involved an adoption of principled nonviolence and personal pacifism, that is not the whole of the story. More importantly, for those who are interested in how nonviolent campaigns can have political consequence, King's evolution also involved a hesitant but ultimately forceful embrace of direct action: broad-scale, confrontational, and unarmed. Just as Sharp's conversion would profoundly impact how nonviolence is studied, King's developing appreciation for the strategic dimensions of nonviolent conflict would have lasting consequence for how it is put into practice.

The campaign that first established King's national reputation, the 1956 Montgomery Bus Boycott, was not planned in advance as a Gandhian campaign of nonviolent resistance. At the time, King did not have a clear sense of the strategic principles behind such a campaign. Rather, the bus boycott came together quickly following the arrest of Rosa Parks in late 1955, taking inspiration from a similar action in Baton Rouge in 1953.

Still a relative newcomer to Montgomery, King was elected by his fellow ministers and community leaders as the president of the Montgomery Improvement Association, formed at the start of the boycott to oversee the campaign. He was chosen in part because he was not identified with any of the established factions among the city's prominent blacks. King was surprised by his selection and reluctant to assume his new role and its burdens. Indeed, the risks were considerable: soon he was receiving phone calls on which unidentified voices warned, "Listen, nigger, we've taken all we want from you. Before next week you'll be sorry you ever came to Montgomery." After such threats resulted in the bombing of King's home in February 1956, armed watchmen guarded against further assassination attempts.[18]

At this point, King's embrace of the theory and practice of nonviolent action was still tentative. In his talks before mass meetings, King preached the Christian injunction to "love thy enemy." Having read Thoreau in college, he described the bus boycott as an "act of massive noncooperation" and regularly called for "passive resistance." But King did not use the term "nonviolence," and he admitted that he knew little about Gandhi or the Indian independence leader's campaigns. As biographer Taylor Branch notes, out-of-state visitors who were knowledgeable about the principles of unarmed direct action—such as Rev. Glenn Smiley of the Fellowship of Reconciliation and Bayard Rustin of the War Resisters League—reported that King and other Montgomery activists were "at once gifted and unsophisticated in nonviolence."[19]

In a famous incident described by historian David Garrow, Rustin was visiting King's parsonage with reporter Bill Worthy when the journalist almost sat on a pistol. "Watch out, Bill, there's a gun on that chair," the startled Rustin warned. Rustin and King stayed up late that night arguing about whether armed self-defense in the home could end up damaging the movement. Rustin believed it could; King was uncertain.[20]

Although today's NRA members might prefer to forget, it was not long before King came around to the position of Rustin and Smiley, who argued for the removal of the firearms. Smiley would make visits to Montgomery throughout the civil rights leader's remaining four years there, and King's politics would be shaped by many more late-night conversations.[21]

In 1959, at the invitation of the Gandhi National Memorial Fund, King made a pilgrimage to India to study the principles of *satyagraha*. He was moved by the experience. Ultimately, he never embraced the complete pacifism of A. J. Muste, Sharp's former employer; in the Black Power years, King made a distinction between people using guns to defend themselves in the home, on the one hand, and the question of "whether it was tactically wise to use a gun while participating in an organized protest," on the other. But, for himself, King claimed non-violence as a "way of life," and he maintained his resolve under conditions that would make many others falter. Although Southern Christian Leadership Conference (SCLC) staffers, fearing that their leader could be assassinated, often implored police and federal authorities to ensure public safety at civil rights gatherings, King regularly refused to travel with an armed guard, and he showed a sometimes-disturbing acceptance of the idea of that he might someday be killed.[22]

In September 1962, when King was addressing a convention, a two-hundred-pound white man, the twenty-four-year-old American Nazi Party member Roy James, jumped onto the stage and struck the clergyman in the face. King responded with a level of courage that made a lifelong impression on many of those in the audience. One of them, storied educator and activist Septima Clark, described how King dropped his hands "like a newborn baby" and spoke calmly to his attacker. King made no effort to protect himself even as he was knocked backward by further blows. Later, after his aides had pulled the assailant away, King talked to James behind the stage and insisted that he would not press charges.[23]

Believers in pacifism often contend that such principled nonviolence represents the high point in a person's moral evolution. They argue that those who merely use unarmed protest tactically—not because they accept it as an ethical imperative—practice a lesser form of nonviolence. Gandhi advanced this position when he claimed that those who forgo violence for strategic reasons employ the "nonviolence of the weak." King echoed the argument when he wrote that "nonviolence in the truest sense is not a strategy that one uses simply because it is expedient in the moment" but rather is something "men live by because of the sheer morality of its claim."[24]

Despite such admonitions, the opposite case can be made: in holding up King as an icon of individual pacifism, we fail to see his true genius. Like Sharp, the civil rights leader made his greatest impact when he championed campaigns of widespread disruption and collective sacrifice.

In time, Martin Luther King Jr. would embrace strategic nonviolence in its most robust and radical form, and this stance produced the historic confrontations at Birmingham and Selma. But it is important to remember that these events came years after his baptism into political life in Montgomery and that they might easily not have happened at all.

Following the success of the Bus Boycott, King sought out ways to spread the Montgomery model throughout the South. He knew there were strategists who had immersed themselves in the theory and practice of broad-scale confrontation, but he acknowledged that this organizing tradition had yet to take root in the civil rights movement. In early 1957, King met James Lawson, a savvy student of unarmed resistance who had spent several years in India. As biographer Taylor Branch relates, King pleaded with the young graduate student to quit his studies: "We need you now," King said. "We don't have any Negro leadership in the South that understands nonviolence."[25]

Despite his desire to employ tactics of nonviolent struggle, the idea of waging widely participatory campaigns of direct action fell far outside of King's organizational frame of reference, and in many ways he remained a reluctant convert to mass action. Founded not long after the Montgomery Bus Boycott, King's Southern Christian Leadership Conference was conceived as a coalition of ministers. It thought of itself, in the words of one historian, as the "political arm of the black church." As Ella Baker biographer Barbara Ransby writes, typical church institutions were none too bold in their push for civil rights, and "the majority of black ministers in the 1950s still opted for a safer, less confrontational political path." Even King and his more motivated cohort "defined their political goals squarely within the respectable American mainstream and were cautious about any leftist associations."[26]

Frustrated that the SCLC's program in the first years involved more "flowery speeches" than civil disobedience, the militant Rev. Fred Shuttlesworth of Birmingham warned that if the organization did not become more aggressive, its leaders would "be hard put in the not too distant future to justify our existence."[27]

The next major breakthroughs in civil rights activism would come not from the SCLC's hesitant ministers but from the student lunch-counter sit-ins that swept through the South starting in spring of 1960, and then from the 1961 Freedom Rides. In each case, when young activists implored King to join them, the elder clergyman—himself just in his early thirties—stalled and equivocated. King told the students that he was with them in spirit. They pointedly shot back, "Where's your body?"[28]

According to John Lewis, then a leader in Student Nonviolent Coordinating Committee (SNCC), King replied to such challenges with irritation, making reference to the site of Jesus's crucifixion: "I think *I* should choose the time and place of my Golgotha," he said.[29]

When King's SCLC did get directly involved in a major campaign of strategic nonviolence, the organization was drawn into an effort that was already under way—the movement in Albany, Georgia, starting in late 1961. Even then, the SCLC did not fully commit until after King and Ralph Abernathy were swept up in an unplanned arrest.[30]

The failure of the protests in Albany, combined with the inspiration of the Freedom Rides and student sit-ins, convinced King that the time had come for a campaign that, in the words of Andrew Young, could be "anticipated, planned and coordinated from beginning to end" using the principles of nonviolent conflict.[31]

King had chosen his Golgotha: Birmingham, 1963.

~

King and Sharp, in their own ways, would each make critical contributions to a lineage that had been growing out of Gandhi and that was about to flourish in the second half of the twentieth century.

Nonviolent action did not start with the Indian independence movement. Sharp documented a variety of earlier precedents, going back to the use of noncooperation by the plebeians of Rome in 494 BC. And there were intellectual forerunners as well. Thoreau produced influential writings in the 1800s, as did Tolstoy—who even carried out a correspondence with the young Gandhi.[32]

Yet, these forebears notwithstanding, it was Gandhi's experiments in South Africa and India that would most profoundly shape the usage of strategic nonviolence in the years that followed. Both King and Sharp saw themselves as standing in his shadow. King, a Christian minister, would describe the influence in religious terms: "Gandhi was probably the first person in history to lift the love ethic of Jesus above mere interaction between individuals to a powerful and effective social force on a large scale," he wrote.[33]

Sharp made a similar observation, using more secular language: "Gandhi," he argued, "was probably the first to consciously formulate over a period of years a major system of resistance based upon the assumption" that "hierarchical systems can be modified or destroyed by a withdrawal of submission, cooperation, and obedience."[34]

For both King and Sharp, Gandhi's efforts in India were not an end point. Instead, Gandhi's campaigns were breakthrough examples of what nonviolent confrontation could accomplish. They suggested the enormous potential of a mode of political engagement that was only starting to influence world affairs. For his part, Gandhi sometimes spoke of nonviolence as a developing science. He saw himself as conducting investigations into its unique laws and properties, going so far as to title his autobiography *The Story of My Experiments with Truth*.

Viewed in this framework, King, like Gandhi, would become an experimenter pushing the frontiers of innovation. Sharp, on the other hand, would take on a different role: that of a taxonomist who documented the most exciting discoveries that were made.

One of the achievements that became a trademark for Sharp—and that showed his penchant for careful cataloguing—was his list of "198 methods of nonviolent action." Originally presented in detail in the second volume of *The Politics of Nonviolent Action*, the list serves as a suggestion of possible tactics for movements. It encompasses widely varied approaches: vigils, fasting, land occupations, "protest disrobings," display of flags and symbolic colors, mock funerals, humorous skits and pranks, deliberate bureaucratic inefficiency, and civil disobedience—in addition to dozens of distinct types of strikes and boycotts.

In a 2003 interview, Sharp explained the origins of his now-famous list. He explained that, around 1960, he began collecting examples of different forms of resistance. At first, he said:

> I think I had 18 methods of nonviolent action. The largest list I had come across previously was 12. When I was in Norway, I drew up a list which I think went up to 65 and took it to a conference in Accra, Ghana. People there were absolutely fascinated by this list.[35]

By the time *The Politics of Nonviolent Action* was published, Sharp's count had grown to 198 tactics.

The list is sometimes misunderstood by Sharp's admirers and his enemies alike. Some readers assume that Sharp somehow invented the nonviolent tactics, when really he merely documented approaches that had already been put into practice by others. As he labored away in the archives, Sharp became buried in examples, and his writing style showed a love of classification that bordered on obsessive. But Sharp's list had great strengths. It encouraged dissidents to be creative in their planning and not to simply repeat previously tried approaches. Sharp likened the 198 methods to the various weapons in the arsenal of a conventional army: each has different range and effects, and each is adapted to distinct circumstances. They can be used separately or together. And their wise selection can help determine the outcome of a battle.

At a time when little attention was granted to nonviolent tactics, Sharp's expansive inventory hinted at a new world of possibility—both for action and for future research. And this was only one part of his project.

Digging through history, Sharp found countless examples of the deployment of nonviolent methods. Yet he saw that, in most cases, activists in diverse countries and time periods were essentially reinventing the wheel. No systematic study existed that might illustrate core principles of launching unarmed uprisings. "Extensive use of nonviolent action has occurred despite the absence of attention to the development of the technique itself," he wrote. When movements undertook nonviolent campaigns, it was usually in haphazard fashion—"partly spontaneous, partly intuitive, partly vaguely patterned off of some known case."[36]

How much more effective could civil resistance be if it were seriously studied? Sharp reasoned that a thorough exploration of how unarmed mass action worked—how uprisings could be sparked and their power harnessed—could have significant, real-world consequences. And so he made this his mission. He conceived of his research as "a very careful examination of the nature, capacities and requirements of nonviolent struggle."[37]

Sharp insisted that nonviolent resistance—with proper knowledge and planning—could produce the kind of major upheavals that are often attributed to the diffuse spirit of the times. Certainly, in any given campaign, many political and economic factors are beyond the control of activists. But that does not mean that people seeking change should sit around and wait until circumstances seem ideal. Sometimes, the combination of careful preparation and tactical daring could upend conventional wisdom about the possibilities for change. "Some nonviolent struggles have succeeded in very poor circumstances because the struggle group compensated for specific unfavorable conditions by developing their strengths and their skills in how to act under such conditions," Sharp would argue.[38]

Pursuing these ideas, Sharp followed a somewhat lonely path. Having broken with traditional peace groups, he made a turn toward scholarship. Yet Sharp never fit particularly well within the professorial mold, and he showed little interest in the sometimes-tedious processes of peer review. Consequently, his ideas were slow to take hold in academia. Had he started his career today, rather than in the 1970s, he could have much more easily found an academic community—thanks to the field of study his writing has done so much to help spawn. Stephen Zunes, a professor at the University of San Francisco and expert in the field, comments that, prior to Sharp, lectures on nonviolent movements took place almost exclusively in religion and ethics courses. Slowly, consideration of such campaigns moved into sociology. And today, the study of nonviolent conflict and civil resistance is a respectable subfield within political science and strategic studies, engaging scholars who would have no interest in a "peace studies" curriculum.[39]

If these developments have taken place too slowly to benefit Sharp's professorial career, he can take some consolation in the traction his studies have gained outside the academy. Sharp's theories are useful enough that they not only have influenced intellectuals but also have been widely adapted for practical application. Trainers who have been inspired by the emerging field of civil resistance—and who have waged campaigns of nonviolent conflict in places such as Serbia, South Africa, Poland, and Zimbabwe—have worked to codify a new organizing tradition based on the lessons gleaned from past mobilizations. As a result, activists today can benefit from the experiences of their predecessors in a way that would have been unimaginable just a few decades ago. Like the Egyptian protester who told the BBC in 2011 that he had been handed a photocopy of the 198 methods, printed without any reference to the list's provenance, many dissidents who have never heard Sharp's name have nonetheless ended up exposed to his thinking.[40]

In his 1973 magnum opus, Sharp made an audacious prediction—a writerly version of Babe Ruth pointing his bat at the ballpark fences. "We are only becoming aware of the past history of this type of conflict and of the vast armory of nonviolent weapons it utilizes," Sharp wrote. Of his investigation he stated, "This is only the beginning," and he expressed the hope that it would initiate a "new stage in the development of nonviolent alternatives."[41]

Remarkably enough, this is exactly what has come to pass.

~

On the ground in Birmingham in 1963, King and other civil rights organizers discovered what it took to actually carry out the type of campaign that Sharp was theorizing. And it was hardly as simple as it might have looked on paper.

It can be easy, with the benefit of hindsight, to overlook how much was unknown to the movement activists in Birmingham as they commenced their high-risk confrontation. Although Project C reflected the SCLC's careful planning and preparation, its creators soon found that following through on their designs would mean taking huge risks and facing tremendous uncertainties.[42]

In the decades since the success of the Birmingham campaign, some writers have suggested that a triumph there was virtually preordained. This tendency was already in full bloom in March 1964, when *Jet* magazine published a glowing profile of Wyatt Walker that lionized the young SCLC administrator as the "Man Behind Martin Luther King Jr." The piece described Walker as "a natty dresser, a tall, handsome movie-idol type with a flashy smile . . . a smooth, convincing, and wondrous wheeler-dealer." According to this story, Walker's planning for Birmingham was so flawless that, when King commenced the campaign, all he "had to do was push the right button that Walker had already connected to the proper detonator."[43]

In more recent times, a different type of determinism has crept into popular versions of the Birmingham story. According to these accounts, the SCLC chose Birmingham because organizers relished a clash with Bull Connor, knowing that the hot-headed commissioner could be relied on to react to protests with violence and would make a perfect villain in the press.

This narrative, however, misses some important complexities. The SCLC did indeed plan on a confrontation with city officials in Birmingham, but organizers had not chosen the site solely based on Connor or the temperament of any single individual. Rather, the SCLC had been impressed by the careful preparation of local activists, led by Shuttlesworth and his Alabama Christian Movement for Human Rights. When they met in Dorchester, King and his advisors had reason to believe that Bull Connor might be removed from power by the time Project C commenced, and indeed they were hoping this would be the case. Connor's longtime position as Commissioner of Public Safety was being phased out, and he was running a closely contested mayoral race against a more moderate candidate, Albert Boutwell. The SCLC twice delayed its campaign so as not to interfere with the election. The local black community fervently wanted Connor to be unseated, and the civil rights organizers shared the wider community's wish: "We too wanted to see Mr. Connor defeated," King wrote in his famous letter from Birmingham's city jail, "so we went through postponement after postponement to aid this community in need."[44]

Such delay was not merely for the sake of local residents. As Ralph Abernathy would later explain: "Our careful restraint was not something we did for Birmingham alone. We were also concerned about our own hides." As he describes their calculus, the activists knew that in the demonstrations to come, "we would be much safer facing a government headed by Albert Boutwell than one headed by Bull Connor, and we would certainly be happier with a new police chief." When the election took place, Boutwell did prevail over Connor, although a lawsuit by the defeated commissioner allowed Connor to retain day-to-day control over the police force as the case wound its way through the courts.[45]

Strategy and preparation were important to the success of Birmingham, to be sure. Project C laid out a course of premeditated disruption and nonviolent escalation. But to stay that course, it took perseverance and creativity. Sociologist Aldon Morris explains, "SCLC strategists decided that the Birmingham movement should be a drama. That is, it would start out slow and low-keyed and then continue to build up, step by step, until it reached a crisis point, where the opposition would be forced to yield." When planning alone was insufficient to create such drama, organizers had to work hard to ensure that the campaign did not stall in its tracks. Their clever, persistent, and skillful maneuvers to keep tension building at times when protest energy might otherwise have died out were another factor belying the idea that successful uprising was a "spontaneous" occurrence.[46]

Indeed, despite their best-laid plans, protest organizers had to make many decisions about their unfolding production under tense conditions, once the demonstrations were already under way. "In the end, Project C was no social science formula," writes King biographer Taylor Branch. "It was a cold plunge."[47]

When the Birmingham campaign officially launched on April 3, 1963, it quickly became clear that conditions for an uprising were hardly as ideal as was hoped. With the start of the campaign, local leaders announced an economic boycott of downtown stores. Mass meetings at prominent African American churches began taking place nightly. And daily lunch-counter sit-ins and marches resulted in the arrest of small groups of demonstrators—a dozen or two people during most of the initial days. However, these events did not amount to everything King and other organizers had dreamed.

The truth was that the SCLC's recruitment of jail-goers required painstaking outreach and had produced only modest results. Those staffers who arrived in Birmingham months earlier encountered less unity than expected among local black ministers and more resistance from members of the city's black middle class, some of whom belittled King as a mere "glossy personality." Moreover, the delays in the campaign's start were costly. As they waited on the mayoral race, the organizers agonized over losing precious weeks that would have allowed them to punish segregationist merchants during the lucrative Easter shopping season.[48]

It took several key developments over the course of the following weeks for the campaign to surmount these difficulties and realize its vision. These involved both savvy moves by top leaders and great courage on the part of local activists.

First, the SCLC worked hard to mend fences in the city's divided black community, winning over previously reluctant leaders such as businessman A. G. Gaston and the Reverend J. L. Ware, president of the city's Baptist Ministers Conference. This did not stop the city's black weekly, *The World*, from continuing its attacks—the paper declared aggressive protests "both wasteful and worthless" on April 10—but the endorsements from the likes of Ware did swell the ranks of participants in evening mass meetings.[49]

Next, with volunteers for arrest still lagging, King resolved that he would go to jail himself on April 12: Good Friday. This was a difficult decision to make. Getting arrested for leading a march meant violating an injunction against further protests that a court had handed down less than two days before. Many of the SCLC's organizers were fearful that the campaign was on the brink of failure and that the movement did not have enough money to cover bail and legal fees of the dozens of people who had already been taken into custody. Some advisors, including King's father, a respected minister, opposed the arrest. They argued that the SCLC president should travel north to raise money for their flagging effort rather than risk a lengthy imprisonment himself. Yet, after careful discernment, King decided, "The path is clear to me. I've got to march."[50]

King's gambit was that, in serving as an example of personal sacrifice, he could both move others to step forward and reassert a sense of escalating drama in the Birmingham drive. He was right. As photos of the arrested minister spread internationally, the Kennedy administration was prompted to intervene. After city authorities arrested King, they placed him in solitary confinement and prevented him from receiving news from the outside. To the general public, this raised the specter that a prominent black citizen might be "disappeared" inside a jail in the Deep South. In hopes of preventing any such mishap, both Attorney General Robert Kennedy and his brother, President John F. Kennedy, made it known that they were monitoring the situation with concern. Both called Coretta Scott King to reassure her that the FBI had determined that Martin was safe. Wyatt Walker made sure that word of these calls became part of the national press coverage of the campaign.

Although King's arrest provided a temporary boost, it took a third major breakthrough for Project C to escalate to its full magnitude. This came with the decision, in what became known as the "Children's Crusade," to allow high school students to join the demonstrations. Early on, James Bevel had recruited scores of teenagers eager to take a stand. Yet older leaders were wary. They were sensitive to criticism about deploying student protesters who were perceived as too young to be on the front lines of the civil rights struggle. Eventually, however, the enthusiasm of the youth and the need to carry forward the campaign's momentum won out.

"We were inspired . . . to give our young a true sense of their own stake in freedom and justice," King would later write. Just shy of one month into the campaign, organizers announced that all people would be allowed to participate, and students overwhelmingly responded to the call. On May 2, the first day of the Children's Crusade, wave after wave of young people flooded Birmingham's streets, singing and joining arms. Project C was no longer a matter of a dozen or two activists risking jail time: in just one day of action, more than five hundred people were arrested by the police.[51]

With space in Birmingham's City Jail rapidly diminishing, Bull Connor turned to more aggressive reprisals, and this marked a last major development that transformed the campaign: the advent of highly publicized police violence.

Connor likely believed that a firm-handed crackdown on "Negro troublemakers" would make him into one of Alabama's most popular politicians. His instincts about what would appeal to his base of supporters in the state may well have been correct. Yet the national perception of his actions would be very different. Although Project C's organizers had not known in advance that Connor would still be leading the Birmingham police, nor that the official response to their determined protests would come in the exact form that it did, they were well aware of the power that images of repression could have. And they were ready to maximize the advantage gained by tactical mistakes on the part of authorities.

Several weeks earlier, shortly after the start of the demonstrations, Bull Connor had already brought out one of his most infamous weapons: the snarling police dog. On April 7, a unit of canines growled at marching protesters. When a bystander taunted one of the animals, the dog lunged and pinned the man. Onlookers from the crowd jumped in to help pull the bystander free, and the dog's attack made national press.[52]

That evening, as they reflected on what had transpired, some of the SCLC organizers were jubilant. In a now-famous encounter, SNCC's James Forman came upon Wyatt Walker and Dorothy Cotton in the Gaston Motel, the movement's command center. As Forman describes it, Walker and Cotton "were jumping up and down, elated. They said over and over again, 'We've got a movement . . . They brought out the dogs. We've got a movement.'" Forman was unsettled by the sight, disturbed that other civil rights campaigners would be excited about police brutality.[53]

But Walker and Cotton were not trivializing the violence of the police dogs. They took the risks of the campaign very seriously. As King had contended, the point of creating a public crisis in Birmingham was not to introduce Connor or other authorities to violence. Rather, it was to expose the violence routinely inflicted upon the black community under Jim Crow segregation. "We merely bring to the surface the hidden tension that is already alive," King wrote. "We bring it out in the open, where it can be seen and dealt with."[54] Walker and Cotton knew that the attacking police dogs would serve as a choice representation of the much more pervasive violence that flourished in the city. In his tactical foolishness, Bull Connor had become an ally in exposing the brutality of white supremacy. And he was just beginning.

∼

Despite tipping his hand early on, Bull Connor did not deploy public violence in earnest until after Birmingham's black youth flooded the streets. On May 3, the day after the first Children's Crusade march, even larger crowds took to the streets. With their jails already filled, Connor's forces decided against mass arrests and instead opened up on demonstrators with batons, dogs, and water hoses. The scenes that resulted were horrifying. Streams from high-pressure fire hoses ripped the clothing from the backs of protesters, who turned and cowered against the force of the blasts. During one confrontation, a jet of water pinned a writhing Fred Shuttlesworth against a wall, and the reverend was taken to the hospital on a stretcher. Doctors treated other demonstrators for dog bites. And at least one black woman, a bystander watching the marches, charged that she had been intentionally knocked to the ground by police, beaten, and kicked in the stomach.

President Kennedy told one group of visitors to the White House that the images of Bull Connor's crackdown made him sick. But rather than dissuading protests, the police action galvanized Birmingham's black community. Seeing that demonstrations were only growing larger, the city's merchants scrambled to find a resolution.[55]

The internationally broadcast images of revolt and repression had brought federal pressure for a settlement. But the downtown store-owners were already convinced: black customers had overwhelmingly stopped patronizing their businesses, and this drop in foot traffic alone was significant enough to make the difference between profit and loss on their ledgers. What was more, the prospect of confrontation was keeping white housewives from the downtown shopping district as well. Over the objection of Connor and the city's racist holdouts, the merchants announced an agreement with civil rights leaders on May 10 that promised the start of desegregation. Less than six weeks after Project C began, it was over, and the city was forever changed.

Given the widespread perception that nonviolence functions as a kind of spiritual force, it is not surprising that its most famous adherents are regularly elevated to the status of saints. King, in particular, is enshrined in this way. At annual celebrations, people mostly remember his soul-stirring sermons and public address. They are less likely to be aware of those traits that made King human—his personal failings (such as marital infidelity), his robust sense of humor, or his tactical cunning. Likewise, the calculations of enterprising lieutenants such as Walker fall out of the story. Such omissions reinforce the idea that outbreaks of resistance owe more to divine intervention than earthly design. And they conceal elements crucial for understanding how movements actually succeed.

Both King and Walker were ministers who drew on their religious faith as a source of courage and resolve. But they also worked consciously to manipulate press coverage of the movement. As David Garrow writes, at least one observer "was astounded by King's emphasis on pragmatic rather than spiritual considerations" when he approved the deployment of youth protesters in the Children's Crusade. "We've got to get something going," King said. "The press is leaving, we've got to get going." And this attitude toward the media was just one example of how the civil rights activists maintained a hard-headed approach to unarmed uprising—one that would later be studied and refined by others.[56]

The Birmingham model proved widely influential. In the wake of Project C, movement activity exploded. Historian Adam Fairclough writes, the "protests in Birmingham also sent shock waves through the South. The fact that white leaders had made concessions in a city notorious for its racial intransigence gave new hope to blacks in Baton Rouge, New Orleans, and other segregationist strongholds."[57] Donations to the civil rights movement flowed in, and thousands of those inspired by what had happened in Alabama launched sit-ins, boycotts, and marches of their own.

Even the unadventurous National Association for the Advancement of Colored People (NAACP) diverged from its typical strategy of pursuing lawsuits and insider lobbying to promote more disruptive approaches. At its annual convention that summer, it made the highly unusual move of calling on its local branches to take up "picketing, mass action protests, [and] selective buying campaigns." Politicians also took note of the surge. For two years prior to the campaign, Fairclough explains, "Robert Kennedy had attempted to deal with each racial crisis on an *ad hoc* basis. Birmingham finally convinced him that the crises would recur with such frequency and magnitude that the federal government, unless it adopted a more radical policy, would be overwhelmed."[58]

King's political genius was in putting the institutional weight of a major national civil rights organization behind an ambitious, escalating deployment of civil resistance tactics. It would have been far easier for an organization of the size and background of the SCLC to turn toward more mainstream lobbying and legal action—much as the NAACP had done. Instead, SCLC organizers and their local allies followed the example of the Freedom Riders and SNCC's student activists in embracing nonviolent confrontation.

To go beyond adhering to pacifism as a personal philosophy, and instead to stake your career and your organization's future on a belief in the power of nonviolence as a political force, requires tremendous determination. It took years of deliberation and delay for Martin Luther King Jr. to take such a step. But when he finally did, the result was decisive: King went from being someone who had been repeatedly swept up in the saga of civil rights—a reluctant protagonist in the battle against American apartheid—to being a shaper of history.

~

As civil resistance has emerged as an organizing tradition, it has sometimes been mistaken for a conspiracy.

In the past two decades, cases in which nonviolent resistance has been used to overthrow undemocratic regimes have proliferated. Among other struggles, scholars have paid special attention to the boycotts against apartheid South Africa; the people power movement in the Philippines; the ouster of Pinochet in Chile; the revolutions of 1989 in Poland, Czechoslovakia, and East Germany; the "color revolutions" in Serbia, Georgia, and the Ukraine; uprisings in Burma in 1988 and 2007, and Iran in and 2009; and the revolts that swept the Arab world in 2011. In some instances, key participants in these movements attended trainings in civil resistance or otherwise familiarized themselves with insights from the tradition. In other cases, activists devised their own versions of the approach without exposure to outsiders. Always, leaders drew on their own distinctive political histories and deep local knowledge to rally broad support in their societies.

In countries where these struggles have taken place, Gene Sharp has consistently attracted interested readers. This interest has also drawn detractors, such as the Iranian government. For an intellectual opponent of autocracy, being featured as an animated character in an Iranian propaganda film surely counts as a high honor. Sharp received this strange accolade in 2008, when Iran aired a video that showed a computer-generated version of him scheming with Senator John McCain and philanthropist George Soros. It accused Sharp of being a CIA agent "in charge of America's infiltration into other countries."[59]

Similar charges have emanated from some sketchy corners of the Left. In 2005, French writer Thierry Meyssan, author of a book entitled *9/11: The Big Lie*, charged that Sharp "helped NATO and the CIA train the leaders of the soft coups of the last 15 years."[60] Unfortunately, Meyssan's suspect publishing history did not stop Venezuelan President Hugo Chávez from swallowing the Frenchman's accusations. In 2007, Chávez publicly denounced Sharp as being part of a US plot to oust his government.

Those who think that Sharp is a CIA tool willfully overlook the fact that principles of civil resistance have frequently been used against US-supported dictatorships and that Palestinian activists drew on them during the first intifada in the 1980s. But, more importantly, conspiratorial claims reflect a fundamental misunderstanding of how civil resistance works. It is true that techniques of unarmed uprising—just like guerilla warfare—can be used by groups with a wide range of ideological orientations. But there is an important difference. At their core, the principles of civil resistance are inherently democratic: nonviolent campaigns require mass public support and participation if they are to succeed.[61]

Civil resistance can just as easily be employed to defend a popular government as to challenge a repressive one. Thus, in response to Chávez's complaints, Sharp wrote the Venezuelan president a letter recommending his book entitled *The Anti-Coup*, which explains how nonviolent action can be used to repel an armed *putsch* by a minority group that does not have the backing of the population.

It is an error to attribute any mass movement to a single person. During the Arab Spring, Middle Eastern analysts criticized portions of the Western media for being too eager to credit Gene Sharp as something like an American "Lawrence of Arabia," responsible for the revolts breaking out. Sharp himself disowned such characterizations. When others tried to credit him, he instead highlighted the agency and creativity of indigenous protesters. Sharp consistently argues that movements must always devise their own strategies. "An outsider like me can't tell you what to do," he advised one group, "and if I did, you shouldn't believe me. Trust yourselves."[62]

As King's experience shows, strategic nonviolence does not offer a secret formula for success, and its development is hardly the work of a single mastermind. Rather, the growth of civil resistance has been the result of practitioners experimenting in diverse and difficult conditions, adding their own refinements to an art that has been developing for more than a century. Sharp has made an important contribution to this process, but his is by no means the only one.

The SCLC's campaigns—and those of the civil rights movement more broadly—have become touchstones for a modern tradition of direct action in the United States. Young people whose politics were shaped by campaigns in the South went on to play important roles in New Left student organizing and in the movement against the war in Vietnam. Their example would influence antinuclear activists and feminist groups in the 1970s; Central American solidarity, antiapartheid groups, and AIDS campaigners in the 1980s; and grassroots environmentalists in the 1990s. A strain of common experience would run through the historic protests against the World Trade Organization in Seattle at the turn of the millennium, the massive demonstrations against the Iraq War under George W. Bush, and the eruption of Occupy Wall Street in the Obama era. Although these efforts had distinctive traits and drew in unique constituencies, they also shared many common characteristics, and it is no accident that they have displayed overlapping vocabularies and tactical repertoires.

As civil resistance has matured in other parts of the world, it has raised intriguing questions for this indigenous strain of direct action in the United States. Can domestic activists combine innovations from international movements with their own tradition in order to create something new and powerful? Can Sharp's ideas, which have focused on unseating dictatorships, be applied in a democratic context? Can versions of civil resistance be used to confront the challenges of climate change, runaway economic inequality, racial injustice, and the corporate hijacking of government?

When Sharp began his career, popular opinion held that nonviolence could not succeed against authoritarian regimes. The technique could only work, the argument went, within democratic societies—against governments that, at least in principle, respected basic civil liberties. Mainstream pundits contended that Gandhi could prevail against the British Empire but would have been wiped out by a fascist foe, just as the civil rights movement relied on the Kennedy and Johnson administrations to constrain Southern racists. Sharp took it upon himself to refute such widespread notions, and that commitment shaped his career.

The situation today, however, is very different. As the list of undemocratic governments ousted by "people power" grows ever more expansive, the conventional wisdom about strategic nonviolence may well have reversed: a common bias might hold that nonviolent conflict can be effective in challenging tyrannies, but it holds little value in places where dissent can be channeled through lobbying and electoral politics. In this context, the onus for US activists is now to show how the same types of tactics used to oust autocrats abroad can be brought to bear at home.

Despite the demonstrated power of mass mobilizations to alter the political landscape, few prominent organizations have been willing to pursue strategies of militant nonviolence. There is a reason for this. As veteran labor movement strategist Stephen Lerner has argued, major organizations have just enough at stake—relationships with mainstream politicians, financial obligations to members, collective bargaining contracts—to make them fear the lawsuits and political backlash that come with sustained civil disobedience. What Lerner says of unions applies equally to large environmental organizations, human rights groups, and other nonprofits: they "are just big enough—and just connected enough to the political and economic power structure—to be constrained from leading the kinds of activities that are needed" for bold campaigns of nonviolent conflict to be successful.[63]

As a consequence, explosive direct actions, from the Nashville sit-ins to the revolution in Egypt, are often led by underfunded upstarts. Such ad hoc groups can risk daring campaigns because they have nothing to lose, but they commonly lack the resources to escalate or to sustain multiple waves of protest over a period of years.

A gulf has emerged that separates established organizations dedicated to slowly winning social change over the long haul from explosive mass mobilizations that use disruptive power to shake the status quo. Often, the divide has resulted in tension, acrimony, and confusion. In recent years, civil resistance has presented a compelling possibility: that this gap, which has often seemed insurmountable, might yet be bridged, and that the fortunes of grassroots organizing might be transformed as a result.

CHAPTER TWO

STRUCTURE AND MOVEMENT

TWO SCHOOLS STAND at opposite poles of thinking about how grassroots forces can promote social change. Each has a champion.

One, Saul Alinsky, is widely regarded as the founding father of community organizing; having cut his teeth bringing people together in the ethnically diverse neighborhoods near Chicago's meatpacking district in the 1930s, he would become an author and troublemaker of national renown by the start of the social upheavals of the 1960s. The other, Frances Fox Piven, is an eminent sociologist who played an influential role in the welfare rights movements of the 1960s and 1970s and who subsequently led a successful push to make it easier for Americans to register to vote.

The two have been grouped together in sometimes creative ways, most prominently by conservative commentator Glenn Beck. In early 2010, the popular radio host and Fox News personality had emerged as a champion of the Tea Party movement, and he was at the height of his influence. One of Beck's preoccupations was mapping the workings of the Left, often making use of impressively arcane diagrams. During one program, he unveiled for viewers the "tree of radicalism and revolution." The chart laid out what he imagined to be a vast left-wing conspiracy to take over the nation. At the root of the tree, Beck placed Alinsky. Meanwhile, on the tree's trunk, he wrote Piven's name—along with that of her late husband and coauthor, Richard Cloward. Although Piven was in her late seventies at the time, Beck argued that she was not merely "an enemy of the Constitution" but one of the "nine most dangerous people in the world."[1]

Beck's paranoid theories contained too many errors and unfounded leaps to easily enumerate. Nevertheless, he was correct to identify both Alinsky and Piven as groundbreaking social movement thinkers. Where he went wrong was in concluding that they were part of a unified and malevolent scheme. In truth, what may be most notable when considering Piven and Alinsky together are not their commonalities but rather the ways in which they disagreed. Although the two have similar commitments to grassroots democracy, they promoted distinctly different methods for creating change. As a result, their followers have sometimes found themselves sharply at odds with one another.

Alinsky was a guru in the art of the slow, incremental building of community groups. Like organizers in the labor movement, his approach focused on person-by-person recruitment, careful leadership development, and the creation of stable institutional bodies that could leverage the power of their members over time. As an organizing tradition, this approach can be described as one based on "structure."

Piven, in contrast, has become a leading defender of unruly broad-based disobedience, undertaken outside the confines of any formal organization. She emphasizes the disruptive power of mass mobilizations that coalesce quickly, draw in participants not previously involved in organizing, and leave established elites scrambling to adjust to a new political landscape. In contrast to the structure-based approach of labor unions and Alinskyite groups, her tradition can be dubbed "mass protest."

The future of social change in this country may well involve integrating these approaches—figuring out how the strengths of both structure and mass protest can be used in tandem—so that outbreaks of widespread revolt complement long-term organizing. The emerging field of civil resistance offers considerable potential in addressing this task, providing tools that can help to create a synthesis between competing traditions. But for that to happen, it is helpful to recognize the unique histories and habits of each school and to understand how the rift between them emerged in the first place.

~

Saul Alinsky passed away in 1972, and although his landmark book *Rules for Radicals* is now nearly forty-five years old, the principles that emerged from Alinsky's work have influenced every generation of community-based activists since. In *Rules for Radicals*, Alinsky presented a variety of tactical guidelines—ideas expressed by memorable quotes such as "ridicule is man's most potent weapon" and "power is not only what you have, but what the enemy thinks you have." But Alinsky's most enduring principles are not contained in such aphorisms. Rather, they are embedded in a set of organizational practices and predispositions, a defined approach to building power at the local level. Hang around social change campaigns for a while and you will no doubt be exposed to the laws of Chicago-style community organizing. In 2014, veteran labor journalist David Moberg described several of them: "Don't talk ideology, just issues. . . . Build organizations, not movements. . . . Focus on neighborhoods and on concrete, winnable goals."[2]

Out of such principles has come a far-flung web of social change groups. The organization Alinsky himself founded, the Industrial Areas Foundation (IAF), is now a national network with more than sixty affiliates, spread over some twenty-two states. Moreover, Alinsky's direct influence is felt in other organizing networks ranging from PICO, Direct Action and Research Training (DART) Center, USAction/ Citizen Action, and the Gamaliel Foundation, to the former branches of the Association of Community Organizations for Reform (ACORN) and the current affiliates of National People's Action—whose member groups include Community Voices Heard in New York, Neighbor to Neighbor Massachusetts, and Iowa Citizens for Community Improvement. Collectively, these organizations claim several million members. Together they have won untold numbers of state and local victories around issues such as affordable housing, local hiring, fair lending, living wages, and community investment.

A Chicago native and son of Russian-Jewish immigrants, Alinsky got his start organizing in the 1930s, inspired by CIO and United Mine Workers leader John L. Lewis. In spite of mentoring from Lewis, Alinsky was convinced that the labor movement had grown lethargic and that American democracy needed "people's organizations" based outside the workplace—citizens' groups with roots in local communities. In his first attempt to create such a group, he founded the Back of the Yards Neighborhood Council, an effort to organize those who lived behind the meatpacking plants featured in Upton Sinclair's muckraking 1906 novel *The Jungle*. To fight the slum conditions facing this neighborhood, Alinsky formed committees of local leaders, packed the offices of bureaucrats with hundreds of angry residents, and steered marches in front of the homes of local officials. It worked. "Many confrontations and several months later," author Mary Beth Rogers writes, "Back of the Yards claimed credit for new police patrols, street repairs, regular garbage collection, and lunch programs for 1,400 children."[3]

By 1940, with the help of funding from wealthy liberal Marshall Field III, Alinsky had created the IAF, tasked with spurring organization in other urban neighborhoods. In the 1950s, Alinsky and Fred Ross worked through one IAF-supported group, the Community Service Organization, to improve living conditions for Mexican Americans in California. There, Ross recruited a young organizer in San Jose named Cesar Chavez and another in Fresno named Dolores Huerta. (Only after years of training did Chavez and Huerta leave to form what would become the United Farm Workers.)

Among Alinsky's other prominent campaigns, he worked in the 1960s with black residents in Chicago's Woodlawn neighborhood to fight exploitative landlords and to challenge school overcrowding, and he would help community members in Rochester, New York, compel the Eastman Kodak Company to create a hiring program for African American workers.

Alinsky taught through stories, usually exaggerated, always entertaining. In 1971 writer Nat Hentoff stated, "At 62, Saul is the youngest man I've met in years."[4] *Playboy* interviewer Eric Norden agreed. "There is a tremendous vitality about Alinsky, a raw, combative ebullience, and a consuming curiosity about everything and everyone around him,"

Norden wrote. "Add to this a mordant wit, a monumental ego coupled with an ability to laugh at himself and the world in general, and you begin to get the measure of the man."[5]

Alinsky's first book, *Reveille for Radicals*, became a best seller when published in 1946. It blasted liberal-minded charity efforts and called for an indigenous American radicalism based in citizen action. *Rules for Radicals: A Pragmatic Primer for Realistic Radicals* came in 1971, near the end of Alinsky's life, and remains popular. Early in the Obama era, it was circulated by Republican Dick Armey's organization Freedom-Works and handed out to Tea Party members who were curious about the book's methods, even if they were opposed to its goals. The book's first chapter begins: "What follows is for those who want to change the world from what it is to what they believe it should be. *The Prince* was written by Machiavelli for the Haves on how to hold power. *Rules for Radicals* is written for the Have-Nots on how to take it away."[6]

Frank Bardacke, author of a sweeping history of the United Farm Workers, recounts how Alinsky's principles for building power solidified into an identifiable organizing tradition: "With Saul as the fountainhead, community organizing has become a codified discipline, with core theoretical propositions, recognized heresies, disciples, fallen neophytes, and splits." Bardacke quotes Heather Booth, founder of the Midwest Academy, an Alinskyite training center for organizers, who calls Alinsky "our Sigmund Freud."[7]

"What Booth means is that both Freud and Alinsky founded schools of thought," Bardacke explains, "but there is another, deeper link: the role of training and lineage. Just as psychoanalysts trace their pedigree back to the grand master (they were either analyzed by Freud or by someone who was analyzed by Freud, or by someone who was analyzed by someone who . . .), so Alinskyite and neo-Alinskyite organizers trace their training back to Alinsky himself."

Beyond spawning networks of community organizing groups that reach across the United States, the tradition has spread internationally, with organizing trainings taking place in Europe, South Africa, and the Philippines. Each of the prominent networks now active, writes sociologist David Walls, is "indebted, in greater or lesser degree, to Alinsky and his early organizing programs in Chicago through IAF."[8]

Well after his death, Saul Alinsky would become known for his indirect influence on prominent figures inside Washington, DC. In the 1980s, Barack Obama, then a recent college graduate, began his professional life as an organizer in an Alinskyite community organization, an initiative on the South Side of Chicago known as the Developing Communities Project. Hillary Clinton, too, took interest in the organizing guru. Her undergraduate thesis at Wellesley College was entitled "There Is Only the Fight: An Analysis of the Alinsky Model." These links eventually attracted the attention of not only Glenn Beck but also other right-wing pundits. Republican presidential candidate Newt Gingrich, for example, regularly used Alinsky as a foil on the campaign trail in 2012.

These beltway associations are ironic, given that Alinsky built his reputation as an antiestablishment radical who largely avoided electoral politics. The Alinskyite tradition held that community organizations should be pragmatic, nonpartisan, and ideologically diverse—that they should put pressure on all politicians, not express loyalty to any. Alinsky himself was not antistate. As sociologist P. David Finks writes, for him "the problem was not so much getting government off our backs as getting it off its rear end." But the focus of Alinsky's efforts was squarely outside the electoral arena. Although a variety of community organizing networks, over the decades, have experimented with taking stands in elections (as did Alinksy himself), the IAF holds a lingering pride in its "independent, nonpartisan" status. The group's desire is to recruit members from across the political spectrum in any given community, not merely to engage the usual suspects of progressive activism with appeals to an ideologically coded platform of beliefs.[9]

Such "nonpartisan" avoidance of ideology relates to perhaps the most interesting precept in the Alinskyite tradition: a stance that distances community organizing from mass mobilizations. As Rutgers sociology professor and former ACORN organizer Arlene Stein wrote in 1986, "Community organizers today tend generally to shun the term *movement*, preferring to see themselves engaged in building *organization*."[10]

Why would someone promoting social change see themselves as wary of movements?

There are several reasons, and the way in which the terms "movement" and "organization" are understood by Alinskyites connects to some defining aspects of their model. For Ed Chambers, Alinsky's successor as IAF director, an aversion to movements is a part of his long-term commitment to community members. As he writes in his book *Roots for Radicals*, "We play to win. That's one of the distinctive features of the IAF: We don't lead everyday, ordinary people into public failures, and we're not building movements. Movements go in and out of existence. As good as they are, you can't sustain them. Everyday people need incremental success over months and sometimes years."[11]

Alinsky, too, saw a danger in expecting quick upheavals. He argued, "Effective organization is thwarted by the desire for instant and dramatic change. . . . To build a powerful organization takes time. It is tedious, but that's the way the game is played—if you want to play and not just yell, 'Kill the umpire.'" Before entering a neighborhood, Alinsky planned for a sustained engagement. He would not hire an organizer unless he had raised enough money to pay for two or more years of the staffer's salary.[12]

Beyond setting expectations for time frame, a dedication to "organizations not movements" is reflected in several other Alinskyite norms. The tradition's connection to churches and other established institutions is one. Its selection of bottom-up demands rather than high-profile national issues is another. And its attitude toward volunteers and freelance activists is a third.

First, Alinsky believed in identifying local centers of power, particularly churches, and using them as bases for community groups. The modern IAF continues to follow this principle, serving as a model of "faith-based" organizing.

Second, instead of picking a galvanizing, morally loaded, and possibly divisive national issue to organize around—as might a mass movement—Alinsky advocated action around narrow local demands. Mark Warren's *Dry Bones Rattling*, a study of the IAF, explains: "As opposed to mobilizing around a set of predetermined issues, the IAF brings residents together first to discuss the needs of their community and to find a common ground for action." Practicing what is sometimes called "stop sign organizing," those working in this vein look for concrete, winnable projects—such as demanding that city officials place a stop sign at a dangerous intersection in a neighborhood. The idea is that small victories build local capabilities, give participants a sense of their power, and spur more ambitious action.[13]

They also meet some of the immediate needs of the community, far preferable, in Alinsky's view, to the far-off calls for freedom and justice that regularly emanate from social movements. Throughout his career, Alinsky spoke the language of self-interest. He looked to build democratic power among people seeking to improve the conditions of their own lives. He was suspicious of volunteer activists who were motivated by abstract values or ideology, individuals drawn to high-profile moral crusades. Such suspicion would become a third norm in the Alinskyite tradition related to its distrust of "movements."

Ed Chambers argues, "Activists and movement types are mobilizers and entertainers, not democratic organizers. Their script is their persona and their cause. They tend to be overinterested in themselves. Their understanding of politicalness is superficial or media-driven." Moreover, Chambers contends, movement activists' expectations for change are far too short-term: "Their time frame is immediate. 'What do we want?' 'Freedom.' 'When do we want it?' 'Now!' 'No justice, no peace,'" he explains dismissively. "Movement activists appeal to youth, frustrated idealists, and cynical ideologues, ignoring the 80 percent of moderates who comprise the world as it is. . . . Organizing is generational, not here today, gone tomorrow."[14]

Chambers's view may seem harsh, but it was common among those drawn to community organizing in the early years. As Stein explains, "The revival of Alinsky-style organizations in the 1970s and 1980s often defined itself against the social movements of the previous decade— especially the civil rights, women's, and student antiwar movements— which it tended to view as promoting collective identity formation over the achievement of strategic goals."[15]

The community organizers who took up Alinsky's mantle were burnt on short-term protest, and they were willing to pursue a less glamorous route to change. What did they want? Lasting, community-based reform. When did they want it? Over the long haul.

~

On June 5, 1966, James Meredith, a former Air Force serviceman who had been the first African American student to attend the University of Mississippi, set out on a one-man "walk against fear" in the South. He planned to cover the more than two hundred miles between Memphis, Tennessee, and Jackson, Mississippi. On the second day of his march, however, a sniper's shotgun blast left Meredith sprawling on the highway. Wounded, he was evacuated to a nearby hospital.

As chance would have it, Meredith's hospital in Memphis became the site of an intriguing encounter that would highlight the tensions between "organization" and "movement." When news broke of Meredith's shooting, a variety of organizers and civil rights figures promptly assembled to show their support for the wounded activist and to make a plan for completing his march. Two of those who arrived at the hospital were Martin Luther King Jr. and Nicholas von Hoffman, a close Alinsky lieutenant.

In Memphis, King pulled von Hoffman aside for a brief conversation about the Southern Christian Leadership Conference's work in Chicago. The previous year, the SCLC had come to Alinsky's home turf to mount its first Northern civil rights drive. "He did not say so, but I had the impression he was worried about it," von Hoffman writes.[16]

The organizer offered King his advice about waging a campaign in Chicago: "I told him I thought it could succeed if he was prepared for trench warfare, which would demand tight, tough organization to take on the Daley operation," von Hoffman writes. "I added it could not be done in less than two years."

"He listened," von Hoffman further notes. "I could not tell if he heard it before and didn't believe it, or if it was so out of his previous experience he didn't appreciate how decisive [the mayor's] organizational advantages were. Then he said we ought to talk again, but it never happened."

As the encounter suggested, the Alinskyites in Chicago were not impressed by King's approach. "Organizing is akin to stringing beads to make a necklace," von Hoffman argues. "It demands patience, persistence, and some kind of design. King's campaign in Chicago was short on beads and bereft of design." Von Hoffman regarded King as a "one-trick pony" who relied too heavily on media-seeking marches and "dramatic gestures" like moving his family into an apartment in one of Chicago's poorest neighborhoods. He did not believe that the SCLC's team had demonstrated the ability to build "the stable, ongoing kinds of organizations which get things done inch by inch, year by year."

Von Hoffman saw the outsiders King brought into Chicago as "a hodgepodge of young white idealists, college kids, and summer soldiers, most of whom had no knowledge of the people they were supposed to recruit." He noted the contrast with his tradition: "It was the antithesis of an Alinsky operation where outside volunteers were generally shooed away not only because they got in the way but also because they didn't have any skin in the game," he wrote. "Laudable as it is to volunteer to help other people wrestle with their problems, effective organizations are built with people who have direct and personal interest in their success."

This type of analysis reflected Saul Alinsky's broader critique of the SCLC's work. In a 1965 interview, Alinsky argued, "The Achilles' Heel of the civil rights movement is the fact that it has not developed into a stable, disciplined, mass-based power organization." He added, with King as his unnamed subject: "Periodic mass euphoria around a charismatic leader is not an organization. It's just the initial stage of agitation."[17]

It was not just with civil rights campaigners that Alinsky and his acolytes would clash in the 1960s; they also butted heads with the era's student activists. For Alinksy, the decision to stress the importance of strong organization was, in part, an effort to bridge a generation gap that had become glaringly evident by the middle of that decade. Those yelling "kill the umpire," in his estimation, were the members of the era's youth-driven New Left.

Alinsky felt that elders his age were partially responsible for the youths' ignorance. In writing *Rules for Radicals*, he sought to communicate with less experienced activists whom he saw as suffering from a lack of mentoring—the result of a missing generation of organizers. Of his own, older cohort, Alinsky argued that too few had made it through the anticommunist witch hunts of the 1950s. Of those who did survive McCarthyism, he wrote, "there were even fewer whose understanding and insights had developed beyond the dialectical materialism of orthodox Marxism. My fellow radicals who were supposed to pass on the torch of experience and insights to a new generation just were not there."[18]

Alinsky believed that, as a consequence, young leftists were too easily seduced by quick fixes. In an afterword to a 1969 reissue of his first book *Reveille for Radicals*, he wrote, "The approach of so much of the present generation is so fractured with 'confrontations' and crises as ends in themselves that their activities are not actions but a discharge of energy which, like a fireworks spectacle, briefly lights up the skies and then vanishes into the void."[19]

The creation of an alternative methodology—what Stein describes as "a highly structured organizing model specifying step-by-step guidelines for creating neighborhood organizations"—was an understandable response, and one that has shown great strengths. Patient base building and membership recruitment, long-term strategy and leadership development, incremental wins. Each of these ingredients would contribute to a lasting and influential model for building grassroots power, a means of using the strength of "organized people" to combat the influence of "organized money," as Alinsky often put it.[20]

The question is whether the model, over time, has grown too inflexible—whether principles that Alinsky originally meant as loose guidelines have since hardened into rigid laws in the decades since his death—and whether community organizations, as a result, have missed opportunities to harness powerful outbreaks of popular discontent.

~

For the most part, the work of social change is a slow process. As Alinsky wisely counseled, if you want to see your efforts produce results, it helps to have a long-term commitment. And yet, sometimes things move more quickly. Every once in a while we see outbursts of mass protest, periods of peak activity when the accepted rules of political affairs seem to be suspended.

In the words of sociologist Frances Fox Piven, these are extraordinary moments when ordinary people "rise up in anger and hope, defy the rules that ordinarily govern their lives, and, by doing so, disrupt the workings of the institutions in which they are enmeshed." The impact of these uprisings can be profound. As Piven writes, "The drama of such events, combined with the disorder that results, propels new issues to the center of political debate" and drives forward reforms as panicked "political leaders try to restore order."[21]

Piven, the eighty-two-year-old Distinguished Professor of Political Science and Sociology at the City University of New York Graduate Center, has made pioneering contributions to the study of how people who lack both financial resources and influence in conventional politics can nevertheless create momentous revolts. Few scholars have done as much to describe how widespread disruptive action can change history, and few have offered more provocative suggestions about the times when movements—instead of crawling forward with incremental demands—can break into full sprint.

Piven grew up in the 1930s in Jackson Heights, Queens, a child of working-class parents who had emigrated from Belarus and who struggled to adjust to life in America. As a precocious fifteen-year-old, she earned a scholarship to attend the University of Chicago. But, by her own account, Piven was not a serious student at that point, avoiding reading and relying on her skill at taking multiple choice tests to pass courses. She spent most of her time waitressing at late-night restaurants such as Hobby House and Stouffer's, hustling to cover the living expenses not provided for in her tuition scholarship.[22]

In the early 1960s Piven moved back to New York City. It was only after working as a researcher and helping to support rent strikes with the Mobilization for Youth, an early antipoverty group on the Lower East Side, that she was ultimately hired to teach at Columbia University's school of social work. At the Mobilization for Youth, she also met sociologist Richard Cloward, who became her husband and lifelong collaborator. (Cloward passed away in 2001.)

"A lot of the people who became welfare rights organizers were entranced with Alinsky," Piven says. "And, as I worked with them, I began to develop a kind of critique." In one of their first major articles together, written in 1963, Piven and Cloward made an argument that reflected what they had observed at the Mobilization. They contended that, since "the poor have few resources for regular political influence," their ability to prompt social change depends on the disruptive power of tactics such as "militant boycotts, sit-ins, traffic tie-ups, and rent strikes." What was important was not the organizational structures these activities built, but the willingness of participants to interrupt business as usual. Protest movements, they explained, gain real leverage only by causing "commotion among bureaucrats, excitement in the media, dismay among influential segments of the community, and strain for political leaders."[23]

Piven has been refining and elaborating this thesis ever since. Indeed, it was only after a decade and a half of further work that the argument would make its most controversial appearance, in 1977's *Poor People's Movements*. In the still-young world of academic social movement theory, this book would be recognized as a daring and original intervention—and also, in many ways, as a heresy.

∾

Once a fringe radical, Alinsky had won significant influence in organizing circles by the 1970s, and likeminded scholars, focused on the importance of popular organizations in leveraging social change, were making inroads in academia as well. Today, social movement theory is a well-established area of focus within sociology and political science. During the Vietnam era, however, it was just barely gaining a foothold in the academy. Stanford professor Doug McAdam tells the story of how, as a student activist in the late 1960s, he sought out classes on social movements at his university, searching the catalogue of the political science department. None were listed. When he finally did find discussion of movement activism, it took place in a very different setting than he had expected: namely, in a course on abnormal psychology.

At the time, McAdam writes, "movement participation was seen not as a form of rational political behavior but a reflection of aberrant personality types and irrational forms of 'crowd behavior.'" As Piven and Cloward put it in a 1991 essay, movements were seen "as mindless eruptions lacking either coherence or continuity with organized social life."[24]

In the 1970s, this view began losing its hold, and something closer to the perspective of structure-based organizers began to take its place. Graduate schools became infused with a generation of New Left scholars who had direct ties to civil rights, antiwar, and women's liberation movements. Coming from a more sympathetic standpoint, they sought to explain social movements as rational forms of collective action. They argued that protests should be seen as politics by other means for people who had been shut out of the system. A leading stream of thought that emerged in this milieu was known as "resource mobilization theory."

In many respects, resource mobilization served as an academic analogue to Alinsky's vision of building power through the steady, persistent creation of community organization. It also lined up with the activities of the labor movement. Scholars in the resource mobilization school put social movement organizations at the center of their understanding of how protest groups effect change. As McAdam and W. Richard Scott write, resource mobilization theorists "stressed that movements, if they are to be sustained for any length of time, require some form of organization: leadership, administrative structure, incentives for participation, and a means for acquiring resources and support."[25]

This viewpoint gradually gained ground. By the early 1980s, "resource mobilization had become a dominant background paradigm for sociologists studying social movements," writes political scientist Sidney Tarrow. Although other schools of thought have since come into favor, McAdam and Hilary Schaffer Boudet argue that the biases and emphases of resource mobilization still guide "the lion's share of work in the field."[26]

∾

When Piven and Cloward published *Poor People's Movements* in 1977, its ideas about disruptive power—which were not rooted in formal organizations—represented a direct challenge to ascendant strains of academic theory. More than that, they also clashed with much of the actual organizing taking place in the country, whether spearheaded by Alinskyite organizations, labor unions, or socialist cadre groups. As the authors wrote in an introduction to their 1979 paperback edition, the book's "critique of organizational efforts offended central tenets of left doctrine."[27]

Their position, however, was based on solid evidence. Piven and Cloward mounted their heterodox assault by means of four detailed case studies. These involved investigation into some of the more significant protest movements in twentieth-century America: the movement of unemployed workers early in the Great Depression, the industrial strikes that gave rise to the Congress of Industrial Organizations (CIO) later in the 1930s, the civil rights movement in the South in the 1950s and 1960s, and the activism of the National Welfare Rights Organization in the 1960s and 1970s. As Piven would later summarize their conclusions, the experience of these revolts "showed that poor people could achieve little through the routines of conventional electoral and interest group politics." Therefore, what remained as their key tool "was what we called disruption, the breakdowns that resulted when people defied the rules and institutional routines that ordinarily governed life."[28]

A structure-based organizer such as Saul Alinsky would not object to building power from outside of electoral politics. Nor would he disagree with the idea of using boisterous action to make a stink. After all, he was a great showman and tactician of disorderly troublemaking. But Alinsky would have sharply parted ways with Piven and Cloward on the need for organization to support change. *Poor People's Movements* irked both resource mobilization theorists and on-the-ground organizers by contending not only that formal structures failed to produce disruptive outbreaks but also that these structures actually detracted from mass protest when it did occur.

Piven and Cloward's case studies offered a take on past movements that was very different from standard accounts. Of the labor activism that exploded during the Great Depression, they wrote that, contrary to the most cherished beliefs of union organizers, "For the most part strikes, demonstrations, and sit-downs spread during the mid-1930s despite existing unions rather than because of them." Their studies showed that "with virtually no exceptions, the union leaders worked to limit strikes, not to escalate them."[29]

They saw a similar pattern in the civil rights movement. There, the authors wrote, "defiant blacks forced concessions as a result of the disruptive effects of mass civil disobedience"—not through formal organization.[30]

Piven and Cloward acknowledged that such conclusions failed "to conform to doctrinal prescriptions regarding constituencies, strategies, and demands." Nevertheless, they were willing to pick a fight on this point, writing that "popular insurgency does not proceed by someone else's rules or hopes; it has its own logic and direction."[31]

Poor People's Movements offered a variety of reasons why, when people were roused to indignation and moved to defy authority, "organizers not only failed to seize the opportunity presented by the rise of unrest, they typically acted in ways that blunted or curbed the disruptive force which lower-class people were sometimes able to mobilize." Most centrally, the organizers in their case studies opted against escalating the mass protests "because they [were] preoccupied with trying to build and sustain embryonic formal organizations in the sure conviction that these organizations [would] enlarge and become powerful."[32]

Across the four different movements that Piven and Cloward examined, organizers showed similar instincts—and these instincts betrayed them. The organizers viewed formal structures as essential, seeing them as necessary for marshaling collective resources, enabling strategic decision making, and ensuring institutional continuity. But what the organizers did not appreciate was that, although bureaucratic institutions may have benefits, they also bring constraints. Because organizations have to worry about self-preservation, they become averse to risk taking. Because they enjoy some access to formal avenues of power, they tend to overestimate what they can accomplish from inside the system. As a result, they forget the disruptive energy that propelled them to power to begin with, and so they often end up playing a counterproductive role. As Piven says of the labor movement, "Mass strikes lead to unions. But unions are not the big generators of mass strikes."[33]

Poor People's Movements also made an argument about the pace of change, challenging the idea that gains for the poor were won through steady, incremental effort. Piven and Cloward stressed that, whatever course of action they take, organizers have a limited ability to shape history. Emphasizing the economic and political causes underlying social phenomena, they argued that popular uprising "flows from historically specific circumstances." The routines of daily life, the habits of obedience people develop, and the threat of reprisals against those who act out—all of these function to keep disruptive potentials in check most of the time.[34]

Periods when the poor do become defiant are exceptional, but they also have a defining impact. Piven and Cloward saw history as punctuated by disruptive outbreaks. Instead of change occurring gradually, they believed, it came in bursts—through "Big Bang" moments, as Piven calls them in her 2006 book, *Challenging Authority*. Such a period can erupt quickly but then fade just as rapidly. While its reverberations within the political system have lasting significance, "insurgency is always short-lived," Piven and Cloward explain. "Once it subsides and the people leave the streets, most of the organizations which it temporarily threw up . . . simply fade away."[35]

∼

The divide between "structure" and "mass protest," or between long-term organization and disruptive uprisings, is by no means a matter of two individuals. Alinsky and Piven provide a useful glimpse into this divide. But, in truth, it runs deep through social movement history, appearing with surprising regularity between different groups of grassroots activists in diverse countries and time periods.

With regard to organizing in the 1950s and 1960s, sociologist Charles Payne has argued that the US civil rights movement consisted of two distinct strains of activity: one, which he calls the "community *mobilizing* tradition," was a lineage "focused on large-scale, relatively short-term public events" such as the famous campaigns in Birmingham and Selma. This strain relied on the energy of mass protest. Payne contrasts this approach with the "community *organizing* tradition," a structure-based lineage associated with the gradual base building and local leadership development carried out by the likes of legendary civil rights organizer Ella Baker.[36]

Sometimes the tension between these strains could erupt into heated disagreements. As Student Nonviolent Coordinating Committee (SNCC) leader Stokley Carmichael would later write, "Organization vs. mobilization was always a serious problem, because every day-to-day tactical decision was affected by the strategic approach. Every one."[37]

The divide produced notable arguments between the students in SNCC and King's staff in the SCLC. By 1963, SNCC organizers, influenced by Baker, were making long-term commitments to building community organizations in sometimes remote outposts in the Deep South. These included places such as Lowndes County, Alabama, and small towns throughout Mississippi, which would famously become staging grounds for the voter registration drives of 1964's Freedom Summer. The SNCC activists were critical of the SCLC, arguing that King's group—by moving from city to city, producing media frenzies, and leaving locals to clean up the mess they left behind—did not do enough to cultivate lasting indigenous leadership. As Carmichael put it: "Here comes SCLC talking about mobilizing another two-week campaign, using our base and the magic of Dr. King's name. They are going to bring in the cameras, the media, prominent people, politicians . . . turn the place upside down, and split."[38]

The critique was accurate in highlighting how the SCLC's mass mobilizations were generally short-lived and produced messy fallout for local organizations. However, as Project C showed, these public confrontations were also extraordinarily powerful, drawing national attention to the issue of racial prejudice, creating some of the movement's most memorable images, and forcefully pushing forward federal legislation.

Stepping back, it is apparent that structure-based organizing and mass protest each have important strengths and weaknesses. Interestingly, although Alinsky and Piven took clear sides in the debate between the two traditions, both had moments in which they recognized the value of the other lineage.

For its part, structure-based organizing is right to contend that mass mobilizations are often fleeting and that different types of organization are needed to institutionalize the progress made through periodic outbreaks of disruption. Critics of Piven and Cloward underscored this argument. Although *Poor People's Movements* was quickly recognized as a milestone in its field, the book also provoked some strongly negative reactions. One review dubbed it an "anti-organizational philippic"; another denounced the volume as a call for "blind militancy," hardly better than the abnormal psychology it aimed to replace.[39]

Because *Poor People's Movements* was a book full of polemical contentions, it is not surprising that it evoked strong reactions. However, Piven's life as a politically engaged citizen has suggested a more subtle appreciation of the benefits long-term organizations can offer. For many decades, Piven has had warm relations with Alinskyite groups. In 1984, Cloward and Piven wrote the foreword to a manual in this tradition; they praised *Roots to Power: A Manual for Grassroots Organizing* by veteran activist Lee Staples as "an exemplary exposition of the knowledge and skills that grow out of community organizing." More recently, Piven celebrated ACORN as "the largest and most effective representative of poor and minority people in this country," lamenting that the Right's successful attacks against the organization produced an immense loss. Similarly, although *Poor People's Movements*, like much of the writing produced by the New Left in the 1960s and 1970s, was critical of the ossifying character of big labor, it acknowledged the importance of unions in defending against the erosion of progress achieved during moments of peak mobilization. Throughout her career, Piven has been a consistent supporter of labor's more scrappy and militant organizing factions.[40]

Piven and Cloward were themselves involved in significant organizational advocacy. In the 1980s, the two formed an organization called Human SERVE, or Human Service Employees Registration and Voters Education, to promote voter registration in low-income communities.

Their work was instrumental in securing passage of the Voter Registration Act of 1993, also known as the "Motor Voter Act," which allows people to register to vote in welfare agencies and when getting driver's licenses. When President Clinton signed the bill into law, Piven spoke at the White House ceremony.

Although the contributions of structure are different from those of mass protest, Piven holds out the possibility for different groups of participants to specialize in different types of dissident activity. "Organizations are not movements," she says. "But organizations can institutionalize and legalize the gains won through disruptive mobilization."[41]

~

The structure-based organizers of the Alinskyite tradition had a point: mass protest movements frequently fail to create means of preserving progress over the long term. But *Poor People's Movements* had criticisms of their tradition that were equally valid.

Piven has been astute in identifying a kind of shortsightedness that is common among many longtime organizers. When moments of widespread defiance arise—outbreaks such as the vast immigrant rights protests of 2006 or the emergence of Occupy encampments— those from the worlds of conventional labor organizing, Alinskyite groups, and mainstream political campaigning are often mystified, and sometimes they are downright hostile. Because mass mobilizations fall outside their established models for bringing about change, they commonly respond with suspicion. Thus, at the very moment when social movements are most visible on the public stage, these organizers offer little constructive input to help mass actions grow larger or to garner greater public sympathy.

Over the decades, a variety of organizers in the Alinskyite lineage have challenged such inflexibility in their tradition's guiding tenets. As one recent example, George Goehl, the executive director of National People's Action, has encouraged the groups in his network to embrace bigger-picture vision and to form ties with emergent movements. It is possible that Alinsky himself would have supported this move. Looking back at the origins of many foundational principles associated with community organizing, it becomes clear that he might have pressed for reconsideration of certain commandments that have grown hallowed since the 1960s.[42]

In other words, if Alinsky were alive today, he might well be breaking his own rules.

It turns out that many of the precepts of community organizing come less from Alinsky himself and more from his successors' subsequent codification of his ideas. After Alinsky's death, IAF leaders Ed Chambers, Richard Harmon, and Ernesto Cortes sat down to assess the factors that contributed to the failure of some earlier organizing drives and to refine their methodology for building community groups. In their assessment, they honored Alinsky's innovations but also offered criticisms. Although the founding father had planted seeds for organizations throughout the country, only a handful survived for longer than three years. As IAF organizer Michael Gecan writes in his book *Going Public*, "Alinsky was extraordinarily effective as a tactician, writer, speaker, and gadfly. He was the first theorist and exponent of citizen organizing in urban communities." But, "While Alinsky had many gifts and strengths . . . he did not create organizations that endured."[43]

This challenge would be left to his protégés, in particular Ed Chambers, who took over as head of the IAF in 1972. "That was Chambers's critical contribution to the world of citizens organizing and to America as a whole," Gecan writes. "He had a talent for teaching people how to organize power that lasted." Chambers systemized the Alinsky model in several key ways. He formalized processes for recruiting and grooming organizers. He improved working conditions among staffers to reduce burnout. He relied less on large foundations for funding. And he strengthened ties to faith-based groups. Other networks of community organizations further developed the model: they brought local groups into national coalitions. And they created their own training programs to refine and spread the rules of grassroots power building.

In many respects, these were necessary changes. Yet they may have come at the cost of some of Alinsky's original creativity. In their focus on building for the long term and creating strong organizational structures, subsequent community organizing leaders have grown less sensitive than their tradition's founder to the potential of exceptional moments of mass protest.

In his organizing practice, Alinsky was far less rigid than the "rules" attributed to him might suggest. Nicholas von Hoffman, in a memoir of his time with Alinsky, describes his former mentor as "one of the least dogmatic and most flexible of men. Alinsky believed that liberty was to be redefined and re-won by every generation according to its circumstances and the demands of the time." For his part, Alinsky liked to tell a story, possibly apocryphal, of sitting in on a university exam designed for students of community organization. "Three of the questions were on the philosophy and motivations of Saul Alinsky," he claimed. "I answered two of them incorrectly!"[44]

Alinsky's flexibility, at least during a few vital moments, extended into his take on mass mobilization. During one such moment in his career, he saw the need to integrate the energy of a movement uprising into the work of one of his community organizations.

In May 1961, von Hoffman was organizing under Alinsky's direction in Chicago's Woodlawn neighborhood when he was contacted by a young activist named Terry Sullivan. A devout Catholic and aspiring journalist originally from Denver, the twenty-three-year-old Sullivan had previously volunteered with the community group that von Hoffman was trying to build. Since then, Sullivan had joined a handful of other young whites in traveling to the South to participate in an innovative and potentially dangerous civil rights campaign being sponsored by the Congress of Racial Equality (CORE)—an effort known as the "Freedom Rides."[45]

In 1961, the Supreme Court decision ordering the desegregation of interstate transit systems had been ignored throughout much of the South—much like long-standing federal measures guaranteeing black Southerners the right to vote. Seating on buses run by commercial operators such as Trailways and Greyhound remained separated by race, as did bus station waiting rooms and restaurants.[46] The idea behind the Freedom Rides was to challenge this illegal discrimination. The first group of riders consisted of six white passengers and seven African Americans, led by CORE director James Farmer. After months of planning, these activists departed on two buses from Washington, DC, on May 4, 1961.

On the tenth day of the ride, May 14, the Freedom Riders crossed state lines into Alabama. In coordination with local police, one hundred Ku Klux Klan members attacked the first bus just outside the city of Anniston. Accusing the Freedom Riders of "race-mixing" and "Communistic plots," Klansmen slashed the bus's tires and firebombed its back end while holding the front door shut. Just when they thought the bus was going to explode, the vigilantes holding the door ran off, allowing the riders to spill out, gasping for air. As the activists called for water and protection, Klansmen instead attacked. Highway patrolmen on the scene allowed the melee to proceed for several minutes before intervening, standing by as locals with baseball bats clubbed riders who were crawling on the ground, still gagging on the smoke in their lungs. Finally, one patrolman ended the assault by firing a pistol into the air and telling the mob casually, "You've had your fun, now go home." One of the few bystanders who came to assist the riders, a twelve-year-old white Anniston resident, later described it as "like a scene from hell." Years later, she would say, "It was the worst suffering I'd ever heard."[47]

With the first bus rendered a charred shell outside of Anniston, the second bus continued to Birmingham. There, it was attacked by the Klan and local white vigilantes, egged on by police commissioner Bull Connor. Anticipating the riders' arrival, the local Klan called on members from across the state to convene and greet the bus. Connor had communicated that they would have a fifteen-minute "grace period" to confront the Freedom Riders, during which authorities would look the other way. A mob of hundreds, armed with iron pipes, was ready to take advantage of this offer. As civil rights activists entered the city's bus terminal, the vigilantes pounced. CBS News reporter Howard K. Smith witnessed the violence: "They knocked one man, a white man, down at my feet and they beat him and kicked him until his face was a bloody red pulp." Charles Person, one of the riders most seriously injured, required fifty-three stitches on his head after being beaten with a lead pipe, and his injuries resulted in a permanent knot at the base of his skull.[48]

Descriptions of the attacks and images of the burned bus quickly made national and even international news. Organizers issued calls for fresh volunteers, black and white, from across the country to continue the rides, and they received a strong response. Over the next three weeks, waves of new buses crossed the Deep South. Amid the escalating drama, Sullivan made a long-distance, collect call from New Orleans to Chicago, reaching von Hoffman at the Woodlawn community organization. Sullivan indicated that several Freedom Riders were interested in making a public appearance in the North, and he requested that von Hoffman's group host an event.

Von Hoffman was initially hesitant. He was doubtful that the event would advance local organizing and mindful of previous civil rights rallies in Chicago that drew only a handful of picketers. Yet he arranged for a talk to be held in a large gymnasium in Saint Cyril's Church. As Alinsky biographer Sanford Horwitt writes, "On a Friday night, two hours before the program was to start, the gym was empty and von Hoffman was nervous—his initial fears seemed about to be confirmed. An hour later, an elderly couple arrived, and then, to von Hoffman's total amazement, so many people turned up that there was no room left in the gym, in the foyer, or on the stairs."[49]

Von Hoffman arranged for loudspeakers to broadcast the talk to the hundreds of people in the streets outside the venue. Later, he left the event reeling. Far more people had come than his group could have possibly mobilized through its organizational structures, and the topic had generated a profound energy in the community. He woke up Alinsky with a middle-of-the-night phone call and explained what happened. Von Hoffman said, "I think that we should toss out everything we are doing organizationally and work on the premise that this is the moment of the whirlwind, that we are no longer organizing but guiding a social movement."[50]

To his surprise, Alinsky responded by saying, "You're right. Get on it tomorrow."

The Woodlawn organization subsequently held its own version of the Freedom Rides—a bus caravan to register black voters. The event, Horwitt recounts, produced "the largest single voter-registration ever at

City Hall," startling the city's powerbrokers. It generated much greater publicity than Woodlawn's typical actions, and it set the stage for further civil rights activism by the group.[51]

Alinsky understood something important when he embraced "the moment of the whirlwind." He saw that using mass mobilization to produce spikes in social unrest is a process that follows a different set of rules than conventional organizing. Many of its principles—embracing demands with wide symbolic resonance, channeling energy and participation from a broad public rather than a carefully cultivated membership, and being willing to present issues in moral and visionary terms—are the opposite of the principles that drive local community organizing. And yet Alinsky was willing to experiment with their possibilities.

～

One reason structure-based organizers are typically wary of movement mobilizations is that the workings of disruptive power are often murky. Can outbreaks of mass defiance really be intentionally triggered and magnified? Advocates like Piven give little sense of how. And this silence contributes to the notion that mass mobilizations owe more to the zeitgeist of an era than to calculated human effort.

Poor People's Movements is visionary in recognizing the explosive potential of bottom-up defiance. At times, it seems almost prophetic in anticipating the course of the uprisings like Occupy and the Arab Spring. But whereas, on one hand, the book appears to encourage such mass mobilization, it stubbornly refuses, on the other, to serve as a guidebook for future action. In fact, because it asserts that activists' best-laid plans more often than not are doomed to failure, it threatens to rob people of their agency altogether. If, as Piven and Cloward argue, "protest wells up in response to momentous changes in the institutional order" and "is not created by organizers or leaders," what are those seeking social change to do with themselves?

In its conclusion, *Poor People's Movements* offered a qualified call to arms: "One can never predict with certainty when the 'heavings and rumblings of the social foundations' will force up large-scale defiance,"

Piven and Cloward wrote. "But if organizers and leaders want to help those movements emerge, they must always proceed as if protest were possible. They may fail. The time may not be right. But then, they may sometimes succeed."[52]

This was a reasonably hopeful note upon which to end. Still, activists can be forgiven if they find *Poor People's Movement*'s advice to be frustratingly vague. In a later essay, Piven and Cloward noted: "Saul Alinsky said organizers must rub raw the sores of discontent, but that does not tell us which sores, or whose sores, or how to inflame them, or what to suggest people should do when they are ready to move into action." This is well put. And yet, most often, Piven and Cloward's writings were even further removed from any direct guidance of social movements. Because of this, it has been left to others to provide more practical insights into how to orchestrate disruptive protest.[53]

Fortunately, the world of social movement thinking is now experiencing a renaissance on this front, with traditions of strategic nonviolence occupying a critical space in the discussion. Civil resistance recognizes both *conditions* and *skills* as relevant in shaping mass mobilization. Its practitioners would not disagree with Piven when she writes that there are "major ways protest movements are shaped by institutional conditions," and that the effectiveness of organizers is often "circumscribed by forces they [do] not control."[54] However, this reality only makes it more important that activists refine their *skills* for addressing the aspects of mobilization that they can influence. These skills include the ability to recognize when the terrain for protest is fertile, the talent for staging creative and provocative acts of civil disobedience, the capacity for intelligently escalating once a mobilization is under way, and the foresight to make sure that short-term cycles of disruption contribute to furthering longer-term goals.

The legacy of *Poor People's Movements* is that, in providing a counterbalance to traditional ideas about organizing, it opens the door for more inventive analysis of movement strategies. The recognition of structure and mass protest as two distinct forms of action allows for dialogue between different schools of thought—and it ultimately creates the potential for a synthesis.

Many new activists are drawn into politics through the energy of a mass mobilization but are disappointed when their movement experiences an abrupt decline. For them, the challenge of how to combine explosive short-term uprisings with long-term organizing that can make movements more sustainable is an exciting one. Coming from the opposite perspective, veteran community organizers who have recently experienced the tremendous momentum that disruptive outbreaks can generate—even if much of it is fleeting—have been willing to reexamine maxims such as "build organizations, not movements." These two groups share a mutual interest bridging the gap between "resource mobilization" and "disruptive power." They recognize that a study of mass protest does not rule out appreciation of what can be accomplished through building institutional structures, just as a focus on disruption does not require that activists wait around until the next "Big Bang" moment in world history arrives before endeavoring to take action.

The emergence of civil resistance is compelling because it presents the possibility of integration—between structure and mass protest, between fast and slow. As an organizing model, strategic nonviolence looks carefully at the question of what activists can do to practically make use of disruptive power. Furthermore, by grappling with questions of institutionalization, it opens a dialogue between activists in the lineage of Alinsky and those more in line with Piven, suggesting ways in which their respective traditions can work in tandem.

Already, campaigns of civil resistance have provided some illuminating models. Without ever having heard of Alinsky or Piven, a group of student revolutionaries in Serbia struggled in the 1990s with their own questions of structure and mass protest. The marriage between the two that they forged would represent a major breakthrough: a form of momentum-driven mobilization that could sustain the energy of uprising over multiple years—and that could prove powerful enough to topple a tyrant.

CHAPTER THREE

THE HYBRID

IT WAS DECEMBER 1996, and tens of thousands of people were filling the avenues and city squares of Serbia's capital. Student leaders at Belgrade University, a key center of the demonstrations, felt that their target was in sight: they were going to take down Slobodan Milosevic, the strongman who had ruled over Serbia since 1989 and whose campaigns of ethnic cleansing had earned him the nickname "the Butcher of the Balkans."

The previous month, a collection of antiregime candidates, working in a coalition known as *Zajedno*, or "Together," had gained clear majorities in more than thirty races across the country, but Milosevic annulled their victories. Outraged, Serbians in dozens of cities and towns began holding daily rallies. By late November, marches in the nation's largest city were regularly drawing more than a hundred thousand people. Foreign reporters noted a carnival atmosphere, with speakers set up on cars blasting music. The crowds of protesters were known for carrying whistles, which they blew loudly at any mention of Milosevic's name, sending cacophonous echoes through the streets.[1]

On December 27, the Organization for Security and Co-operation in Europe (OSCE) added to the momentum of the demonstrations by calling on Serbian officials to seat the local election winners. By then, the protests were attracting excited admirers far beyond Serbia's borders.

Indeed, the 1996 uprising in Serbia may have been the first time when the phrase "Internet Revolution" was excitedly used by tech boosters to describe a revolt against a repressive government.[2]

Many student activists who rallied in 1996 had been involved in previous waves of university-based demonstrations against the regime in 1991 and 1992. This time, however, it seemed like anything was possible. December 31, 1996, saw the largest demonstrations yet, with a massive New Year's Eve rally. "This was the night when Belgrade found its soul again after all those terrible years of war and nationalist darkness," activist Novica Milic wrote optimistically at the time. "This night of complete freedom from fear, of happiness that the future could bring us freedom, will always be our sign that we—the democrats in Serbia—will win!"[3]

Such enthusiasm turned out to be premature.

Demonstrations continued until February 4, when Milosevic finally backed down and acknowledged the opposition's municipal victories. The announcement was a high point for movement forces, and yet winning the local elections was never their ultimate goal—they wanted Milosevic out. That did not happen. Over the next year and a half, the strongman consolidated his power, becoming more entrenched than ever. The regime skillfully amplified discord among the opposition parties, and "Together" quickly split into warring factions.

By the end of 1997, Milosevic had circumvented a term limit and engineered his election as president of Yugoslavia, with one of his close allies taking over as the titular head of Serbia. Shortly thereafter, Milosevic made decisive moves to root out two key pockets of resistance: universities and independent media. He passed a new University Law, increasing government control over faculty, as well as an Information Law that allowed the regime to levy large fines against any journalistic institutions deemed to pose a danger to the country's "constitutional order."[4]

Less than a year after what looked like a victory, the vigor of the mass uprising was a distant memory. All of the ambient, frenetic energy of the protests had fizzled. Worse still, young protest leaders found that they had no mechanism for reviving it. When they tried to call new demonstrations, few responded. The activists were left dejected and burned out after months of sleepless nights. Some left the movement or departed the country altogether; others spiraled into depression or drug addiction.[5]

In late 1997, coming off of the disappointments of the protests, a dozen or so veterans of the previous year's uprising began gathering in drab city center cafés, sparsely decorated student newspaper offices, and each other's apartments—anywhere they could talk. Over countless cigarettes and cups of coffee, they dissected what had gone wrong. One participant described it as a meeting of desperate friends. The activists were determined to find a new approach. In October 1998, they decided to found a group called Otpor, or "resistance" in Serbian.[6]

One of those who attended the meetings was Ivan Marovic. Today, Marovic is a father and self-described "retired revolutionary," living a quiet life in Nairobi, Kenya. But in 1996, he was a student in Belgrade University's mechanical engineering department—a place that became an unlikely refuge for antiregime activists, in part because aspiring engineers were given draft deferrals by the government. First as a student protest leader and then as a founding member of Otpor, Marovic would develop a reputation both as a shrewd strategist and as the movement's prankster-in-chief.

During Marovic's childhood, Serbia had been one of the most open countries in Eastern Europe; its citizens were able to travel and to engage freely in music and the arts—"everything that ordinary people can do," Marovic says. But just as other Soviet bloc nations were loosening restrictions in the late 1980s, the situation in Serbia deteriorated. "Following the breakup of Yugoslavia, Serbia was involved directly and indirectly in four wars, which culminated in the bombing of Serbia by the United States and its Western allies," Marovic explains. "I lived in Belgrade during all that period, and I remember experiencing the biggest hyperinflation in the world since the Second World War. I remember economic sanctions, which totally destroyed our economy . . . I remember the total merging of the criminal segment of the society with the state. Economically and socially it was a bad time to live in Serbia."[7]

"And on top of all that," he says, "Milosevic used very brutal methods in order to keep the opposition in check. We had death squads organized by the secret police that were eliminating people—like Slavko Curuvija, the editor of the biggest newspaper who dared to write something against the government."[8]

Although Marovic entered the university as an apolitical teenager, he found the mass protests to be exhilarating, and by 1996 he was fully immersed. "We were having street demonstrations during the day and parties during the night. I got mononucleosis as a result of that," he says—referring to the so-called kissing disease—"and I met my current wife."[9]

Marovic felt deep disappointment when the high period of resistance ended and the regime solidified its power. "They gave us a little victory, but after that there was a crushing defeat," he explains. "We realized, it's not a sprint, it's a marathon. And for a marathon we needed a different type of organizing."[10]

This realization would have historic consequences. Seeking to spark an unarmed rebellion, Otpor would set out to distinguish itself from the mass protest movements of the past. But it would also organize differently than the structure-based groups in the country—namely, Serbia's opposition political parties and its established trade unions. Forging a middle path, it would use provocative, creative actions to produce a series of crises for the Milosevic regime and eventually accomplish what previous efforts could not.

The model that Otpor developed has been studied by movements in dozens of other countries and adapted to local circumstances in widely varied parts of the world. What it represented was perhaps the most compelling example to date of a hybrid between structure and mass protest—a powerful example of what can be called momentum-driven organizing.

～

For as long as people have experimented with building movements around strategic nonviolence, they have grappled with a dilemma: how to reconcile the explosive short-term potential of disruptive power with the need to sustain resistance to meet long-term goals.

Gandhi struggled throughout his life with creating a hybrid. He was famous for his campaigns of widespread civil disobedience, or *satyagraha*. But he combined these with an ongoing "constructive program," through which local communities could build autonomy, as well as with efforts to build the grassroots reach of the Indian National Congress, which became the country's leading independence organization. The Southern Christian Leadership Council was another attempt at integrating models. Although it specialized in mass mobilization, the SCLC built up an organizational infrastructure that allowed it to engage in a series of successive campaigns. Because of this, King's organization could move from Albany to Birmingham to Selma and beyond rather than disappear after the peak energy of a single wave of demonstrations died down.

With its mixture of structure and mass protest, Otpor provided another innovative example of how dissidents employing militant nonviolent tactics could gradually increase pressure over time, escalating through multiple stages of uprising that were spread over years. Because lessons from the Serbian uprising came at a time when the field of civil resistance was reaching maturity, they could be integrated with the insights from the academic lineage that had grown out of Gene Sharp's work. The result was an important leap forward for strategic nonviolence as an organizing tradition.

Over the past decade, the Serbian activists have been widely celebrated, but not for any one particular thing. Some commentators have noted that Otpor activists were hip and edgy, that they made protest fun, and that they used social networks to draw in large numbers of participants. Others have been impressed by their clever tactics and use of pointed humor. All these things are true, but none are necessarily unique: resistance efforts have long attracted recruits by projecting a sense of coolness; satire has been a perennial tool of dissidents; and all social movements are, by nature, *social*—dependent on interpersonal relationships as much as abstract ideology.

Although they are less frequently recognized, Otpor's most distinctive innovations in fact involve the new type of organization they created: one that was disruptive yet highly strategic, decentralized yet carefully structured.

Throughout their year of coffee shop brainstorming, Otpor's founders centered their discussion on how to create something distinct from the organizing traditions they had previously encountered. All of Otpor's founders had been intimately involved in the revolts of 1996, and they knew well the excitement and energy that mass mobilizations could produce. Several were also veterans of earlier student demonstrations against the regime in 1991 and 1992. With no founding members over the age of twenty-seven, the fact that some had seen at least two sizable waves of movement activity come and go was a testament to the ephemeral nature of such revolts.

"The school of organizing I came from was the student protests," says Marovic. "This organizing school was totally impulsive. It put no emphasis on establishing connections between people. It was about getting the greatest number of people and bringing them out on the street.

"We could draw out 10,000, sometimes 20,000 people, just from the university," he explains. "The problem with this way of organizing is that it couldn't last long, and we couldn't take it outside our familiar terrain"—namely, the prominent college towns.[11]

Having been trained in mass protest, Marovic came from one side of the organizing spectrum. A different set of Otpor founders were individuals who had been reared in structure-based organizing. Various independent trade unions were present in Serbia, patiently trying to build up their membership rolls and exercise power in individual workplaces. Likewise, human rights groups and professional associations mobilized targeted constituencies to push for reforms. But the structure-based approach was best exemplified by the country's long-established political parties. Several of Otpor's founders had been groomed in the youth branches of different opposition parties. They were trained to build up chapters of local party loyalists and were given a glimpse of how they could make a career by rising through the parties' carefully managed hierarchies. The operations that tutored them worked within the constraints of the system to eke out small legislative gains and to serve their members.[12]

"That school of organizing is based on building connections, building networks, and slowly growing an organization," Marovic explains. The young leaders had learned important lessons there, but they were discontent. In the wake of a major electoral defeat in the fall of 1997, the youth criticized their parties. "My friends who had been involved with the political parties were frustrated with their way of organizing," says Marovic, "because it was sluggish, and because it couldn't reach people who weren't already connected to their networks. They couldn't bring in people from the outside like we could with our protests."[13]

The need for integration was an idea that arose organically in the activists' conversations. "It came out of both sides feeling frustrated," Marovic explains. "When the two groups got together, we started thinking of a model that would incorporate elements of each tradition. It wasn't quick; we were meeting for many months. But slowly we came up with a hybrid. And that hybrid was later named Otpor."[14]

～

Otpor's combination of traits usually found in disparate schools of organizing has been the source of confusion for many observers who have been unsure how to classify the movement. Looking back, some have described Otpor as a "genuine populist movement" and a "viral explosive which detonated in the consciousness of like-minded youths." Others, such as sociologist Vladimir Ilic, have seen the group as an organization with "a rather well-developed structure" and "an invisible but efficient hierarchy" of leaders.[15]

Both are right. Otpor developed a type of momentum-driven organizing that is fundamentally based on deploying disruptive power but that takes a deliberate and disciplined approach to mass mobilization. Rather than waiting around for the next "Big Bang" that could send people into the streets, they began building a network with the ability to engineer its own spikes of unrest. They would start small. But they would end with a revolt of historic proportions.

Early on, the organizers decided that Otpor should maintain a firm commitment to using nonviolent tactics. Their reasoning was simple: Milosevic would slaughter them if they took up arms. Whatever rag-tag group they could assemble would be no match for the government's soldiers and secret police—not to mention the regime's partners in organized crime—if they fought on the terrain where those forces felt most comfortable. Instead, the activists set out to make the regime as uncomfortable as possible.

"Initially Otpor was viewed as just another student organization with no real political influence, and neither the regime nor the opposition parties paid much attention to it," write former activists Danijela Nenadic and Nenad Belcevic. "By the time the regime realized the strength, impact, and significance of Otpor, it was too late to stop the momentum of resistance."[16]

From the start, the movement was conscious about its look and messaging. The Otpor founders were savvy in their ability to steal ideas from corporate marketing campaigns to allow their message to reach people who were indifferent to the typical political advertisements and sloganeering of the opposition parties. The earliest and most iconic of these symbols was Otpor's logo: a clenched fist, rendered in stylized fashion by activist Nenad Petrovic. After initially creating the Otpor logo, Petrovic submitted it as an assignment for a design class in branding, and he was given the equivalent of a C. Two years later, Otpor's fist would be one of the most recognizable images in Serbia.

The fist had strong patriotic associations, recalling the icon of the Yugoslav Partisans who fought against Nazi occupiers during the Second World War. The allusion was a bow to the country's older generation, which had first-hand memory of the earlier resistance movement. But it also had pop appeal: the Partisans were the subject of a 1970s TV show beloved by the country's youth, a sort of Serbian version of the A-Team.

Otpor's fist was easy to paint onto walls with a stencil or to slap onto a street sign as a sticker. It quickly began appearing throughout the country, sometimes accompanied by a single word, "Resistance!" T-shirts with the same design became a sought-after commodity, especially for Serbians under thirty.

In March 1999, US and European forces in the North Atlantic Treaty Organization (NATO) bombed Serbia for seventy-eight days in retaliation for Milosevic's war in Kosovo. Despite their hatred of Milosevic, Otpor organizers opposed the bombing of their country, witnessing how it rallied the population in support of the regime. During this time, the organizers—who had been slowly adding to their ranks—laid low. But when the bombing ceased that summer, Otpor reappeared, deploying a series of irreverent stunts that capitalized on public dissatisfaction and mocked Milosevic's pretentions of being a conquering hero despite having suffered an obvious defeat.

At a time when many people did not believe anything could be done to confront the regime, Otpor deployed its members to carry out hundreds of small actions that conveyed a sense that resistance was possible. When asked about their formative influences, Otpor's founders were fond of citing Monty Python's Flying Circus. In the town of Nis, activists held a birthday celebration for Milosevic, offering the president gifts such as handcuffs and a one-way ticket to the International Criminal Tribunal at The Hague. When authorities in the city of Novi Sad tried to surround their postwar reconstruction efforts with official pomp—even though the new bridge the government constructed over the Danube River amounted to little more than a temporary pontoon— activists responded by ceremoniously building their own toy bridge over a pond in one of the city's central parks. The stunt left authorities with two bad options: look cartoonishly repressive by arresting people for playing around with a Styrofoam prop, or let Otpor continue to mock the regime.[17]

In another now-famous prank in Belgrade, a troupe of activists placed a steel barrel emblazoned with Milosevic's image on a busy walkway in one of the city's central pedestrian shopping centers. Next to it, they placed a baseball bat. Signs invited onlookers to either drop a coin into the barrel "for Milosevic's retirement fund" or—if they did not have a coin "because of Milosevic's economic policies"—to take a whack at the barrel. Within 15 minutes, a large crowd had formed of shoppers eager to take turns at bat. Police soon arrived on the scene. But finding no evidence of the activists who set the stage, they were not sure whom they should arrest. Eventually, they took the barrel itself into custody, much to the delight of the independent media.[18]

Such irreverent stunts allowed a growing number of new Otpor participants to undertake acts of defiance that, if they were caught, might typically earn them only a night in jail. None of the pranks secured Otpor much in the way of formal influence—and thus they would have been regarded as wasted efforts in the calculus of conventional politics. But they generated publicity that helped the activists win the sympathy of the public at large. Their aim was to disperse the atmosphere of fear and apathy that had prevailed since the uprising of 1996 sputtered out. Gradually, it was working.

~

By ridiculing the regime, Otpor chipped away at its legitimacy. Milosevic was the continual butt of their jokes: an autocrat to be ridiculed rather than feared. The group's most famous slogans—such as "It's spreading," "He's Finished," or "It's Time"—were not even explicit in naming their target. They did not need to be.

Such messaging was a departure from the appeals of the political parties, which were always written to bolster a selected candidate or advance a specific reform. Otpor's methods would set them apart from the traditional parties in other ways as well. The parties could offer concrete benefits to their members: they could help secure patronage jobs or find some state funding for local projects. Yet the parties' pull within the system, limited as it was, made them averse to taking risks. They might hold demonstrations, and they might contest Milosevic's candidates in elections. But they were cautious about keeping their carefully scripted protests from escalating. They were aware that, if they got too confrontational, their leaders would be subject to arrest—and possibly worse. After all, these leaders were easy to find.

That was not the case with Otpor. Its founders had been burned on the idea of charismatic leadership. Accordingly, they decided that the movement would have no figureheads that would become media celebrities or that authorities could imprison or blackmail if they wanted to shut down the group. Certainly, Otpor had leaders—people who took on greater responsibility and set an example of commitment. But the group constantly rotated its official spokespeople, and it was careful to avoid developing a cult of personality around any individual.

A key element of the political parties was clearly defined hierarchy, with a strong membership base existing to back up top leaders' standing as recognized powerbrokers. In contrast, Otpor created a structure that could allow for local teams of activists to act independently. As it grew, write Nenadic and Belcevic, "Otpor created branches throughout the country and made national calls for coordinated action. Every branch, however, was autonomous and could plan how to carry its own actions to fit local circumstances."[19]

Otpor's appeal was as much cultural as political. With movement activists shut out of the state-dominated mainstream media (except when being denounced as traitors), an alternative rock station called Radio B92 became the leading broadcaster of the resistance. Some of Otpor's largest rallies doubled as rock concerts, with musicians reading pamphlets from the stage between songs.[20]

The audience for these events—the natural fan base of internationally famous acts such as Rage Against the Machine and local favorites such as the Belgrade thrash metal band Eyesburn—skewed young. Yet, although youth would remain at the core of Otpor's supporters, the founders worked hard to reach beyond. "We realized that if we want to win, we need to step out of the university bubble and work with ordinary people," says Marovic. "We needed a truly broad-based push to defeat Milosevic."[21]

At the same time that they wanted to transcend the limited range of past student protests, the Otpor organizers did not see the political parties as having a viable strategy for broad outreach. Like other structure-based groups, the parties were skilled at building up committees of local leaders that could sustain the organization for long periods of time. Some parties had considerable geographical scope. But each was dependent on a narrow constituency for its core support, be it elderly religious conservatives, liberal intellectuals, or some faction of ethnic nationalists. The parties did not reach the great majority of the Serbian population, people who were turned off by the political system as a whole. Their rallies and marches had a predictable flavor, with top operatives taking the podium and loyalists each turning out a small number of followers in order to produce the necessary audience. No one outside of the party would ever show up.

Because they were seeking to maximize their own power, the political parties were always guarding their turf. "They had no common goals and no common sense," remarked Milja Jovanovic, one of Otpor's leaders. Each of the political parties had ambitions to rule, and this meant that they were perpetually arguing among themselves. "One thing they all had in common was that they all wanted to be in charge," Marovic argues. "So they spent a lot of energy fighting each other. A lot of energy was wasted that way."[22]

Otpor had no interest in becoming another feuding party, and it was not concerned with jockeying to place its own members into political office. Therefore, it was willing to work with people from a wide range of ideological backgrounds. "We knew that defeating Milosevic and securing free and fair elections was something we could all agree on," says Marovic. "So we agreed to put our other differences aside until Milosevic was gone." Years later, sociologist Vladimir Ilic conducted a survey of more than six hundred Otpor participants. One respondent described the movement's ideological diversity as a liberating force. Otpor, he explained, "gave you the sort of freedom the political party denies by its very definition, and this is probably why many party members joined in its activities."[23]

When spontaneous outbursts of resistance occurred in rural areas or small towns, Otpor activists worked diligently to magnify these local eruptions. For the political parties, such flashes of discontent were a distraction because they raised tangential issues and did not advance a predetermined agenda. "Traditional organizations and political parties were very strict about the initiative coming from the top," Marovic says. But Otpor valued it when local citizens took initiative, seeing it as an opportunity to expand their outreach to a new section of the public.[24]

By placing local grievances—whether they involved a lack of electricity or problems with a corrupt local official—in the context of a broader fight, Otpor won the commitment of small-town activists, who were acting outside any formal organization. "The beauty of having a resistance movement involved in all this," Marovic explains, "was that everyone started connecting these local problems with the overall problem, which was the Milosevic regime."[25]

"It's spreading," Otpor's defiant slogan, was proving prescient.

~

Since the early 2000s, decentralized organizational structures have attracted great interest, not only in social movements but also in the worlds of business, technology, and political campaigning. Otpor activists were ahead of their time. Their networks were designed to give the greatest amount of autonomy possible to the greatest number of participants. But contrary to the assumption that decentralization means that anything goes, the opposite is arguably true: movements without centralized hierarchies often require even stronger guidelines and more explicit operating procedures if they are to be effective.

On the surface, many things about Otpor's viral protests resembled the student movements of the past, which also used a combination of creative pranks and larger demonstrations. The difference was that Otpor sought to create something at once more diffuse—reaching across the country—and more purposeful, with all localized actions contributing to a unified strategy. As Nenadic and Belcevic write, "While Otpor presented the illusion of fluid organization and ad hoc decisions, in practice it was well organized but decentralized." Without any internal bureaucracy or centralized authority, Otpor succeeded in creating a cohesive movement identity among tens of thousands of Serbians. Two key tools it used to achieve this were frontloading and mass training.[26]

"Frontloading" was a means of creating well-defined norms and practices for the movement without the direct, heavy-handed oversight typical of the hierarchical political parties.

When teenage photographer Nenad Seguljev wanted to help challenge Milosevic, he went to a local opposition party office and offered to dive in. But he quickly found that for a freshly minted activist to dream up and execute a protest from there was virtually unthinkable. "You needed 100 approvals to do something," Seguljev told author Tina

Rosenberg. The response from party higher-ups to his schemes for direct action was always some form of delay: "We'll see, we'll see," they said.[27]

In the movement, he found a very different culture. "Everything [party leaders] forbade me to do was allowed in Otpor," he said. "Every action I could design or think of, I did."

For Otpor's members, autonomy was the rule. Activists could form their own chapters in their schools or communities; they could call a rally, coat their town square with resistance posters, or stage their own guerilla theater production. The possibilities seemed endless.

The reason Otpor leaders could give people freedom, and still be confident that they would take action that was consistent with the goals and messaging of the larger effort, was that they had "frontloaded" the guiding tenets of the movement. The founders had intentionally created a sort of DNA that was replicated as Otpor chapters spread. They established this DNA in many ways: they had a clear strategy, a brand, and a vision of what they wanted to accomplish. They had a distinct set of tactics that people could pick up and use, as well as well-defined boundaries within which local teams expressed their independence.

From the start, Otpor had a single goal: taking down the Milosevic regime. And it had a plan for bringing this about: small acts of defiance were a first step toward building the movement and breaking down public apathy, but these were to be followed by a more specific formula for changing the political system. In short, activists would compel the regime to call elections; they would create massive turnout around a united opposition candidate; they would join other nongovernmental organizations in carefully monitoring election results so they could document their victory; and they would use mass noncompliance—leading up to a general strike—if and when Milosevic refused to step down.

Otpor reached out to other groups with this frontloaded strategy already in place. "We didn't try to build the coalition by bringing everybody to the table and then . . . trying to come up with the common strategy and the common goal, because that would have been a disaster," says Marovic. The group's founders had attended roundtables that attempted such discussions before, only to see them dissolve in acrimony. Their approach instead was to take the most basic demand that everyone could agree on and to build from there.[28]

Initially, other civil society groups told Otpor their formula for ousting the regime was crazy. However, as they saw volunteers flock to lend their support, the insane vision starting looking less absurd. In time, it began to seem almost plausible.

~

The replication of a core DNA is something that happens naturally in mass movements. As protests spread, participants pick up common beliefs, slogans, and practices. But absent conscious deliberation about what the norms of a movement should be, negative habits get passed on along with positive ones. Often, the same tactic that worked at the launch of a movement gets replicated again and again, long after it has lost its novelty in the media and its ability to catch opponents off guard. In this way, an innovative citizen's blockade at a trade summit (the 1999 World Trade Organization protests in Seattle, for example) devolves into an endless series of summit protests, easily contained by the police.

The Serbians were aware of this risk. Because they frontloaded their movement with an overarching strategy, they were not dependent on a single tactic. In November 1999, Otpor held one of its first major rallies in Belgrade. Police descended and violently dispersed the crowd. Amid the clash, fleeing protesters chanted, "Tomorrow! Tomorrow!" vowing a return the next day. But organizers opted for a different tack. Daily rallies had been the hallmark of the protests in 1996, and the Otpor leaders had learned their lesson. "If we do it every day, people will get exhausted after a short while," Marovic told author Matthew Collin. "It's better to show up in a different way than to always give [authorities] the same thing so they know how to deal with you."[29] As it built up to an electoral push that would be backed by mass noncompliance, Otpor avoided centralizing around mass marches in Belgrade; instead, participants kept their actions varied and unexpected.

With the movement's plan progressing, the regime started catching on to the idea that the irreverent troublemaking popping up throughout the country might become more than a mere annoyance. It started intensifying its response. Notwithstanding Otpor's use of humor, resistance could involve serious repercussions. After the organization's first national day of action, in early 2000, sixty-seven activists in thirteen cities were rounded up and interrogated. Overall, between 1998 and 2000, there were more than fifteen hundred arrests of Otpor members. One leader, Srdja Popovic, was pulled off the streets by security forces, questioned, and threatened on several occasions. Once, an officer placed a gun in the activist's mouth and told him that he wished they were in Iraq, where no one would blink if a rabble-rouser were shot. The regime sent the message in other ways as well. Popovic's mother, a prominent journalist who had been editor in chief of TV news at Radio Television Serbia, the state broadcasting service, found herself facing a series of demotions as her son's activism intensified. Nor was Popovic an isolated case. For his part, Ivan Marovic was kidnapped three times by members of the secret police, who once threatened, "We have a wonderful dentist here, a real master who's going to pull out all your teeth."[30]

One of the most notorious attacks on local Otpor members was carried out by Milosevic's son, Marko. The younger Milosevic was a playboy known throughout the town of Pozarevac for his bleach-blond hair, expensive cars, and swaggering machismo. Marko maintained a virtual fiefdom in the area. He ran a string of semisuccessful businesses, including a cell phone shop, a café, and a well-known nightclub, Madona. He was also active in the black market, selling cigarettes and gasoline through the country's illicit trade networks. Needless to say, since Marko's rule over Pozarevac was premised entirely on his father's presidency, he was no fan of Otpor. When a clandestine chapter cropped up in town, Marko went to great lengths to hunt down its leaders.

After luring one suspect into his nightclub, Marko's friends beat the activist with batons and pistol butts. Marko himself pulled out a chainsaw and lifted it close to his victim's head. "You will not be the last one or the first one that I have cut up and thrown in the Morava river," he said by way of a threat. In another incident, Marko's gang savagely beat three Otpor members, leaving their noses broken and faces covered in blood. Marko arrived later in his BMW, yelling "Kill the scum!" as he waved a gun in the air. Adding another layer of injustice to the brutality, the activists were then hauled off to jail, and one of them was charged with attempted murder.[31]

In their attempts to beat down resistance, however, regime loyalists were pursuing a losing strategy. "What they failed to realize is that the detained activists became hero figures in their environments and were particularly looked up to by their peers," writes Ilic. "Their reputation as victims of police repression encouraged ever larger numbers of young people to join the ranks." State violence resulted in public revulsion. After the attacks in Pozarevac, Otpor posters with headshots of the bloodied activists started appearing widely: "This is the face of Serbia," they read.[32]

"We fed on the repression of the regime," one Otpor member told the Serbian print weekly *Vreme*. "In all towns and cities where they arrested our people the movement accelerated its growth. Immediately afterwards we were approached by new people, sometimes even pensioners, prepared to continue with resistance."[33]

∼

The influx of new participants presented a challenge for Otpor: How would it immerse large numbers of people in its organizational culture and have them understand the guidelines that allowed its decentralized teams to be effective?

The organization's answer was mass training.

Mass protest movements commonly fail to absorb the momentum created during periods of peak mobilization. When demonstrations are in the headlines and the buzz surrounding a movement is high, new people come out in droves, inspired and energized by the surge in activity. But when things cool down, these participants can fall away just as easily. Often, those seeking to reenergize the campaign of resistance later have no means of reactivating their new supporters. Their mobilizations end up caught in a very short boom-and-bust cycle.

During the civil rights movement, one main tool used by the SCLC to address this challenge was the nightly mass meeting. Evening assemblies in packed churches in places like Birmingham and Selma were filled with hours of sermons, freedom songs, and tactical briefings.

These gave practical instructions to participants, and they established much of the unifying identity for the movement. They helped to turn a single protest into an escalating campaign that could build pressure over the course of weeks or months.

Otpor, which was trying to sustain momentum for a much longer time, took the process of absorption even further. The group established an extensive series of mass trainings, a program of initiation that allowed them to quickly engage new supporters, to turn casual participants into committed members of the movement, and to continually upgrade the skills of their activists. The mass trainings became a key means through which Otpor could quickly disseminate the common operating procedures that were used throughout its decentralized structure.

The many pranks that activists pulled in the early days did not merely entertain observers and supply the press with ready photo ops. They also provided opportunities to recruit. At each of them, Otpor members would engage passers-by interested in the action and invite them to trainings. These were not the type of nonviolence trainings typically seen in the United States: short, two- or three-hour affairs intended to prepare people for a single demonstration. Instead, they were courses of ten hours or more, designed to empower participants to operate in their own autonomous, local chapters. The movement was a big tent, ideologically speaking. Yet, by the time new participants made it through the initiation, they had internalized the movement's DNA.

A typical training stretched over the course of a week, in Monday-through-Friday evening sessions. Discussions started in an office or classroom often continued at a bar later the same night. (A *New York Times* correspondent called Otpor "part political movement, part social club.") At the end of the week of training, new recruits were asked to plan and execute an action themselves, putting the skills they had just learned to immediate use. Only then were they officially considered members of the movement.[34]

The number of people in a given session might be small—seven or eight participants was typical—but, when repeated hundreds of times, the trainings integrated extraordinary numbers. In a very short amount of time, people could go from being total outsiders to becoming team leaders in their towns. And the training process was exponential. New chapters were outfitted with manuals and toolkits enabling them to host their own trainings. By the time Otpor had twenty thousand members, so many trainings were under way in so many different localities that the obvious locations for gatherings—community centers and youth clubs—were constantly booked. More difficult than finding qualified leaders for the sessions was securing the physical space needed to train.[35]

∿

In February 2000, Otpor held a congress that, for the first time, brought together more than a thousand members from some seventy chapters around the country. At its peak, later in the year, Otpor would claim more than sixty thousand members. When conducting a survey of these members, Vladimir Ilic marveled at "the amount of spare time activists spend in the organization's activities," noting that "an overwhelming majority of them set aside several hours each day."[36]

This dedication translated into genuine clout. By the spring, Otpor was channeling much of the energy it had built throughout Serbia into the next phase of its strategy: uniting the country's opposition parties behind a single contender who could successfully challenge Milosevic at the polls. Otpor was quickly becoming more popular than any political party, which granted the movement considerable sway over the perpetually bickering politicians. Although none of the party leaders could afford to publicly break with Otpor, the movement activists did not need to express loyalty to any individual politician. Instead, Otpor maintained its position that only a unified front could prevail against the regime. In early 2000, eighteen of the parties began forming a coalition that would ultimately be called the Democratic Opposition of Serbia. As Otpor pushed them to support a unity candidate, it sweetened the proposition with the promise that the movement could deliver five hundred thousand votes to whichever candidate the opposition settled on. But it also backed the challenge with a threat: activists pledged that a hundred thousand people would show up on the doorstep of any leader who went back on commitments to the coalition. After much internal debate, the parties ultimately decided on constitutional lawyer Vojislav Kostunica as their candidate.

That summer, Milosevic announced early presidential elections, to be held on September 24. At that point, the opposition parties began to mobilize in earnest, along with a broad network of civil society groups. Otpor joined with them in an effort to spur voter turnout—a drive united under the slogan, "It's Time."

Otpor also launched a more pointed campaign of its own, called "He's Finished!" This two-word declaration began surreptitiously appearing in graffiti throughout the country and on bold, black-and-white stickers that activists placed everywhere: street signs, bus terminals, and even Milosevic's own propaganda posters.

As the elections neared, the government dubbed Otpor an "illegal terrorist organization." Police stormed its offices, carting off computers and file cabinets. The regime also moved to shut down independent radio stations and antiregime outlets such as Studio B television. During one month of peak activity, there was an average of more than seven arrests of activists per day. As Nenadic and Belcevic write, "Almost every protest ended with police intervention."[37]

Once again, official repression failed to stamp out resistance. As the regime detained more and more young people, with less and less evidence that the arrestees had done anything wrong other than voicing their views, it undermined authorities' claims that those being rounded up were traitorous subversives who harbored a hatred for the nation. This was doubly true when the young people were being targeted for wearing shirts that read "Otpor—Because I Love Serbia."

The raiding of Otpor's Belgrade headquarters also provided an occasion for another of the group's famous stunts. Shortly after the police visit, organizers announced they would be restocking their offices with membership files, and they invited the public to come witness their act of resilience. At the appointed time, in front of press photographers and hundreds of spectators, Otpor members began unloading what appeared to be heavy boxes of paperwork. The volunteer movers made a show of straining under the weight of their cargo. Predictably, regime forces quickly moved in to confiscate the materials. To their dismay and public embarrassment, the police officers learned that the file boxes were completely empty. Onlookers cheered the smirking activists as they were taken into custody, and the heavy-handed policing generated a new round of recruits for Otpor's trainings.[38]

~

When Election Day finally came on September 24, 2000, the country saw record turnout, especially among youth. A remarkable 86 percent of voters under thirty cast ballots. And the overwhelming majority of them voted to oust the country's incumbent rulers. The opposition, which had organized ten thousand election monitors to watch the voting, quickly announced the results of its exit polls. They showed that Kostunica had clearly passed the 50 percent threshold required to win the presidency outright. Milosevic, in comparison, had earned approximately 35 percent of the vote.[39]

The mandate was clear. Yet, as expected, the regime did not cede power easily. Its first ploy was to stall for time, arguing that a run-off election was needed. Otpor and other groups were ready, and they commenced their planned campaign of mass noncooperation.

The day after the election, the opposition handed Milosevic a deadline to concede: October 5 at three o'clock. After that time, citizen convoys from provinces across Serbia would enter Belgrade and immobilize the city. Otpor organizers further called for nationwide demonstrations on September 27. Two hundred thousand people poured into Belgrade's Republic Square chanting Gotov Je!, "He's finished!" Thousands more rallied in smaller cities throughout the country.[40]

Next, opposition leaders put out a call to their supporters, instructing them, in the words of the New York Times, to "perform any act of civil disobedience they have at their disposal." Having already participated in droves in the prelude to the elections, Serbians took the call seriously. Forty miles south of Belgrade, seventy-five hundred workers at the Kolubara coal mines, a major power source for the capital city, went on strike on September 29. Copper miners in Majdanpek soon joined them. In various localities, state TV workers interrupted regular programming, demanded fair coverage for the opposition, or called for the firing of regime-friendly editors.[41]

As October 5 neared, the country readied itself for a decisive show-down. The key question was whether the military and the police would open fire on demonstrators, using violence to prevent crowds from re-moving Milosevic from power. Otpor had long anticipated this possi-bility—and endeavored to head it off. Throughout their two years of escalating dissent, the activists consistently worked to cultivate sympa-thy from within the security forces, sending care packages of food and cigarettes to soldiers and commiserating with individual police officers about poor pay and working conditions. The activists' goal was to make sure that, when presented with a hard choice, the army and the police would side with the opposition rather than the regime.

As the sun rose on October 5, long lines of cars, buses, and trucks filled the highways as citizens from throughout the country descended on Belgrade. The police had erected roadblocks to prevent the convoys from entering, and officers had been given orders to shoot. They did not carry out these orders, however. Seeing themselves clearly out-numbered, police abandoned their posts, and demonstrators pushed the blockades from the roads. Indeed, the image of a large, yellow bull-dozer, driven by civilians, plowing through regime barricades would become a defining symbol of the revolution. In total, more than five hundred thousand people amassed in Belgrade's city center. When tear gas failed to disperse the crowd, some members of the riot police be-gan fleeing. Others, seeing that the tide had turned, happily joined the demonstrations.

Some minor skirmishes occurred on October 5, some offices within Parliament were burned, and the downtown police station was ran-sacked. But the mass bloodshed that observers had feared did not take place. That evening, a triumphant Kostunica stood on the balcony of Belgrade's city hall and addressed the crowd. The next day, Milosevic recognized his defeat. Within a year, he would be sent to The Hague to face trial as a war criminal.

∾

By no means did Otpor overthrow Milosevic on its own. The political parties, civil society groups, and the trade unions all intervened at critical moments to propel the resistance forward. Yet Otpor played a vital role as an instigator and catalyst, sparking a much more rapid and broad-based rebellion than was likely to have occurred without it. By doing this, it upended the idea that the most well-established or best-resourced organizations are necessarily the best placed to force major change. Instead, it demonstrated that major groups, precisely because they are firmly established, can be slow to recognize opportunities for disruptive revolt. Sometimes, they must be prodded into action by scrappy upstarts mobilizing outside of the structure of any traditional dissident organization.

Otpor helped to bring about an amazing turn in Serbian life, and its accomplishments would have international reverberations. The group's legacy, however, is not an uncomplicated one, and the aftermath of what has become known as the "Bulldozer Revolution" raises some difficult questions.

Although there have been positive changes in Serbia, Milosevic's ouster was merely a first step toward addressing the country's entrenched problems. As Serbian author and analyst Ivan Vejvoda wrote in 2009, "The institutional, economic, and social devastation left by the Milosevic regime has proven to be an immense challenge." As a result, the progress of democracy in the country has been slow. And yet, there have been some significant alterations: a society that had been plagued by war has been able to begin addressing other issues. Citizens have regularly voted out unpopular governments, and authorities have respected the election results. "The atmosphere of fear that existed before is gone. There's not even remotely the same level of repression as in the past era," says Marovic. Vejvoda further argues, "Citizens in Serbia are alert and watchful of politicians' actions. No one in Serbia, or in the Balkans for that matter, wishes a return to the catastrophe of the 1990s."[42]

Otpor's role in rebuilding the country's democracy after the revolution would be limited, for several reasons. One involved controversy about outside financial support that activists had solicited during their fight against Milosevic. Without a doubt, Serbians themselves had provided the great bulk of the organization's resources—through contributions of time, space for organizing meetings, small cash donations, free taxi rides, and countless other forms of assistance. However, it became public knowledge in the early 2000s that Otpor, along with the opposition parties and many other civil society groups, had also received funding from a variety of foreign governments and nonprofit groups. These included European states and US government-funded institutions such as the National Endowment for Democracy. The funds helped Otpor purchase computers, cell phones, and fax machines and cover printing costs for stickers and posters.

Marovic defends the decision to seek outside help: "It was a tough choice, but important choices are never easy. *These countries bombed us*—talking to the representatives of their governments and heads of their foundations was not without discomfort," he wrote. But Otpor saw taking grants from abroad as preferable to accepting funding from the organized crime syndicates or war profiteers who were backing other parties. "All money in the country was bloody," Marovic contends. "Confronted by that reality, foreign support seemed the lesser evil." He further notes that Vojislav Kostunica, the opposition's candidate, was outspoken in his anti-American and anti–European Union views—hardly a puppet for foreign interests. Marovic himself went on to work with social movements in dozens of other countries, many of which were opposing US-backed regimes.[43]

Nevertheless, the wisdom of Otpor's fund-raising decisions remains a matter of debate, both inside and outside Serbia. The issue was one factor that affected the group's ability to transition into becoming a long-term opposition force.

Another factor was a lack of defining purpose following the revolution in 2000. Otpor participants had been united by a clear mission of overthrowing the regime. With this accomplished, the organization floundered. Although it stayed intact for a time as a watchdog group, its membership waned. In postrevolutionary Serbia, the strong institutional structures of the country's political parties proved more durable than Otpor's decentralized network—with the politicians showing themselves adept at negotiating for the spoils of power and patronage that came with the fall of Milosevic. Otpor could not compete at this type of insider positioning, even if it wanted to. By 2004, when it officially dissolved, the organization's most prominent members had moved on, with some taking posts in nongovernmental organizations, some entering mainstream politics, and others returning to private life.

~

Otpor was unable to answer the question of how to institutionalize after a revolution. That quandary would be left to others. But the hybrid it created was a valuable one—and its power would quickly be recognized internationally. By the time Otpor disbanded, several of its most committed members had become sought-after trainers in nonviolent resistance. Otpor's example was studied closely by the activists who went on to launch the Rose Revolution in Georgia in 2003 and by leaders in the Orange Revolution in the Ukraine in 2004. A slightly tweaked version of the Otpor fist appeared as an emblem of resistance in Georgia, and, in each country, elements of the Serbians' hybrid were adapted and put to use.

In 2004, several of the Serbians founded the Centre for Applied Nonviolent Action and Strategies, or CANVAS. Additional trainers from the Philippines and South Africa joined its roster, prompting one publication to dub the group "a sort of People Power International." As scholar Stephen Zunes has written, Otpor veterans have "disseminated the lessons learned from their successful nonviolent struggle through scores of trainings and workshops for pro-democracy activists and others around the world, including Egypt, Palestine, Western Sahara, West Papua, Eritrea, Belarus, Azerbaijan, Tonga, Burma and Zimbabwe as well as labor, anti-war, and immigration rights activists in the United States."[44]

At the time when they started to organize Otpor, its founders were not familiar with the tradition of civil resistance that was becoming increasingly well established internationally. But when they were ultimately exposed to this lineage, they found that the guiding concepts and strategic principles of civil resistance had uncanny resonance with the dynamics that they were discovering for themselves on the ground.

In spring 2000, while their rebellion was in full bloom, several of Otpor's leaders attended a seminar led by Robert Helvey, a close associate of Gene Sharp. The participants were given several books, including Sharp's *From Dictatorship to Democracy*. Although the seminar did not significantly alter the course of Otpor's work—the activists were already deep into their own experiments in nonviolent uprising—the participants felt that the material presented affirmed their instincts. "It was interesting to hear that there was this whole science behind what we were learning the hard way," Srdja Popovic later told the *Wall Street Journal*. "We'd already been using nonviolent resistance for some time," Marovic adds. "But to find what we were doing written in a book, with everything put in one place, was very valuable."[45]

If the encounter with the field of civil resistance had only a minor impact on how the Serbian revolution unfolded, it would become more consequential as Otpor activists worked after the fact to systematize the knowledge they had gained—reviewing what they had done right and where they went wrong. Like King's SCLC, Otpor demonstrated that mass uprising could be engineered. But the Serbians took things a step further by reflecting on their model and sharing their lessons with others. The importance of developing a hybrid would be a key contribution to emerge from their experience. "I have been in many countries after the failure of a mass protest," says Marovic. "And that's when activists have the revelation: They need both protest and organization."[46]

Those who have led trainings around the world know that you cannot export revolution. Successful nonviolent revolt always depends on local expertise and creativity, with the organizers closest to a struggle developing hybrids of their own. But you can spread skills and expand knowledge of a craft—and this can have important consequences.

Otpor's methods would become a prime example of the craft of momentum-driven organizing, a form of activism that uses strategic nonviolence to navigate a path between structure and mass protest. The practitioners of this craft diverge from traditional organizers and campaign consultants in the way they understand many of the key issues in political life: how advocates can capture public attention, what kind of grassroots support they need to succeed, and when they should declare victory.

But even before addressing any of those concerns, these experimenters in civil resistance take on the most basic question of all: How does social change really happen? Their answer is both challenging and counterintuitive. And it offers a new vision of how democratic participation, taken beyond mere voting and electoral campaigns, can alter some of society's most deeply ingrained prejudices.

CHAPTER FOUR

THE PILLARS

IN SERBIA, IT took social forces pushing from outside the country's oppressive power structure to generate change. The relevance of Otpor's example was quickly recognized by activists struggling against repressive regimes in other nations. But in democratic countries with representative institutions, the conventional wisdom is that the process of altering the status quo looks very different. It means working through officials in high office. It requires prolonged and often painstaking backroom negotiations between various interest groups. And when reforms are achieved, they are never so stark or dramatic as a dictator's fall.

Or are they?

As it turns out, this accepted vision of how political change occurs has serious flaws. At best, it presents an incomplete picture of how progress in our society is won. At worst, it is a wrong-headed story that stubbornly conceals the way in which many of the most significant gains of the past century have been secured, from women's suffrage, to labor laws, to civil rights. It misses how people with few material resources and little access to conventional powerbrokers have sometimes been able to bring about transformations that mainstream politicians consider to be absurd and impractical—right up until the moment when these changes become common sense.

In recent memory, there are few better examples of such a transformation than the victory around same-sex marriage. Not long ago, most supporters regarded the idea that gay and lesbian couples would be able to legally exchange vows throughout the United States as a far-off fantasy. Same-sex marriage was not merely an unpopular cause in America; it was a politically fatal one, a third-rail issue that could end the career of any politician foolish enough to touch it.

It can be difficult to remember how hostile the terrain was for lesbian, gay, bisexual, and transgender (LGBT) advocates in even recent decades. As of 1990, three-quarters of Americans saw gay sex as immoral. Less than a third condoned same-sex marriage—something no country in the world then permitted. Remaining in the closet was by far the safest course for public officials who wanted to keep their jobs, and politicians were much more eager to cozy up with religious conservatives than to risk any associations with the "homosexual lobby." In 1996, the Defense of Marriage Act, which defined marriage as a union between a man and a woman and denied federal benefits to same-sex couples, passed by an overwhelming 85–14 margin in the US Senate. Figures such as Democratic senator and future vice president Joe Biden voted for it. Democratic president Bill Clinton signed the act, affirming, "I have long opposed governmental recognition of same-gender marriages."[1]

When the Vermont Supreme Court ruled to allow civil unions in that state in 1999, Republican presidential candidate Gary Bauer called the decision "in some ways worse than terrorism." The state's voters quickly reversed the court's decision, and the judges' perceived overreach sparked a nationwide backlash. As recently as 2004, conservative strategist Karl Rove, seeing a potent wedge issue, pushed to have "marriage protection" amendments placed on the ballot in thirteen states. All of these passed, in what one newspaper called a "resounding, coast-to-coast rejection of gay marriage." The goal of marriage equality seemed doomed.[2]

Today, these look like scenes from an alternate universe. On June 26, 2015, the Supreme Court issued a ruling that made same-sex marriage legal in all fifty states. Yet even before the decision, a dramatic reversal had already taken place. Some three dozen states allowed same-sex marriages by then, and many of them had enacted it through popular vote or laws passed by elected legislatures rather than through judicial decisions. An ever-growing majority of the public expressed its support for marriage equality in national polls. Surveying the transformed landscape, Republican senator Orrin Hatch, a staunch advocate of "traditional marriage," had conceded in 2014 that "anybody who does not believe that gay marriage is going to be the law of the land . . . isn't living in the real world."[3]

What is striking about this is not just the seeming suddenness of the reversal. It is that the rapidly expanding victory around same-sex marriage defied many common ideas about how change is supposed to happen. This was not a win that came in measured doses but rather a situation in which the floodgates of progress were opened after years of half-steps and seemingly devastating reversals. The change was not enacted thanks to a Senate majority leader twisting arms or a charismatic president pounding his bully pulpit. Instead, it came about through the efforts of a broad-based movement, pushing for increased acceptance of LGBT rights within a wide range of constituencies. Put together, they won the hearts and minds of a critical mass of people, and thus turned the impossible into the inevitable. When the issue tipped and same-sex marriage was demonstrated to be a cause with the majority on its side, change came in a startlingly abrupt fashion.

This is perhaps the most important point: rather than being based on calculating realism—a shrewd assessment of what was attainable in the current political climate—the drive for marriage equality drew on a transformational vision. It was grounded in the idea that if social movements could win the battle over public opinion, the courts and the legislators would ultimately fall in line.

The ousting of Milosevic in Serbia and the triumph of same-sex marriage in the United States might, at first, appear to have little in common. But for the tradition of civil resistance, both are examples of a similar process. At the core of this tradition is a counterintuitive theory of change, an understanding of how power is distributed and how it can be exercised that cuts against mainstream assumptions. When people wake up to the true power they possess, this theory argues, they can often defy the expectations of political experts. And sometimes they can even surprise themselves.

~

In the 1970s, as Gene Sharp wrote his landmark works, he was convinced that nonviolent action could be more than a moral crusade. Indeed, he believed that it could be an exceptionally effective form of political struggle, even against cruel and repressive regimes. But in advancing this position, he did not want to be perceived as a starry-eyed dreamer. Therefore, he presented a detailed explanation of how this form of action works.

When Sharp was still a graduate student at Oxford, it dawned on him that most people held flawed conceptions about the nature of political power. As he later described it, he saw that conventional wisdom regards power as "monolithic and relatively permanent." What he meant was that, according to the standard view, power rests in a small number of hands—specifically, the hands of those at the top: tyrants, presidents, and CEOs. These people seem to hold all the cards. They have authority, influence, and resources. And when push comes to shove, they also have the ability to command heavily armed security forces. This last point is critical: the conventional view holds that power, in the end, "comes from the barrel of a gun." Sharp contended that people living under dictatorships, implicitly schooled in this *monolithic* understanding of power, tend to feel helpless. They are led to believe that there is little anyone can do to challenge the existing regime—unless they somehow have the ear of the tyrant or have amassed a substantial arsenal.[4]

Sharp, however, devoted himself to challenging the thinking behind such despondency. Citing political theorists ranging from the famous (Machiavelli) to the obscure (sixteenth-century French philosopher Étienne de La Boétie), he proposed in his groundbreaking 1973 book, *The Politics of Nonviolent Action*, that the monolithic understanding of power is misleading and that there exists an alternative way of seeing things that is far more useful for grassroots forces seeking change.

Promoting what he has come to call the "social view of power," Sharp argued that people have much more power than they typically realize. "Obedience is at the heart of political power," he wrote. "Rulers or other command systems, despite appearances, [are] dependent on the population's goodwill, decisions, and support." Sharp's idea was straightforward: if people refuse to cooperate with a regime—if civil servants stop carrying out the functions of the state, if merchants suspend economic activity, if soldiers stop obeying orders—even an entrenched dictator will find himself handicapped. And if popular disobedience is sufficiently widespread and prolonged, no regime can survive.[5]

Experience has shown that this message can be a powerful one for dissidents working on the ground. In the case of Serbia, many had taken it to heart. "Even a dictator can't collect taxes on his own," one Otpor activist told author Matthew Collin, giving voice to the *social* view of power. "He can't deliver the mail, he can't even milk a cow: someone has to obey his orders or the whole thing shuts down. The task is to convince them to disobey. When they change sides, the government starts to fall."[6]

Sharp's core proposition has given rise to a rich field of study into the dynamics of popular uprising, and it is clear that the more fluid social view of power can be vital in understanding how popular movements function. Yet, in the years after Sharp first elaborated his theory, a variety of academic critics objected that his approach was overly individualistic and voluntarist. Sharp's discussion of power was too focused on personal consent, they argued, and not enough on how power is embedded in collective systems and institutions.[7]

A concept known as the "pillars of support" made an important contribution to addressing these concerns, and it helped to clarify how the social theory of power could be applied in the real world. The idea was developed by civil resistance trainers, including influential Quaker activist George Lakey, and it was incorporated into the literature of the field in Robert Helvey's 2004 book, *On Strategic Nonviolent Conflict.* With the pillars of support, Helvey explains, power still resides in the general population's willingness to accept the legitimacy of a regime and to comply with its mandates. However, this power finds expression in *institutions* both inside and outside the government.[8]

The military, the media, the business community, the churches, labor groups, the civil service, the educational establishment, and the courts, among others, are pillars that lend structural stability to a political system. These are all bodies that, in one way or another, provide a regime with the backing it needs to survive.

The pillars concept offers a catchy visual metaphor for the social theory of power. Imagine the various institutions of society as columns holding up the roof of a Roman temple. Social movements are pulling at the various columns. If they remove one or two of the pillars of support, the building would be weakened, but it might still stand. However, if people pull out enough of the pillars, the temple is sure to topple, and the movements will triumph.

If we imagine a hated dictator sitting on top of the temple, confidently surveying his dominion, the image of the building's sudden collapse—and the tyrant's resultant tumble—becomes all the more satisfying. In a democratic society, the result of the pillars falling might not be a change of regime, and yet the results can be just as profound: the removal of social supports for the status quo can mean the end of a system such as Jim Crow segregation, for example.

Beyond providing an entertaining exercise in visualization, the idea of the pillars of support is helpful in several ways. As a refinement of Sharp's theory of power, it highlights the fact that people do not merely interact with a regime as individuals. Instead, their decisions about when and how they might cooperate are channeled through their various social and professional roles. The pillars allow for better strategic thinking on the part of those trying to force change. Activists can more clearly predict what it will take for a regime to fall. They can scheme about how they might undermine one or more of the various sources of social support for the system—removing the backing of the clergy, for example, or prodding the press to adopt a more critical posture—and thus place the rulers on an ever-wobblier foundation.

∾

When several Otpor leaders attended a seminar in civil resistance, well after their campaign had begun, the idea of the pillars of support hit home. They found it to be a useful framework to describe a variety of the things they were already doing—and a challenge to be more strategic in reaching out to groups they might not ordinarily target. As their struggle progressed, the Serbians' efforts to undermine Milosevic provided a vivid illustration of what it looks like when the pillars fall in practice.

Independent media was a first important social institution in Serbia to side with the resistance. Broadcast stations such as Radio B92 both spread information and lent Otpor countercultural cachet. In the print media, when the regime tried to punish outlets such as the weekly *Vreme* and the daily paper *Dnevni Telegraf* for positive coverage of Otpor, it had the effect of alienating even mainstream journalists, who grew increasingly critical of Milosevic's attempts to muzzle their profession.[9]

Entertainment and popular music made up another pillar that fell early. In 1999, the entire cast of a play called *Powder Keg* raised their fists in unison on stage following a performance at the National Theater, and they received a standing ovation. Likewise, rock musicians, whose music was already seen as an affront to the more traditional folk tunes favored by the mafia and nationalist conservatives, were consistent friends to activists.[10]

The country's intellectuals and university professors were a third pillar to fall. These individuals threw their support behind resistance efforts in increasing numbers after Milosevic passed a University Law in 1998 curtailing the relative autonomy that the country's institutions of higher learning had previously enjoyed.[11]

Eroding other bases of support for the regime took serious work. For more than a year, Otpor organizers strived to win the loyalties of the army and the police. Gaining converts from the army, made up largely of draftees, was the easier of the two challenges: many disillusioned young veterans from Milosevic's wars joined the movement's ranks, and Otpor made sure they were frequently in the spotlight, giving them prominent platforms to denounce the president at rallies and marches.

Winning over the police would be trickier. These officers were professionals, and insubordination could cost them their jobs. But because Otpor's protests produced a constant trickle of arrests, activists in a given locality were soon on a first-name basis with members of the area police force. "Police got to know the enemy and found out that the enemy was a bunch of kids that wanted a peaceful change of a nondemocratic regime," Marovic recalls. As the resistance started visibly gaining momentum, it became evident that taking orders from commanders close to Milosevic might not be the safest career move for individual officers. Otpor activist Stanko Lazendic reported to author Tina Rosenberg that, as the October 2000 presidential election neared, one policeman asked him, "Will we be able to keep our jobs after you take over Serbia?"[12]

This was a valuable sign that the country had been appropriately readied for a final confrontation. Although chipping away these many pillars was a gradual process, the fall of the temple was quick. When Milosevic refused to accept the results of the election, institutions began to withdraw their support at a furious pace, with union members going on strike and religious leaders calling for the president to step down.[13]

With all of the pillars that had once held them up suddenly weakened beyond repair, the powerbrokers of the old order were forced to come to terms with a new reality. Amid mass demonstrations, members of the army and the police widely refused orders to move against protesters. As Serbian political analyst Ivan Vejvoda writes, "Rumor spread that several army generals' sons and daughters were among the protesters and that they would thus refrain from any major violence. The regime was disintegrating from the inside."[14]

Otpor activists had possessed confidence that mass noncompliance could work, but it took faith to believe that the end was near for the regime. "Being in jail or being in the streets, we didn't realize that," Marovic says. Only after the government monolith snapped could social movements see the extent to which it had been undermined by defections.[15]

～

Milosevic fell when the institutions of Serbian society refused to hold him up any longer. But how can the pillars lend understanding to how the debate over same-sex marriage has unfolded?

In an undemocratic regime, a monolithic perspective sees all power as flowing through the dictator. In a democratic nation, monolithic thinking likewise trains citizens to focus on the top. The vast majority of people are taught early on to hold this view. Most history books chart the rise and fall of business tycoons and ambitious politicians. The message is further reinforced when the bulk of our political reporters spend their time writing about the activities of these same actors. Legislative victories are credited to the policymakers who sign the final bills into law rather than to any movements that might have made passage of the bills possible in the first place. The public absorbs this bias, conflating the process of democratic reform with the decisions of charismatic leaders who manipulate the course of the nation's affairs.

In the monolithic model, if people without privileged political access want to affect the behavior of government in a democracy, the best they can do is try to elect a candidate more sympathetic to their views, with hopes that this person, once in office, will deliver on the issues they care about. Needless to say, this process often ends in disappointment for voters: countless promising new candidates have been quick to distance themselves from grassroots supporters and perpetuate the status quo after they finally breach the corridors of power. Other avenues for gaining influence, such as hiring a lobbyist or filing a lawsuit, depend on the expertise of insiders working the system, and few people can afford to pay the hefty bills that accrue as a result.

A social view of power opens up alternative possibilities for influencing political and economic affairs. Because noncooperation can command the attention of otherwise unresponsive politicians and business leaders, many tactics from the civil resistance canon are relevant across different political contexts. The boycott is a clear example of one that can be used in democracies and autocracies alike. When the United Farm Workers rallied Americans to stop buying table grapes in the 1960s and 1970s, they showed how consumers could exercise power by withdrawing economic participation. The tactic was just as effective in targeting powerful businesses in the United States as it was when applied to a country such as apartheid South Africa.

Both structure-based organizing and momentum-driven campaigns (which seek to deliberately harness the power of mass protest) are based on generating people power outside the formal structures of democratic politics. To that extent, both believe that grassroots sway can be used to challenge monolithic elites. And yet these two organizing traditions use social power in very different ways.

The structure-based approach is fundamentally *transactional*. It employs social power to extract narrow concessions from opponents. If a group of workers threatens to walk off the job, or members of a tenants' association start collectively withholding their rent, they can gain power at the bargaining table. Moreover, if they build up organizational strength, they can use their institutional muscle to leverage further gains. A structure-based organization might target and shake one of the pillars of support in order to demonstrate its strength and gain credibility in negotiations. But it is rarely trying to topple the structure as a whole. The types of victories secured through this approach tend be messy, pragmatic compromises that reflect the consensus about what is politically "realistic" at a given time.

Yet, in its most robust form, a social understanding of power encourages advocates to think bigger. It allows them to break with a solely *transactional* view of politics and instead incorporate a *transformational* perspective on how to generate social change. A transformational approach does not center on using institutional power to leverage what incremental gains might be possible on an issue at a given moment. Instead, this approach attempts to alter the climate of public debate to make much more far-reaching changes possible.

Instead of targeting specific powerbrokers who might be able to grant concessions to social movements, activists pursuing a transformational route seek to influence the public at large. They do so in the belief that, ultimately, the level of popular backing for an issue—both the amount of latent sympathy present and the amount that is translated in active, vocal public support—is what makes powerbrokers act, sometimes in ways these elites would otherwise prefer not to. Author and attorney

Michael Signer notes that "it's hard to thank any single individual for altering history; more often, the ship of state alters course only because tides are vastly shifting underneath." A campaign that is thinking in transformational terms attempts to move these deeper waters. Although it may not abandon transactional considerations entirely, it judges itself by standards that go beyond just its ability to exact favorable compromises in the short term.[16]

The campaign in Birmingham exemplified the approach. There, like in other selected Southern cities, civil rights demonstrators made specific demands on local storeowners and politicians. And yet, the biggest impact of these campaigns was not in eking out small, transactional gains on the local level. Instead, it was in altering public perception on a much wider scale. As Martin Luther King Jr. wrote in 1967, "Sound effort in a single city such as Birmingham or Selma produced situations that symbolized the evil everywhere and inflamed public opinion against it." The result of the shift in public opinion was a far more sweeping change: "Where the spotlight illuminated the evil," King argued, "a legislative remedy was soon obtained that applied everywhere."[17]

Compared with the disobedient campaigns of the civil rights movement, the push for same-sex marriage only sparingly used confrontational protest. Therefore, it does not illuminate many of the facets of how civil resistance works in a democratic context. However, what it does do is provide a powerful example of what happens when a transformational drive turns a politically toxic issue into a mainstream crusade.

To see how change manifests once public opinion has shifted and the pillars give way in the United States, look no further than the spectacle of judges and politicians suddenly embracing a cause that was long considered marginal and doomed.

~

Given that the monolithic view of power is so dominant in our society, it is not surprising that some have tried to place victories around marriage equality within that framework. Such a view sees same-sex marriage as a legal triumph, won through clever action in the courts. The monolithic perspective sees the Supreme Court as the decisive body determining the fate of the issue, and analysts operating from this mind-set have cast the high-power attorneys who have argued before the court—figures such as David Boies and Theodore Olsen—as the key protagonists in their narrative of change.

One book in this mold, *Forcing the Spring* by Pulitzer Prize–winning *New York Times* reporter Jo Becker, opens with the line "This is how a revolution begins." Becker is referring to the 2008 decision of a top-level strategist to launch a legal challenge to California's ban on same-sex marriage, a case that would ultimately reach the Supreme Court in 2013 and set an important precedent.

But that is not how the revolution began. Although Becker's book is an excellent illustration of how a monolithic view of power accounts for the rise of same-sex marriage in the United States, it is seriously flawed. Former *New York Times* columnist Frank Rich tweeted, "For a journalist to claim that marriage equality revolution began in 2008 is as absurd as saying civil rights struggle began with Obama." Likewise, Andrew Sullivan, a prominent conservative libertarian who has long been involved in promoting gay marriage—having written the first national magazine cover story making the case for it in 1989—points to the decades of grassroots work that predated the narrow, transactional effort of the Boies's and Olsen's litigation.[18]

Focusing on a single lawsuit, advanced by powerful insiders, is a wholly inadequate way to explain how same-sex marriage went from being a quixotic cause to a political winner. Sullivan noted that between 1996 and 2007, before the case profiled by Becker even started, public support for same-sex marriage in Gallup polls rose from 27 percent to 46 percent—an enormous shift, and a decisive one in understanding how the issue was finally won. To start an examination of the issue with one of the Supreme Court challenges that happened after this is to observe only the endgame of social change. And it is to miss a far more transformational story.[19]

∾

The Supreme Court's 2013 decisions on same-sex marriage—which struck down both California's ban and the federal Defense of Marriage

Act—were critical milestones, paving the way for the final 2015 ruling. But they were preceded by a long series of state-level legislative and legal fights. These included early legal wins in Hawaii (in 1993) and Vermont (in 1999) as well as the establishment of marriage equality in Massachusetts starting in 2003. They also included acts of civil disobedience such as San Francisco Mayor Gavin Newsom's 2004 decision to marry same-sex couples in defiance of California state law. And they encompassed critical later developments such as the spread of same-sex marriage to New Hampshire, Connecticut, Iowa, and Washington, DC, by 2010.

Viewed incrementally, many of these early efforts were failures: the initial progress in Hawaii and Vermont, for example, was reversed (at least temporarily) by state legislation, and the wins that did hold prompted backlash in other places. Yet their symbolic value was immense. Although early legal challenges and legislative drives did not amount to much in terms of transactional gains, the impact of such initial advocacy could be charted through steady movement in the polls.

"Of course we would lose cases, just as all civil rights movements have, at the start and even in the middle," Andrew Sullivan explains. "But the cases, as in all civil rights movements, could be leveraged into a broader and broader public discussion, which could move the polls, which would increase the chances of winning future cases. And that's the pattern we saw."[20]

The court challenges that did prevail were largely won once a majority of the public had already shifted in favor of gay marriage. Early lawsuits, therefore, were noteworthy less for what they accomplished with judges and more for providing opportunities to rally supporters, educate the public, and make their case in the media. "In the real world, before the courts will act, there is almost always some shift in social legitimacy," writes Linda Hirshman, author of a history of the struggle for LGBT rights in the United States. "Civil rights litigation often speeds up the process of social legitimation, because it forces people to take sides in public, but it is almost never the first step."[21]

Even listing the long series of state-by-state battles that preceded any Supreme Court decision does not convey the breadth and variety of the activism that propelled the issue forward. Prior to any favorable legal rulings, a concerted drive to secure rights, recognition, and respect for LGBT people was well under way. Marriage equality was just one demand of a wider movement—and a sometimes-controversial demand at that. (Many LGBT activists viewed marriage as too limited and advocated a more radical agenda of queer liberation, producing a long history of internal debate on this issue.) And yet, the cumulative efforts of this movement created the changes in public attitudes that allowed the issue to ultimately gain approval in the nation's courts and statehouses.

~

Advocates for same-sex marriage did not rely mainly on civil disobedience and mass protest to generate momentum (although there were notable exceptions, such as Gavin Newsom's actions, marches on Washington in 2000 and 2009, large-scale demonstrations in California around the controversial Proposition 8, and a variety of incidents in which members of the clergy broke official prohibitions to perform same-sex weddings). Nevertheless, activists worked to turn the power of a wide range of social institutions against the conservative status quo. Here, the pillars provide a useful metaphor for showing how different constituencies contributed to the eventual triumph of marriage equality.

In the pillar of entertainment, actors who had remained closeted for fear that their sexuality would cost them roles began coming out in greater numbers than ever before. Perhaps most prominent was Ellen DeGeneres, who appeared on the cover of *Time* in 1997. Popular TV shows and movies began featuring openly queer characters, and by presenting these characters in a sympathetic light they normalized LGBT relationships for millions of Americans. These cultural shifts often went hand in hand with movement activity: speaking before hundreds of thousands of LGBT advocates at the Millennium March in Washington on April 30, 2000, DeGeneres pushed other celebrities to publicly come out. "It is the most important thing you will do to save lives," she said.[22]

Within major religious institutions, there were heated conflicts about whether these organizations would uphold the status quo. With LGBT ministers and church members forcing the issue, mainline Protestant denominations saw battles over whether they would welcome queer parishioners, whether openly gay and lesbian clergy members would be allowed to lead congregations, and whether these leaders would consecrate same-sex unions. Similar debates took place within Conservative and Reform Judaism. Although religious bodies have been seen as leading bulwarks against change (and, indeed, the Mormons, the Catholic Church, the Orthodox Jewish movement, and Christian evangelicals remain some of the most steadfast opponents of marriage equality), this pillar weakened as the number of welcoming congregations gradually expanded.

Progressive lawyers pushed the American Bar Association to pass resolutions in the 1990s supporting adoption by same-sex couples and opposing discrimination in child custody hearings. They succeeded, and a strong consensus in favor of LGBT rights took hold within the legal community—along with a decided skepticism of legal arguments justifying discrimination. This tendency was pronounced enough that Supreme Court Justice Antonin Scalia complained in 2003 that the "law-professional culture has largely signed on to the so-called homosexual agenda."[23]

Experts on parenting and childhood development formed another important pillar that fell early. Conservatives in Congress had long insisted that government has a legitimate interest in preserving heterosexual marriage, because same-sex parents would allegedly endanger the well-being of any children they raised. Yet, the longer conservatives held to this position, the harder they found it to produce credible scholars who would back them on it.[24]

Movements in other countries transformed the international landscape, and this further wore away at conservatives' foundation of support. A landmark court decision in 1999 allowed for civil unions in Canada, and full marriage equality laws passed there in 2005. Belgium and the Netherlands had already acted in favor of same-sex couples by then—as had Spain, a Catholic stronghold. South Africa soon followed.

Finally, youth were a decisive pillar that began to move early in support of gay marriage. Whereas being openly gay in high school had once been almost unthinkable in many parts of the country, LGBT student groups grew in record numbers in the 1990s, creating supportive communities for young people who, in previous generations, would never have come out. The Gay, Lesbian, and Straight Education Network (GLSEN) hired its first full-time staff person in 1995 and held its first national convention in 1997, bringing together such student groups into an expanding activist network. The number of people who reported knowing someone gay rose from 25 percent in 1985 to 74 percent in 2000, with young people being far more likely to fall within the new majority than their parents. And because knowing someone who is gay is a strong predictor of support for marriage equality, young people between the ages of eighteen and twenty-nine were almost twice as likely as people aged sixty-five and older to express approval for change.[25]

For Evan Wolfson, founder of the organization Freedom to Marry and one of the movement's key leaders, such shifts in public attitude were essential. As a lawyer in his thirties, Wolfson worked on the legal case in Hawaii that resulted in landmark legal rulings in 1993 and 1996 in favor of gay marriage in that state. However, after Hawaii's voters approved an amendment to the state constitution in 1998 that reversed these gains, Wolfson was convinced that victory would not be won through legal action alone. What was needed, he argued, was "a true campaign that combined political work and public education."

When he founded Freedom to Marry in 2001, Wolfson described his objectives in transformational terms: "I'm not in this just to change the law," he said. "It's about changing society." He further argued that pushing only for more easily obtainable gains, such as domestic partnerships, was a mistake. "What I [advocate]," Wolfson said, "is that we go into the room asking for what we deserve, telling our powerful stories, and engaging the reachable allies. We may leave the room not getting everything we want, but don't go in bargaining against yourself."[26]

In 2005, when Wolfson and a group of other prominent LGBT organizers met in Jersey City to map out a path to securing same-sex marriage across the country, they believed that the Supreme Court would have the final say in creating a nationwide standard of acceptance. Yet they pushed forward a varied range of fights at the state level to establish a record of public support for the issue. They determined, in the words of historian Josh Zeitz, that to make progress in federal courts they "would need to tip the scales in their favor by committing to a decades-long campaign to win the hearts and minds of ordinary voters."[27]

When state-by-state wins did materialize, many were the result of intensive grassroots mobilization. After a favorable 2003 legal ruling in Massachusetts, writes Zeitz, there was "a protracted struggle of almost four years to stave off initiatives aimed at reversing the judicial decision through constitutional amendment." Advocates for gay marriage, led by MassEquality, the state's largest LGBT rights organization, "built grassroots coalitions of clergy, local business leaders, and small-town notables," Zeitz explains. Moreover, "The movement painstakingly compiled a database of all same-sex couples who had married" since the 2003 ruling, training them as lobbyists and ambassadors. In a similar effort in Maine, canvassers led by young gay activists knocked on two hundred thousand doors, sharing their personal stories and generating conversations with members of their communities. Together with countless others, they were fast creating the environment in which same-sex marriage would prevail nationally.[28]

～

In transactional politics, progress comes through the steady accumulation of small victories. Transformational change, in contrast, often occurs in more dramatically punctuated cycles. Because momentum-driven efforts are focused on changing broad public opinion rather than securing a series of incremental gains, their progress is mainly measurable though polls rather than through a scorecard of more tangible wins. For those not paying attention to the overall climate of debate, the results of movement work can be hard to see until a campaign finally reaches a tipping point. Even if advocates pull out a few pillars, the status quo structure can remain standing. But once the public has moved, and an adequate number of props have been fatally weakened, an edifice that looked inert and immovable can suddenly collapse into rubble.

In the context of a dictatorship, the end can be surprisingly rapid. In this respect, the Serbian experience was no fluke. Instead, the conclusion of that revolution followed patterns that commonly appear at the end of civil resistance campaigns. The sight of police and soldiers disobeying orders, a type of refusal known as a "security defection," is often the last stage of the process. For any dictator, such disobedience is a very bad thing. From the Philippines to Eastern Europe to Tunisia, these defections have been sure signs that the roof is coming down on a regime.

Yet by the time this pillar gives way, other indications that a momentous shift is occurring are usually plentiful. From Milosevic's downfall in Serbia to the revolutions of the Arab Spring and beyond, the signs have been much the same: professors and intellectuals are in open revolt, journalists are disseminating news through underground channels to bypass censors, workers are on strike, judges are asserting that a ruler's abuses of power violate the law, political parties are demanding greater representation in official bodies, religious leaders are preaching about the moral justification for resistance, musicians are singing protest songs at rallies, and youth groups are taking to the streets. The "fear barrier" has been broken, as the Egyptian activists who led the revolt in early 2011 put it. Where gains might have been painstakingly gradual before, defections within different constituencies now follow each other quickly. Rebellion becomes contagious.

With same sex-marriage, the public was treated to a stark portrait of what this same process can look like in the United States.

In 2011, for the first time, polls showed public support for same-sex marriage to be over 50 percent. Starting then, we witnessed something not altogether dissimilar to the last days of a dictatorship. As Gallup reported in 2014, "For proponents of marriage equality, years of playing offense have finally paid off as this movement has reached a tipping point in recent years—both legally and in the court of public opinion." As the temple began to quiver, pillars started falling like dominos, toppling in areas including local government, business, religious organizations, the military, professional sports, and even conservative political groups.[29]

New York, Maine, Maryland, Washington. One after another, between 2010 and 2014, more than a dozen states joined the litany of jurisdictions allowing same-sex marriage. Increasingly, the wins came via legislation and public votes, not merely decisions by judges.

By the time the Supreme Court cases were being debated in 2013, it was hardly a fair fight. As *The Nation*'s Richard Kim wrote, not only did the government opt against defending the Defense of Marriage Act but also "it filed an amicus brief arguing that it violates the Constitution's equal protection clause, essentially leaving the defense of the bill to House Republicans and a sad-sack list of professional homophobes like the Westboro Baptist Church, Concerned Women for America, and the Parents and Friends of Ex-Gays and Gays." Signers of briefs promoting marriage equality went far beyond LGBT advocacy groups; they included professional athletes, libertarian think tanks, and corporations such as Google, Nike, and Verizon.[30]

In the military, the policy of "don't ask, don't tell," which generated intense debate and backlash in the 1990s, was finally rescinded in September 2011, giving way to widespread sentiment in favor of "open service" by gay and lesbian troops. In a once-unthinkable turn, military chaplains began performing same-sex marriages.

In July 2013, Exodus International, the leading ministry that had claimed to "cure" homosexuality, shut its doors after thirty-seven years, sending shockwaves through conservative Christian circles. Exodus's director issued an apology to the LGBT community, stating, "We've been imprisoned in a worldview that's neither honoring toward our fellow human beings, nor biblical."[31]

The Presbyterian Church voted in 2014 to allow its ministers to officiate same-sex weddings in states where it is legal. Meanwhile, the Methodists reinstated a minister who had been defrocked for presiding over his gay son's 2007 wedding. As law professor Michael Klarman notes, the president of the Southern Baptist Theological Seminary acknowledged as early as March 2011 "it is clear that something like same-sex marriage . . . is going to become normalized, legalized, and recognized in the culture" and that "it's time for Christians to start thinking about how we're going to deal with that."[32]

Once-traditionalist politicians suddenly began getting in touch with their more tolerant selves. As of 2005, only two US senators, Ron Wyden of Oregon and Ted Kennedy of Massachusetts, were openly supportive of same-sex marriage. But, after the majority opinion tipped, the public was introduced to the viral phenomenon of politicians "evolving" in their views.[33]

On May 6, 2012, Vice President Joe Biden sat for a high-profile interview on *Meet the Press*, in which he stated that he had changed his position. President Obama completed his evolution shortly thereafter. An electoral fear barrier had broken, and a flood began. In just one week in April 2013, six US senators declared their support for marriage equality. Environmentalist writer Bill McKibben noted with some bemusement that, around the same time, "Bill Clinton, the greatest weathervane who ever lived, finally decided that the Defense of Marriage Act he had signed into law, boasted about in ads on Christian radio, and urged candidate John Kerry to defend as constitutional in 2004, was, you know, wrong. He, too, had 'evolved,' once the polls made it clear that such an evolution was a safe bet." A week later Hillary Clinton joined him in explicitly announcing her support for same-sex marriage, despite having declared in 2004, "I believe marriage is not just a bond but a sacred bond between a man and a woman."[34]

The wave of state-level "marriage protection" amendments that passed in 2004 turned out to be the last gasp of an opposition that had been polarized but was in decline. By 2014, even prominent conservatives had flipped. They included former vice president Dick Cheney, Ohio senator Rob Portman, and former representative Robert Barr, who sponsored the Defense of Marriage Act in 1996.

Same-sex marriage moved to the bottom of the list of major concerns expressed by Republican voters, and even those politicians who had not changed their position preferred to keep quiet about their views. Conservative strategist Steve Schmidt, an advisor to John McCain's 2008 presidential campaign, argued, "I believe Republicans should reexamine the extent to which we are being defined by positions on issues that . . . put us at odds with what I expect will become over time, if not a consensus view, then the view of a substantial majority of voters."[35]

The metaphor of falling pillars shows how, even prior to the 2015 Supreme Court ruling, the gains in the fight for marriage equality had been overdetermined. These advances were triggered in multiple, reinforcing ways. To focus solely on the transactional details of the individual court cases, ballot initiatives, and legislative maneuvers that came at the conclusion of the struggle is to miss a key point: these fights took place in a landscape that had already been transformed. As Richard Kim wrote in 2013, "Gay marriage isn't winning the day because of some singularly persuasive legal argument; it's winning because the battleground has shifted from the court of law to the court of public opinion."[36]

Or, as Wolfson put it, "We had persuaded the country, and the courts followed."[37]

∿

In the court of public opinion, everyone has a say in rendering the final verdict. But there is still a special role for the advocates who make the case before their peers. Both in Serbia and in the United States, a mobilized base was needed to undertake the work of shifting popular opinion. And this reflects a last important point about the theory of change: making the pillars fall is not just about getting a majority of people to passively endorse your cause. It is also essential to create a strong, energized core of participants who are willing to go out of their way to help advance the movement. The type of enthusiasm and dedication possessed by these proponents can be called "active public support."

The data on the difference that active participation makes in determining the success of a nonviolent movement is striking. And this data is available largely thanks to a scholar who never imagined herself becoming an expert in civil resistance.

As an undergraduate at the University of Dayton in the late 1990s, Erica Chenoweth took classes in military science and participated in training activities sponsored by her school's ROTC program; her goal was to become a US Army officer. In the end, Chenoweth decided not to join the military. "I liked the rappelling, the uniforms, map reading, and shooting at the range," she explains. "But I wasn't stoked about getting up in the wee hours of the morning to run until I vomited. I quit, and chose the far less strenuous career of professor."[38]

Chenoweth began a doctoral program at the University of Colorado Boulder, spending her first years as a graduate student writing about political violence. In 2006, she received an invitation from a colleague to attend a workshop sponsored by the International Center on Non-violent Conflict (ICNC). The weeklong seminar was intended to introduce social scientists to the field of civil resistance, with the hopes that the participating academics would use the material in their classrooms. "Skeptical but curious—and more than a little enticed by the free food and books," Chenoweth wrote later, "I applied to the workshop."[39]

Chenoweth had not previously heard of theorists such as Gene Sharp, and she walked away from the workshop unconvinced. "My view of all this stuff was that it was well intentioned, but dangerously naive," she says. Chenoweth found the case studies that had been presented on Otpor, the Indian Independence movement, and other nonviolent struggles to be interesting. However, her background in empirical research left her wary. She believed that the presenters were drawing unduly broad claims from evidence that was merely anecdotal. She was also uncertain about whether the victories claimed by social movements could actually be attributed to people power rather than historical and geopolitical conditions. Throughout the workshop, she needled the presenters with critical questions. "By the end of the week, as you can imagine, I wasn't too popular," she says.[40]

At the conclusion of the seminar, Chenoweth spoke with Maria Stephan, who at that time was serving as the ICNC's academic outreach coordinator. To Chenoweth's surprise, Stephan agreed that too little research had been done to quantitatively reinforce arguments about the effectiveness of civil resistance. After much discussion, the two decided to team up in an effort to correct this. ICNC offered to support a data-driven analysis that would compare the outcomes of struggles that used nonviolent tactics to those of armed uprisings against undemocratic regimes. Chenoweth's participation was secured with the promise that the ICNC would publish the results regardless of what they revealed—even if this meant showing that the unarmed movements were much less effective than true believers in strategic nonviolent action had imagined.

Together, Chenoweth and Stephan began developing what would eventually become the most extensive empirical database ever created on civil resistance. They pored over stacks of encyclopedias, news articles, and historical reports to find their data points. "Whether it was nonviolent or violent," Chenoweth explains, "we would only code a case as 'successful' if it achieved the full removal of the incumbent leader, *de jure* and *de facto* secession, or the expulsion of a foreign military." To be considered effective, a campaign also had to achieve this objective "within a year of its peak."[41]

After two years of research, Chenoweth crunched the numbers. She was surprised by what she saw. Examining the first data set of 323 campaigns, she found that nonviolent movements worldwide were twice as likely to succeed as violent ones. As they added more cases, the new data reaffirmed this finding. Further, Chenoweth and Stephan observed that, over the previous fifty years, nonviolent campaigns had grown both more numerous and more successful, even under brutal authoritarian regimes. Violent insurgencies, meanwhile, had grown "increasingly rare and unsuccessful."[42]

In 2008, Chenoweth and Stephan published these results in an issue of the academic journal *International Security*, and they later expanded their work into a 2011 book, *Why Civil Resistance Works*. Their findings quickly made waves. Within the data-focused quarters of political science and strategic studies, which had previously paid nonviolent conflict little heed, civil resistance began gaining new respectability. *Why Civil Resistance Works* earned the 2012 Woodrow Wilson Foundation Award from the American Political Science Association—the same award that, in 1958, went to Henry Kissinger, someone hardly known for his advocacy of nonviolence. In 2013, *Foreign Policy* named Chenoweth one of the year's "Top 100 Global Thinkers" for, as the magazine put it, "Proving Gandhi Right."[43]

One particularly intriguing finding from Chenoweth's work concerns the level of participation needed to sustain a winning social movement. In their book, Stephan and Chenoweth found a direct correlation between the success of a campaign and the popular involvement it managed to invite. Among the movements they studied, the victorious ones uniformly fostered broad-based public sympathy. And yet, Chenoweth found that the number of supporters who were actively engaged in successful movements could be quite small. She observed a trend that she would later dub the "3.5 percent rule."[44]

As Chenoweth explains, "Researchers used to say that no government could survive if five percent of its population mobilized against it." But she saw that the threshold was not even that high. Reviewing the data, Chenoweth found that, in fact, "no campaigns failed once they'd achieved the active and sustained participation of just 3.5 percent of the population—and lots of them succeeded with far less than that."[45]

This is not an insignificant number: in the United States, 3.5 percent of the population would mean gaining the active support of some 11 million individuals. But that is still a much smaller slice of the population than the approximately 160 million people that would constitute the majority. For a movement, building this minority into a committed base is just as important as swaying the public at large.

Participation entails something considerably more than latent sympathy. The 3.5 percent needed to be people who were moved to actually take a stand. In compiling their data, Chenoweth and Stephan defined participation as the "active and observable engagement of individuals in collective action." Spurring people to this level of engagement is not easy. Nevertheless, the authors found that it could be more obtainable for unarmed social movements than for groups pursuing military strategies. "Civil resistance allows people of all different levels of physical ability to participate—including the elderly, people with disabilities, women, children, and virtually anyone else who wants to," Chenoweth explains.[46]

Whether or not one regards the 3.5 percent rule as a hard-and-fast threshold for creating change, the measure points to an important idea: although the ultimate goal of transformational movements is to win over the support of the majority of a society, an effort's grassroots strength is measured by the number of people who take ownership over the cause.

Active public support, examined more closely, consists of several components. The first is showing up. A movement's active supporters are the people who take to the streets for marches, attend teach-ins, and staff phone banks. Without them, a movement's rallies would be empty. Second, in societies that hold elections, active public supporters vote with the movement. They put the cause at the top of their list of priorities when going to the polls. For these people, a candidate's position on the issue in question—whether it be climate change, abortion rights, gay marriage, or immigration policy—can be enough to swing their vote one way or the other. In other words, in their electoral calculus, the movement's issue outweighs the personalities of the individual political contenders.

A third trait of active public supporters is that they persuade others. Whether they express their opinions on social media or argue with their relatives over Thanksgiving dinner, they attempt to influence the views of those around them.

Finally, active supporters are the type of people who are moved to act independently to advance an issue within their social and professional spheres of influence. This might mean lawyers taking on pro bono work for a cause they believe in, musicians writing songs that celebrate protesters in the streets, teachers bringing lessons on the cause into the classroom, ministers making it the topic of their Sunday sermons, professional athletes or celebrities being spotted in T-shirts that express their beliefs, or store owners putting signs of support in their windows.

Through this last type of advocacy, active supporters help move the pillars to which they are most closely tied. At the start, when an issue is still unpopular, their vocal stances will often earn them scorn from those who judge their passion to be impractical and their techniques to be misguided. The naysayers, however, overlook an important point: without impracticality, underdogs would never win.

∾

Mainstream politicians recognize the benefits of having the backing of the majority, of course. But they go about gaining it in a very different way. The fact that transformative mobilizations cultivate active public support is what distinguishes them from "triangulation" and other insider approaches that try to cobble together a majority by appealing to the political "center."

Triangulation was a strategy most famously pursued by President Bill Clinton in the mid-1990s, under the counsel of then–White House advisor and later Fox News commentator Dick Morris. The strategy was deeply immersed in the logic of two-party politics. In Morris's words, the idea was to "take the best from each party's agenda and come to a solution somewhere above the positions of each party . . . that became a triangle, which was triangulation." By veering to the right on issues such as welfare reform, trade, and military spending, Clinton attempted to woo a majority by presenting himself as pragmatic and above the ideological fray. The Associated Press has described the practice as one of "mak[ing] policy decisions by splitting the difference on opposing views," with the belief that this will create positions that, by virtue of their moderation, are broadly popular with the American public.[47]

Needless to say, the past century's major gains around women's suffrage, economic justice, and civil rights did not emerge from a strategy of triangulation.

Outsider campaigns that attempt to topple the pillars of support and win over majority public opinion through the efforts of a galvanized base take an opposite approach. Writing about climate strategy, environmental journalist David Roberts cites a simple maxim: "If you want to move the center, you have to pull from one end." Advocates in this mode stake out highly principled positions that at first seem unrealistic, and then they work to rally the public behind their viewpoint. Momentum-driven organizing does not limit itself to the political confines dictated by transactional negotiations at any given moment. Instead, it seeks to create possibilities that those maneuvering within the constraints of the system are unable to imagine. It aims to change the terms of debate, creating a new baseline for what is considered politically feasible and expedient.[48]

Pulling from one end is what transformed Milosevic from an entrenched powerbroker into a disgraced and ousted autocrat, and it is what turned gay marriage from an unpopular fringe issue into a civil rights crusade whose time had come. In the case of Serbia in the late 1990s, it was not hard for Otpor and other resistance groups to get a majority of the population to agree that Milosevic should go. A huge portion of the public already detested the regime. With the economy in shambles and the country reeling from a series of disastrous wars, public opinion had already been won. The problem was that people expressed their dissenting views only in whispers, behind closed doors. Although many Serbians wanted change, few believed that it was actually achievable. It took Otpor's active supporters to demonstrate the viability of resistance.

In the case of same-sex marriage, the work of dedicated activists was likewise essential. It was helpful to have families in Middle America approvingly watch *Ellen* or *Will & Grace* in the 1990s. But the vast majority of these people were not going to force the issue in their workplaces or make it their top electoral concern. The few who actually pushed at the pillars—petitioning their churches to accept their same-sex weddings, calling for their employers to extend health benefits to same-sex partners, attending rallies, filing lawsuits, defending same-sex couples at their schools' proms, knocking on doors, and demonstrating the electoral muscle of LGBT voters at the polls—were the movement's active supporters.

The process of promoting change by swaying public opinion is a more circuitous approach than making a narrow demand and targeting it at a specific powerbroker. "In classical politics, you're interested in the direct route to victory," says Marovic. "But in building a movement, you're interested in the more fundamental change that happens through the activation of citizens. It's indirect. And a lot of the things that are going to come from this, you're not going to see in advance." Piven and Cloward likewise argued, "The impact of mass defiance . . . is not so much directly but indirectly felt." Movements at their most transformative produce tectonic shifts that make the ground tremble. Although the impact is undeniable, predicting exactly which buildings or bridges will buckle as a result can be difficult. Because of this, the activists who generate the tremors often do not receive the credit they deserve for the final changes in policy that come about.[49]

Moreover, part of the process of transformational change is that once an issue has won, its righteousness becomes common sense. After this happens, people will commonly deny that the change was ever a big deal to begin with. They will contend that the shift was an inevitable by-product of historical forces, that it would have happened even without a struggle, and that the lessons that one can draw from it are therefore limited. In the case of same-sex marriage, it is not unusual to hear the view that the victory was an easy one because it merely involved a change in cultural attitudes and did not impose significant economic costs on corporations or economic elites. For this reason, the argument goes, the example is not relevant to movements working to address issues such as climate change.

Certainly, it is true that environmentalists squaring off against the world's fossil fuel magnates face formidable opponents and that tackling global warming is a very difficult fight. But this is hardly the end of the story. Conventional wisdom held that the British would never leave India because of the profits generated by colonialism. The Crown was the most powerful force in the world, and it would never be moved, many believed. But the balance of the economic equation shifted, in part due to geopolitical changes and in part due to transformative movements themselves. In retrospect, some historians now argue that it was forever preordained that the Raj was unsustainable and would be evicted. In the future, the severe storms, floods, and ecological dislocations resulting from global warming are set to cause untold billions of dollars in damages. For this reason, there are economic forces lined up on each side of the climate dispute; as the impacts grow ever more extreme and costly, the economic calculus of complying with movement demands continually changes.

If there is a common trait in the most prominent movements of the past century—whether they involved efforts to end child labor, redefine the role of women in political life, or bring down an apartheid regime— it is that they took up causes that established powerbrokers regarded as sure losers and won them by creating possibilities that had not previously existed. As the pillars give way, barriers long seen as too daunting to be overcome suddenly appear surmountable.

With same-sex marriage, a transformative approach triumphed. By the time the Supreme Court ruled, the decision represented the codification of a victory that, in an important sense, had already been won. The change was achieved through a mass withdrawal of cooperation from a past order based on prejudice. It could be felt well before it was written into law and well before it was acknowledged by those elected leaders now struggling to show that they have "evolved." Indeed, like the Serbian regime loyalists caught off guard by an uprising that flooded Belgrade, America's top politicians—the people typically seen as holding power in our society—were among the last to know.

When it comes to the workings of civil resistance, a faith in the monolithic power of those at the top is not the only thing that mainstream operatives get wrong. Just as they regularly fail to appreciate when the pillars holding up the status quo have grown dangerously weak, they often overlook the types of challenges most likely to begin wearing away at these fortifications. Certainly, that was the case with the British Empire's rulers in India. Try as they might, they could not see why Mohandas Gandhi would choose to stake his political career on the most absurd and tangential of issues. Namely: salt.

CHAPTER FIVE

DECLARE VICTORY
AND RUN

IN THE EARLY morning of March 12, 1930, Mohandas Gandhi and a trained cadre of seventy-eight followers from his ashram began a march of more than two hundred miles to the sea. Three and a half weeks later, on April 5, surrounded by a crowd of thousands, Gandhi waded into the edge of the ocean, approached an area on the mud flats where evaporating water left a thick layer of sediment, and scooped up a handful of salt.[1]

History remembers the Salt March as one of the great episodes of resistance in the past century and as an effort that struck a decisive blow against imperialism. Gandhi's act defied a law of the British Raj, as the state of foreign rule was commonly known, which mandated that Indians buy salt from the government and prohibited them from collecting their own. Soon, Gandhi's disobedience inspired much wider resistance, setting off a mass campaign of noncompliance that swept the country and led to more than sixty thousand arrests. In a famous quote published in the Manchester *Guardian* on May 17, 1930, revered Indian poet Rabindranath Tagore described the campaign's transformative impact: "Those who live in England, far away from the East, have now got to realize that Europe has completely lost her former prestige in Asia."

For the absentee rulers in London, Tagore argued, it was "a great moral defeat."[2]

Yet judging by what Gandhi gained at the bargaining table at the conclusion of the drive, it is possible to form a very different view of the salt *satyagraha*. Evaluating the 1931 settlement made between Gandhi and Lord Irwin, the Viceroy of India, analysts Peter Ackerman and Christopher Kruegler have contended that "the campaign was a failure" and "a British victory," and that it would be reasonable to think that Gandhi "gave away the store." There are many precedents for these conclusions. When the pact with Lord Irwin was first announced, it was a bitter disappointment to insiders within the Indian National Congress, an organization that had been founded in 1885 and had risen to nationwide prominence, with Gandhi taking on significant leadership roles starting in 1920. Congress's top officials were hardly thrilled with the agreement that Gandhi had brokered with Irwin. Future Prime Minister Jawaharlal Nehru, deeply depressed, wrote that he felt in his heart "a great emptiness as of something precious gone, almost beyond recall."[3]

That the Salt March might at once be considered a pivotal advance for the cause of Indian independence and a botched campaign that produced few tangible results seems to be a puzzling contradiction. Even stranger is the fact that such a result is not unique in the world of civil resistance. When Martin Luther King Jr. and the Southern Christian Leadership Conference concluded their drive in Birmingham, the campaign presented similarly incongruous outcomes: on the one hand, it generated a settlement that fell far short of desegregating the city, disappointing local activists who wanted more than just minor changes at a few downtown stores. At the same time, Birmingham became one of the key drives of the civil rights movement, doing perhaps more than any other campaign to push forward the historic Civil Rights Act of 1964.

This paradox is worthy of examination. One of the biggest differences between momentum-driven organizing and other forms of politics is its approach to evaluating the success of a campaign. From start to finish—in both the way he structured the demands of the Salt March and the way he brought this drive to a close—Gandhi confounded the more conventional political operatives of his era. Yet the movements he led profoundly shook the structures of British imperialism. Many of the guiding principles of his campaigns remain relevant today, offering lessons both useful and unexpected.

～

With the Salt March, Gandhi showed how momentum-driven movements often use demands in an unorthodox fashion.

All protest actions, campaigns, and demands have both *instrumental* and *symbolic* dimensions. Different types of political organizing, however, combine these in different proportions. In transactional politics, demands are primarily *instrumental*, designed to have a specific and concrete result within the system. In this model, interest groups push for policies or reforms that benefit their members. These demands are carefully chosen based on what might be feasible to achieve, given the confines of the existing political landscape. Once a drive for an instrumental demand is launched, advocates attempt to leverage their group's power to extract a concession or compromise that meets their needs. If they can deliver for their members, they win.

Even though they function primarily outside the realm of electoral politics, structure-based organizations—such as labor unions and community-based organizations in the lineage of Saul Alinsky—approach demands in a primarily instrumental fashion. Alinsky prided himself on being a political realist. He believed that people were not motivated by abstract values or ideology. "In the world as it is," he wrote, "man moves primarily because of self-interest." As author and organizer Rinku Sen explains, Alinsky established a long-standing norm that "Organizing should target winning immediate, concrete changes," taking on issues that speak to the self-interest of the group of people that is organizing. Ideally, the demands should be neither divisive nor ideologically loaded.[4]

A famous example of this type of instrumental objective in community organizing is the demand for a stop sign at an intersection identified by neighborhood residents as being dangerous; by winning the stop sign, the community organization both demonstrates its power and makes a small, tangible improvement in people's lives. But the stop sign is just one option. Alinskyite groups might attempt to win better staffing at local social service offices, an end to discriminatory redlining of a particular neighborhood by banks and insurance companies, or a new bus route to provide reliable transportation in an underserved area. Environmental groups might push for a ban on a specific chemical known to be toxic to wildlife. A union might wage a fight to win a raise for a particular group of employees at a workplace, or to address a scheduling problem.

By eking out modest, pragmatic wins around such issues, these groups get concrete results and bolster their organizational structures. The hope is that, over time, their power will grow and small gains will add up to substantial reforms. Slowly and steadily, social change is achieved.

Momentum-driven mass mobilizations function differently. For activists pursuing a transformational route to change, it is critical to create a narrative about the moral significance of their struggle. Therefore, they must design actions and choose demands that tap into broader principles. In this context, the most important characteristic of a demand is not its potential policy impact or enforceability as a contract provision. Most critical are its *symbolic* properties—how well a demand serves to dramatize for the public the urgent need to remedy an injustice.

The specific policy proposals and legal mechanisms used to enact change are important. However, most of the decisive negotiations over details come in the latter stages of a movement: transactional deliberations take place once public opinion has shifted and powerholders are scrambling to respond to disruptions that activist mobilizations have created. In the early phases, as mass movements gain steam, the key measure of a demand is its capacity to resonate with the public and arouse broad-based sympathy for a cause. In other words, the symbolic trumps the instrumental.

A good example of how the symbolic dimensions of a campaign can become far more significant than its purely instrumental objectives is the Montgomery Bus Boycott, which began on December 5, 1955. Here, it was the symbolic idea of challenging Jim Crow injustice that captured the national imagination—so much so that the limited instrumental goals outlined at the start of the campaign were almost entirely forgotten.

Today, the boycott is remembered as a campaign based around African American citizens' iconic refusal to "go to the back of the bus." But, interestingly, the demands initially presented by civil rights leaders were very modest. The activists proposed a new seating plan that modified but did not eliminate discrimination on buses. The plan mandated that, on any given bus, whites would begin filling the seats from the front to the back, while black riders would take seats from the back to the front, and no one would be asked to give up their seat. Organizers also demanded "a guarantee of courteous treatment" and "employment of Negro bus operators on predominantly Negro routes." In other words, they proposed a kinder, more polite form of segregation.[5]

What galvanized the entire African American community in Montgomery—and resonated throughout much of the nation—was not this limited set of negotiating points but rather the larger cry for dignity embodied in the boycott. Gussie Nesbitt, a fifty-three-year-old domestic worker and NAACP member, recalled her reason for refusing to ride the bus to work, despite having to endure a long daily walk as a result: "Before the boycott, we were stuffed in the back of the bus just like cattle," Nesbitt explained. "I wanted to be one of them that tried to make it better. I didn't want somebody else to make it better for me. I walked."[6]

It was not until the bus boycott had been in force for two months that leaders of the Montgomery Improvement Association, with King as its president, dropped public insistence that "At no time have we raised the race issue in the movement, nor have we directed our aim at segregation laws." They filed a lawsuit with just such an aim. In the time it took for the case to wind its way through the federal courts, the boycott passed its one-year anniversary, retaining strong community support. By then, obstinate city officials might have wished that they had simply agreed to the original demands submitted by civil rights organizers. In December 1956, the Supreme Court sided with the boycotters, ordering Montgomery officials to desegregate the city's bus system entirely.[7]

In the decades since then, a variety of thinkers have suggested that mass movements have good reason to make the symbolic properties of their demands an intentional priority.

Because momentum-driven efforts pursue a more indirect route to creating change, they must be attentive to creating a narrative in which their campaigns are consistently gaining ground and presenting new challenges to those in power. In his 2001 book *Doing Democracy*, Bill Moyer, a veteran social movement trainer, stresses the importance of "sociodrama actions" that "clearly reveal to the public how the power-holders violate society's widely held values." Through well-planned actions—the protests in Birmingham and the creative stunts in Serbia being prime examples—movements engage in a process of "politics as theater." In Moyer's words, this drama "creates a public social crisis that transforms a social problem into a critical public issue."[8]

The types of narrow proposals that are useful in the behind-the-scenes negotiations of transactional politics are generally not the kinds of demands that inspire effective sociodrama. Commenting on this theme, leading New Left organizer and anti–Vietnam War activist Tom Hayden argues that mass movements are propelled by a specific type of symbolically loaded issue—namely, "moral injuries that compel a moral response."[9]

In his book *The Long Sixties*, Hayden cites several examples, including the right to leaflet for Berkeley's Free Speech Movement and the desegregation of lunch counters for the civil rights movement. Although these demands had instrumental consequence, they also had dimensions beyond their immediate practicability. "The grievances were not simply the material kind, which could be solved by slight adjustments to the status quo," Hayden writes. Instead, they posed unique challenges to those in power. "To desegregate one lunch counter would begin a tipping process toward the desegregation of larger institutions; to permit student leafleting would legitimize a student voice in decisions." The measure of these demands was not merely whether they served the short-term self-interest of the group that was organizing; their importance was that they exhibited a powerful moral draw that allowed movements to gain active supporters and engender public sympathy.

Structure-based organizers pursuing an instrumental demand attempt to communicate with narrowly defined audiences: namely, the group of people they are rallying within their organization and the specific powerbroker who might grant their demand. The call for a stop sign at an intersection—just like the need for a scheduling change in a given workplace—serves as a compelling issue for the limited group of people affected, and it is clearly actionable for those in power. But such demands are often too tightly focused or too technocratic in nature to captivate the public at large.

Transformative movements, seeking to build widespread popular support, must dramatize broader dimensions of their struggle. Sometimes they are willing to take on a symbolically loaded fight, even if it yields little of instrumental value in the short term.

Perhaps not surprisingly, the contrast between symbolic and instrumental demands can create conflict between activists coming from different organizing traditions. Saul Alinsky was suspicious of actions that produced only "moral victories," and he derided symbolic demonstrations that he viewed as mere public relations stunts. Ed Chambers, who took over as director of Alinsky's Industrial Areas Foundation, shared his mentor's suspicion of mass mobilizations. In his book *Roots for Radicals*, Chambers writes, "The movements of the 1960s and 70s—the civil rights movement, the antiwar movement, the women's movement— were vivid, dramatic, and attractive." Yet, in their commitment to "romantic issues," Chambers believes, they were too focused on attracting the attention of the media rather than exacting instrumental gains. "Members of these movements often concentrated on symbolic moral victories like placing flowers in the rifle barrels of National Guardsmen, embarrassing a politician for a moment or two, or enraging white racists," he writes. "They often avoided any reflection about whether or not the moral victories led to any real change."[10]

In his time, Gandhi would hear many similar criticisms. Yet the impact of campaigns such as his march to the sea would provide a formidable rebuttal.

~

The salt *satyagraha* is a defining example of using escalating, militant, and unarmed confrontation to rally public support and effect change.

It is also a case in which the use of symbolic demands, at least initially, provoked ridicule and consternation.

When Gandhi was charged with selecting a target for civil disobedience, he made a preposterous choice. That is, according to the political insiders of the time. It was ridiculous, they thought, to treat the salt law as the lynchpin of the Indian National Congress's challenge to British rule. Mocking Gandhi's fixation on salt, the English-language newspaper *The Statesman* noted, "It is difficult not to laugh, and we imagine that will be the mood of most thinking Indians."[11]

In 1930, the instrumentally focused organizers within the Indian National Congress trained their attention on constitutional questions—whether India would gain greater autonomy by winning "dominion status" from the British and what steps toward such an arrangement the Raj might concede. Their preferred demands revolved around these issues. The salt laws were a minor concern at best. It seemed ludicrous that Gandhi would give so much attention to this triviality rather than to critical matters pertaining to when the British would leave.

Gandhi had not made his choice lightly, however. It had emerged from a long study of the principles of mass uprising. At the beginning of his career, Gandhi had been trained as a lawyer, and as a young professional he had been reared in the mind-set of transactional campaigning. As he later explained, "I was a believer in the politics of petitions, deputations, and friendly negotiations." But, as he immersed himself in experimentation with civil resistance—first in South Africa, and then in India—his orientation changed. Biographer Geoffrey Ashe argues that, in 1930, Gandhi's choice of salt as a basis for a campaign was "the weirdest and most brilliant political challenge of modern times."[12]

It was brilliant because defiance of the salt law was loaded with symbolic significance. "Next to air and water," Gandhi argued, "salt is perhaps the greatest necessity of life." It was a simple commodity that everyone was compelled to buy and which the government taxed. Since the time of the Mughal Empire, the state's control over salt was a hated reality. The fact that Indians were not permitted to freely collect salt from natural deposits or to pan for salt from the sea was a clear illustration of how a foreign power was unjustly profiting from the sub-continent's people and its resources.[13]

Because the tax affected everyone, the grievance was universally felt. The fact that it most heavily burdened the poor added to its outrage. The price of salt charged by the government, Ashe writes, "had a built-in levy—not large, but enough to cost a laborer with a family up to two weeks wages a year." It was a textbook moral injury. And people re-sponded swiftly to Gandhi's drive against it.[14]

Indeed, those who had ridiculed the campaign soon had reason to stop laughing. In each village through which the *satyagrahis* marched, they attracted massive crowds—with as many as thirty thousand peo-ple gathering to see the pilgrims pray and to hear Gandhi speak of the need for self-rule. As historian Judith Brown writes, Gandhi "grasped intuitively that civil resistance was in many ways an exercise in political theater, where the audience was as important as the actors." In the pro-cession's wake, hundreds of Indians who served in local administrative posts for the imperial government resigned their positions.[15]

After the march reached the sea and disobedience began, the cam-paign achieved an impressive scale. Throughout the country, huge num-bers of dissidents began panning for salt and mining natural deposits. Buying illegal packets of the mineral, even if they were of poor quality, became a badge of honor for millions. The Indian National Congress set up its own salt depot, and groups of organized activists led nonviolent raids on the government saltworks, blocking roads and entrances with their bodies in an attempt to shut down production. News reports of the beatings and hospitalizations that resulted were broadcast throughout the world.

Soon, the defiance expanded to incorporate local grievances and to take on additional acts of noncooperation. Millions joined a boycott of British cloth and liquor, a growing number of village officials resigned their posts, and, in some provinces, farmers refused to pay land taxes. In increasingly varied forms, mass noncompliance took hold through-out a vast territory. Despite arrests, property seizures, and public whip-pings by British authorities, it continued month after month. Through the summer of 1930, "the Raj was slowly running down," writes Ashe. "Repressive measures went on and on with no end in sight. . . . But in spite of these, and the censorship and propaganda, there were few signs of a return to cooperation."[16]

Sparking such national rebellion was a remarkable feat. Finding issues that could "attract wide support and maintain the cohesion of the movement," Brown notes, was "no simple task in a country where there were such regional, religious, and socio-economic differences." And yet, salt fit the bill precisely. Motilal Nehru, revered two-time president of the Indian National Congress and father of the country's future prime minister, remarked admiringly: "The only wonder is that no one else ever thought of it."[17]

∾

If the choice of salt as a demand had been controversial, the manner in which Gandhi concluded the campaign would be equally so—at least when judged by instrumental standards. By early 1931, after some nine months of protest, the campaign had reverberated throughout the country, yet it was also losing momentum. Repression had finally taken a toll: much of Congress's leadership had been arrested, and tax resisters whose property had been claimed by the government were facing significant financial hardship. Moderate politicians and members of the business community who supported the Indian National Congress appealed to Gandhi for a resolution. Even many militants with the organization concurred that talks were appropriate.[18]

Accordingly, Gandhi entered into negotiations in February 1931 with Lord Irwin, who, as viceroy, was the highest-ranking British official in India. On March 5, the two announced a pact. On paper, many historians have argued, it was an anticlimax. The key terms of the agreement hardly seemed favorable to the Indian National Congress: in exchange for suspending civil disobedience, protesters being held in jail would be released, their cases would be dropped, and, with some exceptions, the government would lift the repressive security ordinances it had imposed during the *satyagraha*. Authorities would return fines collected by the government for tax resistance as well as seized property that had not yet been sold to third parties. And activists would be permitted to continue a peaceful boycott of British cloth.

However, the pact deferred discussion of questions about independence to future talks, with the British making no commitments to loosen their grip on power. (Gandhi would attend a Round Table Conference in London later in 1931 to continue negotiations, but this meeting made little headway.) The government refused to conduct an inquiry into police action during the protest campaign, which had been a firm demand of Congress activists. Finally, and perhaps most shockingly, the Salt Act itself would remain law, with the concession that the poor in coastal areas would be allowed to produce salt in limited quantities for their own use.[19]

Some of the politicians closest to Gandhi felt dismayed by the terms of the agreement, and a variety of historians have joined in their assessment that the campaign failed to reach its goals. In retrospect, it is certainly legitimate to argue about whether Gandhi gave away too much in negotiations. At the same time, to view the settlement merely in instrumental terms is to miss its most important achievements.

∾

If not by short-term, incremental gains, how does a campaign that employs symbolic demands or tactics measure its success?

For momentum-driven mass mobilizations, there are two essential metrics by which to judge progress. Because the long-term goal of a transformative movement is to shift public opinion on an issue, the first measure is whether a given campaign has won more popular support for a movement's overall cause. The second measure is whether a campaign builds the capacity of the movement to escalate further. If a drive allows activists to fight another day from a position of greater strength—with more members, superior resources, enhanced legitimacy and an expanded tactical arsenal—organizers can make a convincing case that they have succeeded, regardless of whether the campaign has yet made significant progress in closed-door bargaining sessions.

Throughout his time as a movement leader, Gandhi stressed the importance of being willing to compromise on nonessentials. As political scientist Joan Bondurant observed in her perceptive early study of the principles of *satyagraha*, one of Gandhi's political tenets was the "reduction of demands to a minimum consistent with the truth." The pact with Irwin, Gandhi believed, gave him such a minimum, allowing the movement to end the campaign in a dignified fashion and to prepare for future struggle. For Gandhi, the viceroy's agreement to allow for exceptions to the salt law, even if they were limited, represented a critical triumph of principle. Moreover, he had forced the British to negotiate as equals—a vital precedent that would be extended into subsequent talks over independence.[20]

In their own fashion, many of Gandhi's adversaries agreed on the significance of these concessions, seeing the pact as a misstep of lasting consequence for imperial powers. As Ashe writes, the British officialdom in Delhi "ever afterwards . . . groaned over Irwin's move as the fatal blunder from which the Raj never recovered." In a now-infamous speech, Winston Churchill, a leading defender of the British Empire, proclaimed that it was "alarming and also nauseating to see Mr. Gandhi . . . striding half-naked up the steps of the Vice-regal palace . . . to parley on equal terms with the representative of the King-Emperor."[21]

The move, he elsewhere claimed, had allowed Gandhi—a man he saw as a "fanatic" and a "fakir"—to step out of prison and emerge on the scene "a triumphant victor."[22]

While Indian National Congress insiders had conflicted views about the campaign's outcome, the broad public was far less equivocal. Subhas Chandra Bose, one of the radicals in Gandhi's organization who was skeptical of the pact with Irwin, had to revise his view when he took in the reaction in the countryside. As Ashe recounts, when Bose traveled with Gandhi from Bombay to Delhi, he "saw ovations such as he had never witnessed before." Bose recognized the vindication. "The Mahatma had judged correctly," Ashe continues. "By all the rules of politics he had been checked. But in the people's eyes, the plain fact that the Englishman had been brought to negotiate instead of giving orders outweighed any number of details."[23]

In his influential 1950 biography of Gandhi, still widely read today, Louis Fischer provides a most dramatic appraisal of the Salt March's legacy: "India was now free," he writes. "Technically, legally, nothing had changed. India was still a British colony." And yet, after the salt *satyagraha*, "it was inevitable that Britain should some day refuse to rule India and that India should some day refuse to be ruled."[24]

Subsequent historians have sought to provide more nuanced accounts of Gandhi's contribution to Indian independence, distancing themselves from a first generation of hagiographic biographies that uncritically held up Gandhi as the "father of a nation." Writing in 2009, Judith Brown cites a variety of social and economic pressures that contributed to Britain's departure from India, particularly the geopolitical shifts that accompanied the Second World War. Nevertheless, she acknowledges that drives such as the Salt March were critical, playing central roles in building the Indian National Congress's organization and popular legitimacy. Although mass protests alone did not expel the imperialists, they profoundly altered the political landscape. Civil resistance, Brown writes, "was a crucial part of the environment in which the British had to make decisions about when and how to leave India."[25]

~

In the case of Birmingham, the settlement reached by King and other organizers with downtown merchants was hardly more impressive than Gandhi's agreement with Lord Irwin. The victory they claimed was a largely symbolic one, but it was no less powerful because of it.

On May 3, 1963, after a month of protests, the young activists who took to the streets as part of the Birmingham movement's "Children's Crusade" were met with police dogs and fire hoses, and the scenes of violence made national and international headlines. The following week the conflict only escalated further. More than a thousand protesters were arrested on May 7, and many others were blasted with the hoses. Bull Connor was not dismayed by the violence. When he learned that one of those slammed by a high-pressure stream of water was Birmingham's most prominent local civil rights leader—the Reverend Fred Shuttlesworth, then forty-one years old—Connor remarked, "I waited a week to see Shuttlesworth get hit with a hose. I'm sorry I missed it."[26]

Local merchants were not so smug. They were keenly aware that the surge of negative media attention was damaging the city's reputation and that the movement's boycott was cutting into their profits. In short, they were ready to settle. When influential city elders began getting personal calls from Kennedy administration officials such as Treasury Secretary Douglas Dillon and Defense Secretary Robert McNamara, they began siding with the merchants and supported a truce.[27]

The pressure generated by the campaign was working. However, after days of intense negotiations, the concessions made by white leaders were relatively minimal. The final settlement between civil rights activists and white Birmingham officials, announced on May 10, outlined only modest changes. Indeed, each of the provisions in the agreement seemed to have a catch. Yes, fitting rooms at some downtown stores would be desegregated, but this had been considered a relatively painless and uncontroversial concession from the start. The city would begin a process to desegregate lunch counters, and it would order that the "Whites Only" signs on restrooms and water fountains be taken down, but it was not clear how these directives would be enforced. Storeowners agreed that they would hire "at least one sales person or cashier" who was black, but a conservative interpretation of this provision held that only one black employee in the entire city would have to be hired, as opposed to one African American employee in every store, as organizers had intended. Public facilities, such as city parks, would be left unchanged.

Needless to say, these terms represented far less than the total desegregation of the city. Given all of the effort and sacrifice—thousands of arrests, scores of hospitalizations, nationwide outreach, and a nearly complete unsettling of normal daily life in the city—the gains seemed almost inconsequential in comparison.

This fact was not lost on the movement's opponents, the media, or even some of the SCLC's own supporters. Sidney Smyer, a powerful businessman and high-profile white negotiator, stated shortly after the agreement that "King won little or nothing." Assessments in the media reinforced this idea. The day after the May 10 announcement of the accord, the *New York Times* reported, "The settlement terms fell far short of those sought originally by Dr. King and other Negro leaders." The remainder of the *Times* article pointed out the various limitations of the deal, including the fact that Birmingham city officials showed little willingness to promptly implement what narrow accords negotiators on both sides had managed to sort out. *Time* magazine hit an equally skeptical note when it called the settlement "a fragile truce based on pallid promises."[28]

Some activists who had put their personal well-being on the line were outraged by the limited reach of the accord. Fred Shuttlesworth, recovering in his hospital room, was notably nonplussed with the agreement; in advance of announcing the deal, King and Abernathy were left scrambling, in the words of author and journalist Diane McWhorter, "to stanch the leaking rumors of his unhappiness with the peace terms."[29]

Although Shuttlesworth had solid ground to be unhappy, in time he would change his view. Critics of the settlement were correct in pointing out that, evaluated using instrumental standards, the deal did not make much headway. In terms of what it would take to eliminate racial divisions in Birmingham, the concessions that movement negotiators accepted could charitably be described as a first step toward ending Jim Crow. Yet they were loaded with symbolism, and they allowed the organizers to negotiate a victory at a time when further protest would have been difficult to sustain. The outcomes of the organization's efforts proved profound. As Garrow argues, the "SCLC had succeeded in bringing the civil rights struggle to the forefront of the national consciousness. This success far outweighed the narrower question of whether the settlement provided for speedy enough desegregation of Birmingham's stores or an acceptable number of black sales clerks."[30]

Just a month after the movement and city merchants came to a settlement, President John F. Kennedy gave a major televised address announcing that he would put forward federal civil rights legislation. "The events in Birmingham and elsewhere have so increased cries for equality," he explained, "that no city or state or legislative body can prudently choose to ignore them." For the civil rights organizers watching, it was a remarkable scene. "No American president had ever made such an unequivocal speech in support of the rights of African-Americans," Andrew Young observed.[31]

In a famous turn of phrase, Shuttlesworth would later argue that "but for Birmingham" what was signed by President Johnson as the Civil Rights Act of 1964 would not have come into existence. Over the past several decades, this maxim has become widely accepted. Although significant instrumental gains were not an immediate result of the activists' campaign, it turned out they were not far off. The civil rights movement's drive in Birmingham did much to propel the passage of legislation at the national level. Within just a few years, as a result of federal action, the city's Jim Crow apparatus was dismantled in a manner speedier and more sweeping than SCLC organizers could have dared to dream when they first met at Dorchester.

As Gandhi had done some three decades earlier, Martin Luther King Jr. accepted a settlement that had limited instrumental value but that allowed the movement to claim a symbolic win and to emerge in a position of strength. King's victory in 1963 was not a final one, nor was Gandhi's in 1931. But its importance very quickly became clear. By the time of the Selma campaign in 1964, Garrow writes, "Birmingham had shown that even small tangible gains could represent extraordinary symbolic victories, even if those people closest to the struggle could not appreciate it at the time."[32]

Adam Fairclough adds, "Birmingham, and the protests that immediately followed it, transformed the political climate so that civil rights legislation became feasible; before, it had been impossible."[33]

∼

The use of symbolically loaded demands and the acceptance of settlements that adhere to the Gandhian rule of the "minimum consistent with the truth" are not hard-and-fast tenets in momentum-driven organizing. Instead, they represent some of the approaches that activists have taken in addressing a broader issue: what might be called "framing the victory."

The truth is that, for all social movements, judgments about whether or not a campaign is winning can be somewhat subjective. In a sports contest, a buzzer goes off and a final score is posted; similarly, in an electoral race, a final vote count comes in after the polls close, allowing the winning candidate to claim victory. But for movements pushing forward an issue, the results of ongoing efforts are usually much murkier. What looks like a defeat in the short run may be judged a triumph by history, or vice versa. Often, victory is in the eye of the beholder.

Political insiders, the general public, and social movement participants all have different ways of determining whether a movement is succeeding. And, many times, their metrics can contradict one another.

For insiders functioning within a transactional framework, victory comes when a final legislative deal is brokered or a settlement is signed. The instrumental gains embodied in such agreements serve as clear evidence of what has been achieved. On its face, this looks simple. And yet, the picture is hardly as clear as it might seem. The kinds of compromises produced by transactional politics are never wholly satisfying. There are always caveats and limitations. Almost inevitably, an individual concession, reform, or piece of legislation is only a fragment of what a movement truly wanted to accomplish at the outset. Was the fragment won in an individual campaign worth all of the resources, time, and effort spent? Or should it be regarded as a disappointment? These questions do not have clear-cut answers. They must be evaluated on a case-by-case basis.

For the general public, a totally different set of criteria determine the success or failure of an activist campaign. Often, perceptions of victory depend on how the media portrays a movement. Positive press coverage of a given protest mobilization or political settlement can create the sense that a movement is triumphant and rising. Meanwhile, press coverage that casts these same events in a skeptical or disparaging light can create a very different impression, fostering the sentiment that a movement is sputtering out and has accomplished little.

Movement participants themselves may judge their progress based on yet another set of standards: whether a demonstration *feels* empowering; whether the campaign is drawing in new people and creating fresh energy; or whether a given settlement lives up to their earlier expectations, which were subjective to begin with.

If transactional insiders, the public, and protest participants all look at victory in different ways, how do different organizing traditions manage these varying perspectives?

Within structure-based organizing, the challenges of framing the victory are addressed through one-on-one organizing and strong internal communication. A union or community group will work closely with its leadership committees to make sure that there is agreement within the organization about what constitutes an acceptable resolution to their demands. Sometimes this can be a contentious process: internal membership votes about whether to accept or reject a proposed union contract, for example, can be hotly contested. But if the organization can achieve consensus among those within its institutional structure, then it can move on, claiming the instrumental settlement as a win. What the public thinks, or what established powerbrokers make of the deal, matters little.

Momentum-driven organizers—who are trying to channel the power of disruptive mass protest—face a very different situation. For mass movements, conveying a sense of forward progress is essential. In politics, everybody likes to be on the winning team. Campaign consultants are fond of citing the aphorism: "When you lose, everything you do is wrong. When you win, everything you do is right." Mass mobilizations gain momentum when they are perceived as being winners and doing things right. To build their movement's capacity and continue winning over public opinion, organizers within this tradition must be able to communicate, both to the movement's own members and to the public at large, that they are successfully moving toward their goals.

∼

The use of symbolic demands and symbolic victories is a first way to achieve these aims, but there are other approaches as well. Serbian activists employed a second method, one that did not depend on concessions from their opponents.

Otpor placed a great emphasis on demonstrating to the public that it had a winning record. The country's repressive political context made this a must. Showing signs of progress was essential if the group was going to illustrate that Milosevic was not invincible and that resistance could prevail. And yet, unlike the country's traditional political parties, Otpor was not attempting to wrestle minor legislative victories or other incremental compromises from the regime. Absent these transactional gains, the movement needed a different way of exhibiting its ongoing success.

Otpor came up with a novel approach: campaigners themselves publicly laid out their standards for what would constitute a win, and then they loudly trumpeted it when they met these objectives, using the publicity to generate momentum. For example, activists might announce a goal of launching ten new chapters. Whether it took weeks or months to accomplish this, they could then make a major show of having met their goal once it happened. Or Otpor might announce the objective of holding simultaneous protests in at least a dozen different cities on a national day of action. Because they set this target themselves, they could be confident that it was attainable. And once it was attained, they again made certain that everybody knew about it. With each completed goal reported in the alternative media or in the movement's own communications, the fear barrier became that much weaker.

The activists referred to the art of publicizing their victories as "doing post-production," and they considered it a core part of their methodology. "Everything you do should be capitalized," one Otpor activist explained to author William Dobson. "First of all, proclaim the victory. Second, be sure that potential members and supporters know about it. You need a victory every week, even small victories. If you are on the defensive, you lose."[34]

A key element of this approach was that activists stayed in the driver's seat. "Claiming victory is an event that you produce on your own," Ivan Marovic argues. "You don't wait for someone to grant you victory or somebody to concede. You have to claim it."[35]

If Otpor members had structured their public relations around making a demand of the regime and allowing the media to judge their success or failure based on the government's response, they would have put themselves at the mercy of their opponents, setting themselves up for failure. "Your adversaries are rarely going to grant full acceptance of your demands," says Marovic. If people's attention is focused on the messy back-and-forth of negotiations, naysayers can always find grounds for complaint and movement supporters rarely emerge inspired. Otpor's method allowed them to avoid that. For publicity purposes, Otpor sought to accentuate when the movement made a show of strength and to let insiders worry about muddling through the aftermath.

The activists sometimes summed up the approach with a crafty aphorism: "declare victory and run."

Perhaps the best example of this method concerned Otpor's relations with the country's perpetually bickering political parties. As one of its key objectives, the movement had announced the goal of uniting these forces behind a single opposition candidate. In the last year of Milosevic's rule, a coalition known as the Democratic Opposition of Serbia, or DOS, formed, bringing the opposition parties into a single network. This was an important step forward; theoretically, it meant that they had agreed to work together. But getting them to actually unite behind a sole candidate for the presidential elections was a far more difficult task.

At an April DOS rally in Belgrade, Otpor forced the issue. Onstage with the opposition party leaders, activist Vlada Pavlov pulled out a flag with the movement's iconic fist. He then demanded that each politician, in turn, hold the flag and affirm that they would support a single challenger to Milosevic. Put on the spot, none of the party leaders wanted to be the first to break publicly with the movement, whose influence was steadily growing. One by one, the prospective candidates took the vow, some enthusiastically, and some with the look of having swallowed a mouthful of sour milk.[36]

Otpor used the occasion to announce that its objective of unifying the opposition had been achieved, and they publicized this as a major victory. With this breakthrough, they had eliminated a major obstacle that had prevented people from challenging Milosevic in the past.

In reality, from an instrumental perspective, the only thing that Otpor had won from the political parties was a very vague and somewhat unofficial pledge of unity. The actual process of sorting out what that pledge would mean took several more months of intensive back-room negotiations. It was not until the middle of July, long after the rally, that the formal terms of cooperation for a unified electoral drive had been determined. "It took three months after we claimed victory for the campaign to really bear fruit," says Marovic.[37]

But Otpor's leaders were not interested in waiting for the instrumental end game to play out. They recognized that, although the precise terms of a unity agreement were of great interest to each of the local party chiefs, the public would have been entirely indifferent to the minutiae of the negotiations. The key breakthrough had occurred in April, and activists wanted to make sure that everyone knew about it. For their mission of building popular support against the regime, the *principle* of unity was the most important thing.

By celebrating the affirmation of that principle, not only was the movement able to add to its winning record but its activists could move on to other tasks while the instrumental details were settled. For them, the best course was clear: declare victory and run.

∼

Gandhi and King accepted limited, instrumental settlements, and then highlighted their symbolic importance. Otpor took a second tack. It did not wait for its opponents to respond. Instead, the young organizers announced their own campaign objectives, and then declared victory when they were met.

A third approach to framing the victory happens at a different level—namely, that of individual protest actions. Whether activists like it or not, the media will often judge the success of a protest based on whether events unfold as organizers intended. If activists advertise that they will produce mass arrests, press reporters will evaluate their success based on whether a significant number of people are actually taken into custody. If organizers claim they will prevent a store from doing business for a day, the media will focus on whether storeowners are able to sell anything during that time. If campaigners vow that they will go twenty-one days without food to protest budget cuts, reporters will judge their success based on whether or not the hunger strike actually lasts the full three weeks.[38]

Never mind that the true point of any of these protests might be to raise public awareness or advance a wider goal. The plan for the demonstration—what is known as the "action scenario"—itself becomes the center of the narrative.

There are countless examples of this dynamic. In 1995, conveners of the Million Man March, led by controversial Nation of Islam leader Louis Farrakhan, attempted to create the largest rally ever in Washington, DC, by bringing African American men to the nation's capital. When the march actually took place, on October 16 of that year, the National Park Service estimated attendance at 400,000, and the low count led to a widespread feeling that the march had failed. The Park Service estimate outraged event organizers. Because the march had promised a million people in its very name, the debate about numbers became the dominant standard by which the event was evaluated. Discussion about whether the mobilization had constructive impact in unifying civil rights groups or focusing national attention on the problems facing black men was largely eclipsed.[39]

In the case of Occupy Wall Street, the mobilization's premise demanded that activists hold public space. Therefore, the idea of "occupation" became decisive—for both participants and outside observers. As long as protest encampments remained intact in places such as Manhattan's Zuccotti Park, the movement was succeeding in its stated goal. But once police evicted the camps, the feeling that the movement had been defeated quickly spread.

This phenomenon cannot be entirely controlled by social movement participants. But organizers who are cognizant of it can sometimes manipulate things to their advantage. Although they were known for a different approach—basing victories on self-determined campaign objectives—Otpor sometimes used individual action scenarios to demonstrate success as well. At one point, as their movement was gaining steam, Belgrade activists announced that they would undertake an audacious feat: blockading one of the area's major international highways in defiance of the regime. They subsequently did so and sent the photographic evidence to the media, which reported their bold accomplishment.

What the activists conveniently neglected to mention was that they carried out their protest at a time of the day when traffic was at a lull, and relatively few vehicles were affected. Moreover, their blockade held for all of fifteen minutes—long enough to take some decent photos, but not so long that the cops had time to bust the participants. These details did not prove to be a problem. The activists had indeed blocked the highway, just as they had promised, and they could mark another win in their ledger. Although the triumph they claimed fell far short of the final goal of ousting Milosevic, it effectively inspired greater defiance.[40]

A movement need not be so roguish about how it claims its successes. But, if it fails to pay attention to how it sets the stage for the story of a protest, it can easily lose control of its dramatic production. Organizers risk allowing the media to define the effectiveness of its protests for them and jeopardizing their ability to generate momentum for the future.

In 1999, protests in Seattle against ministerial meetings of the World Trade Organization exploded into headlines when they accomplished what a key activist slogan promised to do: namely, "Shut It Down." Blockades of people linked arms or chained themselves together with lockboxes, clogging entrances to the convention center and preventing trade delegates from attending the opening session of the talks. In response, police filled the streets with tear gas, officials such as US Secretary of State Madeleine Albright remained sequestered in their hotel rooms, and the opening session was canceled. Although the trade meetings resumed on subsequent days, the protest was hailed as a sensational success.

The same scenario backfired a few months later, however. When a similar blockade was attempted in April 2000 outside the meetings of the World Bank and International Monetary Fund in Washington, DC, the rallying cry of "shut it down" became a liability. In that case, police successfully opened up gaps in the activists' lines. Because the meetings' attendees were able to slip through, many deemed the actions a failure. This despite the fact that the A16 protests, as they were known, drew unprecedented attention to criticisms of World Bank and IMF policy—and that, in time, the wider global justice movement helped produce victories worth billions of dollars around issues such as debt cancelation for countries in the Global South. These wider impacts remained peripheral. The theatrical logic of the action demanded that the blockade keep out the meeting's delegates, and when it did not, a perception of defeat spread widely. Movement participants themselves absorbed much of the media's negativity, and, in the aftermath of the protest, many felt demoralized. Organizers working against the international financial institutions persevered, but they did not receive the same boost in energy and enthusiasm they might have otherwise.

In momentum-driven organizing, the challenge of framing the victory is twofold. First, for the public, the movement must create dramas in which resistance efforts can emerge triumphant at times when instrumental results have not yet been clearly established. Second, within the movement, participants must understand the theory of change so that they are resilient in the face of fickle press coverage. They should feel confident that if the movement is swaying popular opinion and it has emerged with a stronger core of supporters as a result of its actions, their efforts are progressing—regardless of whether reporters present them that way.

It rarely is the case that the demands of a campaign are purely symbolic or purely instrumental—and the same is true of the resolutions negotiated at the end of the movement. Symbolic and instrumental elements are intimately intertwined. But to understand how different organizing models work, it is necessary to recognize the differing emphasis they place on these elements. Structure-based organizers derive benefits from a focus on the instrumental: they are able to achieve concrete gains for their members in the short term, and they isolate themselves from the whims of the news media. However, they also give something up: the ability to rally widespread support for their cause and to force the kind of broad changes that are enabled by major shifts in public opinion.

Momentum-driven organizing necessarily places a greater focus on the symbolic. In their mass mobilizations, activists in this tradition need not abandon a push for concrete gains entirely. But instead of measuring their results only by incremental wins at the bargaining table, they use other metrics as well: movement in opinion polls, growing numbers of active participants, the ability to generate resources through grass-roots channels, and the responsiveness of different pillars of support to their mobilizations. Organizers of civil resistance cannot be content with empty declarations of victory or with merely "speaking truth to power." They must be hard headed in assessing their progress in winning over advocates and sympathizers from outside their immediate networks, always guarding against tendencies to become insular "voices in the wilderness."

Many of the most effective practitioners of strategic nonviolence have intuitively appreciated these dynamics. They have been gifted in creating symbolically resonant shows of resistance and establishing a winning record in the popular consciousness. Serbian activists Danijela Nenadic and Nenad Belcevic write, "Otpor was skillful at getting media attention, framing the issues, and keeping their movement in the public eye." The organizers attracted media attention with actions that "were mostly provocative and designed to raise public consciousness, making people aware of the need to change the regime and mobilizing them to join the struggle."[41]

In doing this, Serbian activists followed in the footsteps of past masters. As historian Adam Fairclough argues, Martin Luther King Jr. "maintained to the end of his life that it was far more important to dramatize the broader issues and generate the pressure for change than to draft precise or specific legislation. The exact manner in which the federal government responded to the problem of discrimination did not greatly concern SCLC. What mattered was that its response should be determined, vigorous, and thorough. The administration responded to pressure, King reasoned, not proposals."[42]

Likewise, Judith Brown writes, "For Gandhi, carefully staged and managed campaigns were as much about creating and manipulating images of moral resistance as about crafting strategies which . . . put pressure on the particular opponent in question." In Gandhi's national *satyagraha* campaigns "there was often no direct and immediate link between non-violent civil resistance and a desired outcome, so in a strict sense they could be considered as 'failures.'" And yet, "These campaigns gathered a greater range of active participation and more passive support than had any previous political movement in India." From this, much more so than Gandhi's personal meetings with Irwin, the Raj never recovered.[43]

Of course, for every protest like the Salt March that bursts into popular consciousness and becomes an internationally renowned phenomenon, there are hundreds of others that die out without ever being noticed. What do the explosive ones most frequently have in common? Mainstream political operatives believe they are those backed with the most resources and the strongest organizational coalitions. Strategic nonviolence suggests something else altogether: that even small and unknown groups can capture the public spotlight, provided they are willing to take the right risks.

CHAPTER SIX

THE ACT OF DISRUPTION

FOR PEOPLE TRYING to understand social change—as well as those trying to create it—the question of why some protests are ignored and forgotten while others break out to become sensational public events is a critical one. And it was a particularly pressing concern after the financial meltdown of 2008.

In the years following the crash, the United States entered into its worst economic crisis in seventy-five years. The unemployment rate reached into double digits, which had not happened since the Reagan era. A record number of homeowners entered into foreclosure, and state governments reported skyrocketing demand for food stamps. Yet by 2011 debate in Washington, DC—influenced by the activism of the insurgent Tea Party—revolved around cutting the budget and trimming social programs. "We were basically having an insane national discussion," remarked economist and *New York Times* columnist Paul Krugman.[1]

It took an outburst of popular action to change this. And that outburst came in an unexpected form.

In the fall of 2011, three years after the economic downturn had begun, political observers such as Krugman had long wondered when worsening conditions would result in public demonstrations against joblessness and foreclosures. Labor unions and major nonprofit organizations had attempted to build mass movement energy around these very issues. A year earlier, on October 2, 2010, the "One Nation Working Together" march—initiated primarily by the American Federation of Labor and Congress of Industrial Organizations (AFL-CIO) and the National Association for the Advancement of Colored People (NAACP)—drew more than 175,000 people to Washington, DC, with demands to combat rampant inequality. The next year, long-time organizer and charismatic former White House staffer Van Jones launched Rebuild the Dream, a major drive to form a progressive alternative to the Tea Party.[2]

According to the rules of structure-based organizing, these efforts did everything right. They rallied substantial resources, they drew on the strength of organizations with robust membership bases, they came up with sophisticated policy demands, and they forged impressive coalitions. And yet, they made little headway. Even their largest mobilizations attracted only modest press attention and quickly faded from popular memory.

What worked was something different. "A group of people started camping out in Zuccotti Park," Krugman explained just weeks after Occupy launched, "and all of a sudden the conversation has changed significantly towards being about the right things.

"It's kind of a miracle," he added.[3]

For students of civil resistance, the abrupt rise of Occupy Wall Street was certainly impressive, but its emergence was not a product of miraculous, otherworldly intervention. The haphazard assembly of activists who came together under the Occupy banner did not follow the time-honored rules of community organizing, but what they did do was highly relevant to those trying to create momentum-driven campaigns. They were willing to craft protests that were significantly disruptive; they put on display a high level of sacrifice among participants; and they escalated their protests, building to greater levels of activity and involvement. Each of these contributed force to their drive, allowing a loose and underfunded collection of protesters to alter the terms of national debate in ways that those with far greater organizational might had been unable to manage.

Time and again, in uprisings that steal the spotlight and illuminate injustices that are otherwise ignored, we see three elements—*disruption*, *sacrifice*, and *escalation*—combining in forceful ways. The persistent re-appearance of these elements provides compelling reason to examine their strange and combustive alchemy.

∾

Disruption is a first key factor in pushing outbreaks of revolt into the headlines. The amount of momentum that a movement generates can consistently be linked to the level of disruptive unrest its actions cause. The more that a protest directly affects members of the public, and the more it interferes with an adversary's ability to do business, the more likely it is to draw widespread attention. Snarling traffic, interrupting a public event, shutting down a convention, stopping a construction proj-ect, making a scene at the mall, or impeding operations at a factory—all of these reflect varying degrees of disruption.

In the corporate-driven media, disenfranchised groups and their so-cial movements are seldom able to make it into the mainstream news cycle at all, and even more rarely are they covered on favorable terms. Moments of unusual unrest provide opportunities for those without money or influence to dispel attitudes of indifference—and to high-light social and political injustices. "Our power is in our ability to make things unworkable," argued prominent civil rights organizer Bayard Rustin. "The only weapon we have is our bodies, and we need to tuck them in places, so wheels don't turn."[4]

Rustin's insight has been echoed in the work of many social move-ment theorists, notably in Frances Fox Piven's theories of disruptive power. For Piven, disruption occurs when people are willing to "break the rules" of social decorum and step out of conventional roles. In *Poor People's Movements*, she and Richard Cloward explain, "Factories are shut down when workers walk out or sit down; welfare bureaucracies are thrown into chaos when crowds demand relief; landlords may be bankrupted when tenants refuse to pay rent. In each of these cases, peo-ple cease to conform to accustomed institutional roles; they withhold their accustomed cooperation, and by doing so, cause institutional disruptions."[5]

Piven has forcefully argued that such unrest is the engine of social change. In her 2006 book, *Challenging Authority*, she contends that the "great moments of equalizing reform in American political history" have been responses to periods when disruptive power was most widely deployed.[6]

Gene Sharp has emphasized similar aspects of noncompliance and disruption. When he devised his now-famous list of "198 methods of nonviolent action," Sharp divided the tactics into three categories.

The first encompasses methods of "protest and persuasion," including public assemblies, processions, displays of banners, and formal statements by organizations. These make up the bulk of routine protest actions in the United States, and they tend to involve minimal disruption.

Sharp's other two categories, however, involve increasingly confrontational measures.

His second grouping, "methods of noncooperation," encompasses economic boycotts, student walkouts, and workplace strikes. And the third category, "nonviolent intervention," includes sit-ins, land seizures, and civil disobedience.

This last category involves not only a refusal to participate in political or economic structures but also intent to actively interrupt normal daily activity. Such interventions, Sharp writes, pose a "direct and immediate challenge." A lunch-counter sit-in, after all, is more urgently troublesome for a storeowner than a more removed consumer boycott. And, Sharp contends, because "the disruptive effects of the intervention are harder to withstand for a considerable period of time," these actions can produce results more swiftly and dramatically than other approaches to nonviolent conflict.[7]

~

In the long run, the breadth of participation in a protest movement matters; but in the short term, a sense of drama and momentum can trump numbers. Because the "One Nation Working Together" march had taken place on a weekend, and because it was viewed as a standard-issue demonstration in Washington, DC—one of several major rallies that took place within just a few months in the nation's capital—it could be easily overlooked, even though it brought out more than 175,000 people.

The scenario for confrontation offered by Occupy Wall Street fell into Sharp's third category, and as a result it possessed a different tenor than the marches and rallies that had come before. Occupy Wall Street involved a much smaller number of people, particularly at its beginning. Yet it set out to generate a much greater level of disruption. Activists intended to go to the investment banks in the heart of Manhattan's financial district and erect an encampment on their doorstep, hampering the daily business of those most responsible for the economic crisis.

Although the protesters ultimately established camp at a location several blocks from Wall Street itself, the occupation at Zuccotti Park effectively posed a dilemma for those in power. Authorities could allow activists to hold the space indefinitely, permitting a staging ground for continual protests against the area's financial institutions. Or police could act on behalf of the country's wealthiest 1 percent and shut down dissent, a move that would perfectly illustrate the protesters' claims about what American democracy had become. It was a no-win situation for the state.

While city officials pondered these unattractive options, the question of "how long will the occupation hold?" fostered a growing sense of dramatic tension for the public.

The tactic of occupation had other advantages as well. One was that it could be replicated. Somewhat jokingly, a few weeks into the mobilization, organizers issued a call to "Occupy Everywhere!" Much to their surprise, people responded in droves: the disruptive impact of Occupy grew as encampments sprung up in cities throughout the country. They even sprouted internationally, as with Occupy London, which set up shop directly outside of the London Stock Exchange.

As Occupy progressed, protesters staged sit-ins at banks and marches that blocked streets and bridges. By the end of the year, Occupy-related actions had resulted in an estimated 5,500 arrests in dozens of cities, big and small—from Fresno, California, to Mobile, Alabama; from Colorado Springs to Honolulu; from Boston to Anchorage—all dramatizing the divide between the "99 percent and the 1 percent."[8]

Such actions propelled Occupy forward. However, like all exercises in disruption, they also posed risks.

Although tactics that interrupt business as usual are the most likely to draw attention, this attention is not necessarily positive. Because these actions inconvenience people and create disorder, they risk inviting a negative response—backlash that can reinforce status quo injustices. Therefore, the use of disruption places activists in a precarious position. In crafting scenarios for political conflict, they must carefully cultivate sympathy, working to ensure that observers recognize the legitimacy of their cause. Strategic judgment is needed to maximize the disruption's transformative potential while at the same time minimizing backlash from the public.

∼

It is precisely for this reason that disruption pairs well with a second key factor that works as kindling for mass uprisings: personal *sacrifice*. Movements are primed to flare up when participants demonstrate the seriousness of their commitment. One main way of doing this is through showing a willingness to endure hardship, to face arrest, or even to risk physical harm in dramatizing an injustice.

As he sought to distance his ideas from the tenets of moral pacifism, Gene Sharp constantly insisted that strategic nonviolence does not avoid confrontation or encourage passivity. On the contrary, going back to Gandhi's experiments in mass mobilization, advocates have noted that it can more accurately be considered as a form of asymmetric warfare.

In *War Without Violence*, an early study of Gandhian strategies published in 1939, Krishnalal Shridharani noted that both war and nonviolent conflict recognize suffering as a core source of power. In the case of war, this notion is straightforward: "By inflicting suffering on the enemy, the warriors seek to break the former's will, to make him surrender, to annihilate him, to destroy him, and with him all opposition,"

Shridharani wrote. "Suffering thus becomes a source of social power which compels and coerces."[9]

The main twist with nonviolent action, of course, is that participants do not seek to impose physical suffering but instead are willing to face it themselves.

"Gandhi's whole theory is based on the concept of suffering as a source of . . . social force," Shridharani explained. "In Satyagraha, it is by inviting suffering from the opponent and not after inflicting suffering upon him that the resultant power is produced. The basic formula is the same, but its application is about-face. It almost amounts to putting the energy in reverse gear."

Leading proponents of civil resistance emphasize that strategic non-violent action can produce serious clashes and that these may result in serious injuries and even casualties. Indeed, advocates have sometimes displayed a notable lack of sentimentality on this point. "Guerilla warfare has huge civilian casualty rates. Huge," Sharp explained in a 2005 interview. "And yet Ché Guevara didn't abandon guerilla warfare because people were getting killed." Sharp saw no reason why nonviolent combatants should behave differently.[10]

For his part, Gandhi was frank about the potential consequences of *satyagraha*. During his drive for Indian self-rule he argued, "No country has ever risen without being purified through the fire of suffering."[11]

There is a strong spiritual component in Gandhi's explanation of how this works. This aspect of his thinking has historically been appealing to religious-minded interpreters and sometimes off-putting to more secular-minded readers. Gandhi invokes ideas ranging from the Hindu concept of ascetic renunciation, *tapasya*, to the Christian emphasis on the redemptive suffering of Jesus—pointing to how forms of self-suffering have motivated religious movements for centuries, often with history-shaping consequences.

The modern tradition of civil resistance has adopted a different emphasis. It has drawn out the more practical side of Gandhi's thinking. Even those not inclined toward spiritual considerations can find impressive results in the empirical record of protests in which participants have been willing to take serious risks—whether by jeopardizing their professional reputation or by potentially inviting bodily harm.

Nonviolent actions involving the possibility of arrest, reprisal, or physical trauma allow those who undertake them to display courage and resolve. When participants must ask themselves how much they are willing to sacrifice for a cause, it clarifies their values and strengthens their commitment. It can become a moment of personal transformation. Within successful social movements, organizers constantly ask members to make sacrifices—to make contributions of time, energy, and resources; to risk tension with neighbors or family members who prefer to avoid controversial issues; or even to endanger their livelihood by standing up on the job or coming out as a whistleblower. Nonviolent confrontations often involve making such sacrifices visible, creating scenarios in which those involved can publicly convey their seriousness of purpose.

Personal acts of sacrifice thus have public repercussions. They both draw attention and invite empathy: a bus boycotter willing to walk five miles to work rather than to ride on segregated public transportation; a teacher going on hunger strike against school budget cuts; an environmentalist who commits to sitting in an old-growth tree for weeks to prevent it from being cut down; or an indigenous rights advocate who chains herself to a bulldozer to prevent construction on a sacred site. Gandhi contended that these displays could effectively activate public opinion, serving to "quicken the dead conscience into life" and "make people think and act." When bystanders see someone in front of them suffering, it is difficult for them to remain detached and uninvolved. The scene compels them to pick a side.[12]

A common misconception about nonviolent action is that it is necessarily focused on touching the heart of the opponent and leading to a conversion. In fact, the impact of sacrifice can have little to do with changing the views of one's adversaries—and much more to do with affecting one's friends. When people decide to risk their safety or to face arrest, their decisions have the effect of mobilizing the communities closest to them.

During the civil rights movement, the students who organized sit-ins at lunch counters in cities such as Nashville, Tennessee, experienced this phenomenon. In February 1960, students from Fisk University, Tennessee State University, and Baptist Theological Seminary who had been trained in Gandhian tactics walked in to downtown establishments such as the city's Woolworth and Kress stores. After making small purchases, they sat down at the stores' lunch counters, quietly reading and doing homework as storeowners predictably refused them service. When employees tried to ignore them, they sat for hours on end, and then returned on repeated days. Tension increased. Inevitably, word of the protests spread through Nashville, and the sit-ins started to attract white mobs. Hecklers taunted the students and poured milkshakes over their heads. At times, the violence got worse. In his autobiography, *Walking with the Wind*, sit-in organizer and future congressman John Lewis recalled a moment when enraged whites began to attack. "I was hit in the ribs, not too hard, but enough to knock me over," Lewis writes. "Down the way I could see one of the white men stubbing a lit cigarette against the back of a guy in our group." Despite their discipline in refusing to respond to these provocations, the victims were arrested for disobeying police orders to vacate the store.[13]

As they faced such reprisals, the students found that their parents, their ministers, and their classmates—many of whom had previously been reluctant to speak out—were drawn in by their actions. As the documentary *Eyes on the Prize* explains: "The local black community began to unite behind the students. Black merchants supplied food to those in jail. Homeowners put up property for bail money. Z. Alexander Looby, the city's leading black lawyer, headed the defense." Family members were especially galvanized. "Parents worried that arrest records could hurt their children's future, and they feared for the safety of their children." In response, they "turned to the power of their own pocketbook," launching an economic boycott in support of the sit-ins. The students' sacrifice had created a virtuous circle, drawing in more participants and allowing for even greater disruption. Soon, the mayor was compelled to intervene to quell unrest. And, within months, Nashville storeowners agreed to begin desegregating their lunch counters for good.[14]

∽

Independently, sacrifice and disruption can each produce forceful results. But together, they form an unusually effective pairing. Sacrifice
helps to address two of the great problems of disruptive protest: the
risk of public backlash and the danger of swift and severe repression.
First, by invoking an empathetic response in the public, sacrifice damp-
ens negative reactions and allows for mobilizations to attempt more
profound ruptures of business as usual. Second, sacrifice can take the
crackdowns that often accompany disruptive protests and turn them
into unexpected assets.

Such was the case with Occupy, where sacrifice complemented
disruption in critical ways. From the start, protesters signaled an intention to endure significant hardship in order to voice an ongoing
objection to Wall Street's misdeeds. One of the first images associated
with the movement, a publicity poster released in advance by the Ca-
nadian magazine *Adbusters*, featured a ballerina atop Wall Street's infamous charging bull. The dancer posed serenely while police in gas
masks amassed in the background. The text below the bull read simply,
"#OccupyWallStreet. September 17th. Bring tent."

The poster's suggestion that camping gear would be required for the
mobilization—and that police reprisal would be a looming danger—
immediately set the action apart from countless other demonstrations,
in which participants might show up for an afternoon with a sign, chant
for an hour or two in a permitted area, and then call it a day and go
home. As Occupy commenced, reporters and participants alike were
drawn to the spectacle of protesters ready to sleep on slabs of concrete
in lower Manhattan's sterile financial district in order to bring populist
discontent to the doors of those who presided over the financial crisis.
The dedication of the initial occupiers drew friends and brought in sympathizers curious about the Zuccotti encampment.

Outside interest did not build immediately, however. As MSNBC's
Keith Olbermann noted, "After five straight days of sit-ins, marches,
and shouting, and some arrests, actual North American newspaper coverage of this—even by those who have thought it farce or failure—has
been limited to one blurb in a free newspaper in Manhattan and a col-
umn in the *Toronto Star*."[15]

It took two further developments to break through the de facto blackout of the protest. Each involved even greater personal suffering, and each ignited outrage about how police handled free speech in America.

～

The first pivotal event occurred on September 24, a hot day that marked the one-week anniversary of the occupation. On that occasion, protesters hiked two-and-a-half miles to Union Square, and then turned around to return to Zuccotti. But before they made it back, police detained groups of marchers and started to make arrests. In total, eighty people were taken into custody.

The arrests themselves were significant, but the most consequential product of the day's activity would be a video of a police officer later identified as Deputy Inspector Anthony Bologna. The video showed two women who had been penned in with orange police netting standing and talking calmly. Unprovoked, Bologna walks up to them, pulls out a can of pepper spray, and lifts it toward their faces. Then he sprays them at virtually point-blank range. Grainy cell phone footage captured the scene of the women dropping to their knees in pain, cupping their eyes, and crying out in agony.

Video of the malicious attack went viral, accumulating over a million views within four days. It became the incident that put Occupy Wall Street on the map nationally, spurring a new flood of articles about the mobilization. Rather than deterring participants wary of facing violence, as one might expect, the video fueled public outrage. It motivated new occupiers to join the assembly in Zuccotti, and it compelled many outside of New York to consider how they could support the movement.

A week later, Occupy was a bona fide news event, and the mobilization was able to stage a much larger march to mark the completion of two weeks of occupation. For this procession, protesters made their way toward the Brooklyn Bridge. As they approached, the NYPD directed marchers onto the bridge's main roadway. There, officers promptly surrounded the assembly and methodically arrested some seven hundred people, binding their wrists with plastic zip-tie cuffs. Several activists on the pedestrian walkway above live-streamed video of the arrests, making the event an Internet sensation even as it was still taking place.

The roundup involved the most arrests by far for Occupy to that date, and it represented one of the largest mass arrests in New York City's history. Yet, like the previous week's video, footage of the police action on the Brooklyn Bridge did not dampen dissent. Instead, it conveyed a sense of escalating momentum and attracted fresh participants. Just a few days later, on October 5, Occupy held its largest march yet, bringing out some fifteen thousand people, including delegations from the city's most prominent labor unions.

The idea that repression can actually help a movement, rather than hurt it, is a notion that stands a conventional understanding of power on its head. And yet, the ability of nonviolent demonstrators to benefit from the zealousness of authorities is a well-studied occurrence within the field of civil resistance. This phenomenon is commonly described as "political jiu-jitsu."

In the martial art of jiu-jitsu, practitioners use the momentum of an opponent's blow to throw the opponent off balance. Strategic nonviolence does something similar in the realm of political conflict.

Dictatorial security states and heavily armed police forces are well prepared to deal with violent outbursts, which conveniently serve to justify heavy-handed repression and legitimate a trend toward militarization. In these cases, the mainstream media is all too willing to play along, with local news stations fixating on acts they perceive as violent and valorizing attempts to restore order.

What confounds and destabilizes authorities is a different type of militancy. Gene Sharp writes, "Nonviolent struggle against violent repression creates a special, asymmetrical conflict situation" in which the use of force by those in power can rebound against them and embolden opposition.

"Harsh repression against nonviolent resisters may be perceived as unreasonable, distasteful, inhuman, or harmful to . . . the society," Sharp explains. Therefore, it turns the public against the attackers, provokes sympathetic onlookers to join the demonstrations, and encourages defections even within those groups that might regularly be opposed to protests.[16]

As Occupy progressed, it had further opportunities to show its skill in this unusual form of combat. One highly publicized incident involved demonstrators at the University of California, Davis. On November 18, 2011, police arrived on the Davis campus in full riot gear and began to remove tents that students had erected. A group of perhaps two dozen students sat down along a walkway, linking arms, to try to stop the eviction.

Within minutes, campus police officer John Pike approached with military-grade pepper spray and began dousing the students. Video showed Pike casually strolling down the line of protesters, spraying toxic fluid, while those seated on the walkway doubled over and attempted to shield their eyes. Once again, footage of the attack began circulating almost immediately. In the aftermath of the soon-notorious incident, outraged students and faculty called for the resignation of university officials responsible for the attack. Nationally, the event helped keep Occupy in the headlines—and turned Lieutenant Pike into an unlikely Internet celebrity. Popular memes on Facebook and Twitter featured photoshopped images of Pike "casually" pepper-spraying everyone from the *Mona Lisa*, to the Beatles, to the founding fathers.

Occupy is hardly unique as a mobilization that grew stronger as a result of efforts to quash protests. Although too many factors are at play in a given protest to ensure that the gains of enduring abuse will be worth the cost, there is a rich history of repression serving as a turning point for movements promoting change.

In the case of Otpor in Serbia, waves of arrests and beatings by authorities brought the movement fresh recruits, as young people saw the state acting in a way that was arbitrary and vindictive. As author Matthew Collin writes, "They felt that their generation was under attack, and had decided that it was time to fight back."[17]

This was also the case in the push for civil rights in the segregated South. As Representative Emanuel Celler, chairman of the House Judiciary Committee, remarked in 1966, "There are times when the civil rights movement has no greater friend than its enemy. It is the enemy of civil rights who again and again produces the evidence . . . that we cannot afford to stand still." Likewise, Saul Alinsky argued, "A Bull Connor with his police dogs and fire hoses down in Birmingham did more to advance civil rights than the civil rights fighters themselves."[18]

∽

Alinsky was right to highlight the importance of Bull Connor's strategic misjudgments. At the same time, he gave the civil rights protesters too little credit for their skill in creating a situation where Connor's brutality would be exposed and widely denounced. The reality is that, despite the demonstrated power of sacrifice and disruption, it is rare that activist groups risk either in significant measure. Even more rare is when social movement participants undertake disruptive and risky actions not once, but on an ongoing basis—endeavoring to carry out ever-bolder displays of noncompliance over the course of a campaign.

This is *escalation*. Added to sacrifice and disruption, it represents a third crucial element in the alchemy of explosive protest.

Within the field of civil resistance, theorists and practitioners have emphasized the idea of the "dilemma action." The idea here is that demonstrations are especially effective when they create a dilemma for those in power, producing situations in which any response the authorities choose helps the movement. The student lunch-counter sit-ins are often cited as an instructive example. If students were permitted to sit at the lunch counters, unmoved, they would have achieved their goal: by virtue of their protest itself, they would have desegregated the store's eatery. On the other hand, if they were removed forcefully, it threatened to create a media spectacle that portrayed Jim Crow defenders in a negative light. It would demolish the myth of a genteel South in which blacks and whites were each happier to remain separate, and it would show racism for what it was: ugly, violent, and pervasive. Faced with these unpleasant alternatives, both police and storeowners squirmed for days, hoping in vain that the protests would just go away.[19]

The dilemma action has had a prominent place in many other civil resistance campaigns as well. Otpor's stunts—which made the Milosevic regime look like it couldn't take a joke and highlighted the fact that authorities were prone to abusing their power—are another example. Likewise, Gandhi's Salt March left the British Raj with no good options. As a nationalist newspaper described the predicament at the time: "To arrest Gandhi is to set fire to the whole of India. Not to arrest him is to allow him to set the prairie on fire. . . . In either case, Government stands to lose, and Gandhi stands to gain."[20]

The dilemma Occupy Wall Street created was not quite so stark as these examples. But to the extent that police had to choose between respecting free speech and acting as enforcers for Wall Street's banks, the movement put them in an uncomfortable position.

The point of the dilemma action is that activists need to devise protests that cannot simply be ignored, and they need to create situations in which they will gain public sympathy if they are attacked or arrested. Disruption and sacrifice can each play a role here. Disruption is a crucial means for making sure that demonstrations are not overlooked. Sacrifice, meanwhile, makes it more likely that observers will side with movement participants rather than those who move against them.

Thinking in terms of creating dilemmas for their adversaries can be a useful way for activists to devise more effective interventions. At the same time, perfect dilemmas are very difficult to construct. In truth, any individual action can only do so much. More important than coming up with a single, brilliantly conceived act of nonviolent resistance is a willingness to string together multiple protests in a way that creates a sense of heightening drama.

This is where escalation becomes significant.

When scholar Joan Bondurant set out to chart the fundamental rules of Gandhi's mass campaigns, she emphasized that movements must progressively advance through new stages of activity, always avoiding stagnation. Gene Sharp, influenced by this analysis, stressed that to sustain a long struggle, activists cannot deploy just one tactic. Rather, they need to create a sequence of actions that builds over time. The goal, he contended, citing prominent rabbi and author Arthur Waskow, is the "escalation of disorder without violence."[21]

Practitioners experimenting with unarmed uprising have come to similar conclusions. The antinuclear movement of the late 1970s was a key moment in the development of the modern tradition of nonviolent direct action in the United States. During this movement, organizers tried to follow what one activist called the "power of ten" rule. As they rallied participants to stage occupations on the site of the proposed Seabrook nuclear power plant in New Hampshire, these organizers aimed to make sure each of their planned disruptions was exponentially larger than the last. They knew this was not easy. But, to their surprise, they succeeded. As historian Barbara Epstein explains, "On August 1, 1976, eighteen people walked down the abandoned railway tracks leading into the site and were arrested. On August 22, in pouring rain, 180 people, some of them from Boston and Western Massachusetts, were arrested." All of this led up to a much larger action the following spring. Starting on April 30, 1977, a group of approximately twenty-four hundred arrived on the Seabrook site and began setting up camp. The National Guard arrested more than fourteen hundred protesters, who were held in several armories around the state for up to two weeks after they refused to pay bail. The fact that the mass disobedience at Seabrook grew in size and militancy throughout the campaign helped make the antinuclear actions a national story.[22]

The track record of what escalation can accomplish is impressive, and still it is rarely attempted, for a variety of reasons. A first is fear: it takes courage to engage in a protest that might involve physical harm or legal sanction. Risking these repercussions once is significant. Doing it repeatedly requires an even more uncommon commitment.

For structure-based groups, there can be severe consequences to disobedience: formal leaders can be sued, assets can be seized, hard-earned access to mainstream powerbrokers can be compromised. These are the factors that veteran labor strategist Stephen Lerner identifies as decisive in limiting the willingness of mainstream unions to experiment with more disruptive strategies: "Unions with hundreds of millions in assets and collective bargaining agreements covering millions of workers won't risk their treasuries and contracts by engaging in large-scale sit-ins, occupations, and other forms of non-violent civil disobedience that must inevitably overcome court injunctions and political pressures."[23]

It is not that unions lack the ability to stage major disruptions. During the rare moments when they commit serious effort and resources to mass noncooperation—for example, during a strike—their powers of mobilization can be impressive. However, the potential for negative fallout from militant nonviolence presents a clear danger, and leaders of established groups rarely see the upside of escalation. Because a mass mobilization might not produce instrumental gains in the short term, transactional organizers may not see the point in pushing it to greater heights.

In short, when confronted with the possibility to escalate, groups have all too many reasons to play it safe. Which is why it is especially remarkable when they opt for a more turbulent course.

~

In the case of Occupy Wall Street, the movement often escalated without having a conscious plan to do so. With its unexpectedly successful invitation to "Occupy Everywhere," tent cities proliferated widely beyond Zuccotti, with occupations springing up from Tahlequah, Oklahoma, to Lagos, Nigeria. One attempt to keep track of the activity listed 1,518 encampments in total. And Occupy escalated in other ways as well. Although the camps themselves were important, they also served as launching pads for other protests. Occupiers disrupted foreclosure auctions, held sit-ins in bank lobbies, and erected blockades to protect families that had been victims of predatory lending schemes from being evicted from their homes. The movement also used partnerships with labor and community groups to stage mass marches. The October 5, 2011, march, for one, was joined by unions such as Service Employees International Union (SEIU), the American Federation of State, County and Municipal Employees (AFSCME), and the Communication Workers of America (CWA), drawing thousands of participants. Throughout that fall, these varied forms of protest combined to create the sense that the movement was continually stepping up its activity.[24]

If Occupy's escalation lacked premeditated design, other prominent campaigns of civil resistance have planned to scale up from the start. In Serbia, Otpor's acts of resistance—which started with cultural defiance and individual creative stunts—were all connected to a grand strategy that built over time. When the movement peaked, massive nationwide disobedience was being used to force Milosevic to recognize the results of the presidential election and cede office.

In Birmingham, organizers also planned for escalation from the outset, and they backed up their intention to go big on repeated occasions as the campaign unfolded. The pressure that civil rights advocates put on city storeowners did not come through a single demonstration but rather through a range of tactics, deployed in a calculated sequence. These included store-based sit-ins, a citywide economic boycott, and large protest marches that resulted in significant numbers of arrests. "The SCLC had anticipated that Birmingham would be a long struggle," writes sociologist Aldon Morris. "Project 'C' was prepared according to a precise timetable designed to produce maximum drama." When this timetable broke down due to unforeseen twists, civil rights organizers had to make tough decisions about how they were going to step up movement activity in the face of challenging circumstances. In other words, many of the pivotal decisions of the Birmingham campaign revolved around questions of escalation.[25]

King's gambit to risk arrest on Good Friday, despite the concerns of his advisors, was one such decision. In the end, his instincts proved sound. In addition to animating local supporters, who came out in large numbers to see King personally face off against Bull Connor, the mere announcement that he would be facing arrest earned the movement front-page coverage in national newspapers.[26]

The burst of energy created by his arrest only lasted for so long, however. Three weeks later, when the campaign was again threatening to stall out, organizers in Birmingham made the difficult and controversial decision to allow high school students—who were clamoring to join the demonstrations—to participate. This ended up becoming the campaign's most critical moment of escalation, allowing the civil rights activists to expose the true depths of Bull Connor's brutality. "Mobilizing the children saved the movement from collapse," historian Adam Fairclough writes.[27]

The salt *satyagraha* in India was another instance in which nonviolent activists progressively turned up pressure on their adversaries. Gandhi's march to the sea was only the first stage of a much wider rebellion that would quickly involve millions of participants. Future prime minister Jawaharlal Nehru wrote, "It seemed as though a spring had been suddenly released." Despite facing heavy repression from colonial authorities, activists reinvigorated the boycott of foreign clothing, British-appointed Indian bureaucrats resigned from their posts, and tax strikes flared across the country's provinces. Soon, prominent officials such as the mayor of Calcutta were being arrested for reading seditious literature in public.[28]

The Salt March, historian Judith Brown writes, sparked a "moral enthusiasm for breaking laws seen as oppressive, even to the point of suffering severe personal injury from police retaliation." In one famous action alone, the nonviolent raid on the saltworks at Dharasana in May 1930, the savage beating of protesters by police resulted in two deaths and at least 320 hospitalizations. Defiance continued throughout the year. Across the country, the number of arrests, by some estimates, rapidly surpassed sixty thousand. Only when Gandhi sensed that the movement could escalate no further did he seek out a settlement with Irwin.[29]

~

Along with disruption and sacrifice, escalation has served as the lifeblood of major civil resistance campaigns. From India, to Birmingham, to Serbia, its impact has been undeniable. But what about with Occupy?

Just as Alinsky gave civil rights campaigners too little credit for their savvy maneuvering in catapulting segregation into the headlines, so Occupy activists often receive slight acknowledgment for their success in propelling inequality to the fore of national discussion. In fact, some have gone so far as to question whether Occupy Wall Street really accomplished anything at all. In mid-2012, political analyst Andy Ostroy concluded that the movement "has had no material impact on

American life." Similarly, the *New York Times*'s Andrew Ross Sorkin, writing on the one-year anniversary of the occupation of Zuccotti Park, argued that Occupy was nothing more than "a fad" and that "it will be an asterisk in the history books, if it gets a mention at all."[30]

It is true that Occupy Wall Street may not get its due in the annals of history. Because its vision was so broad and its ambitions so great, the movement lent itself to disappointment. After all, participants aspired to nothing less than a revolutionary shift in America's economic structures and a grassroots reinvention of political democracy. Observers who compare the actual political reverberations of Occupy with its most grandiose pronouncements can easily conclude that it achieved nothing close to its stated goals.

Even judging by more realistic standards, there is legitimate debate about whether Occupy lived up to its full potential. Momentum-driven organizing distinguishes itself from unstructured mass protest in that it seeks to be deliberate in harnessing and sustaining the power of disruptive outbreaks. Its goal is to allow mobilizations to endure through multiple waves of activity. Occupy fell short in this regard. Like many other mass protests, it was not well equipped to last beyond a brief cycle of revolt. Although it did have general assemblies and working groups through which it organized participants, activists soon experienced the limits of these structures. The movement did not have the frontloading that would have allowed it to convey an overarching strategy. Because it lacked a culture of mass training, methods of transmitting the movement's norms to new participants remained informal. And the diverse crowds of Occupiers never developed a shared theory of how they would leverage change.

Because of this, much of the movement's escalation was accidental. For some, ramping up the confrontation was not even a goal. Their focus was on building community within the occupations, not on creating strategic protests outside of them. They were indifferent or hostile to engaging with the mainstream media or crafting appeals to win over the general public.

Finally, momentum-driven organizing is attentive to ways mass mobilization might collaborate with structure-based institutions; it tries to draw in further support from established groups that are ordinarily reluctant to risk disruptive activity. Many regulars at the Occupy encampments, in contrast, were so wary of "cooptation" that the movement missed opportunities to collaborate with constituencies outside its countercultural base.

Such limits were not only acknowledged by outside critics: after the mobilization died down, some of the most committed Occupy activists, dissatisfied with the movement's organizational models, entered into a period of introspection similar to that experienced by the student activists who went on to form Otpor in Serbia.

Occupy's shortcomings were real. But reflection on them should not obscure the impact that the movement did have. It is important to remember that Occupy was a drive that started with extremely minimal financial resources, no staff, no offices, and no established membership lists. Throughout its peak months, it drew primarily on its own momentum rather than on any sources of outside support. Yet, despite its lack of institutional backing, it accomplished precisely what far more muscular organizations had tried, and failed, to do in the years before. Its mixture of disruption, sacrifice, and escalation ended up having concrete implications, both small and large.

On the level of direct, incremental gains, Occupy could claim a variety of wins, many of which involved fights around housing. When Occupy erupted, it provided a major boost to existing campaigns against foreclosures, generating an influx of attention and volunteer support. In Brooklyn, the group Organizing for Occupation prevented at least one public foreclosure auction by interrupting the court proceeding with chants and song. In Cleveland, movement activists who camped out on the front lawn of a local woman's home helped her to secure a stay of eviction. Occupy Atlanta assisted injured Iraq War veteran Bridgette Walker by guarding her home and pressuring Chase Manhattan. "They got everyday people like myself involved—everyday people contacting Chase and advocating for me, peaceful demonstrations, people calling and writing in," Walker stated after successfully negotiating a loan modification. An umbrella effort, "Occupy Our Homes," tracked cases like these around the country.[31]

Occupy also secured instrumental advances related to consumer banking. Bank Transfer Day, which took place on November 5, 2011, encouraged those who held accounts with major banks—specifically Bank of America—to switch their business over to credit unions. This campaign surged as Occupy gained steam, and when Bank Transfer Day arrived upward of 650,000 customers shifted $4.5 billion in resources from major banks to credit unions. As Salon's Andrew Leonard wrote, riffing on an old joke, "$4.5 billion here, $4.5 billion there, and pretty soon you are talking about real money, even for JPMorgan-Chase." Bethpage Federal Credit Union CEO Kirk Kordeleski told the *New York Daily News*, "These are very good times for credit unions." Conversely, American Bankers Association CEO Diane Casey-Landry called the antibank sentiment generated by Occupy a "reputational kick in the chin."[32]

This was not merely a matter of public relations. When Bank of America announced plans to instate a $5 monthly charge for debit card holders with account balances under $20,000, twenty-two-year-old Molly Katchpole, an underemployed recent college graduate and nanny working two jobs, started an online petition protesting the change. Amid the antibank climate Occupy had created, the drive went viral, quickly garnering three hundred thousand signatures. Katchpole appeared on YouTube cutting up her debit card outside her local branch's lobby, and she was soon getting calls from ABC and CNN. By October 28, Bank of America moved to "redefine" its fee structure and effectively end the monthly charge. Wells Fargo and JPMorgan Chase quickly followed suit.[33]

Finally, the movement contributed to other concrete gains in the realm of union campaigns. Occupy Wall Street maintained a Labor Outreach Committee, which used movement energy and volunteer resources to assist numerous groups of workers. Verizon employees, Longshoremen on the West Coast, HarperCollins publishing house workers, Harvard dining hall employees, and art handlers at Sotheby's all benefited from active relationships with the Occupy movement. For their part, the Longshoremen secured a resolution that allowed some fifty thousand port workers to win their first contract as union members. After the victory, Jack Mulcahy, an officer in the Longshoremen's Portland local, argued that Occupy was "a critical element in bringing [the company] to the bargaining table and forcing a settlement.[34]

"Make no mistake," he added, "the solidarity and organization between the Occupy Movement and the Longshoremen won this contract."

~

Although these direct, on-the-ground victories are not insignificant, the movement's most profound impact was in shifting the national debate, prompting a change that had important ramifications in the realms of policy and electoral politics. Prior to Occupy, in the summer of 2011, congressional Republicans had effectively trained public attention on controlling the federal budget deficit, creating a debt ceiling, and implementing drastic, emergency cuts to government programs and social services. A ThinkProgress report showed that in the month before activists arrived in Zuccotti Park, news outlets such as CNN, MSNBC, and Fox News were mentioning government debt some fifteen times more often than problems of unemployment.[35]

Two months later, with the movement in full bloom, the trend had reversed. *BusinessWeek* reporter Dan Beucke wrote, "Coming out of the summer the economic debate in Washington was dominated by talk of cutting the deficit—not jobs, not the wealth disparity in America, and certainly not the role of money in politics. Today that has shifted. Part of my job here each morning is to aggregate stories about the wealth debate; the volume of candidates is impressive."[36]

The change outlived the encampments themselves. In January 2012, well after Occupy Wall Street's eviction, Richard Morin, a senior editor at Pew Social and Demographic Trends, told the *New York Times*, "Income inequality is no longer just for economists. . . . It has moved off the business pages into the front page." For months after that, database searches showed that mentions of "income inequality" in US newspapers were still double what they had been before Occupy began.[37]

Attempting a similar shift in debate through paid media would have taken tens of millions of dollars in ad buys. When advertisers and conventional political campaigns spend such resources, they have no guarantee that they will have nearly as much influence in shaping popular discussion. But they are willing to spend handsomely because they know that nudging the public even slightly can have major repercussions: it can swing an election, tip a ballot initiative, or dramatically alter sales of a product.

The same autumn that Occupy Wall Street burst onto the scene, conservative lawmakers in Ohio were pushing antiunion legislation strikingly similar to that passed by Republican governor Scott Walker in Wisconsin. If the measure, known as SB 5, had been allowed to stand, it would have curtailed labor's capacity to collect dues from its members in Ohio and decimated the state's public sector unions. The issue was ultimately decided by a referendum on the November ballot, which gave voters a chance to repeal the lawmakers' initiative. Coming off of major defeats in Wisconsin and Michigan, winning the ballot measure was seen as a national priority for the labor movement.

The Occupy movement transformed the dynamics of the campaign. "I spent a week in Ohio in early November interviewing dozens of people and reporting on the run-up to the SB 5 referendum," wrote *Mother Jones* reporter Andy Kroll. "I visited heavily Democratic and Republican parts of the state, talking to liberals and conservatives, union leaders and activists. What struck me was how dramatically the debate had shifted in Ohio thanks in large part to the energy generated by Occupy Wall Street. It was as if a great tide had lifted the pro-repeal forces in a way you only fully grasped if you were there."[38]

When SEIU president Mary Kay Henry went door to door to canvass voters, she told Kroll, "Every conversation was in the context of the 99 percent and the 1 percent, this discussion sparked by Occupy Wall Street." On Election Day, labor emerged triumphant, and SB 5 went down to a resounding defeat. In the aftermath, Henry stated, "The Occupy movement has framed the fight. They've totally changed the debate within a 30-day period."[39]

It wasn't just Ohio. After being targeted by Occupy activists as "Governor 1 Percent," New York's Andrew Cuomo reversed his stance on extending a "Millionaire's Tax" in the state, which gave a tax break to working- and middle-class families by hiking rates for top earners. Once considered a dead measure, the bill came back to life after protesters erected a "Cuomoville" outside the state capitol. As the *New York Times* reported, state legislators "lauded the Occupy Wall Street movement for changing the political climate in Albany, where lawmakers had planned to allow the millionaires' tax to simply expire." California governor Jerry Brown had pushed forth a similar measure in his state the same month, prompting an Associated Press headline reading, "You Can Thank the Occupy Movement for These New Taxes on Millionaires in California and New York."[40]

In Los Angeles, activists helped push forward a "responsible banking" ordinance, forcing banks that conducted business with the city to release data about their lending practices. For years, the *Los Angeles Times* explained, "the ordinance . . . had been languishing, but the arrival of protesters outside City Hall last October brought new momentum to the issue." The measure became law, as did California's Homeowner Bill of Rights, which offered a host of protections for families facing foreclosure. This state-level initiative had likewise been defeated by banking lobbyists in previous years but was pushed forward by housing activists in Occupy.[41]

In each case, one could argue that the movement was not the sole cause of the victory. But it would be myopic to ignore the contribution provided by the surge in grassroots activism. As such initiatives went forward, the *New York Times* reported, "It is apparent that Occupy Wall Street's impact is already being felt."[42]

On the national level, Occupy's messaging seeped into many prominent races, helping to advance candidates such as Elizabeth Warren in Massachusetts, who won her Senate seat after adopting the rhetoric of the "the 99 percent." In his race against Barack Obama, Republican presidential hopeful and multimillionaire Mitt Romney had planned to use his background as head of an investment firm as a major selling point in the 2012 election. Instead, his ties to the private-equity industry became a liability.[43]

Far too many factors shape the outcome of a presidential race for Occupy to claim any defining role. However, some political commentators who are generally skeptical of the movement's impact have given it partial credit. Even while questioning whether Occupy Wall Street made a "deep impact on the political landscape," *Washington Post* reporter Chris Cillizza concluded, "It helped re-frame or re-emphasize the populist messaging that President Obama ran and won on." Similarly, at the *New York Times*, Andrew Ross Sorkin acknowledged that Occupy's "message has subtly been woven throughout the Obama administration's re-election campaign, in the Democrats' position on everything from taxes on the highest earners to the soaring levels of student debt."[44]

Having failed to spark a revolutionary upheaval or uproot the power of the big banks, Occupy's most dedicated participants could hardly declare that their mission had been accomplished—especially since many of them were loath to support the Democrats. But any account of the movement's significance must surely weigh these outcomes against the blasé assertion that Occupy ended with nothing to show for its efforts.

After the financial collapse of 2008, political analysts waited for years for an eruption of mass outrage to begin. Some of the nation's most powerful progressive groups tried diligently to spark revolt, and still popular fury stayed dormant. The outbreak of defiance that finally changed this state of affairs was not without faults. But Occupy showed the power and potential that unarmed uprisings possess when they make use of a vital combination of ingredients: *Disruption. Sacrifice. Escalation.*

Not every exercise in strategic nonviolent conflict generates the type of intense flurry of activity that surrounded Occupy. But the experience of that movement illustrated a phenomenon that has been repeated in many campaigns of civil resistance. At its most successful, momentum-driven organizing creates new spaces of possibility in public life. It produces situations in which the normal rules of politics appear to be suspended, and large numbers of people respond with outpourings of hope and creativity.

Time and again, those who have encountered such situations have found them to be both exhilarating and enigmatic. They are not always certain how to make sense of them. But invariably they are aware that they have lived through something special.

They have experienced the whirlwind.

CHAPTER SEVEN

THE WHIRLWIND

EARLY IN THE afternoon on April 18, 2001, forty-eight members of Harvard's student-labor solidarity group made their way into Massachusetts Hall, the campus building that houses the office of the university president. After securing a conference room, the foyer, one office, a bathroom, and the hallway outside, the students sat down and announced that they would not leave the building until the campus's janitors, security guards, and dining hall workers were paid at least $10.25 an hour. It was the start of the Harvard Living Wage Sit-In.[1]

Over the previous two-and-a-half years, students had conducted extensive research into the local cost of living and the rates paid to campus workers by various subcontractors. They had canvassed dorms and passed petitions. They coordinated with campus unions, and they held countless one-on-one meetings with university staff, faculty, and alumni. They held public speak-outs and private delegations. All of this activity was designed to pressure university president Neil Rudenstine and the members of the Harvard Corporation to address the exploitation of service workers at the world's richest university. At the end of 2000, the same year in which Harvard announced that its endowment had exceeded $19 billion, there were roughly a thousand campus employees, predominantly immigrants and people of color, earning less than $10 per hour. Some made scarcely more than the state's minimum wage of $6.75, an hourly rate that left a parent with one child living below the poverty line.[2]

The contrast between Harvard's immense wealth and the daily difficulties faced by its lowest-paid employees made for a jarring juxtaposition. Carol-Ann Malatesta, a forty-year-old custodian, told her story for an oral history written by one of the sit-in participants. "The work itself sucks, alright?" Malatesta said. "It's very tiring, and it's hard work. But you just clean it all up, hold your nose, and you think to yourself, 'I got three kids, I love my kids, I love my kids. I want the kids to be happy.'

"Financially I'm OK now," Malatesta continued. "I was able to move out of the projects, but, you know, after paying taxes and daycare and car insurance, that's when you start going to food pantries and soup kitchens at night and you start trash-picking for clothes and toys and furniture. . . . I mean, my kids don't really think they're poor. When we go to a soup kitchen, they think they're going to a restaurant. What the hell? It's free food. . . . Waste not, want not."[3]

Frank Morley, a sixty-year-old janitor, spoke about the stress of holding down two jobs: "I work at Harvard until 4:00 pm," he said. "I get on the train, grab a cup of coffee, throw down a donut. Get off the train and walk twenty minutes from the station to my second job—the Supermarket. It doesn't pay a heck of a lot . . . but it helps, so I do bagging and stocking shelves until 10:30 pm. . . . Usually I'm so tired, I hit the pillow and bang, I'm out. But you ever been so tired, you can't go to sleep? That happens sometimes too, and it just drives me nuts. Anyway, I'm up again by four.

"I don't need to be a 50K man . . . all anybody's talking about is a living," Morley concluded. "How does Harvard justify paying a person $8.50 an hour with the kind of money they have? They should be damn well ashamed of themselves."[4]

～

Harvard's administration was unmoved. Although stories like Malatesta's and Morley's lent moral urgency to the campaign, the students' efforts had been met with bureaucratic stonewalling. Previously, the university formed an Ad-Hoc Committee on Employment Policies, made up of administrators and professors close to the president's office. Committee members talked among themselves for a year about the university's role as an employer, only to reject the idea of a living wage standard out of hand. By starting their sit-in, the product of more than two months of planning, the students sought to put an end to such intransigence.[5]

At first, the response on campus was modest. Student organizers recruited supporters to attend daily rallies in Harvard Yard, and members of unions representing campus employees also turned out. Initially, the people who showed up for rallies tended to be those already involved in the union or in progressive student groups. Yet over the next several days, the sit-in slowly began to gain traction.

On the occupation's third day, Senator Ted Kennedy made an unexpected visit to express his support, shaking hands with the students through the windows of Massachusetts Hall. Top officials of the national AFL-CIO also endorsed the campaign during the first week. Finally, even while one team of activists continued to hold the administrative building, organizers outside decided to escalate by setting up a tent city on the carefully manicured grounds of Harvard Yard. Not only did this move make the occupation dramatically more visible but it also annoyed administrators protective of the campus's immaculate landscaping. Soon, the makeshift camp swelled to include more than a hundred tents, occupied not only by students but also members of the surrounding community.

A strange shift began to take place.

Before long, it became clear that the action was generating a level of energy far beyond anything the campus student-labor organization was typically capable of producing. "We tried hard to organize and plan very carefully for the sit-in," says Amy Offner, who was a senior at the time and one of the campaign's leaders. "But by a week in, the whole operation had become so vast that what any one person could know about was only a small fraction of the activity going on."[6]

The campaign started to break into the national media. In the two years leading up to the sit-ins, the students had diligently cultivated contacts in the local and national press. As the sit-in commenced, they worked these contacts relentlessly. When their action began gaining momentum, the effort paid off in a big way. By its second week, the campaign was receiving mention on the evening news broadcasts of major networks. University officials were adamant that they would not yield to student demands, yet they were hesitant to expel the sit-in by force. Tension mounted, and the press took note. Images of activists hanging banners out the windows of the building from which the president had been exiled spread widely. *New York Times* columnist Bob Herbert devoted several columns to championing the sit-in, writing, "However this plays out, the protesters have provided a great service by insisting that we no longer avert our eyes to the continuing assault on the living standards of working men and women, even at a great institution like Harvard."[7]

Prior to the sit-in, the campaign had done insistent outreach to other student groups to get them to endorse the demand of a living wage. Now the dynamic was different. Students who previously thought little about the wages of service workers were actively talking about the subject, and a sizable number wanted to help the campaign. When campus groups had meetings, the sit-in was a top item for discussion, regardless of whether the campaign had requested to be on their agendas. One leader from Harvard's Black Student Association got his group to do a teach-in on race and poverty outside of the Massachusetts Hall occupation. "He did it on his own," says Offner. "He was going to do it whether we were good at reaching out to him or not."

Eventually, the sit-in was covered on every major network and by every prominent paper throughout the country. "We got more press during the sit-in than during the two years cumulatively," says Offner. The general counsel for Harvard, who was on vacation in Asia when the sit-in started and had not been informed of developments, reportedly learned about what was happening on campus when she saw the sit-in featured in a news segment on TV at the Tokyo airport.

Suddenly, associating with the campaign became fashionable, and people wanted to go on record advancing the cause. Supportive professors convinced nearly four hundred of their fellow faculty members to sign on to a full-page ad that ran in the *Boston Globe* endorsing the living wage. In theatrical fashion, several professors also opted to give lectures directly outside the windows of Massachusetts Hall to show their support.

While the student activists were aware in advance that campus unions could not be seen as being legally responsible for the sit-in, workers adopted the campaign as their own. Dining hall servers delivered pizzas to the occupiers, security guards gave testimonials before news cameras, and janitors held independent marches that blocked traffic in Harvard Square. Some three hundred food service workers, who were in the midst of contract negotiations with the university, took a strike authorization vote and then marched into the Yard for a noisy rally alongside the sit-in, their vote raising the specter that administrators might soon be facing a full-blown labor crisis on campus.

With the sit-in entering its third week, around a hundred Harvard alumni planned and executed a one-day solidarity sit-in at New York City's Harvard Club. Graduate students hung banners in the Yard expressing solidarity from various branches of the university, with slogans such as "Law Students Support a Living Wage"; from the education school, "Teachers for a Living Wage"; and, perhaps most memorably, from the Divinity School: "God Supports a Living Wage."[8]

By this time, the encampment outside Massachusetts Hall had taken on a life of its own. "Harvard Yard has mutated from a staid pastoral setting into a massive tent city of supporters so densely populated that there is a waiting list to sleep out," wrote Ben McKean, a junior who was one of the activists inside the administrative building. Increasingly, Tent City was being referred to as its own geographical destination. Before the sit-in was over, the residents of this makeshift metropolis held a mayoral election, and the camp was receiving deliveries from the US Postal Service. At one point, someone decided to host a barbecue in Harvard Yard for the occupation. "It was the craziest thing. To this day, I still have no idea how it was organized," Offner recalls. "A state senator showed up with veggies."[9]

Prior to the sit-in, student-labor activists on campus were accustomed to having perhaps twenty-five attendees at their meetings. "On bad weeks, it was more like 10 to 15 core people," says Offner. In contrast, by the time the sit-in had gained momentum, hundreds of people were actively participating, and the movement was calling rallies that could attract as many as two thousand.

By the third week, President Rudenstine, who had previously declared that he would resign before backing down, was looking for a way to save face. The administration was deep into negotiations with the students, who were being represented pro bono by top lawyers from the AFL-CIO. After twenty-one days, they announced a settlement.

The occupiers emerged from Massachusetts Hall into the sunlight of Harvard Yard to the cheers of a crowd of campus workers, fellow students, and community supporters. The campaign had accepted a symbolic victory: among its main terms, their agreement with the administration stipulated a moratorium on outsourcing and the formation of a committee—one with genuine union and student representation—to recommend new wage and benefit policies. There was no guarantee that this would produce a living wage. But the deal worked. Within a year, negotiations resulted in contracts that guaranteed even the lowest-paid service workers on campus around $11.00 an hour. When colleges resumed classes the following fall, at least forty new living wage campaigns launched on campuses across the country.[10]

⁓

"I don't think I got any sleep for three weeks," Offner recalls, reflecting on the sit-in. "I don't think any of the organizers did." But, in a way, it was expected that the core members behind the campaign, those who had built up the organizational structure of the student-labor group, would be working nonstop. More surprising, she says, were the people who came out of the woodwork and threw themselves into the mobilization. "By two weeks in, what was amazing—it was miraculous, honestly—was to see people who hadn't really been that involved in the campaign, or hadn't been involved at all before, weren't getting any sleep either," she says. "They were spending all of their time doing something like organizing Tent City. It was incredible."[11]

Every so often, we witness a period of intensive protest that seems to defy the accepted rules of politics: where previously apathy had reigned, outbreaks of dissent begin popping up everywhere. Organizers see their rallies packed with newcomers who come from far outside their regular network of supporters. Rather than having to painstakingly work to activate individual supporters, movement veterans are startled to see people motivating themselves to take action. Mainstream analysts, even more taken by surprise, describe something akin to spontaneous combustion. And those in power find that their previously accepted rationalizations for injustice are put under newly intensive scrutiny.

It was during one such moment of peak activity—amid the wave of interest in the civil rights struggle that swelled after the 1961 Freedom Rides—that Saul Alinsky took an excited, middle-of-the-night phone call from protégé Nicholas von Hoffman. After their event with several Freedom Riders at Chicago's Saint Cyril's Church was packed beyond capacity, these two organizers agreed on the need to temporarily set aside their normal structure-based methodologies in order to tap into the energy of that extraordinary time. They dubbed the unusual state a "moment of the whirlwind."[12]

It was an apt phrase. Although moments of the whirlwind happen across many different social movements, they are rarely reflected upon seriously—or even given a name. Yet, just in the new millennium, we have already seen whirlwinds materialize on a variety of scales. The Harvard Living Wage Sit-In electrified a campus, setting off a rash of defiance and public engagement within a single university community. The protests known as the 2011 Wisconsin Uprising centered on a state capital, Madison, but drew support from citizens throughout the state who were outraged by their conservative governor's attempts to destroy public sector unions. Occupy Wall Street created a whirlwind at the national level, with encampments springing up from coast to coast, and some forming in other countries as well. Finally, the Arab Spring, which swept through the Middle East, was a whirlwind of global significance, reminiscent of the Revolutions of 1989 in the former Soviet bloc.

The defining attribute of a moment of the whirlwind is that it involves a dramatic public event or series of events that sets off a flurry of activity, and that this activity quickly spreads beyond the institutional control of any one organization. It inspires a rash of decentralized action, drawing in people previously unconnected to established movement groups.

Individual academics have recognized these atypical states. Political scientist Aristide Zolberg describes them as "moments of madness"—periods of political exuberance when "human beings living in modern societies believe that 'all is possible.'" Most long-time participants in social movements have experienced at least one such moment. Indeed, it is not uncommon to learn that they were first recruited into political activism during such an outbreak. When asked, they will typically recall with wonder the mysterious and invigorating atmosphere that existed at the time.[13]

And yet, moments of the whirlwind remain conspicuously understudied. They do not feature in most models for creating change, and because of this they are more likely treated as freak outliers than as regular characteristics of successful social movement campaigns.

For their part, conventional political analysts contend that outbreaks of mass disruption are the product of broad historical forces. They suggest that no one could consciously engineer such upheavals. Most organizing traditions do little to counter this belief. As theorists of unharnessed disruption, Frances Fox Piven and Richard Cloward consistently emphasize the historical contingency of mass mobilizations, and seldom do they suggest methods through which outbreaks might be intentionally provoked. Participants themselves absorb this bias. When unstructured mass protests erupt, many new demonstrators regard their movement's sudden rise as a uniquely fated uprising—an occurrence without precedent or predictable shape. "Finally, the people have awakened," they think.[14]

Meanwhile, organizers in structure-based lineages of community and labor organizing see these outbreaks as too sporadic and unpredictable to be relied upon. As a consequence, they do not seek to understand whirlwind moments or to determine how they might be strategically incorporated into their work.

Momentum-driven organizing puts forth several propositions that challenge such attitudes. Those immersed in the study of how unarmed uprisings work contend, first, that moments of the whirlwind are not as rare as they might seem; second, that there is an art to harnessing them when they occur spontaneously; and third, that activists willing to embrace a strategy of nonviolent escalation can sometimes set off historic upheavals of their own.

~

If we do not want to be perpetually blindsided by outbreaks of heightened political activity, a first step is recognizing that these are not odd flukes. Rather, they are common, and they play an important role in the ups and downs of social movements.

For activist, educator, and author Bill Moyer, understanding the fluctuations typical in the cycles of movement campaigns became a life's work. Moyer was born in 1933 and grew up in northeast Philadelphia, the son of a TV repairman. As a child, he aspired to one day become a Presbyterian missionary in Africa. But a troublemaking spirit got in the way: as he told it, "In March 1959 I was voted out of the Presbyterian Church because I invited a Catholic and a Jew to talk to the youth group."[15]

The expulsion led him into the arms of the Quakers. At the time, Moyer was just three years out of Penn State, working as a management systems engineer and searching for more meaning in his life. Through one of Philadelphia's active Quaker meetings, Moyer came in contact with a vibrant circle of socially engaged peers, and he was tutored by an elder couple in theories of nonviolence. These encounters altered the course of his career. "I had no idea that it was the start of 'the Sixties,'" Moyer later wrote, "and never suspected that I was beginning my new profession as a full-time activist."[16]

In the 1960s, Moyer would take a job with the American Friends Service Committee in Chicago, helping to convince Martin Luther King Jr. to launch an open housing campaign in the city. Moyer then worked on King's last drive, the 1968 Poor People's Campaign in Washington, DC. In the decade that followed, he spent his energies protesting the Vietnam War, supporting the American Indian Movement at Wounded Knee, and promoting the newly emerging movement against nuclear power.

Even as the study of civil resistance was taking shape as an academic field, Moyer contributed to the development of an American lineage of strategic nonviolence. Throughout the 1970s and 1980s, members of his community—the Philadelphia-based Movement for a New Society— served as active participants in feminist, gay rights, antiapartheid, and Central American solidarity movements, often taking on responsibility for training newer activists. They developed a distinctive strain of non-violent direct action in the United States, one whose norms and tactics would run through the major environmental, global justice, and anti-war mobilizations of 1990s and 2000s.

As he increasingly began training other activists, Moyer saw a gap. "How-to-do-it models and manuals provide step-by-step guidelines for most human activity, from baking a cake and playing tennis to having a relationship and winning a war," he wrote in 1987. Within the world of activism, however, such material was harder to come by.[17]

There was writing about movements produced by academic theo-rists, but it tended to be dry and removed. As Moyer put it, although useful information could be found in these theories, "most do not help us understand the ebb and flow of living, breathing social movements as they grow and change over time." Among activists on the ground, Alin-sky's followers had created training manuals for their specific brand of community organizing. Likewise, materials drawing from Gandhi and King were available for instructing people in how to create individual nonviolent confrontations. But Moyer believed that there was a lack of models that looked at the long arc of protest movements, accounting for the highs and lows experienced by participants.[18]

To address this problem, Moyer created a model charting the stages through which successful movements progress—a framework he called the Movement Action Plan (MAP). It was initially printed in 1986 in the movement journal *Dandelion*, with twelve thousand newsprint cop-ies of the model distributed through grassroots channels. It became an underground hit. Moyer's blueprint was passed hand to hand, trans-lated into other languages, and shared at trainings for well over a decade before taking its final form in the 2001 book *Doing Democracy*, pub-lished shortly before Moyer's death.[19]

During their earliest stages, the model observed, social movements tend to keep a low profile. As a campaign launches, activists attempt to demonstrate that a genuine problem exists and to prove that the use of formal channels has failed to address it. They engage in the type of research, educational work, outreach, and petitioning that the Harvard students had undertaken prior to their Living Wage Sit-In. At this point, the movement's active supporters are few in number, and its organizers have yet to win over substantial swaths of the public.

But Moyer noted that this could change rapidly, due to what he called "trigger events." Moyer described a trigger event as a "highly publicized, shocking incident" that "dramatically reveals a critical social problem to the public in a vivid way." The incident could be any number of things: a natural disaster or a political scandal; a journalistic exposé or an act of war. Such events, Moyer argued, are an essential part of the cycle of every social movement. "Overnight, a previously unrecognized social problem becomes a social issue everyone is talking about," he explained. By thrusting activists into the public spotlight, trigger events create vital opportunities for rallying mass participation and sharply increasing support for a cause.[20]

Examples of triggers abound. A significant one for Moyer was the partial meltdown at the Three Mile Island nuclear power plant on March 28, 1979. The accident transformed nuclear safety from a niche concern into a hot-button issue. Just days later, a previously planned antinuclear rally in San Francisco that ordinarily might have attracted a few hundred participants instead pulled a crowd of twenty-five thousand. Within six weeks, Moyer writes, "Demonstrations across the country culminated when 125,000 protesters marched to the nation's Capitol on May 6, 1979."[21]

There have been countless trigger events since then, including prominent ones in recent years. The Bush administration's clear intention to launch an invasion of Iraq at the start of 2003 was a trigger event that spurred antiwar mobilization. Protest actions included the largest coordinated demonstration in world history on February 15 of that year, which involved as many as twelve million people across nearly eight hundred different cities around the globe. These mass marches were accompanied by acts of nonviolent militancy: after the Iraq War officially started on March 19, 2003, a week of actions in San Francisco effectively shut down the city's financial district, with 1,025 people being arrested on just the first day. Later protests there blocked major intersections, disrupted military recruitment centers, and attempted to occupy the iconic San Francisco Bay Bridge.[22]

For the immigrant rights movement, a critical trigger event occurred a few years later. In mid-December 2005, conservative Republicans in the House of Representatives pushed through the Sensenbrenner Bill, a draconian measure that, among other provisions, would have criminalized people providing food and basic services to undocumented immigrants. In the months that followed, the prospect that such legislation would be passed by the Senate and signed into law ignited a series of massive protests in immigrant communities throughout the nation.[23]

In 2014 and 2015, police killings of African American men, including Michael Brown in Missouri, Eric Garner in New York City, and Freddie Gray in Baltimore, set off successive waves of demonstrations, propelling the #BlackLivesMatter movement to national prominence.

Moyer's account of what happens in the wake of such an incident is prescient: "The trigger event starkly reveals to the general public for the first time that a serious social problem exists and that deliberate policies and practices of the powerholders cause and perpetuate the problem," he explained. "The event instills a profound sense of moral outrage within a majority of the general citizenry. Consequently, the public responds with great passion . . . and is ready to hear more information from the movement."[24]

During these times, new participants are inspired to join in their first demonstrations, and groups that had previously been building slowly find themselves amid a tempest, surrounded by a rush of urgent activity.

Trigger events sometimes happen spontaneously, and often they come as a surprise. After all, no one had expected that Three Mile Island would start to melt down when it did. But not every trigger event is so random or accidental—and some are more complicated than they at first appear.

～

In 1955, a young African American woman boarded a city bus in Montgomery, Alabama. It was getting late, and she was returning home after a long day. She paid her fare and sat down in an empty seat. Gradually, as the bus made stops along its route, it began to fill up. Eventually, the bus's driver asked the woman to give up her seat: she was black, and a white passenger had been left standing. Weary from the day, and even more so from the indignity of being treated as a second-class citizen, she refused to move to the back of the bus. The driver pulled over. Within minutes, police arrived on the scene, and they dragged the black woman off to jail in handcuffs. "All I remember," she said when recalling that day decades later, "is that I was not going to walk off the bus voluntarily.[25]

"I just couldn't move," she added. "History had me glued to the seat."

The woman's name was Claudette Colvin. She has been largely forgotten by history. Nine months later, an almost identical action took place, and the results were very different. Rosa Parks, a well-respected figure in Montgomery's African American community and secretary of the local NAACP, also refused to move to the back of the bus. Her defiance sparked a historic bus boycott, spawned national debate about segregation in America's Deep South, and went down as one of the last century's great acts of individual resistance.

The reality is that, in segregated Montgomery, many local blacks had indignantly declined to give up their seats on the city's buses over the years. In most cases, they were unceremoniously fined, and their punishment simply added to the generalized anger of a community forced to live under Jim Crow. By the time of Colvin's arrest, local civil rights groups had been looking for a test case that they might turn into a focal point of struggle. However, for a variety of reasons—including the fact that Colvin had been charged with assaulting an officer and that she was just fifteen years old—they decided to pass on her case. When Parks was arrested, on the other hand, civil rights leaders judged her an ideal figure to unite the community behind.

This is not a unique example. A trigger event that has spectacular impact in one specific time and place may have little consequence in another. On December 17, 2010, twenty-six-year-old Tunisian street vendor Mohamed Bouazizi took the extreme step of dousing himself in gasoline and lighting himself on fire to protest government harassment. His suicide incited widespread anger and indignation, leading to a rebellion that overthrew the nation's ruling regime and set off the Arab Spring. Yet when forty-three-year-old businessman Yacoub Ould Dahoud took similarly drastic action in Saudi Arabia the next month, his agonizing sacrifice produced no comparable effect in his country. In fact, there have been many self-immolations both before and after Bouazizi's in various parts of the world. The majority of these have passed with little notice, as was the case with Charles Moore, a seventy-nine-year-old Methodist minister who lit himself on fire seventy miles outside of Dallas, Texas, in late June 2014 to protest racism and homophobia within his denomination.[26]

In truth, potential trigger events happen all the time. However, only a small minority of them generate moments of the whirlwind. Oil spills, school shootings, and financial crises take place with distressing regularity. Likewise, investigators are constantly uncovering episodes of outrageous corruption in business and government. Most of these incidents pass briefly through the news cycle or go unnoticed entirely. People might shake their heads in horror, disgust, or exasperation. But then they move on. Usually, nothing much happens.

So, what determines whether a trigger sets off a feeble pop or a thunderous explosion?

Mainstream political experts focus on the social, economic, and geopolitical circumstances surrounding a given event. When mass uprisings burst forth, commentators tend to describe them as the product of historic conditions rather than the decisions of citizens themselves: the moment was ripe, they argue. Given the nature of the times, something like this was bound to happen.

Analysts in the field of civil resistance present a different view. They do not deny the importance that economic and political factors have in creating the context for social unrest. But they emphasize the interplay of such *conditions* with the *skills* of social movement participants. They hold up the agency of activists, as reflected in their strategic choices and practical execution.[27]

Years after the fact, historians have the luxury of looking back on an uprising and identifying the structural forces and historical peculiarities that might have contributed to a successful effort or that might have sunk an unsuccessful one. Activists on the ground, in contrast, never have the benefit of hindsight, and they must make the most of whatever conditions they encounter. As Hardy Merriman, a scholar and trainer in nonviolent conflict, writes, "Agency and skills make a difference, and in some cases have enabled movements to overcome, circumvent, or transform adverse conditions."[28]

In other words, it sometimes happens that the time is ripe only because people have deliberately endeavored to make it so.

Arguably, as in the case of Rosa Parks, the most common difference between a trigger event that fizzles and one that produces a moment of the whirlwind is the presence of a movement that decides to take action. Having an organized group of people consciously choose to rally around an incident can be decisive, especially if the group uses it as a rationale for robust escalation. Their actions turn short-lived public outcry into the kind of sustained agitation that shakes the political system. Moyer noted that more than a dozen years before Three Mile Island, a similar nuclear malfunction occurred at Detroit's Fermi reactor. It passed with little notice, and the Atomic Energy Commission succeeded in suppressing critical details about the potentially disastrous accident, in large part because there was no movement organizing around the issue that was prepared to respond.[29]

Ultimately, neither skills nor conditions are enough on their own. The two work in tandem. At any given time, history might offer up a trigger event that provokes widespread disquiet and sends people into the streets. But it takes dogged escalation on the part of activists to keep the issue at the fore of discussion, to create protest actions involving greater numbers of participants, and to repeatedly reinforce a sense of public urgency.

Chance offers up possibilities for revolt; movements make whirlwinds.

∿

Of course, seizing an opportunity when it happens to come along is one thing. Engineering a viral uprising from scratch is another. It is in navigating this latter challenge that momentum-driven organizing reaches the peak of its ambition.

In a cycle of nonviolent conflict, sacrifice and disruption can make for small, effective actions; they provide an entry point. Escalation can turn isolated protests into a campaign of building tension; it provides a means of continuation. A moment of the whirlwind, although rarely achieved, sees social movements in their most expansive and dynamic state; it is the climax.

Birmingham and the Salt March created textbook moments of peak activity. But these were not triggered by something that happened randomly. On the contrary, acts of disobedience themselves served as trigger events, dramatizing injustices and sparking much larger explosions of defiance. The same was true of the Freedom Rides that took Alinsky and von Hoffman by surprise. And it has been true of outbreaks such as Occupy Wall Street and the Harvard Living Wage Sit-In.

This is where skill comes in. Momentum-driven organizing is based on the principle not only that organizers can hone their talents for guiding and harnessing disruptive outbreaks that are provoked by external events but also that they can develop instincts for how to make their own sparks. By studying how movements themselves set off revolts, they can get better at pulling the trigger.

Mohandas Gandhi and Martin Luther King Jr. were experts in the politics of the unusual. In contrast to conventional politicians, and even to many of the organizers they worked with, they carefully cultivated techniques for creating periods of crisis and rupture. In his 1968 book *Where Do We Go from Here: Chaos or Community?*, King describes civil rights organizations using militant nonviolence as "specialists in agitation and dramatic projects," creating "explosive events" that "attracted massive sympathy and support." He self-critically notes that these events were no substitute for building institutional structures that could sustain the fight for the long haul. Still, the uprisings he helped create in places such as Birmingham and Selma became defining pinnacles in the push for civil rights.[30]

Project C produced a classic rupture, bringing a marked influx of new participants into civil rights activism and spawning a wide array of copycat protests. "A score of Birminghams followed the first," explains organizer James Farmer. By some counts, upward of a thousand demonstrations took place over the summer of 1963, resulting in some twenty thousand arrests. The initial campaign, which had been carefully crafted, gave rise to a rush of decentralized action. Historian Adam Fairclough argues, "The surge of nonviolent protest which swept the South after Birmingham was largely unplanned, uncoordinated, and unforeseen." This is not to say that individual protests were unorganized: beyond the Southern Christian Leadership Conference itself, groups such as Student Nonviolent Coordinating Committee (SNCC), the Congress of Racial Equality (CORE), and local civil rights organizations all adopted Birmingham as a model. Even the normally staid NAACP endorsed direct action in the summer of 1963. But the viral spread of defiance went beyond the membership lists or institutional structures that any civil rights groups had previously established, inspiring remarkable sacrifice even from people not previously active.[31]

Decades before, Gandhi had likewise articulated how nonviolent conflict could be consciously used to provoke social crises. Krishnalal Shridharani's 1939 treatise on Gandhi's campaigns, entitled *War Without Violence*, notes that unarmed uprisings have more in common with war than with routine interest group politics. "Underlying . . . both violence and non-violence," Shridharani writes, "is the basic assumption that certain radical social changes cannot be brought about save by mass action capable of precipitating an emotional crisis, and that the humdrum everyday existence of human life needs shaking up in order that man may arrive at fateful decisions."[32]

Issues of grave injustice, he continues, "must be successfully and sufficiently dramatized in order to arouse mass interest and mass enthusiasm preparatory to reaching a crucial decision. This requires not merely an intense consciousness of the issues involved, but also an emotional crisis in the life of the community."[33]

In 1930, when the Indian National Congress selected Gandhi as the strategist in charge of crafting its direct action challenge to the British

Raj, the group's leaders did not do so because they were his spiritual disciples. In fact, many of them distrusted Gandhi's otherworldly faith in the power of redemptive suffering. Nevertheless, they took the risk of choosing him for a simple reason: he had gained a hard-won reputation for being able to create moments of the whirlwind.

Trigger events are real. But whether they come from external sources or from movements themselves, they are only a beginning. When an uprising truly gains momentum, it is never the result of just one incident. Rather, it is the product of multiple, compounding crises, many of which are the result of deliberate effort. Effective movements create a feedback loop: building from an initial starting point, they use disruptive actions and political jiu-jitsu to make fresh headlines, prompt a reaction from authorities, and attract ever-greater numbers of participants to join in larger and more widely distributed actions.

Seen in this way, the moment of the whirlwind is the end point of escalation. Organizers ratcheting up tension through nonviolent conflict have no guarantee of reaching this state of peak enthusiasm. But they at least have a method for attempting it. And sometimes they succeed beyond their wildest imagination.

None of the student organizers at Harvard would have ever dreamed that their campaign would prompt such a wide range of activity. But their determined escalation—taking Massachusetts Hall, spreading the occupation into Harvard Yard, putting out a call for wider support— allowed for a potent storm to gather.

For student activists, the occupation of administrative buildings has proven to be an effective trigger on many campuses. In the spring of 1999, two years before the Harvard Living Wage Sit-In, antisweatshop campaigners at schools including Duke, Michigan, Arizona, and the University of North Carolina held sit-ins. Their example helped make the next few years periods of rare unrest. In 2000, activists at Johns Hopkins and Wesleyan occupied buildings in support of a living wage for campus workers, creating a template for escalation at Harvard. The Massachusetts Hall takeover, in turn, moved more young dissidents to act.[34]

In a broader context, organizers using civil resistance have some-times been able to find other triggers that are unusually reliable. They have successfully anticipated opportunities by planning around coming events that they know will be focal points for media attention.

The global justice movement of the late 1990s and early 2000s faced a daunting challenge when it came to moving public opinion around its cause: issues of injustice in the global economy could feel too diffuse and far-removed to capture much attention. But high-profile trade summits created an opening. Major news organizations already sent reporters to cover these events, and the presence of world leaders created a hook for discussion. Plans for wide-scale direct action turned these international summits into predictable trigger events. In this way, the ministerial meetings of the World Trade Organization in Seattle; the gatherings of International Monetary Fund and World Bank officials in Prague and Washington, DC; negotiating sessions for the Free Trade Area of the Americas in Quebec City, Miami, and Mar del Plata, Argentina; and the gatherings of G8 ministers in Cologne, Germany, and Genoa, Italy, all served as flashpoints of highly publicized dissent.

In Serbia, activists adopted the technique of using an electoral con-test as a trigger event. Knowing that the falsification of a vote count can serve as a powerful spark for mass defiance, they centered their strategy on prodding Milosevic to hold elections. This approach has since be-come a cornerstone of civil resistance campaigns working under repres-sive regimes. Dictators "assume that in the event they do not win the election, they can steal it," writes author Tina Rosenberg. "But this often fails." Even electoral contests that are supposed to be nothing more than rubber-stamp ratifications of a regime's power can turn into incendiary opportunities. "Elections provide a sharp focus for opposition organiz-ing," Rosenberg explains. "They wake up the citizenry to the question of who runs the country."[35]

This creates a fortuitous situation: knowing that an alarm clock is set for Election Day, organizers can quietly prepare for escalation. A trigger awaits them.

∽

Organizers who take a momentum-driven approach to creating change emphasize moments of the whirlwind because they recognize their peculiar power. And this is a fundamental way in which the organizing model differs from structure-based traditions.

Many Alinskyite community-organizing groups see themselves as specialists in confrontational action. Indeed, they might regularly deploy tactics such as sending busloads of inner-city residents to picket directly outside a slumlord's suburban house or filling the lobby of City Hall with hundreds of people to challenge the mayor. But in their drive to "build organizations, not movements," they limit the scope of their confrontations. They do not seek to escalate to the point of creating a public crisis and spurring activity outside their institutional framework. In the words of longtime Industrial Areas Foundation director Ed Chambers, they push for "incremental success over months and sometimes years," not peaks of activity that appear abruptly and cannot be sustained.[36]

The transactional gains of structure-based organizing produce genuine benefits in people's lives. Slow and steady efforts can pay tangible dividends. And yet, because they are generally suspicious of the sudden energy created by trigger events, organizers in this tradition miss opportunities to tap the vast potential of whirlwinds.

For momentum-driven mobilizations, in contrast, peak moments are critical. In Moyer's model, movements can work for a long time in their early stages to cultivate support and still see only modest gains. But after a triggering incident precipitates a crisis, campaigns can make major leaps forward. "The extensive media coverage of the trigger event and the movement's dramatic nonviolent demonstrations not only makes the public aware of the social problem," he writes, "but also conveys the social movement's position for the first time." As a result, public opinion on the issue moves like it never has before.[37]

For Patrick Reinsborough and Doyle Canning of the Center for Story-based Strategy, "Dramatic crisis situations can challenge underlying assumptions and redefine the conventional wisdom." Major trigger events, ranging from the start of the Iraq War to the flooding of New Orleans, "inevitably disrupt the dominant culture's mental maps and can trigger mass *psychic breaks*: moments when status quo stories no longer hold true." These times are crucial for reorienting public opinion. "Psychic breaks," Reinsborough and Canning write, "open new political space and can provide powerful opportunities for new stories to take root in popular consciousness."[38]

Consistent with a transformative approach to creating change, the impact of these shifts is not always evident immediately—at least in terms of producing instrumental gains. Aristide Zolberg writes, "Stepped-up participation is like a flood tide which loosens up much of the soil but leaves alluvial deposits in its wake." Although it is not yet a time for harvest, the ground has become newly fertile.[39]

Moyer suggests that the goal of movements experiencing a whirlwind is "to create a public platform from which the movement can educate the general public." But, counterintuitively, he contends, "It is *not* a goal or expectation to get the powerholders to change their minds, policies, or behavior at this stage." That change comes later.[40]

To his credit, Saul Alinsky saw the period of unrest that had been created by the Freedom Rides as an opportunity. He recognized it as time to put aside the organizing model he had done so much to champion and instead to experiment, at least for a short while, with a different mode of confrontation. Von Hoffman had suggested, "We are no longer organizing but guiding a social movement," and Alinsky agreed. Trade unionists and community organizers who have been inspired by recent mobilizations such as Occupy and #BlackLivesMatter, and who have thrown themselves into supporting these uprisings, have expressed similar openness and daring.

Recognizing an exceptional moment, they have been willing to leap into the storm.

≈

If whirlwinds represent a climax, what comes next can only be a letdown.

Alinsky said that dramatic confrontations staged by movements will typically produce "a flare-up" that cuts quickly "back to darkness." Piven and Cloward acknowledge that disruptive uprising "erupts, flowers, and withers, all in a moment."[41]

By using the techniques of civil resistance, momentum-driven organizing seeks to address this problem, at least in part. Working to consciously guide and amplify mass protest, it aims to create repeated cycles of uprising. Over the course of a cycle, movements experience periods of peak escalation, absorb their energy through mass training and decentralized structures, then continue to build toward future trigger events. When the process is successful, it results in campaigns of nonviolent confrontation more lasting and powerful than typical eruptions of mass protest.

Nonetheless, emotional ups and downs are unavoidable. With all mass protests, surges of extraordinary participation are followed by fallow stretches. In the down times, activists' numbers dwindle and advocates struggle to draw any attention at all to their work. During these lulls, those who have tasted the euphoria of a peak moment often feel discouraged and pessimistic.

One of the strengths of Bill Moyer's work is its attentiveness to the psychological challenges faced by people struggling to push a cause forward. Moyer was proud when trainers using his materials reported that participants would nearly gasp in recognition when the MAP explained patterns that they had thought were unique to their own experience. Moyer referred to these as "Aha!" moments, and his goal was to create as many of them as possible.

For those encountering Moyer's work for the first time, the biggest "Aha" usually does not come with description of the trigger events and take-off periods that characterize a movement's most exhilarating moments. Instead, the most profound recognition comes with the discussion of what follows: according to Moyer, after a whirlwind's flurry of activity dies down, movements predictably experience what he calls the "Perception of Failure."

Moyer sometimes shared the story of when he first presented his model of movement cycles. In February 1978, he was scheduled to give a presentation at a strategy conference to forty-five organizers from the antinuclear group known as the Clamshell Alliance. This group had conducted the landmark series of direct action protests against the Seabrook power plant in New England. At its peak, the previous spring, the alliance carried out an occupation of Seabrook in which 1,414 people were arrested and spent up to twelve days in jail. As Moyer wrote, "During those two weeks, nuclear energy became a worldwide public issue as the mass media spotlight focused on the activists locked in armories throughout New Hampshire."[42]

They had generated a model whirlwind: in the wake of the Clamshell actions, hundreds of new grassroots groups formed around the country. The Seabrook protest inspired further occupations in places such as the Diablo Canyon nuclear plant in California. Moreover, the organization's methods—its affinity groups, spokescouncils, consensus process, and focus on militant, nonviolent blockades—would ultimately become an influential template for direct action in the United States.

Because of all they had accomplished, Moyer expected that the group at the conference would be upbeat and celebratory. Instead, he encountered the opposite. "I was shocked when the Clamshell activists arrived with heads bowed, dispirited and depressed, saying their efforts had been in vain," Moyer wrote. Because protests had died down and they had failed to reach their short-term transactional goal—stopping construction on the specific plant they had targeted—they felt defeated.[43]

In his presentation, a sketchy version of what would become his MAP model, Moyer scrambled to demonstrate how the activists had made considerable gains. By galvanizing national opposition to the industry, the movement had already reversed the near-universal acceptance of nuclear power that prevailed during the 1960s and early 1970s. Activists were well on their way to establishing majority support for their position—and seeing tangible changes as a result.

Moyer believed that the framework he presented helped the activists better understand their predicament and plan for future stages of activity. Whether or not this is the case, anti–nuclear power campaigns ultimately achieved a resounding victory. By making the safety, cost, and ecological impact of nuclear power into concerns shared by a majority of Americans, they created a situation in which orders for new nuclear power plants ceased. The government was compelled to abandon its goal of having a thousand facilities in operation by the end of the century. And the number of working plants was set on a path of steady decline—a path on which it continues to this day.

By making the "perception of failure" a part of his model, Moyer highlighted a contradiction that was not confined to one group of anti-nuclear activists. After a whirlwind spike in activity subsides, movement participants commonly feel dejected—even though it is at precisely this time that they are poised to secure their most significant gains. With the excitement of the peak moment behind them, many people "burn out or drop out because of the exhaustion caused by overwork and long meetings." Moreover, the mainstream media reinforces an air of negativity by reporting that, because protests have dropped off, the movement is dead and has accomplished nothing. All of this, Moyer wrote, combines to create "a self-fulfilling prophecy that prevents or limits [movement] success."[44]

By identifying the perception of failure as a normal part of social movement cycles, Moyer hoped to blunt its negative force. He argued that activists who look to history will see that they are not alone in experiencing letdown—and that past movements which were able to overcome despondency ended up seeing many of their once-distant demands realized. As campaigners move to later phases that involve institutionalizing their gains and capitalizing on the increased public support they have accumulated, they begin reaping what they have sown.

Because feelings of failure within movements are so seldom acknowledged in other sources, let alone considered thoughtfully, Moyer's discussion of the perception of failure has been widely referenced. Progressives have used it in the aftermath of Occupy Wall Street, while, in 2014, none other than far-right guru and ex–Fox News titan Glenn Beck considered Moyer's observations in some detail in contemplating the future prospects of the Tea Party.[45]

But, we might ask, are perceptions of failure necessarily irrational and misguided? How does one determine when pessimism is misplaced?

Moyer's analysis is consistent with a transformative vision, and it recalls the way in which same-sex marriage was won. Movements succeed when they win over ever-greater levels of public support for their cause and undermine the pillars of support: "Over the years . . . the weight of massive public opposition, along with the defection of many elites, takes its toll," Moyer argues.

If, in desperation, activists become ever more insular and isolated from the wider public, then feelings of failure are warranted. But a movement that is building popular support need not worry if its initial moment in the spotlight passes and the fickle news media turns its attention elsewhere. Instead, its active supporters can ready themselves to ignite fresh waves of protest when the opportunities arise. "The long-term impact of social movements," Moyer contends, "is more important than their immediate material success."[46]

Moyer's work serves as an important reminder that the whirlwind is a critical peak moment of struggle, but it is not the only phase. Prior to the Harvard sit-in, there had been a long campaign by students to raise awareness of the living wage issue. As in Birmingham, activists carefully laid the groundwork for escalation, and they meticulously planned their initial act of civil resistance. Moreover, their work was not completed at the end of the sit-in. When the students left Massachusetts Hall, they had not accomplished much in concrete terms: again like the Birmingham movement, they won minor concessions and a framework for future negotiations. It took a year of intensive organizing after the sit-in before campus workers saw significant transactional gains.

But the Living Wage Sit-In produced a psychic break in the life of the campus. After the whirlwind, the campaign negotiated in an entirely new context. As Offner writes, for a time the sit-in "changed the power relations at Harvard, giving workers, students, and the neighboring community a degree of collective power that could actually match that of the administration and the Harvard Corporation." Past university task forces had made wage decisions with scarcely any input from the people who actually worked as custodians and dining hall servers at the university. Now, conservative critics charged that the voices of these workers were overrepresented in committee hearings. One economics professor complained, "Anyone who speaks publicly against the Living Wage risks being demonized."[47]

It would be more accurate, defenders of the campaign countered, simply to say that those who believed that the world's richest university could not afford to pay more than poverty wages were losing. In the words of participant Ben McKean, the sit-in had served to demonstrate the "consensus of an entire community." And that consensus won out.[48]

∼

Bill Moyer believed that "social movements involve a long-term struggle between the movement and the powerholders for the hearts, minds, and support of the majority of the population." Yet there is a paradox inherent in this belief: While protesters aim to generate popular support, protests themselves can be very unpopular.[49]

Contrary to the campaign-trail pledges of mainstream politicians, who constantly vow to bring the country together, grassroots campaigners serious about compelling change often find that the route forward involves courting controversy. Ironically, the people with some of the keenest insights into the dynamics of divisiveness are those perceived as peaceniks—the planners of nonviolent revolt.

Their message? Togetherness can be overrated. And sometimes it pays to be a "divider."

CHAPTER EIGHT

THE DIVIDERS

ON JULY 3, 1981, the *New York Times* published its first story about a rare and fatal condition that had appeared among homosexuals in the city. Already, the mysterious disease had claimed the lives of forty-one people, young men whose immune systems had been ravaged. Within a few years, hundreds more began overcrowding hospital wings in New York, Los Angeles, and San Francisco, victims of what was then being called the "Gay Cancer." Their bodies were slowly decaying from infections and skin lesions, and they were afflicted by what had been dubbed the three Ds of the disease: "Dementia, diarrhea, and disgrace."[1]

The AIDS crisis had arrived. By 1987, AIDS was spreading exponentially, with more than fifty thousand cases reported in 113 countries. But the disease's early casualties were concentrated in the gay communities of metropolitan New York and California. For a generation of gay men, the diagnosis was fatal. As renowned HIV specialist Dr. John Bartlett remarked, "It was an awful way to live. They got emaciated. They died a lingering death. If you asked me, 'How would you least want to die?' I'd say, 'The way an AIDS patient died.'"[2]

Despite the fact that AIDS was quickly becoming a sweeping epidemic that affected both men and women, regardless of sexual orientation, it was clouded in stigma. For seven years after the emergence of the disease, President Ronald Reagan went out of his way to avoid acknowledging AIDS. His first policy address on the subject came in 1987, near the end of his second term, prior to which he scarcely uttered the word publicly. Behind his silence was a cruel bias. The Reagan administration maintained close ties with the emergent "religious right," in particular the Moral Majority. The leader of that group, the Reverend Jerry Falwell, had stated flatly, "AIDS is not just God's punishment for homosexuals, it is God's punishment for the society that tolerates homosexuals."[3]

In the broader public, fear was prevalent. A December 1986 poll in the *Los Angeles Times* showed that 50 percent of respondents supported a quarantine of AIDS patients, and 15 percent were in favor of tattooing AIDS victims. People diagnosed with the disease were routinely fired from their jobs and evicted from their residences. Children with AIDS were refused access to schools, and when one such child—Ryan White—protested, his family's home was vandalized and the tires of his parents' car were slashed. At least one bishop advised parishioners attending church with people who might have the disease to stop drinking from the communion cup.[4]

Such public scorn and official indifference had serious consequences. Some hospitals refused to take AIDS patients or expand services to meet the growing need. Budgets for AIDS research at organizations such as the National Institutes of Health (NIH) were seriously underfunded, a trend that started early. "Here is a telling comparison," writes sociologist Deborah Gould: "in 1976, the Centers for Disease Control spent nine million dollars within months of the initial outbreak of what became Legionnaires' Disease, an outbreak that killed thirty-four people; in contrast, during the entire first year of the AIDS epidemic, when more than two hundred people died, the CDC spent just one million dollars on AIDS." Making things worse, the federal Food and Drug Administration (FDA) refused to streamline its approval procedures to bring new drugs to market in time to help patients who were dying. When pharmaceutical companies finally did make these drugs available, they were incredibly costly and inaccessible. Patients struggled to get treatment covered by their insurance companies and to collect disability benefits. Many were left impoverished and alone.[5]

If there was a single watershed moment when this began to change, it might well have been March 24, 1987. On that day, 250 protesters gathered on Wall Street to demand that government and corporations act to address AIDS—and that the $10,000 annual price of AZT, the only drug then available to treat HIV, be lowered. Activists lay down to block traffic on Wall Street and Broadway, some with cardboard tombstones, and seventeen were arrested.[6]

The protesters were from a group that had been founded just days before: the AIDS Coalition to Unleash Power, or ACT UP. They were loud. They were abrasive. Their emblem was a pink triangle—the symbol that homosexuals had been compelled to wear in Nazi concentration camps. And their motto was "silence equals death." After continued protest, the pharmaceutical company Burroughs Wellcome cut the price of AZT, and a new template for AIDS advocacy was established.

So much of mainstream politics involves an appeal to togetherness. Politicians perennially pledge to create common ground and help the country's citizens overcome their disagreements. And yet, social movements often take an approach that is almost exactly opposite: instead of bridging differences between groups, they widen them. ACT UP is an important case in point. Unlike other AIDS campaigners, these activists were willing to make enemies and to polarize the issue of how the disease was being addressed. ACT UP members denounced opponents as "Nazis" and "murderers"; they openly confronted religious leaders, politicians, and doctors whom they saw as worsening the crisis; and they cared little if people called them "faggots" and "sinners" in response. Undertaking a notably confrontational strategy, the group stirred strong feelings and often courted backlash.

This strategy did not always make them popular. But it did allow them to stay in the public eye, to expose the injustice of official neglect and disregard, and finally to win broad support for their cause.

Practitioners of nonviolent conflict have regularly shown themselves willing to be intentionally divisive, making use of a complex yet critical phenomenon known as "polarization." In doing this, they grapple with an undeniable tension: broad-based support is vital if campaigns of civil resistance are to prevail. And yet many of the tactics of nonviolent disruption tend to be unpopular. People prefer calm speech and reasoned dialogue to the ruckus of confrontational protest. In many cases, creating a galvanizing crisis around an issue involves inconveniencing members of the general public, potentially alienating the very people that advocates want to win over. Moreover, when a vocal minority speaks out, it can inspire its most ardent enemies to begin organizing in response.

Notwithstanding these dangers, the experience of social movements—from the civil rights movement in the 1960s, to ACT UP in the 1980s and 1990s, to the immigrant rights movement in the new millennium—shows that polarization can also be a powerful friend. By taking an issue that is hidden from common view and putting it at the center of public debate, disruptive protest forces observers to decide which side they are on. This has three effects: First, it builds the base of a movement by creating an opportunity for large numbers of latent sympathizers to become dedicated activists. Second, even as it turns passive supporters into active ones, it engages members of the public who were previously uninformed, creating greater awareness even among those who do not care for activists' confrontational approach. And third, it agitates the most extreme elements of the opposition, fueling a short-term backlash but isolating reactionaries from the public in the long run.

Polarization did not guarantee that ACT UP would win its fight, but it did make the battle lines clear. And in a climate where silence and indifference had become fatal, this was a decisive advance.

∾

ACT UP was certainly not the first organization formed in response to the growing challenge of AIDS. In San Francisco, West Hollywood, and New York City, the communities of those most affected by the disease had mobilized to fill the vacuum left by an indifferent public health system. Groups such as Gay Men's Health Crisis (GMHC) provided education, peer support, legal aid, and care for those suffering from AIDS. Some of the people who ran or donated to these organizations—such as GMHC president Paul Popham, an ex–special forces officer and successful Wall Street banker—brought privileged connections and access to money, because they themselves were closeted members of the socio-political elite. But their standing made them reluctant to risk exposure by publicly challenging governmental and corporate institutions.[7]

Larry Kramer, an openly gay author and Academy Award–nominated screenwriter, had been one of the founders of GMHC in 1982. But, over time, he grew frustrated with the increasingly institutionalized and professionalized nature of the organization. "Everything had to have a job description and approval by this, and approval by that," Kramer later recalled. "It became the Red Cross."

This ethos meant avoiding politics: "They wouldn't go after anybody," Kramer explained. "They wouldn't criticize anybody. They wouldn't picket, they wouldn't protest—any of those things."[8]

On March 10, 1987, Kramer found himself delivering a speech on short notice at New York's Lesbian and Gay Community Center after scheduled speaker Nora Ephron fell ill. The talk drew a large crowd, and Kramer gave what one observer called "one of the most moving and impassioned speeches of the AIDS era." Kramer castigated the NIH, the FDA, and even GMHC. He told those assembled that if they didn't stand up and fight, many of them would be dead in just a few years. At the end, he called for the creation of an organization devoted solely to political action. The room filled with cries of assent, and two days later ACT UP was born.[9]

Over the next decade, the group staged some of the most creative and militant nonviolent protests in US history. It organized hundreds of dedicated volunteers through chaotic general assemblies and decentralized affinity groups. As *The New Yorker* later reported, "Dozens of chapters were formed, from San Francisco to Bombay. Each was filled with desperate, aggressive, and often exceptional young men who, in the end, made Gay Men's Health Crisis look like a sleepy chapter of the Rotary Club."[10]

In the following years, members of ACT UP returned to Wall Street and—in an unprecedented coup—successfully shut down trading on the floor of the New York Stock Exchange. They chained themselves inside pharmaceutical corporations and blockaded offices at the FDA, plastering posters with bloody handprints to the outside of the agency's headquarters. They stopped traffic on the Golden Gate Bridge and interrupted mass at Saint Patrick's Cathedral. Using fake IDs to enter CBS headquarters, they jumped onscreen during Dan Rather's nightly news broadcast, reeling off a string of chants before the network cut to a long, unplanned commercial break.[11]

ACT UP draped a giant yellow condom over the Washington home of Senator Jesse Helms, one of the movement's most ardent and homophobic adversaries. And during a 1992 memorial in Washington, the group's members held a procession to scatter the ashes of friends and lovers who had died of AIDS onto the White House lawn. Public health administrators ACT UP members disliked were sometimes hung in effigy at protests.[12]

Unsurprisingly, not everyone was enamored of these actions. ACT UP's brazenly confrontational demeanor, a *Rolling Stone* reporter wrote in 1990, "caused many to write off the group as radical lunatics." The *New York Times* described the group's tactics as "a mixture of the shrill and the shrewd," remarking that "to the businesses, bishops, and bureaucrats that they accuse of slowing the fight against AIDS, they often seem rude, rash, and paranoid, and virtually impossible to please."[13]

Meanwhile, the *Washington Post* wrote, "Kramer, a very public face of an increasingly public disease, was in everyone's face," and elsewhere he was described as the "angriest man in America." Even within the gay community, critics argued that ACT UP's strident demonstrations only gave ammunition to the rising religious right, which used fear about homosexuality to swell its ranks.[14]

Asked in 2005 if he thought ACT UP's tactics had been alienating, Kramer responded with characteristic indignation: "Who gives a shit? I'm so sick of that. You do not get more with honey than you do with vinegar. You just do not."[15]

As is characteristic of polarizing movements, ACT UP had a different effect on different groups of people. Most directly, it took a community at the center of the crisis—AIDS patients, their lovers, and friends—and transformed them from passive victims into a potent political force. A growing number of disciplined activists found their voice within the working groups that emerged from ACT UP's decentralized structure. In short, the organization's high-profile actions and vibrant meetings generated a strong base of active public supporters.

Michael Petrelis, a New Jersey native and ACT UP stalwart who had been openly gay since high school, contended that this had a ripple effect in the wider gay community: "Because we're in the streets being the radicals, everyone else can take another step and still seem moderate," he argued. Members of the public at large were moved toward activities such as supporting AIDS charities and promoting sex education, even if they were not inclined to approve of activists' more abrasive tactics.[16]

ACT UP was only one factor that shifted the spectrum of opinion around AIDS. But over the decade when the group was most active, public attitudes underwent a profound transformation. Where stigma had previously prevailed, increased awareness about the disease led to much greater compassion for its victims. Joining the fight against AIDS became a popular celebrity cause, and ordinary people flocked to AIDS Walk benefits. Patients who were HIV-positive were included in government protections against discrimination. And, as author Randy Shaw writes, "Federal spending on AIDS rose from $234 million in 1986 to nearly $2 billion in 1992, a nearly tenfold increase in only six years." Eventually, such funding gained broad bipartisan support.[17]

On the negative side, there is no doubt that ACT UP produced backlash. Religious conservatives used the group's attacks on religious leaders to convey the sense that Christian America was under assault by advocates of a "homosexual lifestyle." But by holding their opponents publicly accountable for their bigoted views of AIDS patients, ACT UP ultimately succeeded in isolating them from the mainstream. In the early 2000s, even Jesse Helms repented, saying he regretted his previous stance opposing funding for AIDS research and treatment.[18]

To what extent any single organization can claim credit for prompting the seismic shifts in public opinion around AIDS is questionable. But it is certain that ACT UP made a vital contribution. The high levels of disruption and sacrifice embodied in the group's demonstrations prompted a stream of headlines that kept people talking about the disease. "It's hard to overestimate the impact of these protests," the *Washington Post*'s Jose Antonio Vargas wrote in 2005. "Silence = Death" became the central rallying cry of the forces that established AIDS as a true public crisis. Companies targeted by die-ins made previously unaffordable drugs more accessible, and hospitals acquiesced to demands to treat patients with more respect and care.[19]

Members of ACT UP's Treatment Action Group proved themselves to be knowledgeable experts about the on-the-ground success of various drug therapies and treatment regimens. Soon they were invited guests at major conferences, establishing a key role for patients themselves in helping to set the direction of public policy. Gran Fury, the renowned design and art collective within the organization, created a new iconography for the fight against AIDS. Its "Kissing Doesn't Kill: Greed and Indifference Do" posters became a landmark in public awareness about the disease. Meanwhile, its stickers with ACT UP's slogan and pink triangle, wrote one reporter in 1990, became "ubiquitous reminders on cash machines, newsstands, tollbooth buckets, and pay phones" throughout New York City.[20]

Dr. Anthony S. Fauci, director of the NIH's program on infectious disease and a past target of activists' ire, acknowledged, "ACT UP put medical treatment in the hands of the patients. And that is the way it ought to be."[21]

ACT UP prompted major changes in the federal government's procedures for testing and distributing new drugs, allowing AIDS patients to receive life-saving medications far more quickly than they would have otherwise. "They helped revolutionize the American practice of medicine," *The New Yorker*'s Michael Specter wrote in 2002. "The average approval time for some critical drugs fell from a decade to a year, and the character of placebo-controlled trials was altered for good. . . . Soon changes in the way AIDS drugs were approved were adopted for other diseases, ranging from breast cancer to Alzheimer's."[22]

A *New York Times* headline from January 3, 1990, perhaps put it best: "Rude, Rash, Effective," it read, "ACT UP Shifts AIDS Policy."[23]

~

Members of ACT UP prided themselves on being aggressive and out-spoken. But the controversy surrounding the group, and the range of responses its protests provoked, is not unique. Indeed, it is only a somewhat magnified example of the reactions that all campaigns of nonviolent protest tend to generate.

In 2012, the *Los Angeles Times* reported, "Polls have shown that the public generally supports Occupy's message but not its disruptive tactics." The next year, Salon published a story with the headline, "Study: Everyone hates environmentalists and feminists." It reported, "People tend to hold negative views of political and social activists," preferring "nonabrasive and mainstream methods" over activities "such as staging protest rallies."[24]

The Salon article drew a moral from the negative perception of protesters: "The message to advocates is clear," the story concluded: "Avoid rhetoric or actions that reinforce the stereotype of the angry activist." This message echoed the well-intentioned counsel that campaigners hear constantly: that they should be more moderate and friendly, and that embracing a less antagonistic route toward pursuing change will produce better results.

Certainly, activists can work to be creative in their actions and present themselves in ways that break with typical protest clichés. But the idea that they should avoid negative reaction by being less "angry" is folly. The major social movements of the past two centuries have consistently proven wrong the advice that activists do better to appear civil and minimize confrontation. The most well-known quote from famed abolitionist Frederick Douglass eloquently addresses this very topic: "If there is no struggle, there is no progress," Douglass stated in 1857. "Those who profess to favor freedom and yet depreciate agitation are men who want crops without plowing up the ground, they want rain without thunder and lightning. They want the ocean without the awful roar of its many waters."[25]

True, disruptive actions are polarizing. But this is not an unintended consequence. It is central to how they work. The dynamics of divisiveness are not easy to master, and they do not always play out in completely predictable fashion. Nevertheless, across many movements, some instructive patterns have appeared.

In recent years, the phenomenon of polarization has rarely received in-depth reflection within the field of civil resistance. However, its importance was recognized early on. In his 1973 work, *The Politics of Nonviolent Action*, Gene Sharp wrote, "With the launching of nonviolent action, basic, often latent, conflicts between . . . groups are brought to the surface and activated." The start of public demonstrations, he wrote, "will almost always sharpen the conflict, cause the conflicting groups to become more sharply delineated, and stimulate previously uncommitted people to take sides."[26]

Try as they might, activists have little hope of avoiding such an effect: "This polarization," Sharp observed, "seems to be a quality of all forms of open conflict."[27]

On the positive side, Sharp noted, "As tension increases, morale rises and large numbers of formerly passive people become determined to take part in the coming struggle." Unfortunately, there are less desirable consequences as well. The "previous period of indifference," Sharp noted, is replaced by one where there is "active antagonism." Reactionaries who are opposed to the movement's cause will rise to defend the status quo, mobilizing a backlash. In instances when the backlash is powerful, it can look like activists are worse off for having picked a fight—especially if vocal opposition is accompanied by repression from the state.[28]

One might ask: If the discord generated by confrontational protests spurs both supporters and detractors, what is actually gained?

For polarization to pay off, the positive must outweigh the negative. And here the reaction of the general public—those not already aligned with either side—is critical. Acts of sacrifice and political jiu-jitsu can help to foster an empathetic reaction: they convince the undecided to side with communities in resistance rather than forces of repression. When the process works, members of the public are alienated by the extremism of reactionary opponents, and they acknowledge that something needs to be done to address the movement's grievances. They become passive sympathizers.

Interestingly, a significant portion of these people will still be turned off by the movement's *tactics*—they will plead for peace and reasoned negotiation rather than continued disruption. But even when they do not like a movement's methods, these new sympathizers will agree with the justice of its cause. In the civil rights movement, these people may have disliked the fact that impatient students started sitting in at segregated lunch counters in Southern cities rather than going through official channels. Yet they were loath to identify with the racist mob members who poured milkshakes over the activists' heads or put out lit cigarettes on the backs of the students' jackets. Even as the moderate observers wished for an end to conflict, they acknowledged the injustice of Jim Crow and insisted that officials provide a remedy.

"The first public reaction to the nonviolent challenge may well be negative," Sharp notes. Yet, over time, "successful nonviolent campaigns produce a strengthened solidarity among the nonviolent militants, a growth of wider support for correction of the grievance, and a fragmentation and disintegration of support for the opponent." As a campaign progresses, the ranks of its active supporters swell and passive goodwill toward the activists' position becomes dominant. Meanwhile, the opposition shrinks down to an ever-smaller core of enraged and embittered extremists, and the public increasingly recognizes their views as isolated and obsolete.[29]

Working independently from Gene Sharp and others in the field of civil resistance, Frances Fox Piven identified polarization as a critical common factor in dozens of social movements in US history. Indeed, she presents polarization as a core function of these mobilizations. As they "force people to ask themselves how they stand on the issues of contention," she argues, movements create stark divides among voters, compelling politicians to offer concessions as a means of restoring order in the electoral landscape.[30]

Piven writes in her book *Challenging Authority*, "Protest movements threaten to cleave the majority coalitions that politicians assiduously try to hold together. It is in order to avoid the ensuing defections, or to win back the defectors, that politicians initiate new public policies." For this reason, Piven contends, "conflict is the very heartbeat of social movements." Even if protests are seen as distasteful, protesters can win.[31]

～

Time and again, patterns of polarization appear in democratic movements in the United States and abroad. Looking back from the safe remove of history, it can be easy to imagine that landmark social and political causes of the past—whether they involved ending slavery, securing the franchise for women, or establishing standards of workplace safety—were popular and widely celebrated. But the truth is that, in their time, these issues generated tremendous controversy. In promoting them, activists had to make the difficult decision to invite division and acrimony before they achieved their most impressive results.

The civil rights movement is a key instance in which agitation was widely depreciated. Although it is now universally admired and honored, the fight against Jim Crow was not always regarded with such reverence. In fact, the movement was incredibly polarizing.

Today, Martin Luther King Jr.'s "Letter from Birmingham City Jail" is viewed as an eloquent explanation of the aims and methods of the struggle against segregation. It stands as one of the most significant and closely studied essays written by one of America's national heroes. It is less commonly remembered, however, that King did not write the letter as a response to racist opponents. Instead, he was addressing would-be supporters who criticized the movement's approach as too pushy and impetuous.

On April 12, 1961, in the second week of Project C, King, along with his close friend Ralph Abernathy and forty-six other demonstrators, was arrested for kneeling down in prayer in front of Birmingham's City Hall, a clear violation of the recently instated injunction against public demonstrations in the city. The day after the arrest, eight clergymen, prominent white liberals from Alabama, published an open letter in the *Birmingham News* voicing their opposition to the direct action tactics being used by King, the Southern Christian Leadership Conference, and the local Alabama Christian Movement for Human Rights.[32]

Uncomfortable with the heedless confrontation of the civil rights campaign, the ministers wrote, "We recognize the natural impatience of people who feel that their hopes are slow in being realized. But we are convinced that these demonstrations are unwise and untimely."[33]

"When rights are consistently denied," the ministers further argued, "a cause should be pressed in the courts and negotiations among local leaders, and not in the streets."

Jail was one of the things King feared most. Having been placed in solitary confinement, he was unnerved by the isolation of imprisonment. Yet when he was permitted news from the outside and he saw the ministers' open letter, he focused his attention. He promptly began writing a reply on whatever scraps of paper he could find.

The clergymen had chided protesters for joining sit-ins and marches rather than pursuing negotiation. In response, King charged that the ministers preferred order to justice. "You are exactly right in your call for negotiation," King wrote. "Indeed, this is the purpose of direct action. Nonviolent direct action seeks to create such a crisis and establish such creative tension that a community that has constantly refused to negotiate is forced to confront an issue."[34]

Previously, city fathers had balked at implementing a plan for negotiated progress, King explained. Accordingly, civil rights protesters had little choice but to take up direct action "whereby we would present our very bodies as a means of laying our case before the conscience of the local and national community."[35]

Soon, a righteous impatience was emerging from beneath the formal politeness of King's letter. "I have almost reached the regrettable conclusion that the Negro's great stumbling block in the stride toward freedom is not the White Citizen's Counciler or the Ku Klux Klanner, but the white moderate . . . who constantly advised the Negro to wait until 'a more convenient season,'" King wrote. "Shallow understanding from people of good will is more frustrating than absolute misunderstanding from people of ill will. Lukewarm acceptance is much more bewildering than outright rejection."[36]

King's rebuke to his liberal critics on this occasion was especially forceful. But it was only one of the many times in his career he had been called upon to defend the civil rights movement from people who thought that its tactics were too loud and aggressive. In May 1961, a Gallup poll asked Americans, "Do you think that 'sit-ins' at lunch counters, 'freedom busses,' and other demonstrations by Negroes will hurt or help the Negro's chances of being integrated in the South?" The respondents were overwhelmingly negative: 57 percent believed that the nonviolent actions were counterproductive, with just 27 percent expressing confidence in the tactics' effectiveness.[37]

A year earlier, speaking on the popular Sunday morning political talk show *Meet the Press*, King faced a barrage of questions related to the student sit-ins in Nashville. The program's producer, Lawrence Spivak, a smartly coiffed Harvard graduate, kicked off the discussion on a combative point. Noting that former president Harry Truman, generally held to be "an old friend of the Negro," had recently denounced the students' tactics, Spivak asked bluntly, "Isn't this an indication that the sit-in strikes are doing the race, the Negro race, more harm than good?"[38]

King responded with unflappable calm. "No, I don't think so, Mr. Spivak," he said. "Now, I do not think this movement is setting us back or making enemies; it's causing numerous people all over the nation, and in the South in particular, to reevaluate the stereotypes that they have developed concerning Negroes, so that it has an educational value, and I think in the long run it will transform the whole of American society."

As part of the civil rights movement's struggle with polarization, activists had to face the fact that hard-core opponents were galvanized by their protests. In the South, civil rights demonstrations were a major boon for organizations such as the White Citizens' Councils and the Ku Klux Klan. In *The Rise of Massive Resistance*, historian Numan Bartley writes that, with the launch of the Montgomery Bus Boycott in 1955, "white Alabamians flocked to join the resistance," and "Montgomery quickly became a bastion of Council influence." A month after the start of the boycott, Montgomery mayor W. A. Gayle joined the Council, proclaiming, "I think every right-thinking white person in Montgomery, Alabama, and the South should do the same. We must make certain that Negroes are not allowed to force their demands on us." The next month, the group's membership doubled.[39]

Tellingly, the Council's surge in Montgomery tapered off after the Bus Boycott ended in late 1956. Yet racist resistance continued to spike in other locations where the civil rights movement focused its energies, such as neighboring Mississippi.[40]

Developments in electoral politics added to these troubling trends. As challenges to segregation intensified, race became an ever more crucial electoral issue for Southern politicians. Civil rights activism buoyed the fortunes of staunchly anti-integrationist politicians in the mold of Mississippi governor Ross Barnett and South Carolina senator Strom Thurmond. Politicians who had not previously been vocal on the issue of segregation found it in their best interest to adopt openly discriminatory platforms. Alabama governor and future presidential candidate George Wallace had initially been a fairly progressive Southern Democrat in the style of Louisiana populist Huey Long. But after being defeated in the 1958 gubernatorial primary by an overtly racist candidate riding the wave of anti–civil rights backlash, Wallace vowed, "I will never be out-niggered again." Four years later, he ran for governor once more, this time on a strictly segregationist platform, and he won with a stunning 96 percent of the vote. It was then that Wallace famously declared, "Segregation now, segregation tomorrow, segregation forever!"[41]

Finally, backlash entailed more than political setbacks: it also meant extremist violence. One historian called the two years after the passage of the 1964 Civil Rights Act a "period of terrorism," during which more than two thousand black churches were burned.[42]

If King preferred outright rejection to lukewarm acceptance, the defenders of the old order were offering it as clearly as they knew how.

～

The tactics of the civil rights advocates were often unpopular, and they fueled backlash from the defenders of segregation. But this movement also provides an example of the positive effects of polarization. In the end, these positive effects allowed civil rights activists to triumph.

From the Montgomery Bus Boycott, to the student lunch-counter sit-ins, to the Freedom Rides, to Birmingham, and beyond, high-profile movement campaigns led to a marked increase in levels of participation in resistance efforts, attracting people who were previously supportive but had been reluctant to join in. When the Bus Boycott in Montgomery began, Donie Jones, a forty-seven-year-old mother of six who cooked and cleaned for white families across town at Maxwell Air Force Base, marveled at the overwhelming turnout at mass meetings. "When we had the first meeting, the church was so full, there were so many people," she explained. "It was like a revival starting."[43]

Writing about the launch of the lunch-counter sit-ins in 1960, sociologist Aldon Morris similarly notes, "The sit-ins pumped new life into the civil rights movement." The daring actions "pulled many people, often entire communities, directly into the movement, making civil rights a towering issue throughout the nation. Consequently, the sit-ins produced more experienced activists and provided the movement with more funds, because blacks as well as sympathetic whites sent money to the movement following the dramatic sit-ins."[44]

Beyond activating the African American community, resistance in the South was formative for white college activists nationwide. Kirkpatrick Sale, author of a history of Students for a Democratic Society, writes that after sit-ins started, "civil rights activity touched almost every campus in the country: support groups formed, fund raising committees were established, local sit-ins and pickets took place, campus civil rights clubs began, students from around the country traveled to the South."[45]

While polarization turned passive supporters into increasingly active ones, the movement's campaigns also affected people in the middle of the political spectrum who had not previously taken a stand. Historian Michael Kazin's contention that Bull Connor's attacks on protesters "convinced a plurality of whites, for the first time, to support the cause of black freedom" is supported by visible movement in the polls. Starting in the wake of the Birmingham campaign in 1963, the percentage of the public that identified civil rights as "the most urgent issue facing the nation" sharply increased.[46]

As public opinion moved in favor of the movement, the opposition grew isolated and fractured. Actions of the Klan and the White Citizens' Councils became a liability for segregation's more mainstream defenders, who found it increasingly difficult to defend racist practices in national debates. Previously, Southern legislators in Washington had made their case based on a genteel defense of states' rights. Polarization around racial injustices made this position untenable. The unabashed extremism on display at the local level, in addition to shifts in the center toward civil rights advocates, left them little ground on which to stand.

Just as the pillars of support would fall years later in Serbia against the Milosevic regime and in the United States around gay marriage, major social institutions began abandoning the racist order in the 1960s once majority support for civil rights was established.

Keen to preserve the public image of their states and ward off national boycotts, moderate business leaders in the Deep South openly turned against embattled segregationists. "On February 3, 1965, the Mississippi Economic Council (the statewide Chamber of Commerce) came out in favor of 'order and respect for the law,' fair administration of voting laws, support for public education, and compliance with the newly enacted Civil Rights Act of 1964," writes political scientist Joseph Luders. "This shift toward moderation pitted rearguard defenders of the old order, aligned with the Citizens' Council and Delta plantation interests, against urban industrialists, bankers, and others espousing relatively greater willingness to countenance change."[47]

Politicians started experiencing defections within their own ranks. In January 1965 the Democratic Party's whip in the Senate, Louisiana's Russell Long, shocked segregationists in his state by announcing his support for federal voting rights legislation. The previous year, the senator had been one of the most impassioned voices inveighing against the 1964 Civil Rights Act.

As Long explained his shift, "I've been able to recognize that things move, they change, and to adjust myself to a changing world, and I think that all southerners will have to do that."[48]

Eventually, public opinion would swing so thoroughly that even some of the most stubborn segregationists of the civil rights era were moved to acknowledge their past errors. As his health failed in the 1990s, George Wallace himself sought repentance. He arranged meetings with figures such as John Lewis and Ralph Abernathy, and he even attended a twentieth anniversary march from Selma to Montgomery.

According to the former governor's obituary in the *New York Times*, "Sometimes he even managed to use the magic words 'I'm sorry.'"[49]

~

Few alive in the twenty-first century defend the apartheid system that existed in the US South prior to the 1960s. But plenty will still take a hard line on immigration. And, indeed, the current struggle around immigrant rights provides a vivid illustration of how past patterns of polarization still hold today.

Immigration reform advocates argue that the millions of undocumented immigrants living in the country should be recognized for their contributions to America's communities and afforded a pathway to citizenship. Yet this proposition has stirred intense controversy. Detractors say that "illegals" are no better than common criminals, that they should be deported, and that the border should be sealed, even if it requires militarized means to do so.

By pursuing high-profile protest in recent years, immigrant rights activists have only deepened divisions between these groups—leading a variety of commentators to declare their movement a failure. Yet those who understand the power of polarization will see things very differently: the politicization of the Latino community, brought about in no small part through mass social movement mobilizations, is becoming one of the most significant developments in US politics since the turn of the millennium.

The trigger event for mass action around immigrant rights, starting in 2006, is sometimes invoked with a single word: Sensenbrenner.

In late 2005, Republican representative James Sensenbrenner of Wisconsin proposed a reactionary piece of immigration legislation that would have instated harsh penalties for unauthorized presence in the United States, erected a seven-hundred-mile fence along the border between the United States and Mexico, and criminalized those assisting undocumented immigrants in obtaining food, housing, or medical services. The Sensenbrenner Bill passed through the House in December, and the prospect that it might subsequently clear the Senate in early

2006 set off unparalleled alarm in the Latino community, giving rise to several national days of action.[50]

By April 10, protests spread through more than 140 cities in 39 states. With as many as two million total participants, the news program *Democracy Now!* dubbed it the "Largest Wave of Demonstrations in U.S. History." This was matched by another flood of marchers on May 1, when as many as one million people poured through downtown Los Angeles with the message "No human being is illegal." The spring's mobilizations produced huge crowds in cities such as Chicago, Dallas, Phoenix, New York, and Washington, DC. But perhaps even more remarkably, dozens of smaller cities and towns such as Fresno, California, and Garden City, Kansas, saw the largest demonstrations ever recorded in their localities. Protesters carried American flags and signs that read "We Are America."[51]

These actions drew significant attention in the mainstream press: "Over and over again," the *New York Times* reported, "construction workers, cooks, gardeners, sales associates, and students who said they had never demonstrated before said they were rallying to send a message to the nation's lawmakers." Yet this attention was dwarfed by coverage in the Spanish-language media, which treated the movement as a top story for months. Students across Texas, Nevada, and California added to the drama by marching out of class to protest Sensenbrenner, with school districts in Los Angeles County witnessing a thirty-six-thousand-person-strong walkout.[52]

"It got the word out that we're not going to be quiet," a sixteen-year-old Salvadoran immigrant named Christian Dorn told the *Washington Post*, likening the protests to the civil rights revolts of the 1960s. "We shouldn't be treated like criminals."[53]

Author Randy Shaw called the demonstrations "a social earthquake rumbling across the American landscape."[54]

There was a problem, however: the transactional impact of the quake was not immediately evident—and some doubted whether the movement had made any gains at all. Although the Senate version of the Sensenbrenner Bill did not pass, neither did any positive immigration reform that would have legalized the status of undocumented immigrants or created a pathway to citizenship. The next several years showed little sign that gridlock on the issue in Washington could be broken. By 2011, *Fortune* magazine used the immigrant rights mobilizations as an example of how movements "can peter out without achieving meaningful change."[55]

Just as civil rights activists had invigorated the White Citizens' Councils, one of the effects of the 2006 protests was to activate hardline anti-immigrant sentiment. The Minuteman Project, founded in 2005 by a few hundred people who vowed to maintain "citizen patrols" along the Mexican border, spawned more than three hundred likeminded local organizations by 2010, drawing in tens of thousands of volunteers.[56]

In 2005, reporter David Holthouse visited a camp of Minuteman volunteers in Cochise County, Arizona, and recorded the conversation. "It should be legal to kill illegals," said one sixty-nine-year-old retiree and army veteran. "Just shoot 'em on sight. That's my immigration policy recommendation. You break into my country, you die."

Another volunteer added, "The thing to do would be to drop the bodies just a few hundred feet into the U.S. and just leave them there, with lights on them at night. That sends the message 'No Trespassing,' in any language."[57]

Such fringe groups enjoyed the support of mainstream conservative pundits such as Lou Dobbs of Fox News, who warned that hordes of unwashed immigrants would bring plagues of tuberculosis, malaria, and even leprosy.[58]

Perhaps even more distressing, conservative state legislatures in Utah, Arizona, Georgia, Alabama, Indiana, and South Carolina pushed forward regressive legislation targeting undocumented immigrants. The American Civil Liberties Union (ACLU) charged that these measures, modeled after Arizona's notorious "Show Me Your Papers" bill, invited "rampant racial profiling against Latinos, Asian-Americans, and others presumed to be 'foreign' based on how they look or sound."[59]

In the wake of this wave of conservative backlash, some immigrant rights groups experienced a perception of failure. By 2010, with comprehensive reform legislation stymied in Washington and regressive state-level laws moving forward, they looked back at the legacy of the 2006 protests feeling demoralized.

~

At the time, it seemed that anti-immigrant forces were growing more powerful and aggressive. And in some parts of the country, they were. In heavily white, rural areas of the South and Southwest, immigrant rights advocates were losing—just as civil rights forces faced setbacks in places where the White Citizens' Councils expanded. But this is only half the picture.

Polarization also had a positive side, and this would increasingly translate into tangible gains for the movement. In short order, a galvanized immigrant community created an ongoing crisis for conservatives at the polls. Even as they rallied in the spring 2006 demonstrations, immigrant rights activists had vowed electoral action. "Today we march," they chanted. "Tomorrow we vote!" And by that fall, the movement contributed to one of the more swift and consequential electoral shifts in recent memory.[60]

Prior to 2006, a variety of anti-immigrant actions—for example, high-profile raids on factories that led to scores of deportations—had produced generalized fear and anger in Latino communities. The difference with Sensenbrenner was that the mass mobilization channeled community discontent in a clearly political direction. Throughout the summer and fall of 2006, We Are America, a national alliance of more than a dozen labor, faith, and civil rights groups that formed out of the demonstrations, ramped up an effort to register new voters and oust anti-immigrant candidates in that year's midterm elections. In the end, the effort contributed to a disastrous defeat for the Republicans in 2006, as the party lost control of both the House and the Senate.[61]

Massive turnout among Latinos far exceeded typical patterns for midterm elections. As conservative *Miami Herald* columnist Andres Oppenheimer explained, "Hispanics said 'adiós' to President Bush's Republican Party in Tuesday's midterm elections, voting in much greater numbers than expected for Democratic candidates in an apparent rejection of the ruling party's efforts to blame much of the nation's problems on undocumented migrants.[62]

"Many experts had predicted that Hispanics would not turn out in big numbers on Tuesday," Oppenheimer added; instead, these experts expected "that it would take until the 2008 elections for the largely Hispanic 'today we march, tomorrow we vote' protests of earlier this year to translate into the naturalization and registration of large numbers of foreign-born Latino voters."

The experts were wrong, and the exit numbers in the midterms showed the kind of swing that can make veteran poll-watchers do a double take: 73 percent of Hispanics voted for Democrats, up from 55 percent in the 2004 presidential election.[63]

Savvy Republicans, who saw the potential of serious long-term harm to their party, scrambled to do damage control. In the summer of 2006, top presidential advisor Karl Rove showed up at the national convention of La Raza, the country's largest Latino civil rights organization, and attempted to distance the White House from the anti-immigrant wing of his party. Rove would later warn conservatives, "An anti-Hispanic attitude is suicidal."[64]

No doubt, the protests of 2006 were only one element affecting voting patterns. However, the record in this case provides an impressive testimonial to the power of mass protest: huge numbers of people took to the streets; their actions captured national attention and dominated the Spanish-language media for months; the protesters vowed to turn out votes against anti-immigrant Republicans; and they ended up delivering to a far greater extent than top electoral analysts had predicted.

The shift has had lasting consequences. In 2008 the trend established in the previous election held, and any gains George W. Bush had made in wooing Latinos to the Republican Party in 2000 and 2004 were long gone. In 2012 Republican presidential hopeful Mitt Romney managed to attract just 27 percent support from Latino voters—the lowest of any presidential candidate since Bob Dole in 1996—while record turnout in immigrant communities provided a significant boost for President Obama's reelection. Republican senator Lindsay Graham called the Republicans' loss in 2012 a "wake up call" for the party.[65]

As the Latino voting bloc grows each year, conservatives find themselves in an impossible bind. Looking toward the 2016 presidential race, *Vox* correspondent Dara Lind pointed to the "massive prisoner's dilemma the GOP faces on immigration." If right-wing candidates appeal to the anti-immigrant extreme in an attempt to win primary contests, they enter into general elections facing down an energized bloc of the immigrant rights movement's active public supporters—and their anti-immigrant statements increasingly fly in the face of mainstream opinion as well. It is a losing recipe for conservatives and a winning one for pro-immigrant advocates.[66]

Put another way: polarization is paying dividends.

~

In the summer of 2012, Javier Hernandez and Veronica Gomez had run out of patience with the White House. They decided to go after President Obama by focusing on an operation that they knew would be sensitive: his campaign for reelection.

On June 5, the two walked into the Denver office of Obama for America carrying bags laden with bottled water and Gatorade. They announced that they would stay for the duration of a hunger strike. Until Obama agreed to take executive action to allow young immigrants to remain in the country, they would subsist only on H_2O and electrolytes.

Hernandez, of Denver, and Gomez, living in California, came from similar backgrounds. When they were still toddlers, both of their families had entered the United States from Mexico on visas now long expired. Despite having grown up in the United States, Hernandez and Gomez were undocumented. Because of this, their act of civil disobedience entailed risking something much graver than arrest: they faced possible deportation from the only country they had ever truly known. "We are Americans," Gomez told one reporter, "even without paperwork."[67]

Hernandez and Gomez were part of a group of determined immigrant youth known as the DREAMers. They advocated a piece of legislation, the DREAM Act, designed to provide legal status for young people who had been brought to the country as children, who had spent their formative years living in the United States, and who were seeking to attend college or serve in the armed forces. The moral case for allowing them to formalize their status as Americans was clear. Although the DREAM Act would not create comprehensive immigration reform covering the estimated 11.2 million immigrants living in the United States, the measure would serve as an important first step. It had major instrumental significance for millions of people. And beyond that, it would also provide a critical symbolic victory for the movement.[68]

In the summer of 2012, with the pressure of election season building, DREAMers selected Obama for America offices as prime targets for activism. Even as Hernandez and Gomez carried out their six-day hunger strike in Denver, the movement deployed sit-ins in more than a dozen cities, with actions spread from Oakland, California, to Dearborn, Michigan, to Cincinnati, Ohio. The National Immigrant Youth Alliance, a prominent DREAMer organization, reported that Obama for America offices in Georgia and North Carolina preemptively closed down "once they caught wind of the protests."[69]

As the New York Times commented, Obama suddenly faced the real prospect of "alienating the Latino voters who may be pivotal to his re-election bid."[70]

Starting in 2010, the DREAM Act students had emerged as a disciplined, energized core of activists, carrying forward the energy of earlier mass protests into targeted and vocal confrontations. In one prominent action, four students marched fifteen hundred miles from Miami, Florida, to Washington, DC, attracting press coverage all along the way. Throughout 2011, demonstrations flared: ten undocumented students in Charlotte, North Carolina, were arrested as part of a three-hundred-strong group blocking a major downtown intersection. A group of six young immigrants in Atlanta, Georgia, held up traffic that June, when, donning caps and gowns, they sat on a busy street with a banner reading "Our Dreams Can't Wait." In Washington, student activists convinced Illinois congressmen Luis Gutiérrez to join them in getting arrested during a July rally for the DREAM Act outside the White House.[71]

In one of the most powerful aspects of these protests, the DREAMers drew from the gay rights movement: they made a public display of young activists "coming out" as undocumented—putting themselves at risk by making their status known and asserting their identity as Americans. Jonathan Perez, a twenty-three-year-old student at Pasadena City College who traveled from Colombia with his family at age three, told the Huffington Post, "We need to live without fear because the fear paralyzes us. If we stay quiet, we stay in the shadows."[72]

Legislatively, the DREAM Act, which singled out a very sympathetic subset of undocumented immigrants, seemed like the most likely reform measure to make it through the obstacle course that confronted any immigration legislation in Congress. Near the end of 2010, the act passed through the House of Representatives and gained majority support in the Senate—but was not able to secure the sixty votes needed to overcome a filibuster. It took another year and a half of pressure before the White House was moved to circumvent Congress.

Threats to Obama's reelection prospects proved decisive in making that happen. Previously, the president had insisted that he did not have the legal power to unilaterally grant the DREAMers' demands, despite the fact that the movement had produced more than ninety immigration law professors who argued the contrary. But just ten days after the hunger strike in Denver began, and with pro-immigrant allies in Washington needling the president with increasingly aggressive questions about the issue, Obama announced that his administration would implement a de facto version of the DREAM Act by executive order.[73]

On June 15, 2012, President Obama directed federal immigration authorities to follow a set of guidelines that would allow young residents who met the DREAM Act's criteria to receive renewable work permits. The action allowed as many as 1.2 million young undocumented immigrants to live and work freely in the United States, and it was later expanded to include millions more. For young activists who had submitted their families to great anxiety and uncertainty, risking their futures in the country they knew as home, the announcement represented a great vindication: "We were all watching and listening and screaming out in joy," said one DREAMer.[74]

Polarization was doing its work. After the mass mobilizations of 2006, active supporters of both pro- and anti-immigrant positions had increased. But strong evidence emerged that immigrant rights forces were the ones prevailing in terms of winning over ever-larger blocs of passive sympathizers. Prior to the protests, an August 2005 CBS News poll found that just 32 percent of Americans thought that immigrants who are in the country illegally should "be allowed to apply for work permits which would allow them to stay and work in the United States." In April 2006, with wide-scale demonstrations under way, a similar CBS poll showed 49 percent in favor—a major shift.[75]

Other polls have shown a significant rise in public support for humane immigration reform in the years since, and, for the first time, advocates have been able to demonstrate majority backing for creating a path to citizenship.

Between 2007 and 2009, even amid the growth of extremist border-patrol groups such as the Minutemen, the proportion of people who believed that undocumented immigrants "should be allowed to stay in the U.S. and eventually apply for citizenship" rose from 38 percent to 44 percent of Americans polled. It rose further in the years after. Since 2014, this number has consistently exceeded 50 percent—reaching a record 57 percent in May 2015.[76]

In this context, important changes have taken place. Border vigilante groups such as the Minutemen have dwindled, with the Southern Law Poverty Center's Mark Potok telling the *Christian Science Monitor* in April 2014, "The movement is one-tenth the size that it used to be." Lawsuits by pro-immigrant organizations have succeeded in striking down the discriminatory provisions of reactionary state laws. By the time Alabama settled the remaining legal challenges to its anti-immigrant measure in October 2014, policy experts argued that the move was "part of a broader shift around the country away from harsh anti-immigrant laws on the state and local level." Instead, one news report explained, "more and more states are passing what [advocates] called 'pro-immigrant, inclusive' legislation, such as laws granting driver's licenses to undocumented immigrants or in-state tuition for DREAMers."[77]

In late November 2014, President Obama announced an even farther-reaching executive action, using his power to enact a major overhaul of the immigration system. His initiative created a mechanism for some five million additional immigrants, including those who are parents of US citizens, to live and work in the country legally. The *Washington Post* characterized it as a major coup for advocates, commenting that "the sweeping magnitude of Mr. Obama's order is unprecedented."[78]

It remains to be seen whether Americans will ever see James Sensenbrenner reverse himself in the manner of Jesse Helms or George Wallace, using the magic words "I'm sorry" to make amends with the DREAM Act students. But it is possible that the polarized extremism of the Minutemen may soon look just as archaic and bigoted as the White Citizens' Councils that thrived, for a brief moment, thanks to the "unwise and untimely" clashes generated by the civil rights movement.

∽

Whatever the evidence of polarization's power, it is a process that makes people uncomfortable. Mainstream organizations, particularly those trying to maintain relationships with elected officials, consistently try to avoid it, preferring to look moderate and reasonable. For this reason, groups that are willing to risk divisiveness can expect to receive flack for their boldness.

ACT UP, born of a crisis in which the consequence of silence was death, used vinegar rather than honey to change the course of the fight against AIDS. The civil rights movement ended Jim Crow by refusing to wait for "a more convenient season" to protest. And the DREAM Act students forced the hand of an administration that was fearful of losing the support of a polarized electorate. With the passage of time, successful movements are often celebrated as heroic and noble. But, while they are still active, their tactics are never beloved by all. Accepting that reality is part of using conflict and disruption as tools for change.

Yet there is a danger here. For polarization to work to the advantage of a social movement, advocates cannot delude themselves into thinking that public reaction does not matter or that "anything goes" is a viable strategy. Activists can take the risk of being called rude and rash as a result of pursuing confrontation. But if a movement is to remain effective, it must be another thing as well: disciplined.

CHAPTER NINE

THE DISCIPLINE

EARTH FIRST! WAS in a crisis.

On May 8, 1987, a recently married twenty-three-year-old named George Alexander was working in a lumber mill run by the Louisiana-Pacific logging company in Cloverdale, California. Suddenly, the massive band saw he was operating hit a metal spike and exploded. A twelve-foot piece of the saw tore through Alexander's protective face-mask, shattered his jaw, and cut into his jugular.

Had the blade rotated slightly, Alexander would have been decapitated. "The saw hit me flat," he later explained. "If it had hit me with the teeth I'd be dead. I'm only here because my friend Rick Phillips held my veins together in the hour before the ambulance came."[1]

In the wake of the accident, the logging company and county sheriff quickly blamed environmentalists for placing the metal spike in the tree being cut and thus causing the saw to break. Activists were flooded with a wave of public disgust and recrimination.

Earth First! had attracted controversy before, but this was different. The group was formed seven years earlier, and it had made an important contribution to revitalizing the defense of the nation's forests. Its founders were staffers who had been working for mainstream national environmental groups, but who had been horrified by "Big Green's" willingness to cut a deal in Washington, DC, that allowed for logging throughout the majority of the still-roadless areas on public lands. In the spring of 1980, a small group of these disaffected organizers, including Dave Foreman, Bart Koehler, and Mike Roselle, took a camping trip to Northern Mexico. There they came up with the idea for a new grassroots organization that would be less respectful of Washington's insider process and unafraid to employ confrontational tactics.

The group's name, Earth First!, included an exclamation point to convey urgency. Its slogan, "No Compromise in Defense of Mother Earth," pointedly set the group apart from Big Green's dubiously conciliatory operating procedure.

From the start, Earth First!ers worked to create an image that would distinguish them from other branches of the environmental movement. Having met while working in Wyoming, founders such as Roselle and Foreman called themselves "Buckaroos." Roselle, originally from Louisville, Kentucky, had moved to northwest Wyoming in the late 1970s with a desire to spend more time in the wilderness after being burnt out on anti–Vietnam War activism in California. Within a few years, he had formed a construction business and was building his own house when he was drawn into antilogging protests by Friends of the Earth. Dave Foreman, an Albuquerque native, identified as both a "redneck" and a Republican, although he had pretty much given up voting that way. The two wore cowboy hats, guzzled beers, and tried to distance themselves from the hippie stereotype that the public associated with environmentalists.[2]

Some of Earth First!'s earliest actions were flashy media stunts: in one famous 1981 protest, activists unrolled a three-hundred-foot banner, painted to look like a crack, down the face of Arizona's Glen Canyon Dam. The dam was widely viewed as an environmental monstrosity. Its "cracking" symbolically echoed Edward Abbey's 1975 novel *The Monkey Wrench Gang*, in which a band of eco-saboteurs conspires to blow up the dam.

Indeed, that novel would become influential for Earth First! Early media coverage, such as a 1983 *Outside* magazine article, portrayed the grassroots gang as a real-life version of Abbey's posse. For his part, Dave Foreman published a book called *Ecodefense: A Field Guide to*

Monkeywrenching, which advocated acts such as pulling up survey-ors' stakes, downing billboards, and putting sand in the gas tanks of bulldozers.

In the early years, the group's decentralized activists had the rep-utation of being "loveable but mischievous vandals," in the words of journalist Dean Kuipers. That changed, however, as attention began fo-cusing on their most controversial tactic. Tree spiking involved driv-ing long metal nails into old-growth trees. This did not harm the trees, but it made cutting them dangerous for loggers, who risked damaging their saw blades and hurting themselves. Groves of spiked trees meant frustration and delay for timber companies—and, for activists, that was precisely the point.[3]

Did tree spiking work? Although advocates such as Foreman took it as an article of faith that it did, some others in Earth First! came to the hard conclusion that his insistence on the tactic's effectiveness could not be backed up. Although there were many incidents in which the nails in spiked trees did indeed break saw blades and endanger workers, logging executives considered this safety hazard an acceptable cost of doing business. As Roselle commented about the cutting of one spiked grove, the prospect of hitting nails "barely slowed them down."[4]

For the timber corporations, controversy surrounding tree spiking had a plus side: it was a chance to demonize and discredit their envi-ronmentalist opposition. Particularly after the Cloverdale incident, they took full advantage of this opportunity.

Earth First! had generally taken pains to ensure that its monkey-wrenching was designed to disable equipment, not to hurt people. And there were several reasons to believe that the group might not have been to blame for Alexander's broken saw: for one, the spike he hit had been placed in a relatively small, second-growth tree; Earth First!'s campaigns, in contrast, focused on ancient wood being extracted from previously roadless areas. Second, activists had typically spray-painted the trees they did spike as a way of leaving a calling card and creating a deterrent against logging. Finally, there were signs that the spiking was not carried out by an organized group at all but instead may have been the work of a disgruntled local resident, possibly one upset about the company threatening the area water supply.[5]

Nevertheless, having championed the spiking tactic, Earth First! was vulnerable to an onslaught of popular revulsion.

After the accident, the logging company did not shut down its mill or abandon its determination to strip old-growth forests. But it did launch an aggressive media blitz that cast a pall over environmentalism throughout the region. The Mendocino County Sheriff's office issued a press statement accusing the group of a "heinous and vicious criminal act." Following this lead, the *Eureka-Times Standard* ran stories with headlines such as "Earth First! Blamed for Worker's Injuries," while the *Santa Rosa Press Democrat* decried "Tree-Spiking Terrorism." Politicians such as Idaho senator James McClure clamored to make spiking a federal offense.[6]

Roselle, who publicly disavowed the tactic a few years later, realized that the group was "facing a major PR disaster."[7]

∼

Earth First!'s dilemma pointed to a larger problem. Disruptive movements that attempt to use polarization to their advantage must perform a careful balancing act. By creating confrontational scenes and trying to generate a public crisis around an issue, they knowingly defy the widely held preference for calm and quiet over discord and tension. Activists are aware that many people will not like them, but they pursue conflict in the belief that polarization can activate their base, draw passive supporters to their cause, and isolate their opponents. With ACT UP, the civil rights movement, and the DREAM Act students, this is exactly what happened.

But polarization can also go bad. For movements to benefit from a state of heightened conflict, its participants must make sure of two things: first, that they are drawing in more active supporters than their opponents, and, second, that even if their methods are perceived as extreme or impatient, the tide of public opinion is pushing toward greater acceptance of their views. This requires strategic judgment. A willingness to court controversy does not mean that anything goes. If a movement's tactics are so divisive and widely condemned that they overshadow the issue at hand and foster sympathy for the opposition, polarization fails.

So, where should movements draw the line?

The merits of any individual tactic must be evaluated based on a variety of factors, including the norms and values of the society in which a social movement is functioning. Even when deployed with care, disruption does not always produce the desired results. Some of ACT UP's most controversial actions, such as interrupting mass at Saint Patrick's Cathedral in New York City in December 1989, produced much greater public backlash than anticipated—and thus prompted intense debate among AIDS advocates about whether they had misfired.

But if there are areas of uncertainty with regard to polarization, some trends are clear. In the United States, one of the most consistent and predictable has been the overwhelmingly negative public response to tactics that are perceived as violent.

In the late 1980s, Earth First! experienced a situation in which polarization harmed a movement. But the group also showed how activists were able to turn the tide. Embracing a radical program of strategic nonviolence and mass civil disobedience, the group launched a landmark drive that helped make saving the California redwoods a winning public issue.

The person most responsible for this change was not one of the Buckaroos but rather a five-foot-tall eco-feminist, single mother, and former union organizer. Her name was Judi Bari.

∼

Tellingly, Roselle's first words when he heard the news of the Cloverdale accident were, "Judi's not going to like this."[8]

Judi Bari had cut her teeth as an activist in the movement against the Vietnam War, rallying fellow students on the campus of the University of Maryland before ultimately dropping out. Taking on low-wage work at a supermarket to pay her bills, she quickly became a steward in her union, and she spent the next several years as a labor organizer. In 1979, Bari moved with her then-husband to Northern California, and by the mid-1980s she was a divorced mother of two girls, making a living as a carpenter. She had never given much thought to the idea of forest defense until one day when she was building a country home for a wealthy executive. Having admired the fine grain redwood she was installing, Bari was outraged to learn from her supervisor that it came from millennia-old trees being torn down by logging companies in that same area. The moment served as what she would call her "environmental epiphany." In 1988, Bari joined an Earth First! affiliate in Mendocino County.[9]

Darryl Cherney, an activist and musician who would become one of her main collaborators, noted the boost that Bari provided to anti-logging organizing. "When Greg King and I were organizing demonstrations," Cherney said, mentioning another Earth First! member, "dozens, maybe hundreds of people turned out. But when Judi got involved, thousands came."[10]

Previously, Earth First!'s strategy was largely nomadic, premised on small groups of activists—usually fewer than a dozen people, mostly men—traveling to remote wilderness areas and setting up blockades or tree sits. Bari thought that such acts were courageous, but inadequate. Bari believed that if environmentalists were going to win in the long run, they needed a movement that could go beyond a few dedicated squads of activists and could instead gain broad popular backing.[11]

"There is no way that a few isolated individuals, no matter how brave, can bring about the massive social change necessary to save the planet," Bari explained. "So we began to organize with local people, planning our logging blockades around issues that had local community support."[12]

Coming from a labor background, Bari also strove to build alliances across the traditional blue–green divide that separated working-class communities and environmentalists. Although Earth First!'s founders had a tendency of treating timber employees as villains, Bari did not see front-line workers as the problem. She believed that tree-huggers and roughneck loggers could come together around a shared enemy: logging company executives. Deforestation, after all, affected not only the trees but also the workers who made their living from the woods, many of whom had strong critiques of the corporations for which they worked. "The timber companies treat them the same way they treat the forest," Bari argued, "as objects to exploit for maximum profit."[13]

When George Alexander was nearly killed in the Cloverdale mill, Dave Foreman was dismissive. He commented, "I think it's unfortunate that someone got hurt. . . . [But] nobody is forcing people to cut those trees." Not all Earth First! members were so callous, however. Judi Bari was horrified at the accident, and later she would seek out the logger and his wife, sitting down with them for an interview. Bari learned that, although it was never reported by the press, Alexander had been as critical of his employer's lax safety standards as he had been of Earth First! When the company asked him to go on tour denouncing environmental activists, Alexander refused. "I'm against tree spiking," he told Bari, "but I don't like clear-cutting either."[14]

Within a few years, Alexander was no longer a Louisiana-Pacific employee. "They used my name all over the country," he said. "Then they laid me off when the mill closed down."

Beyond her outreach to workers, Judi Bari also changed Earth First!'s culture by opening space for women to take on more leadership roles. In an essay entitled "The Feminization of Earth First!," Bari reflected, "It is not surprising that I, a lifetime activist, would become an environmentalist. What is surprising is that I, a feminist, single mother, and blue-collar worker, would end up in Earth First!, a 'no compromise' direct action group with a reputation of being macho, beer-drinking eco-dudes.

"Little did I know," she continued, "that combining the more feminine elements of collectivism and nonviolence with the spunk and outrageousness of Earth First!, we would spark a mass movement."[15]

～

To set off this spark, Earth First! needed to move away from tree spiking. By 1990, Bari and a variety of other likeminded activists argued that it was time to renounce the tactic once and for all. Bari based her position as much on pragmatic grounds as moral ones: "The forests that Earth First! had been instrumental in saving in this area (Trout Creek,

Cahto Wilderness, Headwaters Forest, Albion, and Owl Creek)," she later wrote, "have all been saved through blockades and public organizing campaigns, often combined with lawsuits." If anything, tree spiking was slowing down the efforts.[16]

Earth First! had always insisted that its tactics did not involve violence, but its informal local chapters had been hesitant to make explicit statements of nonviolent discipline. "After all, that would contradict the he-man image that Earth First! was founded on," Bari explained. Yet she argued forcefully that a formal declaration was essential. As she later wrote, "Those of us who are out on the front lines . . . can't afford to be isolated and discredited by something as ineffective and incendiary as tree spiking. If we are serious about putting the Earth first, we need to choose tactics because they work, not because they are macho or romantic. That's what no compromise really means."[17]

Others in the group, having heard the concerns of lumber workers, agreed with these sentiments. In late April 1990, Northern California and Southern Oregon Earth First! activists officially disavowed tree spiking in a press conference. Of the corporations that were cutting down the forests, they stated, "These companies would think nothing of sending a spiked tree through a mill, and relish the anti–Earth First! publicity that an injury would cause."[18]

The political and cultural changes that Bari ushered in caused a split in Earth First!'s leadership—prompting Foreman to cut ties with the group. The cofounder charged that Earth First! had been simultaneously taken over by hippies and "class-struggle leftists," and he adamantly defended the old tactics and identity of Earth First! In response, Bari wrote, "Dave Foreman would like to keep the movement small and pure. But profound social changes don't happen without mass movements, and I think we need a whole lot more of us to bring about even the modest reforms we need to save the redwoods."[19]

Foreman moved on, later leading a faction of anti-immigrant environmentalists at the Sierra Club.

Meanwhile, Bari and her fellow Earth First!ers announced a bold initiative: Redwood Summer. The drive took inspiration from the Student Nonviolent Coordinating Committee's 1964 Freedom Summer, when young people from around the country traveled to Mississippi to defy Southern racists and register African Americans to vote. For the summer of 1990, Bari and others embarked on a national speaking tour calling for nonviolent direct action to save California's largest remaining stretch of unprotected old-growth redwood trees. As Bari recalled, "Requests for info started coming in from all over, and we realized this thing was bigger than we thought."[20]

Not everything went as planned, however. Faced with the summer's impending confrontation, opponents of Earth First! again tried to use the taint of violence to discredit the movement—this time in a most twisted fashion.

Starting in April, just weeks after Redwood Summer was announced, key organizers began receiving death threats, which local police refused to investigate. Then, on May 24, while Bari and Cherney were driving through Oakland doing outreach for Redwood Summer, a pipe bomb wrapped in nails exploded under Bari's car seat, tearing into her pelvis and nearly killing her. Cherney was also hurt, but escaped major injury. The FBI was on the scene within minutes. Despite the fact that the two were leading proponents of nonviolence, federal agents accused them of manufacturing the bomb themselves. Officers placed the critically injured Bari under arrest while she was still on the operating table. Presenting no evidence, the FBI argued that Cherney and Bari were transporting explosives to use against logging companies.[21]

Antienvironmentalist groups spread the same message. A right-wing organization that called itself the "Sahara Club" distributed a flyer with a diagram of how to make a bomb, falsely claiming that it had come from an Earth First! manual.[22]

While the press initially ran with the story of left-wing bomb making, Earth First! activists worked to disprove the charges and affirm their commitment to nonviolent direct action. In 1994, Bari and Cherney filed a civil rights suit against the FBI. Through the course of depositions, their lawyers revealed that the FBI had conducted a "bomb school" for its agents just weeks before the 1990 attack, setting off test explosions in several cars in the California woods. An FBI expert also acknowledged that the pipe bomb in Bari's car had been triggered by a sophisticated motion-sensing device, a fact hardly consistent with the notion that activists had accidentally bombed themselves. Although no government involvement in planting the bomb was ever proven, to many it smelled like a repeat of the FBI's notorious 1960s-era COINTELPRO program.[23]

The attack on Bari and Cherney was not the end for Redwood Summer. In the wake of the bombing, volunteers for the campaign poured in. As Bari recovered from her wounds, new Earth First! leaders—largely women who had been inspired by her example—stepped up to take her place in coordinating the next several months of activity. The drive ended up being a milestone. As scholar Douglas Bevington writes, "Thousands of people participated in demonstrations in support of Headwaters, leading to the largest mass civil disobedience for forest protection in U.S. history."[24]

In almost daily actions throughout the summer, participants sat in trees, blocked logging roads, chained themselves to equipment, and confronted corporate leaders at executive meetings. In all, 3,000 participants joined in the campaign over the summer—up from 150 the year before—and there were more than 250 arrests. Unlike with monkey-wrenching tactics, which required secrecy, Earth First!ers were able to openly organize in the community, and they earned the active support of local sympathizers. In one inventive show of solidarity, several Mendocino County residents using the name "Breakfast First!" enlisted gourmet chefs to host a champagne brunch in the middle of a high-traffic logging road.[25]

The nonviolent direct action of Redwood Summer allowed participants to shine a light on the true violence taking place in the woods: both the horrific destruction of the forest, and the repression of those who resisted it. On several occasions, protesters were attacked by logging crews, and on one occasion a timber executive risked injuring demonstrators by ramming a car through a picket line.

In the end, Redwood Summer did not produce immediate legislative gains; a statewide ballot proposition designed to protect old-growth areas was defeated that November. Nevertheless, Earth First!'s campaign was responsible for identifying the destruction of the Headwaters as a critical public issue and turning it into a mainstream cause that drew

national and even international attention. The group's call to halt logging in old-growth forest, previously seen as an impractical demand,
became widely adopted, and politicians began citing Headwaters protection as a top environmental priority. Ultimately, the summer of action fortified a multidecade campaign that resulted in the preservation
of a substantial portion of Northern California's Headwaters Forest. After Redwood Summer, Roselle writes, new Earth First! chapters, in the
United States and abroad, "were springing up like mushrooms after a
spring rain."[26]

Tragically, Judi Bari lived in pain for the rest of her life owing to the
bombing of her car, and she died in 1997 after suffering from an aggressive form of cancer. To the end, she worked for justice in her civil rights
suit, even filming a deposition to be delivered posthumously. Before her
death, she made Cherney promise not to settle out of court. He did not,
and the two won. After they went to trial in 2002, a jury determined that
the FBI and the Oakland Police Department had violated the activists'
civil rights in their mishandling of the case. A judge ordered the agencies to pay $4.4 million to the pair, the largest amount the Bureau has
ever been made to pay for a civil rights violation. The next year, Oakland's City Council passed a resolution declaring May 24 Judi Bari Day,
encouraging schools and public institutions to memorialize her work.[27]

Bari's legacy also lived on in a revitalized wave of direct action forest defense in the Pacific Northwest that took place throughout the
1990s and into the new millennium. Much more so than lobbying from
big-budget environmental groups in Washington, the model adopted
and refined in the Headwaters Campaign was critical in securing some
of the most important victories in US forest protection in the past
quarter century: in multipronged assaults by activists, blockades and
nonviolent interventions at logging sites pushed back the immediate
destruction of threatened groves, while also shining a public spotlight
and creating political pressure. Meanwhile, scrappy legal action groups
supported and sustained by the movement pursued aggressive lawsuits
to establish longer-term protections.

This combination of protest and litigation produced stunning results: overall, between 1988 and 1999 there was a 78 percent drop in

logging in national forests, resulting in large part from activists working outside of national environmental organizations.[28]

"It took the major environmental groups decades to come out against logging in the old-growth forests," Roselle argued in 2009. "The nonviolent campaigns by Earth First! and other grassroots groups across the country finally forced the hand of Big Green when their members began to voice support for such campaigns.

"Meanwhile," he continued, "it was the grassroots direct action effort that stopped logging in ancient forests, by spending day after day, year after year, blocking illegal roads."[29]

～

When it comes to questions of whether social movements should use violent tactics, the tradition of civil resistance takes a different stand from what many outsiders might expect.

Pacifists have long argued back and forth with defenders of revolutionary violence about the morality of using violent methods to advance political ends. Likewise, advocates of sabotage and property destruction commonly argue these tactics should not be considered "violent," because they target inanimate objects and are not designed to cause physical harm to people.

For activists using strategic nonviolence, these exchanges are beside the point. The relevant question is: What tactics work best in growing a movement and winning popular support?

Here, the philosophical definition of what constitutes violence is largely irrelevant. What matters is the response of the public at large to a tactic—whether the wider society in which a social movement exists judges an action to be violent, and how it reacts as a result. From a strategic perspective, which tactics are classified as "violent" or "nonviolent" is determined by this public perception, not by the outcome of any abstract debate.

Once a movement accepts that gaining broad popular backing is essential to its success, a strong argument can be made for the effectiveness of maintaining strict nonviolent discipline.

Many of the movements that adopt civil resistance as a means of struggle, especially those confronting authoritarian regimes, do so for a specific strategic reason: because they have determined that they cannot win through military conflict. Certainly, this was the case in Serbia, where Otpor activists saw that the Milosevic regime and its paramilitary allies would quickly wipe them out if they took up arms.

In a US context, leftist author and activist Michael Albert puts it this way: "It's really quite simple. The state has a monopoly of violence," he writes. "What that means is that there is no way for the public, particularly in developed First World societies, to compete on the field of violence with their governments. That ought to be obvious. Our strong suit is information, facts, justice, disobedience, and especially numbers. Their strong suit is lying and especially exerting military power."

Although Albert rejects philosophical pacifism, he nevertheless concludes: "A contest of escalating violence is a contest we are doomed to lose. A contest in which numbers, commitment, and increasingly militant nonviolent activism confronts state power is a contest we can win."[30]

The use of tactics widely perceived as violent is a recurring issue in social movements. Short of armed guerilla warfare, various dissident groups on the US left since the 1960s have burned down animal testing laboratories and attacked research facilities with connections to the military, while groups on the right have bombed abortion clinics and federal office buildings. In the context of large demonstrations, some activists, especially those from traditions of anarchist insurrectionism, have consistently argued for an anything-goes approach euphemistically known as "diversity of tactics." Rejecting agreements that would set guidelines for behavior at mass protests, they seek to allow for tactics of property destruction—such as smashing storefront windows or lighting cars on fire—as well as throwing Molotov cocktails and fighting with police.

The moral implications of these different acts may vary considerably. But from a strategic perspective they have something in common: they directly interfere with the processes through which movements using nonviolent conflict are able to build support and leverage change.

Those who argue that mass movements should undertake property destruction or brawls with police often claim that routine marches and polite petitions do not accomplish anything. This position ignores the fact that the repertoire of civil resistance includes a vast range of tactics—many of which can be highly disruptive and confrontational. The tools of nonviolent conflict include boycotts and workplace strikes, blockades and occupations, as well as art and creative resistance. Deployed in escalating fashion, these tactics can profoundly impede the regular daily functioning of the status quo.

Yet the use of violence by activists gives authorities a clear means of defusing such escalation, providing a justification for repressive force. In other words, it can stop the momentum of an uprising in its tracks.

When Gene Sharp set out to make an argument for nonviolent discipline, he based his position on the fact that different forms of action work in contradictory ways and therefore cannot function together effectively. "Violent action and nonviolent action possess quite different mechanisms, and induce differing forces of change in society," Sharp observed. Whereas authorities are well prepared to handle violent attacks, nonviolent confrontation creates a type of asymmetrical conflict that throws them off balance. "This is part of the reason why it is important for the actionists to maintain nonviolent discipline even in face of brutal repression," he explained. "If the nonviolent group switches to violence, it has, in effect, consented to fight on the opponent's own terms and with weapons where most of the advantages lie with him."[31]

Nonviolent conflict allows activists to highlight the systemic violence that exists in society and that usually goes unrecognized—the violence, for example, of routine and persistent police brutality, of economic displacement and exploitation, of wanton environmental destruction, or of racist criminalization and imprisonment of entire communities. As Martin Luther King Jr. argued, nonviolent direct action allows activists to "bring to the surface the hidden tension that is already alive." Yet, if activists turn to violence themselves, it allows authorities to institute expanded repression in the name of restoring a state of "peace" in which systemic abuses are once again submerged.[32]

Although King was a believer in moral nonviolence, he also voiced a clear strategic argument for nonviolent discipline. "Anyone leading a violent rebellion must be willing to make an honest assessment," he wrote, "regarding the possible casualties to a minority population confronting a well-armed, wealthy majority with a fanatical right wing that would delight in exterminating thousands of black men, women, and children."[33]

Judi Bari recalled that, shortly before being bombed, she told a friend, "I wasn't a Gandhian who considered nonviolence to be the only way ever." Expressing solidarity with the struggle against death-squad governments in Central America, she stated, "I would never tell a Salvadoran to use nonviolence only." Moreover, given her deep love of the forest, Bari had sympathy with people carrying out clandestine acts of sabotage against development projects. But, always an organizer, she was equally clear that such tactics would have disastrous consequences if used as part of a mass movement.[34]

"People who put their bodies in front of the bulldozer are depending on prevailing moral standards and the threat of public outrage to protect them from attack," Bari wrote. "Unfortunately, prevailing public opinion in the country, at least in the timber region, is that if sabotage is involved, they have a license to kill. Until that changes, mixing civil disobedience and monkey-wrenching is suicidal."[35]

∼

By adopting the liberal rhetoric of "diversity," the argument for "diversity of tactics" is designed to sound unobjectionable. But this agreeable phrasing masks a profound problem: social movements need strategy, and strategy requires discipline.

The measure of success for a polarizing movement is whether it draws ever-greater numbers of active supporters and whether it builds popular support for its cause. However, for at least the past half century of US history, tactics perceived as violent have been overwhelmingly unpopular with the American public.

Social movements on the right wing of the political spectrum have experienced this reality. In the mid-1980s, a rash of clinic bombings by opponents of abortion rights resulted in near-universal condemnation. In a joint CBS News–*New York Times* poll from early 1985, a full 82 percent of respondents said the attacks on reproductive health facilities were "the same thing as terrorism," compared to just 5 percent who thought that the arson "should be treated as a forceful kind of political protest." A decade later, the *Washington Post* reported that the Reverend Flip Benham, director of Operation Rescue, went so far as to argue that "those in the abortion-providing industry" had themselves engineered most of the violence that had occurred against clinics "in an attempt to discredit the anti-abortion movement."[36]

Although sabotage and damage against property fall in a very different moral category than violence against human targets, the public tends to conflate these categories. And they have some rational grounds for doing so: like tree spiking, arson may be meant to target property only, but it puts people at risk. Historically, there have been all too many cases when people have been unintentionally injured or even killed when bombs go off and buildings burn. In street demonstrations, those interested in breaking store windows or smashing cop cars also tend to be willing to actively fight with police, especially if it allows them to escape capture.

Whether or not the public perception of these actions as violent is warranted, mass mobilizations have seen detrimental consequences as a result of their use. The tactics tend to limit the numbers of a movement's active supporters, turn off potential sympathizers, and boost the opposition. In other words, they contribute significantly to negative polarization.

In the fall of 2012, rapper and longtime Oakland resident Boots Riley commented on community reaction to the repeated use of Black Bloc tactics by groups associated with Occupy Oakland. The Black Blocs involved groups of disproportionately young, white men who dressed in all black and engaged in activity that included trashing parked cars, breaking windows at businesses, and clashing with police. The blocs had the effect of visibly alienating the predominantly African American base of residents in the city. "If 'the job of the revolutionary is to make the revolution seem irresistible,'" Riley wrote, "the use of black bloc has been making a revolutionary movement pretty damn resistible in Oakland, CA.[37]

"When almost every conversation I have with folks from Oakland about Occupy Oakland has the smashing of windows brought up as a reason people don't like that grouping," Riley argued, "scientifically it means the tactic is not working. It doesn't matter that technically it's only smashing corporate windows. It matters that people don't want to join because of that."

∼

Knowing that violence can cause harm to movements and provide an ideal pretext for repression, governments and reactionary groups have actively tried to encourage it. Highlighting this tendency, Gandhi put forth a willfully counterintuitive proposition: for a member of a mass protest movement to resort to violence, he argued, was to "cooperate with the Government in the most active manner."[38]

In many cases when activists do not initiate violence, governments have worked to provoke them. Across a wide range of countries and time periods, authorities have sent infiltrators into activist organizations to serve as *agent provocateurs*—people who attempt to instigate activity that damages the targeted movements.

In the United States, the public will never know the full extent of the government's use of provocateurs, because agencies such as the FBI closely guard information about the activities of paid informers and undercover operatives. It took journalist Seth Rosenfeld two decades of lawsuits to uncover even a small portion of FBI files on the bureau's attempts, in the words of Director J. Edgar Hoover, to "disrupt and neutralize" the movements of the 1960s and early 1970s. Among the discoveries published in his 2012 book *Subversives*, Rosenfeld found that it was a paid informant of the FBI who had supplied the Black Panthers with some of their first firearms.[39]

Also during the 1960s, there were multiple instances of infiltration and provocation on the part of authorities seeking to neutralize the movement against the Vietnam War. One infamous case involved an undercover police officer in upstate New York known as "Tommy the

Traveler," who infiltrated an area chapter of Students for a Democratic Society. As author and attorney Michael Linfield writes, Tommy "constantly urged students to undertake violent actions," showing them how to use guns and make bombs. In early 1970, he persuaded two 19-year-old students to firebomb an ROTC office at Hobart College. Not only did the bombing result in the arrest of the students who carried it out, but also public backlash from the incident became a significant setback for Hobart's antiwar movement, effectively squelching activism on campus by incriminating its leaders. In another incident, a paid FBI informer and Vietnam veteran named Larry Grathwohl helped teach bomb making to the Midwest collective of the Weather Underground.[40]

Such activity by authorities is not limited to a bygone era, many decades in the past. To the contrary, examples of infiltration and probable provocation have already been exposed in the new millennium.

In July 2001, at the height of the movement against corporate globalization, leaders of the G8 industrialized nations met in Genoa, Italy, attracting a large protest mobilization. There is strong evidence that one of the Black Blocs that formed amid the demonstrations was actually made up of authorities and right-wing provocateurs. An Italian member of parliament claimed that he spotted members of this bloc gearing up at a local police station with black garb and iron clubs, and the *Guardian* reported video evidence of men in black deploying from police vans near the protests. Activists accused these provocateurs of ransacking storefronts and torching cars during a three-hundred-thousand-person protest outside the summit.[41]

Although they denied provoking violence in the streets, police later admitted to disguising officers as Black Bloc members. Moreover, during a parliamentary inquiry into police action, senior officer Pietro Troiani confessed that authorities planted two Molotov cocktails in a school building that Genoa activists were using as a dormitory—a location that was then raided by security forces.[42]

In the absence of explicit agreements setting guidelines for people taking part in the demonstrations, movements have little means of calling out and containing fake protesters. In Genoa, police took advantage of the confusion their agents had helped create. They unleashed what radical anthropologist Jeffrey Juris described as an "indiscriminate campaign of state terror," during which authorities "used the excuse of militant violence to attack violent and nonviolent protesters alike." One protester in Genoa was shot and killed by police, and hundreds were injured. Commenting on the decision by factions of militants to enact "performative violence," Juris noted, "Paradoxically, tolerance for certain tactics"—namely, property destruction, Molotov cocktails, and brawls with police—showed that it could "undermine the ability of other protesters to implement more innovative direct-action practices."[43]

Nor have recent cases of provocation been limited to Europe. On the eve of 2012's May Day protests, five young anarchists who had been involved in Occupy Cleveland were arrested in an alleged plot to blow up the Brecksville-Northfield High Level Bridge. It soon came to light that they had been encouraged in this scheme by a thirty-nine-year-old FBI informant, Shaquille Azir. Among other acts, this informant arranged logistics and provided transportation so that the activists could meet with a merchant to buy explosives. In truth, the supposed arms dealer was an undercover FBI agent, and, on the night of the action, Bureau officers swept in moments before the planned detonation to arrest the group. Amid sensationalistic headlines, police moved to evacuate the entire Occupy Cleveland encampment, one of the movement's longest-standing camps.[44]

~

Governments may sometimes be eager to provoke violence. But they do not do it alone. Attempts at instigation only succeed in environments where nonviolent discipline has not been established. As one sociologist writes, "Provocateurs must move in a movement that tolerates their wild talk and wild action."[45]

By the late 1960s, the movement against the Vietnam War and the broader radical student movement had become such settings. Even if the government had not attempted to infiltrate and provoke, there were groups of activists who believed that revolutionary violence could prevail in the United States, or at least that violent strikes against symbols of US power could help slow down the government war machine. Their actions in pursuit of this belief went far in crippling one of the leading forces of antiwar mobilization in the country.

In 1969, a small faction that later became the Weather Underground succeeded in taking control of Students for a Democratic Society, or SDS—the largest mass organization of the antiwar student movement. In the fall of 1969, leaders of this faction, including former Columbia University student Mark Rudd, called for activists to descend on Chicago for what would be dubbed the "Days of Rage." Their mission was to "bring the war home" by sparking a violent clash with police. In a series of confrontations spread between October 8 and 11, a few hundred activists smashed windows of cars, homes, and businesses in the affluent Gold Coast neighborhood of Chicago and in the city's downtown Loop. Chicago's police department met them in force, deploying thousands of officers to pummel, gas, and arrest the demonstrators. Despite predictions by organizers that fifteen thousand activists would attend, the Days of Rage involved only a tiny fraction of that number. Moreover, a wide range of movement groups denounced the protest, including Chicago's Black Panthers. Panther leader Fred Hampton called the actions "opportunistic," "adventuristic," and suicidal.[46]

Large swaths of American society as a whole were also repelled; yet this was hardly an accident. In their most militant phase, the Weathermen were actively opposed to winning majority popular support. They saw most of the American public—and indeed most of the rest of the antiwar movement—as too bourgeois and compromised to contribute to a genuine revolutionary struggle. Reflecting with several decades of hindsight, Mark Rudd would later conclude, "I had purposely excluded the millions of moderate, nonviolent, middle-of-the-road people who now were willing to publicly demonstrate their opposition to the war." The rhetoric at the time was more blunt. Bernardine Dohrn, another of the group's leaders, stated: "We're about being crazy motherfuckers and scaring the shit out of honky America."[47]

By the time the Weathermen backed off this ultramilitant line and sought to create broader alliances with other movement and countercultural groups, they had already done significant damage.

By some estimates, SDS at its peak could claim more than 350 chapters and 80,000 members. Yet rampant sectarianism and out-of-touch tactics would quickly destroy the organization. In the months after the Days of Rage, a torrent of chapters disassociated from the national office; some disbanded altogether, with members turned off from the movement. An FBI report later released through the Freedom of Information Act noted gleefully, "The SDS has been deeply fractured in the last four months. Its pre-eminence as the leader of the young radical left in the USA is now questionable. . . . Rudd and his colleagues have alienated a large segment of potential and heretofore willing followers."[48]

"I couldn't have said it any better," Rudd himself would later write. "The anonymous FBI analyst and his superiors must have had a long laugh over the gift we'd handed them.[49]

"We might as well have been on their payroll," he concluded.[50]

Indeed, with SDS in peril, a few of the Weathermen, deeming the organization insufficiently revolutionary, decided to destroy it altogether. "The SDS is not serious enough," Rudd had exclaimed in a speech; "I want it to die." In January 1970, the Weathermen closed SDS's national office in Chicago. The next month, Rudd and fellow activist Ted Gold loaded boxes full of mailing lists and organizational files from SDS's New York office in a Volkswagen van, drove to the pier at Manhattan's West 14th Street, and dumped their cargo onto a city sanitation barge.[51]

A few months after that, in March, Gold was one of three people killed when an attempt at bomb making in a Greenwich Village townhouse went awry and resulted in an explosion that destroyed the building. Subsequently, the Weathermen became a tiny, clandestine organization that carried out bombings of courthouses, banks, police stations, and public buildings.

Even some of the international movements with which New Left activists had aligned watched this self-destruction with dismay. According to Rudd, a diplomat from the Cuban Mission had argued that the Chicago Days of Rage action was a terrible idea and that student radicals needed to unite the largest possible number of Americans in opposition to government interventionism. His advice was disregarded.[52]

∼

Although the Weathermen represent an extreme case, factions often exist within movements that are consciously antagonistic toward other activists. There are strains of anarchist insurrectionism, for example, that explicitly reject efforts of other activists to build long-term organization—even efforts by antiauthoritarians with other strategic perspectives, whom they sometimes dismiss as "not real anarchists."

These insurrectionists are willing, and sometimes even enthusiastic, to undermine organizing that they deem to be too bureaucratic or reformist. Moreover, they spurn the idea of appealing to the wider public or paying attention to media coverage of protest tactics. They argue that concern for public opinion stands in the way of "real action," which they define as specific attacks on governmental and corporate institutions.[53]

Within social movements, this presents a clear conflict. To simply advocate for a "diversity" of approaches in this context, without reckoning with how some of those approaches are diametrically opposed to one another, is to abandon strategic thinking altogether.

Likewise, some tactics just do not mix. Or, rather, they are actually poisonous when mixed together. Activists who have locked themselves to the entrance of a building to prevent politicians or business leaders from carrying out undemocratic trade negotiations, for example, are put in grave danger if insurrectionists a few blocks away decide to begin trashing stores and cars. Those engaging in property destruction may be able to run to safety and evade arrest, but those locked down will be forced to bear the unmitigated brunt of a police attack, with the public likely to view even harsh repression as justified.

This is not an uncommon dilemma, as advocates of controversial tactics often take cover in larger crowds that do not willingly choose to support their activities. In response to Black Bloc mobilizations in Oakland, activist and author Rebecca Solnit writes, "If you wish to do something the great majority of us oppose, do it on your own." Unfortunately, that is not what typically happens. As Solnit comments, "These small violent bands attach themselves to large nonviolent movements, perhaps because there aren't any large violent movements around." In the context of larger protests, trashing stores or brawling with authorities can endanger people who are seniors, who have physical disabilities, or who have children with them, and thus are unable to easily run away in the event of indiscriminate police repression.[54]

A second reason that not all tactics mix well is that some methods, rather than lending themselves to public outreach, promote insularity. Earth First! cofounder Mike Roselle ultimately rejected both violence and property destruction, in part for this reason. "As a tactic, the use of violence is corruptive, requires secrecy, and generally isolates its practitioners from the very people and places they wish to serve," Roselle writes. "I've learned this the hard way, not in some university course."[55]

A final reason that some tactics do not mix well involves the issue of defectors. As social movements successfully remove the pillars of support for the status quo, they encourage dissension and splits within the ranks of opponents. Particularly important for activists living under undemocratic regimes are "security defections," moments when soldiers and police officers refuse orders to attack protesters—or even decide to take the side of popular forces.

This process is endangered by an anything-goes approach. "Resistance violence is especially likely to restore loyalty and obedience among any of the opponent's troops or police becoming disaffected," Sharp explains. "In nonviolent struggles in which success and failure hinge on whether the opponent's troops can be induced to mutiny, violence against them may spell defeat."[56]

Even in democratic states, absent political jiu-jitsu and broad public sympathy to push back against official crackdowns, activists can be exposed to the full impact of the state's repressive apparatus. And despite militaristic posturing, those who have called for violent escalation can find themselves the most isolated and vulnerable.

Advocates of sabotage and property destruction have often been taken by surprise by the severity of the response from the state. In 1990, a cohort of disaffected activists had taken to calling Earth First!'s California campaign "Deadwood Bummer." They believed that organizers were "leading lambs to the slaughter" by subjecting recruits to violence at the hands of the logging industry. Some of these activists and their friends would later become active in the likeminded Animal Liberation and Earth Liberation Fronts, which undertook campaigns of arson in the 1990s and early 2000s against targets including facilities connected to the fur industry and SUV dealerships. Although their actions never attracted a mass following, the reaction they prompted from authorities was extreme. Sadly, it turned out that they were the ones presenting themselves for slaughter.[57]

In the 2001 PATRIOT Act and the subsequent 2006 Animal Enterprise Terrorism Act, the federal government explicitly defined the kind of attacks perpetrated by the eco-anarchists as terrorism. In 2005, the arrest of fourteen accused arsonists resulted in a highly unromantic scene in which militants scrambled to inform on their fellow activists in order to avoid the draconian, one-hundred-plus-year jail sentences the government had authorized itself to impose.

Looking back on their strategy, several participants later renounced their former approach and argued that environmental radicals should pursue nonviolent tactics that can be more effective. One prominent activist, Rod Coronado, called on movements working to defend forests and protect animal rights to "Let our opposition who believe in violence carry the burden of its justification."[58]

∼

Among activists and academics alike there is an idea that more radical approaches to resistance can have a constructive effect by making moderate reformers look less extreme. If those trying to negotiate with business leaders or reluctant politicians can point to militant activists who are bolder in their tactics and more uncompromising in their demands, this argument goes, they can present themselves as a sensible alternative. The more moderate elements can implicitly pose the question, "Who would you rather deal with: us or them?"

In social movement theory, this is known as the "radical flank" argument, and scholars of civil resistance have studied the phenomenon. "A positive radical flank occurs when . . . the presence of a radical wing makes moderate demands and strategies appear more reasonable, and radicals may create crises that are resolved to the moderates' advantage," writes sociologist Kurt Schock. Meanwhile, "a negative radical flank effect occurs when . . . radicals discredit an entire movement's activities and goals," making it more difficult for moderates to extract concessions.[59]

Radical flanks relate directly to the dynamics of polarization. Once again, the challenge is to maximize the positive effects while avoiding the negative ones.

Schock points out that radical flanks need not be violent. ACT UP, for one, provided a militant pole that indirectly helped bolster the ranks of more temperate AIDS groups and boosted their lobbying efforts. The question, therefore, is not whether a radical flank can be helpful for a movement; it is whether escalating civil resistance can be more adept than revolutionary violence at creating positive flank effects and pushing the spectrum of political debate.

The best quantitative evidence available on this issue suggests that radical flanks are more effective when they exert pressure through nonviolent conflict. Political scientist Erica Chenoweth reviewed hundreds of cases in order to compile a groundbreaking data set on the track record of resistance efforts that have challenged undemocratic regimes in the past century. She found that, empirically, movements in which a violent flank was present were more than 20 percent less likely to achieve their goals than nonviolent movements without such a flank. Rather than increasing the size and prominence of wider efforts, violent factions tended to decrease participation—something that her research found was vital to movement success.[60]

Chenoweth might well have chosen to echo Judi Bari's words: "There is no way that a few isolated individuals, no matter how brave, can bring about the massive social change necessary to save the planet." That requires a wider revolt.

∿

Creating discipline within a movement is at once a difficult task and an essential one.

Where structure-based organizations such as labor unions and community-organizing outfits operate through clearly defined hierarchies, mass mobilizations rely on activating loose, broad networks of supporters. This creates a unique challenge for momentum-based organizers. Invariably, some of those drawn in from the outside will want to pursue tactics or advance agendas that contradict the aims of the movement. Mass mobilizations must find means of inviting creative, broad-based participation, while also being able to distance the movement from destructive actions that contribute to negative polarization.

Hybrid organizations offer some solutions to this dilemma: like Otpor and the SCLC, those working to intentionally spark, guide, and sustain mass protest can frontload adherence to nonviolent tactics as one of their movement's norms. And they can create a culture of training to foster a greater unity of strategic vision. In Redwood Summer, modeled on the civil rights movement, participation was premised on an explicit commitment to nonviolent direct action. This agreement set the tone for a wealth of resistance that was simultaneously creative, daring, and disciplined.

The key common link among all the activities in a momentum-driven movement is that they must be designed, in the long run, to build mass support. It is with this common goal in mind, and with the importance of nonviolence established, that activists can adopt a diversity of roles and approaches.

There is no single type of dissident, and no single style of organizing, that alone will carry a movement to the final realization of its goals. After moments of peak involvement, social movements must attempt to reap what their escalating disruption has sown. The energy of mass mobilization must be channeled back into long-term structures that can formalize and preserve the gains brought about by high-profile drives. And here, a new array of skills is required.

Once the whirlwinds die down, another struggle begins.

CHAPTER TEN

THE ECOLOGY OF CHANGE

"TAHRIR BROUGHT TEARS to my eyes," says Ahmed Salah. "We had tried before. But nothing was like this."[1]

Salah, a veteran youth organizer, had worked for years to drum up resistance to the autocratic thirty-year regime of Hosni Mubarak, the eighty-two-year-old president of Egypt. In 2004, Salah had helped form a movement called Kefaya, or "Enough." More recently, he was a co-founder of the April 6 Youth Movement, which had called for protests on January 25, 2011, in Cairo and other cities throughout the country.

The time seemed opportune. Just a few months earlier, Egypt had gone through elections that human rights groups called "the most fraudulent ever." As Salah explains, "Mubarak's National Democratic Party swept parliamentary elections through a process so rigged that no effort was made to hide the fraud. When one member of my family went to the polls, he discovered that he had already voted—his ballot had been fraudulently cast for the ruling party." Salah further notes, "The consensus view among Egyptians was that Mubarak was grooming his son Gamal to take his place, which would turn Egypt into a hereditary dictatorship."[2]

The electoral fraud had given rise to widespread public disgust. Still, Salah had little expectation that the January demonstrations could turn into a full-fledged rebellion. "I had hopes, but I never really thought that I'd see it," he says.[3]

What actually happened on the day of protest made Cairo's Tahrir Square into a global sensation. On the heels of a revolution in neighboring Tunisia, Egyptians responded in huge numbers to the January 25 call to action, and they kept coming out in the days that followed. "We had millions on the streets on that very first day, and these numbers doubled and tripled," says Salah. "It was incredible afterwards. You could see in Cairo alone between five and seven million protesting in the streets of just this city. Maybe in Alexandria a million or two, and all over the country hundreds of thousands in every city."[4]

Just a few weeks later, Mubarak was gone. News of his resignation on February 11, 2011, marked the climax of what was quickly recognized as one of the most sudden and significant upheavals of the twenty-first century. As the *New York Times* reported, "The announcement, which comes after an 18-day revolt led by the young people of Egypt, shatters three decades of political stasis and overturns the established order of the Arab world." Citizens in Egypt, along with sympathizers throughout the world, rejoiced.[5]

Mubarak's ouster was one of the high moments of the Arab Spring. And yet, within a few short years, the euphoria of those times evaporated. In Egypt's first free elections, disorganization among the secular democratic opposition resulted in the election of Mohamed Morsi, a leader of the Muslim Brotherhood, an Islamist group that had only belatedly joined the uprising. Then, in the summer of 2013, Egypt's military, under the command of General Abdel Fattah al-Sisi, took power by overthrowing Morsi. Not long after, prominent political scientist Amr Hamzawy described his nation as "a country in fear" that was experiencing a "fast recovery of authoritarianism."[6]

Others would concur, noting a shattering reversal of progress. "The streets are empty. The prisons are full," reported Amnesty International in early 2015. "The fourth anniversary of Egypt's '25 January Revolution' is passing largely in silence, with many of the young activists who led it now firmly behind bars."[7]

Without a doubt, the revolution in Egypt presents a troubling case. The toppling of the Mubarak regime in 2011 was initially held up as a triumph of civil resistance, a fresh and exciting example of how a non-violent mass mobilization could prevail over a force with far greater military might. However, as the country slid back into a repressive and undemocratic state, that rosy appraisal faded. More recently, Egypt's situation has given fuel to cynics who argue that things would have been better if the revolution had never happened, as well as those who more generally doubt the power of nonviolent movements to secure change.

In truth, the Egyptian revolution is best seen as neither an uncomplicated success nor a mere justification for pessimism. It is far more valuable when recognized as something different: a perfect case study of what can be accomplished by mass mobilizations that harness the power of disruptive protest—and of the limits of these mobilizations.

Egypt shows that widespread revolts can do amazing things, but uprising alone is not enough. From Gandhi, to US labor unions in the 1930s, to the civil rights movement, to ACT UP, organizers using non-violent escalation have grappled with how to put in place lasting mechanisms that can sustain the progress generated by their most high-profile campaigns. This is the challenge of institutionalization. In addressing it, these activists have found that the talent for creating mass unrest must be combined with the skills and perspectives of other organizing traditions in order to formalize and protect the gains won by popular mobilizations.

Institutionalization, moreover, is part of a wider dynamic. Peak moments do not exist in isolation. Instead, social movements progress through different stages. They contain actors who can play distinct roles, the relative importance of which fluctuate based on what stage of its life span a movement is in. At different times, the skills that various organizing traditions offer come to the fore.

Not all efforts to create change prevail over the long term. But those that do tend to see themselves as part of an ecology that is made healthier when different traditions each contribute: mass mobilizations alter the terms of political debate and create new possibilities for progress;

structure-based organizing helps take advantage of this potential and protects against efforts to roll back advances; and countercultural communities preserve progressive values, nurturing dissidents who go on to initiate the next waves of revolt.

∾

Egypt's case is helpful in illustrating what mass mobilizations do well, and what they do not. But to understand why, it is first necessary to answer a more basic question: How did a small, loosely organized group of Egyptian young people end up setting the terms for their country's revolution?

If anyone should have spearheaded a successful revolt against Mubarak's rule, it was the Muslim Brotherhood. Having existed for more than eighty years, the group had organized hundreds of thousands of members, despite being officially banned for decades. Moreover, the group's influence extended beyond its membership rolls. The Muslim Brotherhood established a strong reputation as a social service provider, operating a nationwide network of schools, food banks, hospitals, and programs for orphans and widows. As public health researcher Nadine Farag reported in 2011, an Egyptian woman, regardless of politics or religion, could pay the equivalent of $175 to give birth in a well-staffed and well-equipped hospital run by the Brotherhood, or she could pay $875 in a private hospital. Salah calls the organization "by far the largest and best-organized opposition group in Egypt."[8]

Yet, despite this unique strength, the Muslim Brotherhood did not take the lead in sparking revolution. The success of groups such as the April 6 Youth Movement shows how momentum-driven efforts, in launching nonviolent rebellions that capture the public imagination, often take the more well-structured organizations on a given political scene by surprise. The upstart groups have far fewer resources and much weaker institutional structures than conventional labor unions, political parties, or community-based organizations. But they use these traits to their advantage, organizing *outside* the confines of any established group.

Although it may seem strange, the same factors that made the Brotherhood powerful—the strengths of its structure-based organizing model—also made its leaders hesitant to risk all they had built in a mass confrontation with Mubarak. It was evident to them what they had to lose. Because the Brothers had clearly identified leadership and hierarchical membership, they were easily targeted for repression by the state. Because they had created a strong framework through which they could patiently amass power, they felt less urgency to force a public crisis around the regime. And because they were experts in person-to-person networking among their Islamist base, they were less adept at advocating for widely popular political demands that would be supported by other segments of society.

Consistent with momentum-driven campaigns, social media–savvy organizations such as April 6 and the followers of popular activist Facebook pages in Egypt operated differently. Although these recently formed groups had tens of thousands of online "members"—sometimes gathered in a matter of weeks after a high-publicity event—organizers often knew little more about a given follower than an Internet username. Rather than mastering the arts of long-term leadership development, they focused on confrontation and public spectacle. Their strength was telling stories: publicizing pictures of police abuse and rallying outrage.

The regime gave them plenty to work with. The youth organizers posted videos of Egyptian civilians being beaten by police, and they shared pictures of people who had been tortured in custody. In these images, the victims showed how electrocution had created patches of congealed blood underneath their skin, leaving blotchy pink stains.

One particularly well-trafficked hub of online activity, the "We Are All Khalid Said" Facebook page, was named after a twenty-eight-year-old man who, in June 2010, was beaten to death by authorities after posting a video of police misconduct. As journalist David Wolman recounts, two detectives confronted Said at a cybercafe and "slammed his head on a table before the owner told them to take the fighting outside." Police then "pulled Said out to a building entryway where they kicked him and smashed his head against an iron gate until his body went limp."[9]

When a picture of Said's dead body was circulated online, it became a catalyst for indignation. "Maybe it was because he was a well-known and educated guy with many friends," one student told Wolman. "And the picture. I mean, he was so completely disfigured. I don't know what it was exactly, but it spread like fire."

When it came time to mobilize citizens for a mass demonstration on January 25—the day that would become the start of the revolution—the approach of the youth organizers was more akin to concert promotion than the building of neighborhood organizations. They put forth symbolically loaded demands to engender the broadest possible sympathy, adopting a slogan that had already been made famous in Tunisia: "The people demand the fall of the regime."

The call to action generated buzz. In another viral video, twenty-six-year-old Asmaa Mahfouz, a cofounder of the April 6 Youth Movement, positioned herself directly in front of her computer's camera and announced that she would attend the protests. Forgoing the safety of online anonymity, she brazenly implored others to join her: "As long as you say there is no hope, then there will be no hope," Mahfouz argued. "But if you go down and take a stance, then there will be hope."[10]

The experience of January 25 proved her right. Salah describes the march that formed that day in his neighborhood to head toward Tahrir Square: "This was my neighborhood, my home, and during my 10 years as an activist I had met hundreds of people in and around the activist community. Yet the streets were filled with men and women I had never seen. And they were leading chants! As I lifted my voice to join them, I thought to myself: *My God! Where have you been? We've been waiting for you!*"[11]

～

After the initial confrontation on the twenty-fifth, the uprising advanced quickly. For a time, the Egyptian media branded all youth organizing as the work of the April 6 Youth. The group had created a mobilization that was less a concrete institution than an open movement, one with which people across the country could identify. According to Salah, the group had only a few dozen physical members as of early 2011, and yet a vast range of autonomous activity was soon associated with the organization's efforts, ranging from neighborhood-level organizing, to online advocacy, to mobilization on the part of the country's emergent independent labor movement. "It became the brand name," Salah says of the April 6 Youth Movement. "We were successful in making it the icon of change."[12]

Like other momentum-driven efforts, the organizers' canny use of disruptive escalation gave them weight that could never have been justified on the basis of their true institutional size or strength. Not only did they spark early demonstrations but also they exerted lasting influence as the protests grew. When, several days in, groups such as the Muslim Brotherhood and the National Association for Change—led by the Nobel Laureate and former head of the International Atomic Energy Agency Mohamed ElBaradei—finally decided to amplify a political eruption that had become too large to ignore, these experienced actors showed deference to the methods and the messages that the young people had established from the outset. The latecomers overwhelmingly adopted the slogans and framing of the existing revolt, making the effort resolutely nonsectarian.[13]

April 6 and other youth groups were able to spark a contagious uprising precisely because they were not based on rigid structures. They did not have organizational assets that could be seized by the regime. They did not have established political turf to defend or factional interests that would cast them as partisan or self-interested. They did not have well-established chapters that could be easily infiltrated. And so they could take on a broad-scale, symbolically loaded campaign, geared toward maximum support and maximum disruption.

Certainly, on February 11, 2011, when authorities announced Mubarak's resignation and the activists cried with joy in the square, storm clouds loomed. When revolutionaries talked about the future, there were already indications that their coalition was fragile. But for the moment, they had accomplished something that few in the world could have predicted, and something that the best organized group in the country could not pull off: they unseated the tyrant who had ruled for longer than many of them were alive.

They overthrew Mubarak.

～

Once a moment of the whirlwind passes, activists must be attentive to how the gains they have won can be institutionalized and made durable. And here the habits of structure-based organizing become very useful.

Youth organizers had brought people onto the streets in staggering numbers by "breaking the fear barrier," as a popular expression among Egyptian activists put it. They had rallied mass public sympathy and ousted an entrenched regime. All these were remarkable accomplishments. Yet, just as the momentum-driven organizing model of April 6 and other youth groups gave them disproportionate influence in shaping the uprising, the well-engineered structures of the Muslim Brotherhood proved critical in defining what would come next.[14]

Momentum-driven groups thrive on broad, transformative demands that have symbolic resonance and can inspire support from the general public. For the purposes of creating a crisis of legitimacy for Mubarak, the importation of "The people demand the fall of the regime" was perfect. But such broad-based appeals were not nearly as effective in promoting the rise of new leaders or pushing forward specific reforms to the system of governance. In contrast, the Muslim Brotherhood's transactional demands, although not useful in instigating revolt, allowed them to leverage the institutional power they had accrued to influence the new governing bodies that were being established after the revolution.

Youth organizers took it as a point of pride that they did not sink into the muck of party politics and instead focused on broadly resonant issues such as freedom and ending police brutality. In the Oscar-nominated documentary *The Square*—released in January 2014 to coincide with the third anniversary of the revolution—two youth leaders discussed how this focus became a problem after the fall of Mubarak:

"Politics is not the same as a revolution. If you want to play politics, you have to compromise. And we're not good at this . . . at all," said

Khalid Abdalla, a British-Egyptian activist and actor known for his role in *The Kite Runner*.

"We're terrible at it," agreed Ramy Essam, a musician who performed regularly before rallies in Tahrir, earning renown as the "singer of the revolution."[15]

The Muslim Brotherhood was in a very different position. For its leaders, negotiating for institutional advancement in a postrevolutionary climate came naturally. With a framework for a political party already in place and an organized bloc of voters at the ready, the Brotherhood moved to the fore. Whereas the younger and more secularly minded activists generally favored allowing time for the drafting of a constitution and the formation of new parties, the Brotherhood pushed for quick elections.

Abdul-Fatah Madi, an Egyptian analyst writing for *Al Jazeera*, explained that prior to Mubarak's defeat, the youth-led factions "preoccupied themselves with acquiring knowledge on how to topple tyrannical regimes as well as spreading information about human rights violations." But as the postrevolutionary transition began, they failed to engage in "the intricacies of state-building and political projects that would serve as an alternative to the authoritarian regime."[16]

In the absence of a more structured challenge by the groups who had sparked the revolution, the Muslim Brotherhood dropped any pretense of a movement coalition. Six months after Mubarak fell, it ordered its members out for mass rallies. The disciplined crowds now took up much more partisan chants: "Islamic rule, Islamic rule" and "The Qur'an is our constitution."

The secular youth, champions of momentum, had been outmaneuvered. For all their success in targeting the former regime, a lack of structure meant that they lost control after their primary goal of removing the autocrat was realized.

Structure-based organizing and momentum-driven movements are not inherently in conflict. Ideally, the two models can complement one another. Established groups that share the goals of a mass uprising can benefit from the burst of energy and the increased interest in a cause that comes with a high-profile mobilization. In turn, the more

established organizations can lend their prestige and resources to outbreaks of resistance when they arise. This happened when the Muslim
Brotherhood decided to back the Tahrir revolt—bringing microphones
to the square, turning out its members, arranging garbage collection—
and when it joined the push for a coalition government. But when the
constituencies split, putting secular revolutionaries at odds with the Is-
lamists, the main beneficiary was the military.

The armed forces, which had refused to crack down on behalf of
Mubarak during the January 2011 uprising, were regarded by the public
as heroes after the revolution. Capitalizing on this good will, the military
emerged as the force that controlled the structures of the old regime.
With Mubarak gone, it competed with the Muslim Brotherhood for
dominance. Over the next year and a half, the Supreme Council of the
Armed Forces attempted to delay handing over power to a civilian government. In response, reinvigorated protests—brandishing the slogan,
"A new revolution all over again"—forced it to cede to popular rule. This
allowed the Brotherhood's Mohamed Morsi to take office as the country's first democratically elected president in the summer of 2012.

However, during his year in office, Morsi granted himself ever
more-expansive powers, prompting a public backlash. Having already
dethroned Mubarak and the Supreme Council, Egyptians took to the
streets to rally against a third ruling power—the Muslim Brotherhood.
Graffiti artists changed their stencils: those who once marked red Xs over
spray-painted images of Mubarak began using cutouts of Morsi instead.

In the summer of 2013, amid a new wave of mass antigovernment
protests, the military stepped in and forced the Muslim Brotherhood
from power. At first, liberals were hesitant to call it a coup. But hopes
for more open and pluralistic governance were once again thwarted. In
following months, the army escalated repression, clamping down on
both its Islamist and secular opponents. By the revolution's third anniversary, Amnesty International warned of authorities "using every resource at their disposal to quash dissent." Things appeared bleak.[17]

Today, the path ahead looks very difficult. Those who led
momentum-driven mass mobilizations in Egypt recognize that, if they
are to succeed in the future, they will need not only the skills to initiate

widespread disruption but also the ability to hold on to their gains in the aftermath. In 2012, leaders of the April 6 Youth Movement vowed to embark on a five-year plan to develop alternative institutions. Since then, repression from the military has made progress difficult, and many leaders have been jailed.[18]

If there is hope for the future, it is that the 2011 uprising has unleashed a spirit of communal self-determination that cannot be easily subdued. By early 2014, Ahmed Salah was living in exile and dealing with the trauma of repression. "I feel that this is the worst time," he said. "Most people have been brainwashed into thinking that the only way to save Egypt is through military rule."

And yet he reported that his pessimism was balanced by another impulse. "I also feel confidence," Salah said. "Each group that has been in the leading position in the country has tried to retain power. Yet we Egyptians were able to bring down three regimes: Mubarak, the Supreme Council, and the Muslim Brotherhood.

"What we did before," he concluded, "we can do again."[19]

∼

When it comes to mass upheaval, momentum-based campaigns do not wait for moments of unrest to spontaneously occur. Rather, they seek to consciously generate whirlwinds, to take advantage of outside trigger events when they occur, and to sustain periods of peak activity. Hybrid organizations such as Otpor and the Southern Christian Leadership Conference were successful at doing this, enabling them to endure multiple waves of revolt. By the time they finished their campaigns, they had gained enough active support that their allies were many and their enemies were fractured. As a result, they scored critical wins.

But even groups that carry out disruptive action for long periods must understand their efforts in a larger context. How can movement activists absorb the energy of revolt into lasting structures? How can they protect the gains they have secured? And how can they spark new cycles of disruption that propel further change?

The greatest practitioners of civil resistance have answered these questions by drawing on the strengths of different social change traditions.

Although mobilizing unusual moments of peak unrest demands a unique methodology, this does not negate the value of skills from other approaches. Indeed, these skills become critical in various stages of social movements. When mass mobilizations, established organizations, and alternative communities see themselves as complementary, they can create a movement ecosystem that allows diverse approaches to promoting change to flourish.

Focusing on movements outside the United States, the tradition of civil resistance acknowledges that strategic nonviolent action against authoritarian regimes must function as part of a wider drive to build up the kind of healthy civil society institutions that can keep a democracy intact. "No one should believe that with the downfall of the dictatorship an ideal society will immediately appear," Gene Sharp wrote a decade before mass protests in Tahrir Square. "The disintegration of the dictatorship simply provides the beginning point . . . for long-term efforts to improve the society and meet human needs more adequately."[20]

For this reason, Sharp contended, "careful precautions must be taken to prevent the rise of a new oppressive regime out of the confusion following the collapse of the old one."

No doubt, this is easier said than done. But the challenges of establishing a more just social order after a revolution do not apply only to nonviolent movements. Instead, they afflict all turbulent changes of state power, whether armed or unarmed.

Studies have found that, at least since the 1970s, when regimes are toppled, the posttransition states have been far more likely to become democratic if the movements that brought about the change employed tactics of strategic nonviolence—such as strikes, mass boycotts, and large-scale demonstrations. In the case of a guerilla uprising against an undemocratic state, revolutionaries still have to fill the vacuum left by the old regime. And because the armed force that carried out the overthrow is often the best-organized institution of the resistance, its hierarchical structures are primed to take over. The result, as in many postcolonial African states, is often a new dictatorship led by guerilla commanders.[21]

Upheavals prompted by civil resistance do not face this difficulty, and therefore they have a better likelihood of producing positive

long-term results. Still, problems after the fall of an undemocratic regime are common. Although countries might not experience a rever-
sion to autocratic rule, as Egypt did, they must nonetheless confront a
host of challenges in making new political leaders live up to progressive
ideals. In Serbia and in several "color revolutions" in the former Soviet
bloc—such as the 2003 Rose Revolution in Georgia and the 2004 Orange Revolution in the Ukraine—young people played a critical role in
leading quickly swelling mobilizations. But in all these cases, they were
unprepared for later events. Matthew Collin, author of *The Time of the
Rebels*, a study of these uprisings, writes that there "seemed to be no
blueprint for what, if anything, these youth movements could achieve
after their revolutions.[22]

"In all cases, most of the rank-and-file activists simply drifted away,"
Collin explains. "They could help to change their countries, but they
found it harder to ensure that the politicians who came to power afterwards remained true to the principles they had espoused at the moment
of revolution." In such cases, institutionalizing progress after momentum dies down has remained a persistent difficulty.

For social movements in the United States, the challenge takes a
different form, but it is no less relevant. Groups attempting to create
change in a democratic context do not typically have to deal with the
complexities of setting up a new ruling order after a revolution. But they
must still work to see that the changes they win are safeguarded after
momentous upheavals subside, and they must retain the capacity to
launch new mobilizations after the goals of earlier efforts are met.

∼

It was a classic moment of the whirlwind: in late 1936, with the pain
of the Great Depression still lingering, a strike hit the heart of the au-
tomobile industry. Flint, Michigan, was home to the central production facility of the powerful General Motors. Starting on December 30,
workers at several GM sites sat down and occupied their factories. Ultimately, they brought production to a standstill for forty-four days, creating what the BBC would later describe as "the strike heard round the
world."[23]

There is debate over who deserves credit for building the disciplined organizational networks that guided the Flint strike—whether the fledgling United Auto Workers, independent rank-and-file leaders in the factories, or socialist cadre groups of various stripes. But it is clear that the strike was an impressively managed affair. Workers within the factories organized committees to handle everything from food and sanitation to rumor control and entertainment. Meanwhile, groups on the outside such as the Emergency Women's Brigades took responsibility for walking picket lines, coordinating deliveries of provisions, and facing down police.[24]

The action in Flint gave rise to a rush of decentralized activity that expanded far beyond the reach of any established organizational structure. On the heels of the initial sit-down, the GM strike spread throughout the company's factories, not only in Detroit, but also to plants in Ohio, Indiana, Wisconsin, and even Georgia.[25]

On February 11, 1937, General Motors accepted defeat. In a historic victory for labor, the company announced that it would bargain with the UAW, something that ultimately resulted in major pay increases and an expanded voice for workers on the job. And over the next year, the wave of action continued to spread. Sit-down strikes became a genuine national phenomenon as employees clamored to replicate the success in Flint. Labor historian Jeremy Brecher cites data from the Bureau of Labor Statistics showing sit-downs involving nearly four hundred thousand workers in 1937. In one month alone, March 1937, there were 170 industrial sit-downs recorded. "In the mood of the time, any grievance could become a trigger," Frances Fox Piven and Richard Cloward write. Nor was the fever limited to just factory workers: hotel employees in Michigan, students in New York and North Carolina, and even prisoners in Illinois and Pennsylvania all used the tactic to demand that their grievances be addressed.[26]

"After the sit-down strike," reflected former UAW president Leonard Woodcock, "people organized themselves. They came by literally the tens of thousands, and all kinds of people. . . . It was a crusade."[27]

The genius of John L. Lewis, president of the national Committee for Industrial Organization (CIO), was not in sparking the strike wave.

Rather, Lewis's genius was in using recently passed federal labor law—specifically, the protections that labor had demanded and won in the 1935 Wagner Act—to give the unions a means of institutionalizing the energy of a mobilization that had spread beyond organizers' wildest aspirations. Not only did Lewis appreciate the opportunity created by the sit-downs but also he was willing to invest heavily in seizing it—risking his union's treasury to hire phalanxes of new organizers, including talented local radicals and Communist Party members, who signed up rank-and-file supporters en masse. Within a year of the victory in Flint, the autoworkers' union, a CIO affiliate, grew from thirty thousand members nationwide to a quarter million, and union membership in other industries similarly skyrocketed. It was a landmark moment in the formation of the modern US labor movement.[28]

As this experience showed, mass mobilizations can be critical in bolstering organizations. Established groups, for their part, can help to support new waves of disruption. However, this type of mutually supportive behavior does not always happen. In fact, structure is often hostile to mass mobilization. A variety of historians argue persuasively with regard to the strike wave of the late 1930s that union leaders often worked to cool the sit-down strikes rather than to fuel them. They placed an interest in organizational preservation ahead of continued unrest. Piven and Cloward write that, especially once workers were signed up for the union, labor leadership scrambled to "curb work stoppages and maintain production," believing that the strength of its bargaining position was based on its ability to temper disobedience in the shops.[29]

The tension extends far beyond the labor movement. With reference to nonprofit groups, Bill Moyer notes, "The large budgets, professional staff, board of directors . . . and reliance on foundations for funding make almost all of the large professional opposition organizations politically cautious and on the conservative side of the political spectrum of the left." Professionalized groups tend to be averse to risking negative polarization. And, because they usually focus their work on instrumental demands that benefit their members, they might see little point in symbolic appeals to the public at large. Because of this, during moments when mass mobilizations begin taking off, the instinct of more professionalized groups is often to guard their turf and undercut the upstart efforts.[30]

The friction here is real. But recognition of how different approaches can contribute during various stages of movement activity can help ease tensions. A firm advocate of disruptive power, Frances Fox Piven is wary of organizational bureaucracies because of their tendency of trying to dampen or contain outbreaks of revolt. Yet she, too, acknowledges that structured institutions can play a role. "Organizations can preserve a legacy," she says. "They can institutionalize and legalize the gains won through disruptive mobilization." Furthermore, she and Cloward have written that "quiescent periods" and "periods of reaction" are "times when organization-building makes sense." During these stages, established groups can be critical in fighting off the backlash that typically comes from elites.[31]

Piven and Cloward are critical of the labor movement for accommodating itself to America's mainstream establishment after it rose to prominence, especially during the Cold War, and they contend that bureaucratized unions too rarely exercise the power of the strike. Nevertheless, the authors argue, "To be sure, the unions that emerged in the 1930s did become permanent; and . . . they have been useful in protecting the interests of workers." Industrial unionization, Piven and Cloward write, was a victory worth winning, resulting in higher pay, shorter hours, greater job security, and workplace safety protections—changes that made significant differences in the lives of millions of American families.[32]

If adopting professionalized structures can inhibit an organization's willingness to embrace disruptive uprising, there is an opposite danger for momentum-driven activity. Groups that are unable to institutionalize can find themselves at a dead-end when the energy of a revolt runs out or an initial demand is fulfilled.

The successful growth of industrial unions in the wake of the sit-down strikes stands in contrast to the case of US farmworkers in California and the Northwest. Over the past several decades, these workers have experienced repeated waves of wildcat strikes involving thousands of people, spread over hundreds of farms and orchards. But, given that farmers can change crops from year to year, that agricultural employees are constantly rotating, and that workers in the fields do not benefit from many of the protections of existing labor law, organizations such as the United Farm Workers have had great difficulty retaining a stable membership base and enforcing ongoing contracts. Consequently, many of the wage increases and improvements in working conditions granted as a result of strikes have proven extremely challenging to maintain. Today, the largely immigrant workforce that helps harvest America's crops remains one of the most exploited in the country.

As uprisings swell, there is no problem with established groups seeking to capitalize on the unrest or using the new energy to advance long-term goals that are broadly consistent with the movement's aims. The problem comes if organizations act in ways that belittle or impede rising movement efforts. To avoid this, structured-based groups can treat moments of peak activity as times for experimentation. This is what Alinsky did in the wake of the Freedom Rides, when he agreed with his protégé Nicholas von Hoffman. "I think that we should toss out everything we are doing organizationally," von Hoffman had said, "and work on the premise that this is the moment of the whirlwind, that we are no longer organizing but guiding a social movement."[33]

This perspective matches the insights of Piven and Cloward. By adopting a temporary focus on "mobilizing disruptive acts rather than organizing members," the theorists argue, established organizations can "work *with* the tides of popular defiance rather than against them."[34]

Although she recognizes the tension that often exists between structured organizations and decentralized movements, author and community organizer Rinku Sen argues that each is essential. Sen writes, "While organizations of all sorts produce incremental victories that help prevent backsliding, shifts in core values that shape policy take place through social movements that involve large numbers of people."[35]

In the end, Sen argues, "A systematic challenge" to status quo injustices "will come from people who have been exposed to a number of organizing models, who can debate big ideas, and who can forego direct benefits to their own organization in terms of reputation and money."[36]

∾

Until his death, Martin Luther King Jr. remained a champion of the Birmingham model of civil resistance, and he sought to apply the tactics of nonviolent escalation to new contexts. However, late in his life, he also acknowledged that groups, including his own SCLC, faced limitations if they remained only "specialists in agitation and dramatic projects."[37]

In 1967, King wrote of his group's campaigns in places such as Birmingham and Selma as being akin to emergency measures. They had served as a "crisis policy and program," advanced through "explosive events." The campaigns helped secure critical legislative advances. But King believed that, for new stages of struggle, crisis mobilizations must be supplemented by ongoing, daily commitment. "We will have to build far-flung, workmanlike, and experienced organizations in the future," he wrote, "if the legislation we create and the agreements we forge are to be ably and zealously superintended."[38]

King had been developing this line of thinking for some time. In 1966 he wrote, "More and more, the civil rights movement will become engaged in the task of organizing people into permanent groups to protect their own interests and to produce change in their behalf." The end goal was that people would be organized to work together in what King called "units of power."[39]

These units could span a wide range of political and economic relationships. King saw the units of power including tenant associations, voters' leagues, groups of the unemployed, and labor organizations. Even as he planned for major mobilizations such as the Poor People's Campaign—which envisioned a multiracial brigade of three thousand people spearheading an occupation of the National Mall to advance demands for economic justice—King believed that institutionalization into these units was critical to long-term racial and economic justice.[40]

King's assassination prevented the world from witnessing how his integration of nonviolent revolt and long-term institution building might take shape. But his concept of units of power is intriguing, both because it encouraged collaboration between a diversity of groups and because it envisioned permanent organization that could be mobilized in support of mass action when needed.

If disruptive mobilizations refashion the landscape of political possibility, other approaches to change become important once the new terrain of debate has been established. Over the past century, movements have found a variety of ways to institutionalize and preserve their legacies. The structures they created have not always realized King's ideal of integration between long-term organizing and support for new campaigns of nonviolent escalation. Yet, by and large, they have contributed to creating a rich ecology in which social movements can function.

The industrial unions that gained prominence in the 1930s are a mode of long-term organization that continues to have a major impact on American life. As embattled as these unions might be, the fact that they are funded by their members not only makes them self-sustaining but also gives them a critical level of independence. Owing to this, they serve as the country's most reliable institutional counterbalance to the influence of unchecked wealth and privilege on the nation's politics. In cases such as the civil rights movement, unions sometimes provided pivotal funding and support for disruptive campaigns—including Project C in Birmingham.

Outside of organized labor, some movements have institutionalized by creating watchdog groups to monitor and enforce gains around an issue. The Harvard Living Wage Sit-In was part of a larger wave of student-labor activism in the late 1990s and early 2000s. Campus groups drew attention not only to the plight of low-wage service workers on US campuses but also to the sweatshop conditions in factories overseas where college sweatshirts and other branded items are typically made. These conditions could be disturbing. A prominent *New York Times* article from 1998 profiled one factory producing Nike goods in Vietnam. There, employees were forced to work sixty-five hours per week for a total of just ten dollars, with no overtime pay—and they were "exposed to carcinogens that exceeded local legal standards by 177 times in parts of the plant."[41]

In 2001, students, workers, and labor experts came together to form the Workers Rights Consortium (WRC), which student-labor groups began pushing their universities to join. Membership in the body requires true independent monitoring of factories: third-party inspectors make unannounced visits to ensure that workplaces follow proper ventilation and fire safety standards, that factories are free from child labor and forced overtime, and that employees have the freedom to form a union if they so choose.[42]

Since the group's founding, the WRC has grown to include more than 180 affiliated colleges and universities. Because participating colleges are each required to pay membership dues ranging from $1,500 to $50,000, based on their licensing revenue, the advocates have created a stable, ongoing advocacy group that operates with a significant budget.[43] Although the antisweatshop movement now gets less national attention than in the late 1990s, chapters of the United Students Against Sweatshops have continued to launch new campaigns, expanding the WRC and creating fresh waves of campus sit-ins in 2008 and 2011.

As another means of institutionalization, movements can influence official bodies—and sometimes take them over. ACT UP derived its power from being confrontational. But one of its main accomplishments was securing a voice for AIDS patients within the very institutions it was targeting. As public funding to address the disease dramatically increased, thanks in part to movement efforts, a variety of ACT UP members moved into new roles, helping to administer grants, hammer out state and federal policies, and run treatment programs. Although ACT UP itself became far less prominent over time, this shift in funding and administration transformed day-to-day care for more than a million patients around the country.[44]

A third approach to institutionalization is to make a direct bid for state power. In some places—Poland, South Africa, and Bolivia being prominent examples—mass movements have formed political parties. This has resulted in triumphant scenes of resistance leaders such as Lech Walesa and Nelson Mandela becoming the first democratically elected heads of state in their countries, and social movement icon Evo Morales emerging as the first indigenous president of Bolivia. More recently, parties such as Syriza in Greece and Podemos in Spain have worked to channel the energy of popular uprisings into parties that can attempt to directly alter the ruling policies of their countries.

However, the seizing of state power does not diminish the importance of disruptive movements. Even in the most successful cases of institutionalization through political parties, elected officials have run up against limits in their ability to challenge establishment elites. The changes they secure through governmental channels inevitably fall short of the original goals that animated grassroots resistance. And then, of course, there is the problem of politicians selling out: as the energy of mass mobilization drops off, once-fervent champions of popular democracy risk becoming complacent insiders who start defending the status quo for personal gain. For all these reasons, even if former movement leaders take office, there remains a need for further waves of uprising that create fresh pressure.

"Specialists in agitation and dramatic projects," as King called them, can rarely find a convenient time to retire.

~

The need for disruptive movements to reignite on a persistent basis raises the question of how even very committed people can sustain their efforts over the course of decades and generations. One way to do this is to build communities that reach beyond the realm of traditional political struggle.

"New movements arise from prophetic minorities at the margins, culturally, economically, and politically," writes longtime activist and prominent 1960s student leader Tom Hayden. Hayden further adds that, when movement participants come together, they "develop communities of meaning to enrich their lives during the ups and downs of the long journey." These communities might share bonds of common music and art, or they might they have religious or spiritual ties. Often they create alternative institutions, such as squats, co-ops, community kitchens, and radical bookstores.[45]

Such countercultural or "prefigurative" communities are another part of the ecology that sustains social movements—and they are critical in laying the groundwork for future revolts.

Although the building of alternative communities and institutions can be a potent force in social movements, it can also present challenges.

Activists have long debated the question: Should we fight the system or "be the change we wish to see"? Should we push for transformation within existing societal structures, or should we model in our own lives a different set of social and political relationships that might someday form the basis of a new society? Going back centuries, different movements have incorporated elements of each approach, sometimes in harmonious ways and other times in ways that create conflicts between groups.

Various academic and political traditions discuss the two differing approaches using overlapping concepts: these include "cultural revolution," "dual power," and—most controversially—"lifestyle politics." The term "prefigurative politics," coined by political theorist Carl Boggs and popularized by sociologist Wini Breines, emerged out of analysis of the movements of the 1960s. Rejecting both the Leninist cadre organization of the Old Left and conventional political parties, members of the decade's "New Left" attempted to create activist communities that embodied the concept of participatory democracy, an idea famously championed in the 1962 Port Huron Statement of the Students for a Democratic Society.[46]

Instead of waiting for revolution in the future, the New Left sought to experience it in the present, through the movements it built. Breines argued that the central imperative of prefigurative politics was to "create and sustain within the live practice of the movement, relationships and political forms that 'prefigured' and embodied the desired society."[47]

Wini Breines defended prefigurative politics as the lifeblood of 1960s movements. But at the same time, she distinguished prefigurative action from a different type of politics—*strategic politics*—that attempts to "achieve power so that structural changes in the political, economic, and social orders might be achieved." Despite their differences, both structure-based organizing and mass mobilization share this strategic orientation. They both attempt to change the dominant institutions that affect peoples' lives, and both can sometimes clash with prefigurative politics.

The tension between waging campaigns to modify the existing political system, on the one hand, and creating alternative institutions and communities that more immediately put radical values into practice, on the other, long predates the 1960s. In the 1800s, Marx debated utopian socialists about the need for revolutionary strategy that went beyond the formation of communes and model societies. Similarly, advocates such as Gene Sharp, who worked to establish nonviolence as a strategic practice, contrasted their efforts with people whom they saw as espousing a lifestyle of pacifism, but not building effective political movements.

In the recent past, a clash between prefigurative politics and attempts to influence dominant institutions could be seen within the Occupy movement. Whereas some participants pushed for concrete political reforms—greater regulation of Wall Street, bans on corporate money in politics, a tax on millionaires, or elimination of debt for students and underwater homeowners—other Occupiers focused on the encampments themselves. They saw the liberated spaces in Zuccotti Park and beyond, with their open general assemblies and communities of mutual support, as the movement's most important contribution to social change. These spaces, they believed, had the power to prefigure a more radical and participatory democracy.

Strain between prefigurative politics and organizing traditions that focus on changing existing societal institutions persists for a simple reason: although they are not always mutually exclusive, these approaches have very distinct emphases. They present sometimes contradictory notions of how activists should behave at any given time.

Where structure-based organizing and momentum-driven campaigns attempt to alter the direction of mainstream politics, prefigurative groups function outside of the mainstream. They lean toward the creation of liberated public spaces, community centers, and alternative institutions. Activists with a strong prefigurative orientation may be involved in mass protest or civil disobedience. However, they approach such protest in a unique way. Instead of designing their actions to sway public opinion, prefigurative activists are often indifferent, or even antagonistic, to the attitudes of the media and of mainstream society. They tend to emphasize the expressive qualities of protest—how actions express the values and beliefs of participants rather than how they might affect a target.[48]

Countercultural clothing and distinctive appearance—whether it involves long hair, piercings, punk stylings, keffiyehs, or any number of other variations—help prefigurative communities create a sense of group cohesion. They reinforce the idea of an alternative culture that rejects conventional norms. Meanwhile, groups engaging in what Breines calls "strategic politics" look at the issue of personal appearance very differently. Saul Alinsky, in his book *Rules for Radicals*, takes the strategic position when he argues, "If the real radical finds that having long hair sets up psychological barriers to communication and organization, he cuts his hair."[49]

Community organizations and momentum-based drives often seek to build pragmatic coalitions as a way of more effectively pushing forward demands around a given issue. During the course of a campaign, these activists might reach out to more established unions, nonprofit organizations, or politicians to make common cause. Prefigurative politics, however, is far more wary of joining forces with those coming from outside the distinctive culture a movement has created. This is especially true if prospective allies are part of hierarchical organizations or have ties with established political parties. The extreme fear of "co-optation" among some Occupiers reflected this tendency, and it often interfered with possibilities for institutionalization in the movement. Instead of welcoming it when mainstream groups or politicians began to champion the issues of "the 99 percent," they saw this behavior as a threat.

All this highlights a certain contradiction: new movements may arise from the margins, but if they want to make change for the majority, they should not aspire to stay there.

~

There are perils in prefigurative politics, but also great strengths.

In terms of pitfalls, one problem is that, if the project of building alternative community totally eclipses attempts to communicate with the wider public and win broad support, it risks a type of self-isolation that limits possibilities for creating social and political change. Exploring this danger, writer, organizer, and Occupy activist Jonathan Matthew Smucker describes what he calls the "political identity paradox."

"Any serious social movement needs a correspondingly serious group identity that encourages a core of members to contribute an exceptional level of commitment, sacrifice, and heroics over the course of prolonged struggle," Smucker writes. "Strong group identity, however, is a double-edged sword. The stronger the identity and cohesion of the group, the more likely people are to become alienated from other groups, and from society."[50]

Experiencing this paradox, groups focused on prefiguring a new society—and preoccupied with meeting the needs of an alternative community—can become cut off from the goal of building bridges to other constituencies and winning public support. Instead of looking for ways to effectively communicate their vision to the outside world, they are prone to adopt slogans and tactics that appeal to hardcore activists but alienate the majority. These tendencies become self-defeating. As Smucker writes, "Isolated groups are hard-pressed to achieve political goals."

In the 1960s, a divide emerged between the "movement" and the "counterculture." While movement "politicos" organized rallies against the Vietnam War and were interested in directly challenging the system, members of the youth counterculture saw themselves as undermining establishment values and providing a vigorous, living example of an alternative.

This split is vividly illustrated in the documentary *Berkeley in the Sixties*. Barry Melton, lead singer for the popular psychedelic rock band Country Joe and the Fish, tells of his debates with his Marxist parents.

"We had big arguments about this stuff," Melton explains. "I tried to convince them to sell all their furniture and go to India. And they weren't going for it. And I realized that no matter how far out their political views were, because they were mighty unpopular—my parents were pretty left wing—that really they were [still] materialists. They were concerned about how the wealth was divided up."[51]

Melton's passion was for something different, a "politics of hip," in which "we were setting up a new world that was going to run parallel to the old world, but have as little to do with it as possible." He explains, "We just weren't going to deal with straight people. To us, the politicos—a lot of the leaders of the anti-war movement—were straight people because they were still concerned with the government. They were going to march on Washington. We didn't even want to know that Washington was there. We thought that eventually the whole world was just going to stop all this nonsense and start loving each other, as soon as they all got turned on."

The 1960s counterculture—with its flower children, free love, and LSD trips into new dimensions of consciousness—is easy to parody. Yet prefigurative impulses did not merely produce the flights of utopian fantasy seen at the countercultural fringes. This approach to politics also made some tremendously positive contributions to social movements. Melton's example aside, movement and counterculture were often intertwined. And the desire to live out a vibrant and participatory democracy produced groups of dedicated citizens willing to make great sacrifices for the cause of social justice.

The Student Nonviolent Coordinating Committee is one example of this. In SNCC, participants spoke of the desire to create the "beloved community"—a society that rejected bigotry and prejudice in all forms and instead embraced peace and compassion. This was not merely an external goal; rather, SNCC militants saw themselves as creating the beloved community within their organization. They built an interracial group that, in the words of historian Cheryl Greenberg, "based itself on radical egalitarianism, mutual respect, and unconditional support for every person's unique gifts and contributions. Meetings lasted until everyone had their say, in the belief that every voice counted." The strong ties fostered by this prefigurative community encouraged participants to undertake bold and dangerous acts of civil disobedience—such as SNCC's famous lunch-counter sit-ins. In this case, the aspiration to a beloved community both facilitated strategic action and had a significant impact on mainstream politics.[52]

As another example of the positive influence of prefigurative groups, alternative communities have historically been crucial in providing the first recruits for mass movements. The Quakers, a religious tradition with strong social justice and antiwar norms, are a key example. Going back to the seventeenth century, "The Quakers had little political power or influence and were a marginalized group," write authors Ori Brafman and Rod Beckstrom. "But their marginalization ultimately gave the Quakers a different kind of power. Because they were outsiders, they were forced to form their own culture, business relationships, and community."[53]

This community's prefigurative values led members to take up a variety of causes at a time when they were still ignored or despised by the general public. Perhaps most notably, Quakers served as the backbone of the movement against slavery in both the United States and Great Britain. As Claudine Ferrell writes in her book *The Abolitionist Movement*, the early story of antislavery advocacy "is, with few exceptions, the history of Quaker arguments, publications, pronouncements, and activists." Later on, Quakers would play important roles in the women's suffrage, civil rights, antiwar, and antinuclear movements.[54]

When combined thoughtfully with methods of structure-based organizing and momentum-driven revolt, prefigurative politics can be a vital component of an integrated approach to change. More than the work of any other individual, it was Gandhi's experiments in nonviolent escalation that laid the foundation for the modern field of civil resistance. But to sustain his work over a period of more than fifty years, Gandhi used a full range of social movement approaches, including structure, momentum-driven organizing, and the creation of prefigurative community.

In Gandhi's method, the Salt March and other campaigns of *satyagraha* in India produced defining whirlwinds for the cause of independence. Meanwhile, the Indian National Congress, in which Gandhi played important leadership roles, became a critical structure-based mechanism for institutionalization; indeed, it would become the country's ruling party after the end of the British Raj. Finally, with his prefigurative "constructive program," Gandhi advocated for a distinctive vision of self-reliant village life, through which he believed Indians could experience true independence and communal unity. He modeled this program by residing communally with others in a succession of *ashrams*, or intentional communities that melded religion and politics.

All these ingredients blended with one another, and together they made up a potent recipe for transformation. Members of Gandhi's *ashrams* not only prefigured new possibilities for communal life but also served as trusted nonviolent shock troops in the campaigns of *satyagraha*. Campaigns of mass disruption fed into both structure and intentional community: when these campaigns escalated, they increased the organizational clout and political sway of the Indian National Congress, and they also drew in new converts interested in collective models of living and working. Finally, when momentum died down, Congress and the ashrams were each strong enough to survive on their own through fallow periods, and they could therefore help to seed future moments of the whirlwind.

At different points in his life, Gandhi placed varying emphasis on these different modes of activism. But one of the most compelling aspects of his legacy is his interest in unifying all three. At the same time that Gandhi told his followers that they must change their own ways of living in the world, he also insisted that they organize and mobilize the wider community—and that they sometimes take the risk of rising up to do so.

⁓

The great movements of the past century have won by taking issues that were unpopular and changing the boundaries of the politically acceptable, so that advances which previously seemed impossible were made inevitable. But even after they have prevailed, movements have still had to battle for their contributions to be acknowledged. A healthy movement ecology preserves the memory of how past transformations in society have been achieved—and it draws sustenance from this history.

A peculiar irony arises when social movements are most successful. Even as an activist cause becomes accepted in the mainstream of society, many of its most longstanding advocates are erased from history. Bill Moyer notes that, in the late stages of a movement, once a firm majority of the population is convinced to support an issue, it creates a setting in which opportunists flourish. Mainstream politicians, centrist organizations, former critics, and once-recalcitrant powerbrokers all scramble to take credit for gains that have been won. Notwithstanding years of stonewalling, silence, and timidity, these people insist they, too, are repelled by segregation; that they are truly committed to expanding voting rights; that they strongly believe in marriage equality; and that the war they once had endorsed was actually the mistaken folly of their political opponents.

As sociologist Sidney Tarrow argues, "Cycles of contention are a season for sowing, but the reaping is often done in periods of demobilization that follow, by latecomers to the cause, by elites and authorities."[55]

Activists are notoriously poor at celebrating their victories. And mainstream commentators, steeped in a monolithic view of power, are notoriously stingy in recognizing the importance of grassroots efforts, preferring to point to ripe historical conditions or enlightened politicians as the source of change. "In this version of managed memory," Tom Hayden writes, "it is the Machiavellians who are credited for great reforms, never the radicals who created the climate making those reforms necessary." In the conventional top-down narrative, Hayden contends, "Abraham Lincoln abolished slavery, Woodrow Wilson passed the suffrage amendment . . . and Lyndon Johnson declared that we would overcome."[56]

Furthermore, social movement participants are the most likely to have a pained awareness of the work that still remains to be done—and therefore the least likely to feel celebratory about the gains that have been secured. For this reason, they are often missing from the victory parties.

It requires deliberate effort for movements to champion the story of what their struggle has made possible. But this effort is vital, because without it future victories are harder to achieve. In societies where history is a tale of presidents and senators, generals and CEOs, the social view of power too often remains in the shadows. The potential for what can happen when people refuse to obey must constantly be learned anew.

CONCLUSION

BY 1963, THE Dorchester retreat center near Savannah, Georgia, had emerged as a buzzing hub of activity for the civil rights movement in the American South. The site where Project C was hatched was also the home of a thriving social movement ecology.

With the help of veteran organizers at the Highlander Folk School, the Southern Christian Leadership Conference had renovated the facilities at a former missionary school located just a few miles off Georgia's Atlantic coast. Starting in 1961, the SCLC used the Dorchester center, nestled in a campus lined with moss-covered oaks, for a regular series of "citizenship schools" run by Dorothy Cotton and Septima Clark. When these educators brought in adult students from communities throughout the South for weeklong trainings, their method was rooted in the person-to-person leadership development of structure-based organizing. After a week of intensive courses, local activists were prepared to go home to run trainings in democratic rights and resistance techniques in their own towns and cities. The trainees, including such storied leaders as Fannie Lou Hamer, helped to create an infrastructure for a slow-and-steady building toward racial justice.[1]

These elements of long-term community organizing blended with a prefigurative vision of what America could become. Civil rights activists brought people together across boundaries of race, class, age, and educational attainment. And in doing this, they modeled the relationships of an integrated society in their own movement. They bound people together in a spirit of awakening and determination, and they reinforced their community through the sharing of freedom songs. One of the Dorchester trainees, Bernice Johnson Reagon, would later go on to be a central force in preserving the movement's music, through her group Sweet Honey in the Rock.

Finally, Dorchester was a place where strategies of engineered revolt were drafted and refined. In September 1963, King's inner circle returned to the retreat center to reflect once again on the state of their movement. Having experienced a remarkable victory in Birmingham four months before, they watched protests erupt throughout the South over the summer, revolts that were inspired by the success of Project C. At the September retreat, Wyatt Walker made a presentation that he called "How to Crack a Hard Core City." It represented a codification of the lessons that SCLC had learned in its experiments in nonviolent escalation, and it outlined key elements needed for a successful campaign.

In the blueprint Walker presented, "Planning in detail" was one important prerequisite; another was building tension "so great that a crisis be created." The two went hand in hand.[2]

"Spontaneous." "Unplanned." "Uncontrolled." "Emotional." When an outbreak of mass unrest captures the public spotlight, the media reaction is remarkably consistent. But those who gathered at Dorchester saw things differently. The suggestion of Walker's presentation was that the public crises that are critical in propelling change do not burst forth randomly. Rather, his talk proposed that unarmed uprising involved skills that could both be mastered by experienced practitioners and taught to new ones.

Saul Alinsky argued there "are no rules for revolution any more than there are rules for love or rules for happiness, *but* . . . there are certain central concepts of action in human politics that operate regardless of the scene or the time. To know these is basic to a pragmatic attack on the system." Within his tradition of community organizing, generations of advocates have worked to record and refine these concepts. They have created a strong base of knowledge about the processes of building structured groups made up of people who, by themselves, have little power, but who together can effectively push for justice.[3]

Following the example of Dorchester, the lineage of civil resistance has endeavored to do the same for a different mode of resistance. It has worked to fashion an ever-deeper understanding of the art of unarmed revolt. Breaking from earlier traditions of moral pacifism, its adherents have taken a most impractical idea—one previously associated merely with lofty ideals of peace and compassion—and they have demonstrated how it can have the most profound of practical impacts.

Along the way, a variety of key lessons have emerged. Momentum-driven organizing uses the tools of civil resistance to consciously spark, amplify, and harness mass protest. It highlights the importance of hybrid organizations, such as Otpor and SCLC, which can build decentralized networks to sustain protest mobilizations through multiple waves of activity. It goes beyond transactional goals by also advancing a transformational agenda, and it wins by swaying public opinion and pulling the pillars of support. It is attentive to the symbolic properties of campaigns, showing how these can sometimes be just as important as instrumental demands, if not more so. It uses disruption, sacrifice, and escalation to build tension and bring overlooked issues into the public spotlight. It aspires, at its peak, to create moments of the whirlwind, when outbreaks of decentralized action extend far outside the institutional limits of any one organization. It is willing to polarize public opinion and risk controversy with bold protests, but it maintains nonviolent discipline to ensure that it does not undermine broad-based support for its cause. And it is conscious of the need to work with other organizing traditions in order to institutionalize gains and foster alternative communities that can sustain resistance over the long term.

In advancing all of these ideas, momentum-driven organizing contends that the study of mass mobilization has been too often neglected and that reversing this neglect can be essential to the success of future social movements in the United States and beyond. Many different kinds of activity are needed for citizens to provoke, secure, and sustain social progress. The point of momentum-driven organizing is not to deny the contributions of other approaches. But it is to suggest a simple and urgent idea: that uprising can be a craft, and that this craft can change our world.

Those who practice it tell us that outbreaks of widespread disruption, although commonly misunderstood, are neither flukes nor fleeting failures. Rather, they are forces that can be guided with the exercise of conscious and careful effort. Indeed, if the growing legion of these practitioners is right, few forces will have as significant a role in shaping the contours of public life in the years to come.

ACKNOWLEDGMENTS

This Is an Uprising was made possible by a rich community of friends, family members, organizers, colleagues, and social movement thinkers who provided guidance and assistance in innumerable ways as this project developed over a period of more than a decade. The authors would like to express their deep gratitude to all those who helped make this book a reality.

We would like to give special thanks to our dedicated team of readers for thoughtful edits and suggestions that greatly improved our drafts of the manuscript: Rebecca Tuhus-Dubrow, Rajiv Sicora, Joshua Joy Kamensky, Stephanie Greenwood, Eric Augenbraun, and Arthur Phillips. Additionally, Stephen Zunes, Ivan Marovic, Jeremy Varon, and Mladen Joksic provided expert review of chapter drafts, and their insights into social movements were invaluable.

Eric Stoner offered critical feedback at many stages, and we benefited from his editorial leadership at *Waging Nonviolence*, a flagship publication for thinking about civil resistance. Eric graciously provided housing for Paul on frequent trips to New York City, and these visits offered occasion for formative conversations about the theory and practice of strategic nonviolence. The authors would also like to thank the editors at *Dissent*, *Yes! Magazine*, and the *New Internationalist* for providing space for us to develop ideas about processes of social change that were later incorporated into the book.

Sam Pullen and the community at the Center for the Working Poor have been constant sources of support over many years. Paulina

Gonzalez and Kai Newkirk served as a sort of brain trust at the center; they worked intensively both to develop ideas about integrating structure-based organizing and mass mobilization, and to apply these ideas in practice—first in the immigrant rights movement and later in 99Rise. Kai also provided essential input during the drafting and editing of the book. We are grateful for all of these contributions.

Carlos Saavedra, a true master of social movement pedagogy, helped to develop and clarify many of the concepts presented in this book, and he was a driving force behind the creation of the Momentum Training. Other members of the training's founding team—including Belinda Rodriguez, Max Berger, Mirja Hitzemann, Kate Werning, and Guido Girgenti—made great contributions in thinking about how to most effectively teach different organizing models to a wide range of activists. In addition, Lissy Romanow and the Ayni crew have provided crucial assistance. We also thank Brooke Lehman, Gregg Osofsky, and the team at the Watershed Center for their support of these ideas and the training.

Kate Aronoff and Yessenia Gutierrez, the research assistants who worked on this book during the most intensive period of writing, each contributed in countless ways, and we thank them for their talent, creativity, and resourcefulness. Apinya Pokachaiyapat and Madeleine Resch provided additional assistance, for which we are grateful.

We thank Anna Ghosh for skillfully helping to guide this book from conception to publication, as well as Alessandra Bastagli and the team at Nation Books for their commitment to this project and their hard work in bringing it to life.

This book was a family project in more ways than one. We thank our mom, Joan, for all of her love and care, and our brother, Francis, for his consistent support and his many insights into organizing and political struggle. Without the generosity of Nan Beer, David Wuchinich, and Sarah Wuchinich, it would not have been possible to meet the final deadline for completion of the manuscript, and we thank them for their generosity and selflessness.

Finally, we owe a deep debt to Rebekah Berndt and Rosslyn Wuchinich, who, among many other contributions, provided resolute emotional support, steady encouragement, and insightful chapter readings. We are profoundly grateful for their belief in our work. This book is a better one as a result of their efforts.

NOTES

INTRODUCTION

1. Various historians and civil rights movement veterans provide slightly different tallies of the number of participants in the retreat. See Andrew Young, *An Easy Burden: The Civil Rights Movement and the Transformation of America* (Waco, TX: Baylor University Press, 2008), 188; Taylor Branch, *Parting the Waters: America in the King Years 1954–63* (New York: Simon & Schuster, 1988), 688; and David J. Garrow, *Bearing the Cross: Martin Luther King, Jr., and the Southern Christian Leadership Conference* (New York: Random House, 1986), 225.

2. News sources as quoted in Garrow, *Bearing the Cross*, 213, 216. On the Albany Movement, see Lee W. Formwalt, "Albany Movement," New Georgia Encyclopedia, February 3, 2015, http://www.georgiaencyclopedia.org/articles/history-archaeology/albany-movement; Anthony Phalen, "1961: The Albany Movement campaigns for full integration in Georgia (Fall 1961–Summer 1962)," Global Nonviolent Action Database, November 6, 2009, http://nvdatabase.swarthmore.edu/content/albany-movement-campaigns-full-integration-georgia-fall-1961-summer-1962; and "Albany GA, Movement (Oct. 1961–Aug. 1962)," Civil Rights Movement Veterans, http://www.crmvet.org/tim/timhis61.htm#1961albany.

3. See Aldon D. Morris, *The Origins of the Civil Rights Movement: Black Communities Organizing for Change* (New York: The Free Press, 1984), 254; and Adam Fairclough, *To Redeem the Soul of America: The Southern Christian Leadership Conference and Martin Luther King, Jr.* (Athens: University of Georgia Press, 1987), 166–169.

4. On the attack on Cole, see *Encyclopedia of African American Music*, Vol. 3, ed. Emmett George Price (Santa Barbara, California: ABC-CLIO, 2011), 211; Brian Ward, "Civil Rights and Rock and Roll: Revisiting the Nat King Cole Attack of 1956," *OAH Magazine of History* 24, no. 2 (April 2010): 21–24, April 2010, http://maghis.oxford journals.org/content/24/2/21.extract; and "In Birmingham: Negro Singer Nat (King) Cole Attacked; 6 White Men Held," *Florence Times* 97, no. 12 (April 11, 1956), http://news.google.com/newspapers?nid=1842&dat=19560410&id=ZgQsAAAAIBAJ&sjid=jsYEAAAAIBAJ&pg=1533,1109350. On the closing of public parks, see Diane

McWhorter, *Carry Me Home: Birmingham, Alabama: The Climactic Battle of the Civil Rights Revolution* (New York: Simon & Schuster, 2001), 229.

5. As quoted in Garrow, *Bearing the Cross*, 229.

6. Martin Luther King Jr., "Letter from Birmingham City Jail," in *A Testament of Hope: The Essential Writings and Speeches of Martin Luther King, Jr.*, ed. James M. Washington (New York: HarperCollins Publishers, 1986), 291, 295.

7. Morris, *Origins of the Civil Rights Movement*, 274.

8. See "Wyatt Tee Walker," in *Voices of Freedom: Oral History of the Civil Rights Movement from the 1950s Through the 1980s* (New York: Bantam Books, 1990), 126; Andrew Manis, interview with Dr. Wyatt Walker, conducted at Canaan Baptist Church, New York City, Birmingham Public Library: Digital Collections, April 20, 1989, http://cdm16044.contentdm.oclc.org/cdm/ref/collection/p15099coll2/id/69; and Branch, *Parting the Waters*, 690.

9. Martin Luther King Jr., *The Autobiography of Martin Luther King, Jr.*, ed. Clayborne Carson (New York: Warner Books, 1998), 174.

10. Young, *An Easy Burden*, 138.

11. In Davis W. Houck and David E. Dixon, *Rhetoric, Religion, and the Civil Rights Movement 1954–1965* (Waco, TX: Baylor University Press, 2006), 539.

12. Young, *An Easy Burden*, 188.

13. Michael Kazin, "Stop Looking for the Next JFK," *Dissent*, November 21, 2013, http://www.dissentmagazine.org/blog/stop-looking-for-the-next-jfk.

14. See Ishaan Tharoor, "Occupy Wall Street Protests Spread," *Time*, December 7, 2011, http://content.time.com/time/specials/packages/article/0,28804,2101344_2101369_2101667,00.html; Marc Fisher, "In Tunisia, Act of One Fruit Vendor Sparks Wave of Revolution Through Arab World," *Washington Post*, March 26, 2011, http://www.washingtonpost.com/world/in-tunisia-act-of-one-fruit-vendor-sparks-wave-of-revolution-through-arab-world/2011/03/16/AFjfsueB_story.html; and H.D.S. Greenway, "Of Men and Last Straws," *New York Times*, April 19, 2011, http://www.nytimes.com/2011/04/20/opinion/20iht-edgreenway20.html.

15. See "Milosevic Under Pressure to Quit," *The People* (London), October 1, 2000, http://www.thefreelibrary.com/MILOSEVIC+UNDER+PRESSURE+TO+QUIT.-a065627113; Greg Bloom, "U.S. Can't Buy Revolution," *Moscow Times*, December 23, 2004, http://www.themoscowtimes.com/sitemap/free/2004/12/article/us-cant-buy-revolution/226153.html; and Karin Brulliard, "More Immigration Demonstrations Planned," *Washington Post*, August 31, 2006, http://www.washingtonpost.com/wp-dyn/content/article/2006/08/30/AR2006083003161.html.

16. Morris, *Origins of the Civil Rights Movement*, vi, xiii.

17. Branch, *Parting the Waters*, 825.

18. King, *Autobiography of Martin Luther King, Jr.*, 153.

19. See King, *Autobiography of Martin Luther King, Jr.*, 167; and Branch, *Parting the Waters*, 631.

20. King, *Autobiography of Martin Luther King, Jr.*, 167.

21. "Pride and power of nonviolence" quote can be found in King, *Autobiography of Martin Luther King, Jr.*, 211.

CHAPTER ONE: THE STRATEGIC TURN

1. Einstein letter as quoted in Mairi Mackay, "A Dictator's Worst Nightmare," CNN, June 25, 2012, http://www.cnn.com/2012/06/23/world/gene-sharp-revolutionary /index.html.

2. See James VanHise, interview with Gene Sharp, "Nonviolence and Civilian-Based Defense," *Fragments*, June 1983, http://www.fragmentsweb.org/fourtx/sharpint.html; and Jeff Severns-Guntzel, interview with Gene Sharp, "Lessons from the Godfather: Interview with Gene Sharp," *UTNE*, July–August 2010, http://www.utne.com/Politics /Gene-Sharp-Interview-Power-of-Nonviolence.aspx.

3. As quoted in Philip Shishkin, "American Revolutionary: Quiet Boston Scholar Inspires Rebels Around the World," *Wall Street Journal*, September 13, 2008, http:// online.wsj.com/article/SB122127204268531319.html.

4. "Indeed, the greatest practitioners of nonviolence have viewed it not so much as a way to encounter adversaries, or even to change the world," wrote historians Alice Lynd and Staughton Lynd in a 1966 appraisal that was typical for the era, "but rather as a journey in search of truth." Staughton Lynd and Alice Lynd, eds., *Nonviolence in America: A Documentary History* (Maryknoll, NY: Orbis Books, 1995), xlv.

5. Metta Spencer, interview with Gene Sharp, "Gene Sharp 101," *Peace Magazine*, July–September 2003, http://peacemagazine.org/archive/v19n3p16.htm.

6. See Gene Sharp, *Gandhi as a Political Strategist* (Boston: Porter Sargent Publishers, 1979), 252, and Gene Sharp, *The Politics of Nonviolent Action: Part One—Power and Struggle* (Boston: Porter Sargent Publishers, 1973), vi. As noted later, Sharp himself avoids using "nonviolence" as a noun, preferring to use the word as an adjective. Instead of seeing himself as a proponent of "strategic nonviolence," he advocates "strategic nonviolent action."

7. Gene Sharp, *Waging Nonviolent Struggle: 20th Century Practice and 21st Century Potential* (Boston: Porter Sargent Publishers, 2005), 21.

8. "Waging of 'Battles'" quote in Sharp, *Politics of Nonviolent Action: Part One*, 67.

9. Gene Sharp, *The Politics of Nonviolent Action: Part Three—the Dynamics of Nonviolent Action* (Boston: Porter Sargent Publishers, 1973), 556, 755.

10. As quoted in Sharp, *Politics of Nonviolent Action: Part Three*, 681.

11. See Paul Buhle (editor), Sabrina Jones, Gary Dumm, and Nick Thorkelson (artists), *Radical Jesus: A Graphic History of Faith* (Harrisonburg, VA: Herald Press, 2013), 111.

12. Sharp, *Waging Nonviolent Struggle*, 436.

13. Sharp, *Politics of Nonviolent Action: Part Three*, 635.

14. Ibid., 741.

15. On Sharp's arguments with pacifist groups, see Sharp, *Gandhi as a Political Strategist*, 251.

16. See Adam Winkler, "MLK and His Guns," Huffington Post, January 17, 2011, http://www.huffingtonpost.com/adam-winkler/mlk-and-his-guns_b_810132.html.

17. For an example of the appropriation of Martin Luther King by pro-gun groups, see: "Martin Luther King, Jr.—Man of Peace but No Pushover," Gun Owners of

America, http://gunowners.wordpress.com/2013/01/21/martin-luther-king-jr-man-of-peace-but-no-pushover/.

18. Phone threat as quoted in Martin Luther King Jr., *The Autobiography of Martin Luther King, Jr.*, ed. Clayborne Carson (New York: Warner Books, 1998), 77.

19. See King, *Autobiography of Martin Luther King, Jr.*, 54; David J. Garrow, *Bearing the Cross: Martin Luther King, Jr., and the Southern Christian Leadership Conference* (New York: Random House, 1986), 68, 72; and Taylor Branch, *Parting the Waters: America in the King Years 1954–63* (New York: Simon & Schuster, 1988), 179.

20. Garrow, *Bearing the Cross*, 73.

21. Branch, *Parting the Waters*, 180.

22. For King on Muste, see Branch, *Parting the Waters*, 179. For King on Black Power, see King, *Autobiography of Martin Luther King, Jr.*, 317. On nonviolence as a "way of life," see King, *Autobiography of Martin Luther King, Jr.*, 68. On armed guards, see Garrow, *Bearing the Cross*, 232.

23. Clark as quoted in Michael Eric Dyson, *April 4, 1968: Martin Luther King, Jr.'s Death and How It Changed America* (New York: Basic Civitas Books, 2008), 8. Details of the attack on King also in Garrow, *Bearing the* Cross, 221.

24. King, *Autobiography of Martin Luther King, Jr.*, 68.

25. Branch, *Parting the Waters*, 205.

26. Barbara Ransby, *Ella Baker and the Black Freedom Movement: A Radical Democratic Vision* (Chapel Hill: University of North Carolina Press, 2003), 175. Ransby quotes Aldon Morris on the SCLC's self-image as the "political arm of the black church."

27. As quoted in Garrow, *Bearing the Cross*, 116.

28. See Branch, *Parting the Waters*, 466.

29. See John Lewis with Michael D'Orso, *Walking with the Wind: A Memoir of the Movement* (New York: Simon & Schuster, 1998), 166.

30. See Andrew Young, *An Easy Burden: The Civil Rights Movement and the Transformation of America* (Waco, TX: Baylor University Press, 2008), 186.

31. Ibid., 186.

32. Sharp cites early precedents for nonviolent action in *Politics of Nonviolent Action: Part One*, 75–78. For discussion of Tolstoy's influence on Gandhi, see Sharp, *Gandhi as a Political Strategist*, 47; Mohandas K. Gandhi, *An Autobiography: The Story of My Experiments with Truth* (Boston: Beacon Press, 1957), 137; and Anthony J. Parel, "Gandhi and Tolstoy," in M. P. Mathai, M. S. John, Siby K. Joseph, *Meditations on Gandhi: A Ravindra Varma Festschrift* (New Delhi: Concept, 2002), 96–112.

33. Martin Luther King Jr., *Stride Toward Freedom: The Montgomery Story* (New York: HarperCollins, 1958), 97.

34. Sharp, *Gandhi as a Political Strategist*, 57.

35. As quoted in Metta Spencer, interview with Gene Sharp, "Gene Sharp 101," *Peace Magazine*, July–September 2003, http://peacemagazine.org/archive/v19n3p16.htm.

36. Sharp, *Politics of Nonviolent Action: Part One*, 101.

37. Ibid., vi.

38. Sharp, *Waging Nonviolent Struggle*, 437.

39. Stephen Zunes, interview with the authors, June 21, 2013.

40. See Ruaridh Arrow, "Gene Sharp: Author of the Nonviolent Revolution Rule-book," BBC News, February 21, 2011, http://www.bbc.co.uk/news/world-middle -east-12522848.

41. Sharp, *Politics of Nonviolent Action: Part Three*, 808–810.

42. Among historians there is debate about how well formed the SCLC's scheme actually was, particularly at the time of the initial Dorchester retreat. The cloak-and-dagger codename of "Project C" reflected Wyatt Walker's flair for the dramatic, and some scholars, led by Glenn Eskew, charge that Walker's after-the-fact interviews about his preparations also contain an element of theatrical self-aggrandizement—a streak that has colored the historical record ever since. These scholars take issue with the account provided in Taylor Branch's monumental biography of King. Relying on interviews with Walker, Branch suggests that, after Walker presented the plan at the Dorchester retreat, "not a comma of the blueprint was altered." See Glenn Eskew, *But for Birmingham: The Local and National Movements in the Civil Rights Struggle* (Chapel Hill: University of North Carolina Press, 1997), 209–229, 376nn40, 42; and Branch, *Parting the Waters*, 690.

43. John H. Britton, "Man Behind Martin Luther King Jr.: Tough-Minded Cleric Is Fuel," *Jet*, March 12, 1964, http://books.google.com/books?id=68EDAAA AMBAJ&pg=PA3&dq=jet&source=gbs_toc&cad=2#v=onepage&q=jet&f=false.

44. Martin Luther King Jr., "Letter from Birmingham City Jail," in *A Testament of Hope: The Essential Writings and Speeches of Martin Luther King, Jr.*, ed. James M. Washington (New York: HarperCollins, 1986), 291.

45. See Ralph David Abernathy, *And the Walls Came Tumbling Down: An Autobiography* (New York: HarperCollins, 1989), 235.

46. See Aldon D. Morris, *The Origins of the Civil Rights Movement: Black Communities Organizing for Change* (New York: The Free Press, 1984), 260.

47. Branch, *Parting the Waters*, 707.

48. See Adam Fairclough, *To Redeem the Soul of America: The Southern Christian Leadership Conference and Martin Luther King, Jr.* (Athens: University of Georgia Press, 1987), 118.

49. See Garrow, *Bearing the Cross*, 240.

50. Ibid., 242.

51. See King, *Autobiography of Martin Luther King, Jr.*, 206.

52. The details of this incident are disputed, varying somewhat between different historical accounts. Descriptions can be found in: Branch, *Parting the Waters*, 710; Diane McWhorter, *Carry Me Home: Birmingham, Alabama: The Climactic Battle of the Civil Rights Revolution* (New York: Simon & Schuster, 2001), 312; and Eskew, *But for Birmingham*, 226. See also: statement by Leroy Allen, "On the Use of Police Dogs During the 1963 Palm Sunday Demonstrations in Birmingham," Documents on Human Rights in Alabama, April 27, 1963, http://www.archives.state.al.us/teacher/rights/lesson3 /doc6-4.html.

53. Garrow, *Bearing the Cross*, 239–240.

54. King, "Letter from Birmingham City Jail," 295.

55. See Garrow, *Bearing the Cross*, 250.

56. Ibid., 247.

57. Fairclough, *To Redeem the Soul of America*, 135.

58. Ibid., 134–135.

59. As quoted in Sheryl Gay Stolberg, "Shy U.S. Intellectual Created Playbook Used in a Revolution," *New York Times*, February 16, 2011, http://www.nytimes.com /2011/02/17/world/middleeast/17sharp.html.

60. Thierry Meyssan, "The Albert Einstein Institution: Non-Violence According to the CIA," VoltaireNet.org, January 4, 2005, http://www.voltairenet.org/article30032 .html.

61. On the use of Sharp's work in Palestine, see Amitabh Pal, "Gene Sharp's Nonvio-lent Impact," *The Progressive*, February 17, 2011, http://www.progressive.org/ap021711 .html.

62. As quoted in Mackay, "A Dictator's Worst Nightmare."

63. Stephen Lerner, "A New Insurgency Can Only Arise Outside the Progressive and Labor Establishment," *New Labor Forum* 20, no. 3 (Fall 2011): 9–13.

CHAPTER TWO: STRUCTURE AND MOVEMENT

1. See Peter Dreier, "Glenn Beck's Attack on Frances Fox Piven," *Dissent*, January 24, 2011, http://www.dissentmagazine.org/online_articles/glenn-becks-attack-on-frances -fox-piven; and Glenn Beck, "Cloward, Piven and the Fundamental Transformation of America," Fox News, January 5, 2010, http://www.foxnews.com/story/2010/01/05 /cloward-piven-and-fundamental-transformation-america/. Image available at http:// www.pubtheo.com/images/beck-revolution.jpg.

2. Moberg offered this list when reflecting on the work of National People's Action. See David Moberg, "New Rules for Radicals: How George Goehl Is Transforming Com-munity Organizing," *In These Times*, February 12, 2014, http://inthesetimes.com /article/16144/new_rules_for_radicals. Quotes from Saul Alinsky appear in *Rules for Radicals: A Pragmatic Primer for Realistic Radicals* (New York: Vintage Books, 1989), 126–130.

3. Mary Beth Rogers, *Cold Anger: A Story of Faith and Power Politics* (Denton: Uni-versity of North Texas Press, 1990), 85.

4. As quoted in Eric Norden, interview with Saul Alinsky, *Playboy*, March 1972, http://britell.com/alinsky.html.

5. Ibid.

6. Alinsky, *Rules for Radicals*, 3. On the use of Alinsky by FreedomWorks, see Eliza-beth Williamson, "Two Ways to Play the 'Alinsky' Card," *Wall Street Journal*, January 23, 2012, http://online.wsj.com/article/SB10001424052970204624204577177272926154 002.html.

7. Frank Bardacke, *Trampling Out the Vintage: Cesar Chavez and the Two Souls of the United Farm Workers* (London: Verso, 2011), 68.

8. David Walls, "Power to the People: Thirty-Five Years of Community Organizing," *The Workbook*, Summer 1994, 52–55. Updated version as posted at http://www.sonoma .edu/users/w/wallsd/community-organizing.shtml.

9. See P. David Finks, *The Radical Vision of Saul Alinsky* (Mahwah, NJ: Paulist Press, 1984), 261.

10. Arlene Stein, "Between Organization and Movement: ACORN and the Alinsky Model of Community Organizing," *Berkeley Journal of Sociology* 31 (January 1, 1986): 96, http://www.jstor.org/stable/41035376.

11. Edward T. Chambers, *Roots for Radicals: Organizing for Power, Action, and Justice* (New York: Bloomsbury Academic, 2003), 80–81.

12. See Alinsky, *Rules for Radicals*, xx; and Nicholas von Hoffman, *Radical: A Portrait of Saul Alinsky* (New York: Nation Books, 2010), 155.

13. See Mark R. Warren, *Dry Bones Rattling: Community Building to Revitalize American Democracy* (Princeton, NJ: Princeton University Press, 2001), 31.

14. Chambers, *Roots for Radicals*, 107.

15. Stein, "Between Organization and Movement," 94.

16. Von Hoffman quotes on King in, *Radical*, 68–74.

17. As quoted in Sanford D. Horwitt, *Let Them Call Me Rebel: Saul Alinsky—His Life and Legacy* (New York: Knopf, 1989), 469, and in von Hoffman, *Radical*, 72.

18. Alinsky, *Rules for Radicals*, xiii–xiv.

19. Saul Alinsky, *Reveille for Radicals* (New York: Vintage Books, 1989), 228.

20. See Stein, "Between Organization and Movement," 98.

21. Frances Fox Piven, *Challenging Authority: How Ordinary People Change America* (Lanham, MD: Rowman & Littlefield, 2006), 1.

22. See Frances Fox Piven, *Who's Afraid of Frances Fox Piven: The Essential Writings of the Professor Glenn Beck Loves to Hate* (New York: The New Press, 2011), 244–245.

23. Francis Fox Piven quote from interview with the authors, March 5, 2015. Piven and Cloward quotes from Piven, *Who's Afraid of Frances Fox Piven*, 9, 17.

24. See Doug McAdam and Hilary Schaffer Boudet, *Putting Social Movements in Their Place: Explaining Opposition to Energy Projects in the United States, 2000–2005* (Cambridge: Cambridge University Press, 2012), 4; and Frances Fox Piven and Richard A. Cloward, "Collective Protest: A Critique of Resource Mobilization Theory," *International Journal of Politics, Culture, and Society* 4, no. 4 (Summer 1991): 435, http://www.jstor.org/stable/20007011.

25. Doug McAdam and W. Richard Scott, "Organizations and Movements," in *Social Movements and Organization Theory*, ed. Gerald F. Davis, Doug McAdam, W. Richard Scott, and Mayer N. Zald (Cambridge: Cambridge University Press, 2005), 6.

26. See Sidney Tarrow, *Power in Movement: Social Movements and Contentious Politics* (Cambridge: Cambridge University Press, 1998), 16; and McAdam and Boudet, *Putting Social Movements in Their Place*, 17.

27. Frances Fox Piven and Richard A. Cloward, *Poor People's Movements: Why They Succeed, How They Fail* (New York: Vintage Books, 1979), xv.

28. Frances Fox Piven, "Symposium: Poor People's Movements: Retrospective Comments," *Perspectives on Politics* 1, no. 4 (December 2003): 707.

29. See Piven and Cloward, *Poor People's Movements*, 96; and Piven, "Retrospective Comments," 709.

30. Piven and Cloward, *Poor People's Movements*, xv.

31. Ibid., xi.

32. Ibid., xxi–xxii.

33. Chris Maisano, "From Protest to Disruption: Frances Fox Piven on Occupy Wall Street," Democratic Socialists of America, October 2011, http://www.dsausa.org /from_protest_to_disruption_frances_fox_piven_on_occupy_wall_street.

34. Piven and Cloward, *Poor People's Movements*, xi.

35. Ibid., xxi.

36. Charles M. Payne, *I've Got the Light of Freedom: The Organizing Tradition and the Mississippi Freedom Struggle* (Berkeley: University of California Press, 1995), 3 (emphasis added).

37. Stokely Carmichael, *Ready for Revolution: The Life and Struggles of Stokely Carmichael (Kwame Ture)* (New York: Scribner, 2003), 445.

38. Ibid., 445.

39. As quoted in Sanford Schram, "The Praxis of *Poor People's Movements*: Strategy and Theory in Dissensus Politics," *Perspectives on Politics* 1, no. 4 (December 2003): 715.

40. See Frances Fox Piven and Richard A. Cloward, "Foreword," in *Roots to Power: A Manual for Grassroots Organizing*, 2nd ed., ed. Lee Staples (Westport, CT: Praeger, 2004), xvi; and Joseph G. Peschek, "American Politics Today: An Interview with Frances Fox Piven," *Common Dreams*, September 19, 2010, http://www.commondreams.org /view/2010/09/19-4; and Piven and Cloward, *Poor People's Movement*, xvi, 174.

41. Frances Fox Piven, interview with the authors, March 5, 2015.

42. In her book *Stir It Up*, Rinku Sen provides a history of such internal challenges: Rinku Sen, *Stir It Up: Lessons in Community Organizing and Advocacy* (San Francisco: Jossey-Bass, 2003), xlix–lxv. See also Stein, "Between Organization and Movement," 111–112. More recently, David Moberg profiled George Goehl's efforts in "New Rules for Radicals."

43. See Rogers, *Cold Anger*, 95–96; and Michael Gecan, *Going Public: An Organizer's Guide to Citizen Action* (New York: Anchor Books, 2004), 9.

44. See von Hoffman, *Radical*, xiii, 167; and Alinsky, *Rules for Radicals*, 169.

45. See Stanley Nelson, "Roster of Freedom Riders," in *Freedom Riders* (American Experience Films, 2011), documentary film, http://www.pbs.org/wgbh/americanexperi ence/freedomriders/people/roster; and Terry Sullivan, "The Freedom Rides: Were They in Vain?," *The Register: Diocese of Peoria Edition*, July 22, 1962, http://www.crmvet.org /riders/frvain.htm.

46. See Gavin Musynske, "Freedom Riders End Racial Segregation in Southern U.S. Public Transit, 1961," Global Nonviolent Action Database, December 2009, http:// nvdatabase.swarthmore.edu/content/freedom-riders-end-racial-segregation-southern -us-public-transit-1961.

47. Stanley Nelson, "Transcript," in *Freedom Riders* (American Experience Films, 2011), documentary film, http://www.pbs.org/wgbh/americanexperience/freedom riders/about/transcript.

48. See Charles Person, video interview, in *Freedom Riders—Charles Person* (PBA30, May 3, 2011), http://video.pba.org/video/1907104380/; and "Transcript," in *Freedom Riders*.

49. Horwitt, *Let Them Call Me Rebel*, 400.

50. Ibid., 401.

51. Ibid., 401–404.

52. Piven and Cloward, *Poor People's Movements*, 358–359.

53. Piven and Cloward quote Alinsky in their foreword to Lee Staples, *Roots to Power*, xv.

54. See Piven and Cloward, *Poor People's Movements*, 37; and Piven, "Symposium," 708.

CHAPTER THREE: THE HYBRID

1. See David S. Bennahum, "The Internet Revolution," *Wired*, April 1997, http://archive.wired.com/wired/archive/5.04/ff_belgrad_pr.html; Chris Hedges, "100,000 Serbs Take to Street Against Milosevic," *New York Times*, November 26, 1996, http://www.nytimes.com/1996/11/26/world/100000-serbs-take-to-streets-against-milosevic.html; and "Serb Protesters Festive Amid Signs of Military Backing," CNN, December 29, 1996, http://www.cnn.com/WORLD/9612/29/yugo/.

2. On the OSCE, see Srdja Popovic, Slobodan Djinovic, Andrej Milivojevic, Hardy Merriman, and Ivan Marovic, *Canvas Core Curriculum: A Guide to Effective Nonviolent Struggle* (Serbia: CANVAS, 2007), 269. The phrase "The Internet Revolution" was used in a *Wired* magazine feature of that name by David S. Bennahum. As with virtually every other use of the phrase since, the actual importance of online technologies in organizing and propelling the uprising is disputed. It may be telling that this prominent early appearance of the phrase ended up being hyperbole, because the mass protests of 1996–1997 fizzled.

3. As quoted in Bennahum, "The Internet Revolution."

4. See Matthew Collin, *The Time of the Rebels: Youth Resistance Movements and 21st Century Revolutions* (London: Profile Books, 2007), 11–12.

5. See Tina Rosenberg, *Join the Club: How Peer Pressure Can Transform the World* (New York: W. W. Norton, 2011), 220.

6. See Rosenberg, *Join the Club*, 221.

7. Ivan Marovic, "Yes Lab Creative Activism Thursdays with Ivan Marovic," April 10, 2010, https://youtu.be/dleNVu0PNsI.

8. Ivan Marovic, "Tavaana Interview: Ivan Marovic, Part 2," Tavaana, May 3, 2010, https://www.youtube.com/watch?v=iQMPtV00Gtw.

9. Marovic, "Yes Lab Creative Activism Thursdays."

10. Ivan Marovic, interview with the authors, February 26, 2015.

11. Ivan Marovic, interview with the authors, September 20, 2013.

12. Regarding groups other than the political parties, analyst Ivan Vejvoda lists a variety of prominent civil society organizations operating in Serbia in the 1990s. See Vejvoda, "Civil Society versus Slobodan Milosevic: Serbia, 1991–2000," in *Civil Resistance and Power Politics: The Experience of Non-violent Action from Gandhi to the Present*, ed. Adam Roberts and Timothy Garton Ash (Oxford: Oxford University Press, 2009).

13. Ivan Marovic, interview with the authors, September 20, 2013.

14. Ibid.

15. See Collin, *Time of the Rebels*, 4; and Danijela Nenadic and Nenad Belcevic, "Serbia—Nonviolent Struggle for Democracy: The Role of Otpor," in *People Power: Unarmed Resistance and Global Solidarity*, ed. Howard Clark (London: Pluto Press, 2009), 26. Vladimir Ilic as quoted in Nenadic and Belcevic.

16. Nenadic and Belcevic, "Serbia—Nonviolent Struggle for Democracy," 28.

17. See Collin, *Time of the Rebels*, 22; and Rosenberg, *Join the Club*, 231.

18. See "Barrel of Laughs," Narco News TV, June 15, 2011, https://www.youtube.com/watch?v=vc1CcxHwypE.

19. Nenadic and Belcevic, "Serbia—Nonviolent Struggle for Democracy," 29.

20. On Radio B92, see Vejvoda, "Civil Society versus Slobodan Milosevic," 298.

21. Ivan Marovic, interview with the authors, February 26, 2015.

22. Jovanovic as quoted in Tina Rosenberg, *Join the Club*, 220. Ivan Marovic quoted from "Tavaana Interview: Ivan Marovic, Part 3," Tavaana, May 14, 2010, https://www.youtube.com/watch?v=Q87fu530bfo. See Rosenberg, *Join the Club*, 220–221.

23. Ivan Marovic as quoted in "Interview with Tavaana," May 13, 2010, https://www.youtube.com/watch?v=Kbfbip-JOsw. Vladimir Ilic's research published in Ilic, "Otpor—In or Beyond Politics," *Helsinki Files No. 5* (Belgrade, Serbia: Helsinki Committee for Human Rights in Serbia, 2001), http://www.helsinki.org.rs/hfiles02.html.

24. Ivan Marovic, interview with the authors, February 26, 2015.

25. Marovic, "Tavaana Interview, Ivan Marovic, Part 3."

26. Nenadic and Belcevic quoted from "Serbia—Nonviolent Struggle for Democracy," 28.

27. As quoted in Rosenberg, *Join the Club*, 242–243.

28. Marovic, "Tavaana Interview, Ivan Marovic, Part 4," Tavaana, May 14, 2010, https://www.youtube.com/watch?v=WQkq_qtB8YE.

29. As quoted in Collin, *Time of the Rebels*, 24.

30. The arrest of "Sixty-seven activists in thirteen cities" cited in Collin, *Time of the Rebels*, 30. Regarding other arrest numbers, Danijela Nenadic and Nenad Belcevic cite 1,559 arrests by October 2000 in "Serbia—Nonviolent Struggle for Democracy," 32. Tina Rosenberg cites at least 2,500 arrests of Otpor activists in *Join the Club*, 249. Threats against Popovic reported in Rosenberg, *Join the Club*, 221, 226, and in Collin, *Time of the Rebels*, 17. The threat against Marovic is as quoted in Collin, *Time of the Rebels*, 46.

31. The timing of Marko's arrival in the latter incident is a matter of some debate. One account can be found in Collin, *Time of the Rebels*, 36–37. "You will not be the last one . . . ," as quoted in Collin, *Time of the Rebels*, 37.

32. Ilic quoted from "Otpor—In or Beyond Politics." Otpor posters as described in Rosenberg, *Join the Club*, 251–252.

33. As quoted in Joshua Paulson, "Removing the Dictator in Serbia—1996–2000," in *Waging Nonviolent Struggle: 20th Century Practice and 21st Century Potential*, ed. Gene Sharp (Boston: Porter Sargent Publishers, 2005), 323.

34. "Part political movement, part social club" from Roger Cohen, "Who Really Brought Down Milosevic?," *New York Times*, November 26, 2000, http://www.nytimes.com/2000/11/26/magazine/who-really-brought-down-milosevic.html.

35. Ivan Marovic, interview with the authors, April 24, 2015.

36. Attendance numbers for Otpor's Congress cited in Paulson, "Removing the Dictator in Serbia," 319. The number of Otpor members overall is debated. Vladimir Ilic

cites 60,000 as the number claimed by Otpor's Belgrade office, but he believes this count to be inflated; see Ilic, "Otpor—In or Beyond Politics." Ivan Vejvoda cites 18,000 members throughout the country; see Vejvoda, "Civil Society versus Slobodan Milosevic," 308. On the higher side, Roger Cohen cites 70,000 Otpor members in Cohen, "Who Really Brought Down Milosevic?"

37. On the repression of Otpor and allied media outlets, see Collin, *Time of the Rebels*, 39, and Rosenberg, *Join the Club*, 264. "An average of more than seven arrests of activists per day" as cited in Rosenberg, *Join the Club*, 249. Nenadic and Belcevic quoted from "Serbia—Nonviolent Struggle for Democracy," 31.

38. See Collin, *Time of the Rebels*, 52; and Rosenberg, *Join the Club*, 230–231.

39. On voter turnout among youth, see Paulson, "Removing the Dictator in Serbia," 326; and Rosenberg, *Join the Club*, 272.

40. See Paulson, "Removing the Dictator in Serbia," 327.

41. The *New York Times* as quoted in Joshua Paulson, "Removing the Dictator in Serbia," 328. Regarding the Kolubara coal mines, Paulson cites 7,500 workers on strike in "Removing the Dictator in Serbia," 329; Ivan Marovic cites September 29 as the beginning of the strike in "What Happened on October 5th: How Did the Plan Play Out?," Retired Revolutionary, February 1, 2012, http://www.retiredrevolutionary.com/2012/02/how-plan-played-out.html. On the copper miners in Majdanpek, see Paulson, "Removing the Dictator in Serbia," 332.

42. See Vejvoda, "Civil Society versus Slobodan Milosevic," 316. Ivan Marovic quote from interview with the authors, May 8, 2015.

43. Ivan Marovic, "In Defense of Otpor," openDemocracy, December 6, 2013, https://www.opendemocracy.net/civilresistance/ivan-marovic/in-defense-of-otpor; see also Nenadic and Belcevic, "Serbia—Nonviolent Struggle for Democracy," 33; and Jorgen Johansen, "External Financing of Opposition Movements," in *People Power: Unarmed Resistance and Global Solidarity*, ed. Howard Clark (London: Pluto Press, 2009), 198–205.

44. "A sort of People Power International" quoted from Jesse Walker, "The 50 Habits of Highly Effective Revolutionaries," Reason.com, September 21, 2006, http://reason.com/archives/2006/09/21/the-50-habits-of-highly-effect/print. Stephen Zunes quoted from Zunes, "Serbia: 10 Years Later," Foreign Policy In Focus, June 17, 2009, http://fpif.org/serbia_10_years_later/.

45. Popovic as quoted in Philip Shishkin, "American Revolutionary: Quiet Boston Scholar Inspires Rebels Around the World," *Wall Street Journal*, September 13, 2008, http://online.wsj.com/article/SB122127204268531319.html. Marovic as quoted in Adam Reilly, "The Dictator Slayer," *The Boston Phoenix*, December 5, 2007, http://thephoenix.com/Boston/news/52417-dictator-slayer/.

46. Ivan Marovic, interview with the authors, July 18, 2013.

CHAPTER FOUR: THE PILLARS

1. Statistics from 1990 as cited by Michael J. Klarman, "How Same-Sex Marriage Came to Be: On Activism, Litigation, and Social Change in America," *Harvard Magazine*, March–April 2013, http://harvardmagazine.com/2013/03/how-same-sex-marriage

-came-to-be. Bill Clinton quoted from "President's Statement on DOMA," September 20, 1996, http://www.cs.cmu.edu/afs/cs/user/scotts/ftp/wpaf2mc/clinton.html.

2. "In some ways worse than terrorism" and "resounding, coast-to-coast rejection of gay marriage" as quoted in Klarman, "How Same-Sex Marriage Came to Be."

3. As quoted in Roberta Kaplan, "Gay Marriage Battle Hinged on a Great Love Story," CNN, June 25, 2014, http://www.cnn.com/2014/06/25/opinion/kaplan-doma-edie -windsor/.

4. See Gene Sharp, *Waging Nonviolent Struggle: 20th Century Practice and 21st Century Potential* (Boston: Porter Sargent Publishers, 2005), 26–27.

5. See Gene Sharp, *The Politics of Nonviolent Action: Part One—Power and Struggle* (Boston: Porter Sargent Publishers, 1973), 16; and Sharp, *Waging Nonviolent Struggle*, 28.

6. As quoted in Matthew Collin, *The Time of the Rebels: Youth Resistance Movements and 21st Century Revolutions* (London: Profile Books, 2007), 5.

7. See Brian Martin, "Gene Sharp's Theory of Power," *Journal of Peace Research* 26, no. 2 (1989): 213–222; and Kate McGuinness, "Gene Sharp's Theory of Power: A Feminist Critique of Consent," *Journal of Peace Research* 30 (1993): 101–115.

8. See Robert L. Helvey, *On Strategic Nonviolent Conflict: Thinking About the Fundamentals* (Boston: Albert Einstein Institution, 2004), 9–18.

9. The Centre for Applied Nonviolent Action and Strategies (CANVAS), "Chronology of Events—a Brief History of Otpor," http://www.canvasopedia.org/images/books /OTPOR-articles/Chronology-OTPOR.pdf?pdf=History-of-Otpor-Chronology.

10. On the "Powder Keg" incident, see CANVAS, "Chronology of Events."

11. See Ivan Vejvoda, "Civil Society versus Slobodan Milosevic: Serbia, 1991–2000," in *Civil Resistance and Power Politics: The Experience of Non-violent Action from Gandhi to the Present*, ed. Adam Roberts and Timothy Garton Ash (Oxford: Oxford University Press, 2009), 308. Vejvoda writes, "Many academics were ousted from the university at this time for siding with the protesters. As a reaction they set up the Alternative Academic Education Network . . . which was in essence a parallel university." This network "quickly established itself as a hub of academic excellence and a gathering point for students and professors."

12. Ivan Marovic quoted from "Why Didn't They Shoot?," Retired Revolutionary, January 25, 2012, http://www.retiredrevolutionary.com/2012/01/why-didnt-they-shoot .html. Stanko Lazendic as quoted in Tina Rosenberg, *Join the Club: How Peer Pressure Can Transform the World* (New York: W. W. Norton, 2011), 259.

13. Analyst Joshua Paulson writes, "One of the major differences between the opposition demonstrations of 1996 and those of October 2000 was that the former included few, if any, workers. The fact that miners had gone out on strike against the Socialist regime of President Milosevic had an important symbolic effect similar to that produced by the workers of Poland's Solidarity movement when they struck against a workers' state in 1980." See Joshua Paulson, "Removing the Dictator in Serbia—1996–2000," in *Waging Nonviolent Struggle: 20th Century Practice and 21st Century Potential*, ed. Gene Sharp (Boston: Porter Sargent Publishers, 2005), 332–333. On religious leaders, see Serbian Orthodox Church statement, cited in the *New York Times*, September 27, 2000, A10, also quoted in Paulson, "Removing the Dictator in Serbia," 327.

14. Vejvoda, "Civil Society versus Slobodan Milosevic," 314.

15. Ivan Marovic, "Tavaana Interview: Ivan Marovic, Part 4," Tavaana, May 14, 2010, https://www.youtube.com/watch?v=WQkq_qtB8YE.

16. Michael Signer quoted from Signer, "How the Tide Turned on Gay Marriage," Daily Beast, June 20, 2014, http://www.thedailybeast.com/articles/2014/06/20/house -votes-to-defund-nsa-backdoor-searches0.html.

17. Martin Luther King Jr., "Where Do We Go from Here: Chaos or Community?," Chapter 5, as printed in *A Testament of Hope: The Essential Writings and Speeches of Martin Luther King, Jr.*, ed. James M. Washington (New York: HarperCollins, 1986), 612.

18. Frank Rich (frankrichny) wrote on Twitter, "For a journalist to claim that marriage equality revolution began in 2008 is as absurd as saying civil rights struggle began with Obama." April 17, 2014, https://twitter.com/frankrichny/status/4568489321615 89248. Andrew Sullivan responded to Becker's work at Sullivan, "Jo Becker's Troubling Travesty of Gay History, Ctd," The Dish, April 17, 2014, http://dish.andrewsullivan .com/2014/04/17/jo-beckers-troubling-travesty-of-gay-history-ctd/.

19. See Andrew Sullivan, "Jo Becker's Troubling Travesty of Gay History,"; and Justin McCarthy, "Same-Sex Marriage Support Reaches New High at 55%," Gallup, May 21, 2014, http://www.gallup.com/poll/169640/sex-marriage-support-reaches-new-high .aspx.

20. Andrew Sullivan, "Dissent of the Day," *The Dish*, April 18, 2014, http://dish .andrewsullivan.com/2014/04/18/dissent-of-the-day-57/.

21. Linda Hirshman, *Victory: The Triumphant Gay Revolution* (New York: Harper-Collins, 2012), 315.

22. As quoted in Marc Sandalow, "Exuberant Gay March in D.C. / Hundreds of Thousands Join Call for Equality," *San Francisco Chronicle*, May 1, 2000, http://www .sfgate.com/news/article/Exuberant-Gay-March-in-D-C-Hundreds-of-3240157.php.

23. As quoted in Adam Liptak, "A Tipping Point for Gay Marriage?," *New York Times*, April 30, 2011, http://www.nytimes.com/2011/05/01/weekinreview/01gay .html?pagewanted=all&_r=0.

24. See Linda Hirshman, "DOMA Laid Bare," Slate, March 10, 2011, http://www .slate.com/articles/news_and_politics/jurisprudence/2011/03/doma_laid_bare.html.

25. Statistics as cited in Klarman, "How Same-Sex Marriage Came to Be" and Justin McCarthy, "Same-Sex Marriage Support Reaches New High at 55%."

26. Wolfson as quoted in Peter Freiberg, "Wolfson Leaves Lambda to Focus on Freedom-to-Marry Work," *Washington Blade*, March 30, 2001, http://www.geocities.ws /evanwolfson/ftm_washblade.htm, and in Josh Zeitz, "The Making of the Marriage Equality Revolution," *Politico Magazine*, April 28, 2015, http://www.politico.com /magazine/story/2015/04/gay-marriage-revolution-evan-wolfson-117412_full.html #.VUd7-GbcOGM.

27. Josh Zeitz, "Making of the Marriage Equality Revolution."

28. Ibid.

29. See McCarthy, "Same-Sex Marriage Support Reaches New High at 55%."

30. Richard Kim quoted from Kim, "Why Gay Marriage Is Winning," *The Nation*, July 2, 2013, http://www.thenation.com/article/175091/why-gay-marriage-won.

31. See Ed Payne, "Group Apologizes to Gay Community, Shuts Down 'Cure' Ministry," CNN, July 8, 2013, http://www.cnn.com/2013/06/20/us/exodus-international -shutdown/.

32. President of the Southern Baptist Theological Seminary as quoted in Klarman, "How Same-Sex Marriage Came to Be." See also Gram Slattery, "After Years-Long Debate, Presbyterians Allow Gay Marriage Ceremonies," *Christian Science Monitor*, June 20, 2014, http://www.csmonitor.com/USA/USA-Update/2014/0620/After-years -long-debate-Presbyterians-allow-gay-marriage-ceremonies-video; and Scott Neuman, "Methodists Reinstate Minister Who Officiated at Son's Gay Marriage," NPR, June 24, 2014, http://www.npr.org/blogs/thetwo-way/2014/06/24/325331463/methodists -reinstate-pastor-who-officiated-at-sons-gay-marriage.

33. See Dylan Matthews, "In 2011, Only 15 Senators Backed Same-Sex Marriage. Now 49 Do," *Washington Post*, April 2, 2013, http://www.washingtonpost.com/blogs /wonkblog/wp/2013/04/02/in-2011-only-15-senators-backed-same-sex-marriage -now-49-do/.

34. Regarding President Obama: On the campaign trail in 2008, Obama had claimed that he was opposed to gay marriage for religious reasons. Top advisor David Axelrod, in a 2015 memoir, revealed that Obama never actually held any such religious objection but considered it politically expedient to say that he did. A few short years later, political winds were blowing in the opposite direction, and Obama, with the approval of his aides, deemed it appropriate to begin revealing his "true" position. See Zeke J. Miller, "Axelrod: Obama Misled Nation When He Opposed Gay Marriage in 2008," *Time*, February 10, 2015, http://time.com/3702584/gay-marriage-axelrod-obama/. On Bill Clinton, see Bill McKibben, "Is the Keystone XL Pipeline the 'Stonewall' of the Climate Movement?," Grist, April 8, 2013, http://grist.org/climate-energy/is-the-keystone -xl-pipeline-the-stonewall-of-the-climate-movement/. On Hillary Clinton, see Alan Rappeport, "Hillary Clinton's Changing Views on Gay Marriage," *New York Times*, April 16, 2015, http://www.nytimes.com/politics/first-draft/2015/04/16/hillary -clintons-changing-views-on-gay-marriage/; and Sam Biddle, "Remember When Hillary Clinton Was Against Gay Marriage?" Gawker, June 26, 2015, http://gawker.com /remember-when-hillary-clinton-was-against-gay-marriage-1714147439.

35. As quoted in John Nichols, "Not Just Hillary Clinton: Why So Many Republicans Are Embracing Marriage Equality," *The Nation*, March 19, 2013, http://www.thenation .com/blog/173405/not-just-hillary-clinton-why-so-many-republicans-are-embracing -marriage-equality.

36. Kim, "Why Gay Marriage Is Winning."

37. As quoted in "From DOMA to Marriage Equality: How the Tide Turned for Gay Marriage," NPR, July 9, 2015, http://www.npr.org/2015/07/09/421462180/from -doma-to-marriage-equality-how-the-tide-turned-for-gay-marriage.

38. Erica Chenoweth, "My Talk at TEDxBoulder: Civil Resistance and the '3.5% Rule,'" Rational Insurgent, November 4, 2013, http://rationalinsurgent.com/?s=My+ Talk+at+TEDxBoulder&submit=Search.

39. See Erica Chenoweth, "About," http://www.ericachenoweth.com/; and Chenoweth, "The Origins of the NAVCO Data Project (or: How I Learned to Stop Worrying and Take Nonviolent Conflict Seriously)," Rational Insurgent, May 7, 2014, http://

rationalinsurgent.com/2014/05/07/the-origins-of-the-navco-data-project-or-how-i
-learned-to-stop-worrying-and-take-nonviolent-conflict-seriously/.

40. Chenoweth, "My Talk at TEDxBoulder."

41. Chenoweth, "Origins of the NAVCO Data Project."

42. The research found that nonviolent campaigns boasted a 50 percent success rate, while violent struggles saw victories just 26 percent of the time. See Erica Chenoweth and Maria J. Stephan, *Why Civil Resistance Works: The Strategic Logic of Nonviolent Conflict* (New York: Columbia University Press, 2011), 7–9.

43. "The Leading Global Thinkers of 2013: Erica Chenoweth: For Proving Gandhi Right," *Foreign Policy*, 2013, http://2013-global-thinkers.foreignpolicy.com/chenoweth.

44. Chenoweth, "My Talk at TEDxBoulder."

45. With regard to the idea that "researchers used to say that no government could survive if five percent of its population mobilized against it," Chenowith cites Will H. Moore, "The 5% Rule and Indiscriminate Killing of Civilians," Will Opines, July 19, 2012, https://willopines.wordpress.com/2012/07/19/the-5-rule-and-indiscriminate -killing-of-civilians/; and Mark I. Lichbach, *The Rebel's Dilemma* (Ann Arbor: University of Michigan Press, 1998). "No campaigns failed once they'd achieved the active and sustained participation of just 3.5 percent . . . " quoted from Chenoweth, "My Talk at TEDxBoulder."

46. On the "active and observable engagement of individuals in collective action," see Chenoweth and Stephan, *Why Civil Resistance Works*, 30.

47. Dick Morris as quoted in "Chapter 4: The Clinton Years," PBS, http://www.pbs .org/wgbh/pages/frontline/shows/clinton/chapters/4.html. The Associated Press quoted from Ryan J. Foley, "Obama Says No to Triangulation Politics," *Washington Post*, October 15, 2007, http://www.washingtonpost.com/wp-dyn/content/article/2007/10/15 /AR2007101501049_pf.html.

48. David Roberts quoted from Roberts, "Supply, Demand, and Activism: What Should the Climate Movement Do Next?" Grist, February 22, 2013, http://grist.org /climate-energy/supply-demand-and-activism-what-should-the-climate-movement -do-next/.

49. Ivan Marovic quoted from interview with the authors, September 3, 2014. Frances Fox Piven and Richard Cloward quoted from *Poor People's Movements: Why They Succeed, How They Fail* (New York: Vintage Books, 1979), 24.

CHAPTER FIVE: DECLARE VICTORY AND RUN

1. See Geoffrey Ashe, *Gandhi: A Biography* (New York: Cooper Square Press, 2000), 286–287.

2. Regarding arrest numbers, Geoffrey Ashe cites the figure of 100,000 arrested: Ashe, *Gandhi*, 293. Judith Brown cites the lower figure of 60,000 people imprisoned: Judith M. Brown, *Gandhi: Prisoner of Hope* (New Haven, CT: Yale University Press, 1989), 242. Tagore as quoted in Ashe, *Gandhi*, 290, and in Louis Fischer, *The Life of Mahatma Gandhi* (New York: Harper and Brothers, 1950), 274.

3. See Peter Ackerman and Christopher Kruegler, *Strategic Nonviolent Conflict: The Dynamics of People Power in the Twentieth Century* (Westport, CT: Praeger, 1994), 195,

200. Nehru as quoted in Stanley Wolpert, *Nehru: A Tryst with Destiny* (Oxford: Oxford University Press, 1996), 126; and Arthur Herman, *Gandhi and Churchill: The Epic Rivalry That Destroyed an Empire and Forged Our Age* (New York: Bantam Books, 2008), 354.

4. Saul Alinsky quoted from Alinsky, *Reveille for Radicals* (New York: Vintage Books, 1989), 225. Rinku Sen quoted from Sen, *Stir It Up: Lessons in Community Organizing and Advocacy* (San Francisco: Jossey-Bass, 2003), xlvi, lvi. See also Arlene Stein, "Between Organization and Movement: ACORN and the Alinsky Model of Community Organizing," *Berkeley Journal of Sociology* 31 (January 1, 1986): 93–115, http://www.jstor.org/stable/41035376.

5. See Martin Luther King Jr., *Stride Toward Freedom: The Montgomery Story* (New York: HarperCollins, 1958), 109.

6. As quoted in Henry Hampton and Steve Fayer, *Voices of Freedom: Oral History of the Civil Rights Movement from the 1950s through the 1980s* (New York: Bantam Books, 1990), 25.

7. "At no time have we raised . . . " as quoted in David J. Garrow, *Bearing the Cross: Martin Luther King, Jr., and the Southern Christian Leadership Conference* (New York: Random House, 1986), 59.

8. Bill Moyer quote from Moyer, *Doing Democracy: The MAP Model for Organizing Social Movements* (Gabriola Island, BC, Canada: New Society Publishers, 2001), 50. More generally, social movement writers Joshua Kahn Russell, Jonathan Matthew Smucker, and Zack Malitz make two distinctions in discussing these dynamics. They distinguish between the *concrete* and *communicative* aspects of protests as well as ways in which different tactics advance both *expressive* and *instrumental* ends. See Joshua Kahn Russell, "Principle: Make Your Actions Both Concrete and Communicative (but Don't Confuse the Two)," *Beautiful Trouble: A Toolbox for Revolution*, ed. Andrew Boyd and Dave Oswald Mitchell (New York: OR Books, 2012), 154–155; and Jonathan Matthew Smucker, Joshua Kahn Russell, and Zack Malitz, "Theory: Expressive and Instrumental Actions," in *Beautiful Trouble*, 232–233.

9. Tom Hayden, *The Long Sixties: From 1960 to Barack Obama* (Boulder, CO: Paradigm Publishers, 2009), 9.

10. Edward T. Chambers, *Roots for Radicals: Organizing for Power, Action, and Justice* (New York: Bloomsbury Academic, 2003), 131.

11. As quoted in Gopalkrishna Gandhi, "The Great Dandi March—Eighty Years After," *The Hindu*, April 6, 2010, http://www.thehindu.com/opinion/op-ed/the-great-dandi-march-eighty-years-after/article388858.ece.

12. Gandhi as quoted in Gene Sharp, *Gandhi as a Political Strategist* (Boston: Porter Sargent Publishers, 1979), 11. Geoffrey Ashe quoted from Ashe, *Gandhi*, 284.

13. Mohandas Gandhi as quoted in Gandhi, "Great Dandi March."

14. See Ashe, *Gandhi*, 285.

15. Statistics on crowd size from Herman, *Gandhi and Churchill*, 336. Judith Brown quoted from Brown, "Gandhi and Civil Resistance in India, 1917–47: Key Issues," in *Civil Resistance and Power Politics: The Experience of Non-violent Action from Gandhi to the Present*, ed. Adam Roberts and Timothy Garton Ash (Oxford: Oxford University Press, 2009), 50. On the resignation of local administrators, see Ashe, *Gandhi*, 286.

16. Ashe, *Gandhi*, 292.

17. See Brown, "Gandhi and Civil Resistance in India," 50.

18. See Peter Ackerman and Jack Duvall, *A Force More Powerful: A Century of Nonviolent Conflict* (New York: Palgrave, 2000), 100–101.

19. For discussion of the terms of the settlement, see Ackerman and Kreugler, *Strategic Nonviolent Conflict*, 195.

20. Joan Bondurant quoted from Bondurant, *Conquest of Violence: The Gandhian Philosophy of Conflict* (Berkeley: University of California Press, 1965), 38.

21. Geoffrey Ashe quoted from Ashe, *Gandhi*, 297. Churchill as quoted in Herman, *Gandhi and Churchill*, 359.

22. As quoted in Herman, *Gandhi and Churchill*, 357.

23. Ashe, *Gandhi*, 298.

24. Fischer, *Life of Mahatma Gandhi*, 274–275. Although they present a generally critical-minded assessment of the Salt March's outcomes, Ackerman and Kruegler write, "Strategic nonviolent conflict mounted a significant challenge to the British Raj and did lay the groundwork for subsequent struggles for independence that ended in success." Writing about the Salt March, they acknowledge, "Most rational observers from this point onward considered eventual independence inevitable." Ackerman and Kruegler, *Strategic Nonviolent Conflict*, 199–200.

25. Brown, "Gandhi and Civil Resistance in India," 54.

26. As quoted in Diane McWhorter, *Carry Me Home: Birmingham, Alabama: The Climactic Battle of the Civil Rights Revolution* (New York: Simon & Schuster, 2001), 387.

27. See McWhorter, *Carry Me Home*, 388.

28. Smyer as quoted in Garrow, *Bearing the Cross*, 262. The *New York Times* quoted from Claude Sitton, "Birmingham Pact Sets Timetable for Integration," *New York Times*, May 11, 1963. *Time* magazine as quoted in Adam Fairclough, *To Redeem the Soul of America: The Southern Christian Leadership Conference and Martin Luther King, Jr.* (Athens: University of Georgia Press, 1987), 129.

29. McWhorter, *Carry Me Home*, 403.

30. Garrow, *Bearing the Cross*, 264.

31. President Kennedy as quoted in Fairclough, *To Redeem the Soul of America*, 134. Andrew Young quoted from Young, *An Easy Burden: The Civil Rights Movement and the Transformation of America* (Waco, TX: Baylor University Press, 2008), 252.

32. Garrow, *Bearing the Cross*, 351.

33. Fairclough, *To Redeem the Soul of America*, 134.

34. William J. Dobson, *The Dictator's Learning Curve: Inside the Global Battle for Democracy* (New York: Doubleday, 2012), 250–251.

35. Ivan Marovic, interview with the authors, September 3, 2014.

36. See Tina Rosenberg, *Join the Club: How Peer Pressure Can Transform the World* (New York: W. W. Norton, 2011), 266.

37. Ivan Marovic, interview with the authors, September 3, 2014.

38. Patrick Reinsborough and Doyle Canning of the Center for Story-Based Strategy (formerly called *smart*Meme) use the concepts of "action logic" and "meta-verbs" to explain this principle. They write: "Action logic means that the actions you take have an overarching self-evident narrative logic that speaks for itself and tells a story. . . . Action

logic is frequently summarized through the shorthand of a single action-oriented meta-verb that is part of how the action or campaign is publicized. The meta-verb you choose—Protest! Rally against! Shut down! Mobilize! Stop! Transform!—will likely become the benchmark of the action's success, not only to the participants, but also to media observers and the general public." See Patrick Reinsborough and Doyle Canning, *Re:Imagining Change: How to Use Story-Based Strategy to Win Campaigns, Build Movements, and Change the World* (Oakland, CA: PM Press, 2010), 62.

39. This was just as well from the perspective of progressive critics who had previously taken issue with the march's politics on a variety of fronts, ranging from the event's exclusion of women to Farrakhan's adoption of conservative tropes about the need for black men to accept "personal responsibility" for problems in their communities. For comments from critics, including Adolph Reed and Michelle Boyd, see Don Terry, "Black March Stirs Passion and Protests," *New York Times*, October 8, 1995, http://www.nytimes.com/1995/10/08/us/black-march-stirs-passion-and-protests .html.

40. Ivan Marovic, interview with the authors, April 24, 2015.

41. Danijela Nenadic and Nenad Belcevic, "Serbia—Nonviolent Struggle for Democracy: The Role of Otpor," in *People Power: Unarmed Resistance and Global Solidarity*, ed. Howard Clark (London: Pluto Press, 2009), 29.

42. Fairclough, *To Redeem the Soul of America*, 136–137.

43. Quotes from Brown, "Gandhi and Civil Resistance in India," 50, 54, and 44, respectively.

CHAPTER SIX: THE ACT OF DISRUPTION

1. "Show Transcript: Countdown with Keith Olbermann," The Countdown Library, October 21, 2011, http://www.countdownlibrary.com/2011_10_21_archive.html.

2. On the One Nation, Working Together march, see Peter Rothberg, "One Nation Working Together," *The Nation*, September 21, 2010, http://www.thenation.com /blog/154943/one-nation-working-together.

3. "Show Transcript: Countdown with Keith Olbermann."

4. As quoted in Henry Louis Gates Jr., "Who Designed the March on Washington?" PBS, http://www.pbs.org/wnet/african-americans-many-rivers-to-cross/history /100-amazing-facts/who-designed-the-march-on-washington/.

5. Frances Fox Piven and Richard A. Cloward, *Poor People's Movements: Why They Succeed, How They Fail* (New York: Vintage Books, 1979), 24.

6. Francis Fox Piven, *Challenging Authority* (Plymouth, United Kingdom: Rowman & Littlefield, 2006), 21.

7. Gene Sharp, *The Politics of Nonviolent Action: Part Two—The Methods of Nonviolent Action* (Boston: Porter Sargent Publishers, 1973), 357.

8. See "Number of Occupy Arrests," OccupyArrests.com, http://stpeteforpeace.org /occupyarrests.sources.html.

9. Krishnalal Shridharani, *War Without Violence: A Study of Gandhi's Method and Its Accomplishments* (New York: Harcourt Brace, 1939), 283–284.

10. As quoted in Laura Secor, "War by Other Means," *Boston Globe*, May 29, 2005, http://www.boston.com/news/globe/ideas/articles/2005/05/29/war_by_other _means?pg=full.

11. As quoted in Shridharani, *War Without Violence*, 284.

12. Gandhi as quoted in Norman G. Finkelstein, *What Gandhi Says: About Nonviolence, Resistance and Courage* (New York: OR Books, 2012), 51–52.

13. Lewis quoted from John Lewis and Michael D'Orso, *Walking with the Wind: A Memoir of the Movement* (Delran, NJ: Simon & Schuster, 2015), 99. On the Nashville sit-ins more generally, see Aly Passanante, "Nashville Students Sit-In for U.S. Civil Rights, 1960," Global Nonviolent Action Database, January 1, 2011, http://nvdatabase .swarthmore.edu/content/nashville-students-sit-us-civil-rights-1960.

14. See *Eyes on the Prize: American's Civil Rights Movement 1954–1985* (American Experience Films, 1987), documentary film. Transcript available at: http://www.pbs .org/wgbh/amex/eyesontheprize/about/pt_103.html.

15. As quoted in Randy Shaw, *The Activist's Handbook: Winning Social Change in the 21st Century*, 2nd ed. (Berkeley: University of California Press, 2013), 17.

16. Gene Sharp, *Waging Nonviolent Struggle: 20th Century Practice and 21st Century Potential* (Boston: Porter Sargent Publishers, 2005), 405–408.

17. Matthew Collin, *The Time of the Rebels: Youth Resistance Movements and 21st Century Revolutions* (London: Profile Books, 2007), 41–42. Danijela Nenadic and Nanad Belcevic similarly write, "Increased repression, rather than frighten off supporters, backfired. Instead it motivated people (including those previously passive) to offer greater support." Danijela Nenadic and Nenad Belcevic, "Serbia—Nonviolent Struggle for Democracy: The Role of Otpor," in *People Power: Unarmed Resistance and Global Solidarity*, ed. Howard Clark (London: Pluto Press, 2009), 31.

18. Celler as quoted in Gene Sharp, *The Politics of Nonviolent Action: Part Three—the Dynamics of Nonviolent Action* (Boston: Porter Sargent Publishers, 1973), 690. Alinsky as quoted in Sanford D. Horwitt, *Let Them Call Me Rebel: Saul Alinsky—His Life and Legacy* (New York: Alfred A. Knopf, 1989), 468.

19. An important early developer of the concept of the "dilemma demonstration" is George Lakey. See Lakey, *Powerful Peacemaking: A Strategy for a Living Revolution* (Philadelphia and Santa Cruz: New Society Publishers, 1987), 103–109.

20. Dennis Dalton, *Mahatma Gandhi: Nonviolent Power in Action* (New York: Columbia University Press, 1993), 112, citing *The Bombay Chronicle* March 28, 1930, 6. Dalton is also cited in Peter Ackerman and Jack Duvall, *A Force More Powerful: A Century of Nonviolent Conflict* (New York: Palgrave, 2000), 88.

21. Of her nine "fundamental rules governing the campaign" of Gandhian *satyagraha*, Bondurant's fifth rule is "*Progressive advancement of the movement* through steps and stages determined to be appropriate within the given situation"; see Joan V. Bondurant, *Conquest of Violence: The Gandhian Philosophy of Conflict* (Berkeley: University of California Press, 1965), 38. In *The Politics of Nonviolent Action*, Sharp stresses, "In a long struggle phasing is highly important, and the choice and sequence of methods may be the most important single factor in that phasing"; see Sharp, *Politics of Nonviolent Action: Part Three*, 503.

22. See Barbara Epstein, *Political Protest and Cultural Revolution: Nonviolent Direction Action in the 1970s and 1980s* (Berkeley: University of California Press, 1991), 65.

23. Stephen Lerner, "A New Insurgency Can Only Arise Outside the Progressive and Labor Establishment," *New Labor Forum* 20, no. 3 (Fall 2011): 9–13.

24. Tally of Occupy encampments at "Occupy Directory," http://directory.occupy .net/. Regarding the October 5 march, see Christina Boyle, Emily Sher, Anjali Mullany, and Helen Kennedy, "Occupy Wall Street Protests: Police Make Arrests, Use Pepper Spray as Some Activists Storm Barricade," *Daily News*, October 5, 2011, http://www .nydailynews.com/new-york/occupy-wall-street-protests-police-arrests-pepper -spray-activists-storm-barricade-article-1.961645; and Ryan Nagle, "SEIU's Statement of Support for Americans Occupying Wall Street," Service Employees International Union, October 5, 2011, http://www.seiuhealthcaremn.org/2011/10/05/seiu-statement -of-support-for-americans-occupying-wall-st/.

25. Aldon Morris quoted from Morris, *The Origins of the Civil Rights Movement: Black Communities Organizing for Change* (New York: The Free Press, 1984), 260.

26. See Diane McWhorter, *Carry Me Home: Birmingham, Alabama: The Climactic Battle of the Civil Rights Revolution* (New York: Simon & Schuster, 2001), 324.

27. Adam Fairclough, *To Redeem the Soul of America: The Southern Christian Leadership Conference and Martin Luther King, Jr.* (Athens: University of Georgia Press, 1987), 125.

28. Nehru as quoted in Frank Morales, *Jawaharlal Nehru* (Mumbai, India: Jaico Publishing House, 2007), 167.

29. Judith Brown quoted from Brown, *Gandhi: Prisoner of Hope* (New Haven, CT: Yale University Press, 1989), 241. Casualty and arrest statistics as cited in Geoffrey Ashe, *Gandhi: A Biography* (New York: Cooper Square Press, 2000), 291–293.

30. Andy Ostroy quoted from Ostroy, "The Failure of Occupy Wall Street," Huffington Post, May 31, 2012, http://www.huffingtonpost.com/andy-ostroy/the-failure-of -occupy-wal_b_1558787.html. Andrew Ross Sorkin quoted from Sorkin, "Occupy Wall Street: A Frenzy That Fizzled," *New York Times*, September 17, 2012, http://dealbook .nytimes.com/2012/09/17/occupy-wall-street-a-frenzy-that-fizzled/.

31. On the Cleveland action, see Josh Eidelson, "Now What?," *American Prospect*, November 17, 2011, http://prospect.org/article/now-what-0. Bridgette Walker as quoted in "VICTORY: Occupy Atlanta 'Occupy Our Homes' Turning Point," OccupyOurHomes, December 20, 2011, http://www.occupyourhomes.org/blog/2011/dec/20 /brigitte-walker-victory/.

32. Statistics on Bank Transfer Day cited in Jeff Gelles, "Bank Transfer Day a Boon to Credit Unions, Small Banks," Philly.com, November 6, 2011, http://www.philly.com /philly/news/133311428.html. Andrew Leonard quoted from Leonard, "Why Bank Transfer Day Is Only the Beginning," Salon, November 4, 2011, http://www.salon. com/2011/11/04/why_bank_transfer_day_is_only_the_beginning/. Kirk Kordeleski as quoted in Robert Dominguez, "Credit Unions See Huge Spike in Business Due to Debit-Card Fee Backlash Ahead of 'Bank Transfer Day,'" *Daily News*, November 4, 2011, http://www.nydailynews.com/news/money/credit-unions-huge-spike-business-due -debit-card-fee-backlash-bank-transfer-day-article-1.972525#ixzz1cyOUldb8. Diane Casey-Landry as quoted in Simon van Zuylen-Wood, "How Bank Transfer Day Will

Help the Banks It's Trying to Hurt," *New Republic*, November 4, 2011, http://www
.newrepublic.com/article/politics/97033/occupy-wall-street-bank-transfer-day.

33. See Ian Shapira, "Grad Katchpole, Who Sparked Bank of America Debit Fee Protest, Needs a Job," *Washington Post*, November 6, 2011, http://www.washingtonpost
.com/local/art-grad-who-sparked-bofa-protest-could-use-some-cash-flow/2011/11/04
/gIQA4uvMtM_story.html; and Martha C. White, "Occupy Wall Street, One Year Later:
Did It Make a Difference?" *Time*, September 17, 2012, http://business.time
.com/2012/09/17/occupy-wall-street-one-year-later-did-it-make-a-difference/.

34. These various campaigns were covered in such reports as: Josh Eidelson, "How
Occupy Helped Labor Win on the West Coast," Salon, February 24, 2012, http://www
.salon.com/2012/02/24/occupy_helps_labor_win_on_the_west_coast/; Mercer R.
Cook, "'Occupy' Bolsters Workers' Cause in Midst of Contract Negotiations," *The Harvard Crimson*, November 15, 2011, http://www.thecrimson.com/article/2011/11/15
/occupy_bolsters_workers_cause/; Josh Eidelson, "Occupy Verizon, Occupy the Labor
Movement," *The Nation*, October 24, 2011, http://www.thenation.com/article/164144
/occupy-verizon-occupy-labor-movement; Emily Witt, "Occupy Book Publishing!
HarperCollins, This Means You," *Observer*, November 11, 2011, http://observer
.com/2011/11/occupy-book-publishing-harpercollins-this-means-you/; and Jenny
Brown, "Ending Lockout, Teamsters Wrap Agreement with Sotheby's," *Labor Notes*,
June 1, 2012, http://www.labornotes.org/2012/06/ending-lockout-teamsters-wrap
-agreement-sotheby%E2%80%99s. Jack Mulcahy as quoted in Cate Patricolo, "Occupy
and ILWU Declare Victory as Contract Finalized with EGT," *Portland Occupier*, February 14, 2012, http://www.portlandoccupier.org/2012/02/14/occupy-and-ilwu
-declare-victory-as-contract-finalized-with-egt/.

35. Zaid Jilani, "CHART: Thanks to the 99 Percent Movement, Media Finally Covering Jobs Crisis and Marginalizing Deficit Hysteria," ThinkProgress, October 18, 2011,
http://thinkprogress.org/special/2011/10/18/346892/chart-media-jobs-wall-street
-ignoring-deficit-hysteria/.

36. Dan Beucke, "Occupy Wall Street After 2 Months: A Scorecard," Bloomberg,
November 17, 2011, http://www.businessweek.com/finance/occupy-wall-street
/archives/2011/11/scorecard_occupy_wall_street_after_2_months.html. See also Dylan
Byers, "Occupy Wall Street Is Winning," Politico, November 11, 2011, http://www
.politico.com/blogs/bensmith/1111/Occupy_Wall_Street_is_winning.html.

37. Richard Morin as quoted in Sabrina Tavernise, "Survey Finds Rising Perception
of Class Tension," *New York Times*, January 11, 2012, http://www.nytimes.
com/2012/01/12/us/more-conflict-seen-between-rich-and-poor-survey-finds.html. On
numbers of mentions of "income inequality" in US newspapers, see Jackie Smith and
Patrick Rafail, "Media Attention and the Political Impacts of Occupy Wall Street,"
Common Dreams, May 8, 2012, http://www.commondreams.org/views/2012/05/08
/media-attention-and-political-impacts-occupy-wall-street.

38. Andy Kroll, "Tomgram: Andy Kroll, Occupy Wall Street's Political Victory in
Ohio," TomDispatch, November 20, 2011, http://www.tomdispatch.com/post/175470
/tomgram%3A_andy_kroll,_occupy_wall_street%27s_political_victory_in_ohio/.

39. As quoted in Meghan Barr and David Caruso, "Now What? Few Tangible Effects
of Wall St Protests," Bloomberg, November 16, 2011, http://www.businessweek.com
/ap/financialnews/D9R27I4G1.htm.

40. On Cuomo's reversal, see Michael Gormley, "New York Tax Bill, Backed by Governor Cuomo, Hits Millionaires and Helps Middle-Class," Huffington Post, December 8, 2011, http://www.huffingtonpost.com/2011/12/08/new-york-tax-bill-backed-_n _1136579.html; and Thomas Kaplan, "Albany Tax Deal to Raise Rates for Highest Earners," *New York Times*, December 6, 2011, http://www.nytimes.com/2011/12/07 /nyregion/cuomo-and-legislative-leaders-agree-on-tax-deal.html?pagewanted=all. The Associated Press quoted from, "You Can Thank the Occupy Movement for These New Taxes on Millionaires in California and New York," Business Insider, December 10, 2011, http://www.businessinsider.com/occupy-taxes-millionaires-2011-12.

41. *Los Angeles Times* quoted from Andrew Tangel, "Occupy Movement Turns 1 Year Old, Its Effect Still Hard to Define," *Los Angeles Times*, September 15, 2012, http:// articles.latimes.com/2012/sep/15/business/la-fi-occupy-anniversary-20120915. For a partial record of Occupy Our Homes victories, see "Occupy Our Homes," Occupy Our Homes, October 16, 2012, http://occupyourhomes.org/stories/2012/oct/16/ooh -victories/. On the California Homeowner Bill of Rights, see "California Homeowner Bill of Rights," State of California Department of Justice, http://oag.ca.gov/hbor. See also "California Passes Homeowners Bill of Rights," Foreclosure Nation, http:// foreclosurenation.org/democrats/california-passes-homeowners-bill-of-rights/; and Carlos Marroquin, "Occupy Homeowners Advocates Key to Passage in California Homeowners Bill of Rights," Occupy Fights Foreclosures, July 2, 2012, http://www.occupy fightsforeclosures.org/occupy_homeowners_advocates_key_to_passage_in_california _homeowners_bill_of_rights.

42. Cara Buckley, "Beyond Seizing Parks, New Paths to Influence," *New York Times*, November 15, 2011, http://www.nytimes.com/2011/11/16/nyregion/occupy-wall -street-organizers-consider-value-of-camps.html?pagewanted=2&_r=2&hp.

43. See Tavernise, "Survey Finds Rising Perception of Class Tension."

44. Chris Cillizza quoted from Cillizza, "What Occupy Wall Street Meant (or Didn't) to Politics," *Washington Post*, September 17, 2013, http://www.washingtonpost.com/ blogs/the-fix/wp/2013/09/17/what-occupy-wall-street-meant-or-didnt-to-politics/. Andrew Ross Sorkin quoted from Sorkin, "Occupy Wall Street: A Frenzy That Fizzled."

CHAPTER SEVEN: THE WHIRLWIND

1. See Amy Offner, "Winning a Sit-In," *Labor Notes*, January 4, 2010, http://www .labornotes.org/blogs/2010/01/winning-sit; Victoria A. Baena, "A Decade Ago, Another Occupation," *The Harvard Crimson*, December 1, 2011, http://www.thecrimson.com /article/2011/12/1/2001-occupy/; and "The Harvard Living Wage Campaign in the Media," The Harvard Living Wage Campaign, http://www.hcs.harvard.edu/pslm /livingwage/media.html.

2. See Amy C. Offner, "The Harvard Living Wage Campaign: Origins and Strategy," *Employee Responsibilities and Rights Journal* 25, no. 2 (June 2013).

3. The testimonials were first printed on the website of the Harvard Living Wage campaign and subsequently published as a book by oral historian and photographer Greg Halpern. The online posting used pseudonyms ("Jane Mawson" for Carol-Ann Malatesta and "David Morrissey" for Frank Morley), while the book used real names.

See "Workers' Words," Harvard Living Wage Campaign, http://www.hcs.harvard.edu /pslm/livingwage/newworkers.html; and Greg Halpern, *Harvard Works Because We Do* (New York: Quantuck Lane Press, 2003), 29.

4. See "Worker's Words"; and Greg Halpern, *Harvard Works Because We Do*, 138.

5. The May 2000 report of the Ad-Hoc Committee on Employment Policies concluded, "Harvard provides very generous compensation and benefit packages and a favorable work environment." As quoted in Xavier de Souza Briggs and Marshall Ganz, "The Living Wage Debate Comes to Harvard," April 2002, http://marshallganz.com /files/2012/08/Living-Wage-A.pdf.

6. Amy Offner, interview with the authors, May 1, 2015.

7. Bob Herbert, "In America; Harvard's Heroes," *New York Times*, May 3, 2001, http://www.nytimes.com/2001/05/03/opinion/in-america-harvard-s-heroes.html.

8. See "Old Announcements," Harvard Living Wage Campaign, http://www.hcs .harvard.edu/~pslm/livingwage/announce.html.

9. McKean quoted from Benjamin L. McKean, "At Harvard, Living Wage Meets the Ivy League," *Los Angeles Times*, May 6, 2001, http://articles.latimes.com/2001/may/06 /opinion/op-59888. Offner quoted from interview with the authors, May 1, 2015.

10. As cited in *Occupation: The Harvard University Living Wage Sit-In*, documentary film, October 3, 2003, http://www.spike.com/video-clips/dsfkhh/occupation-the -harvard-university-living-wage-sit-in.

11. Amy Offner, interview with the authors, May 1, 2015.

12. Sanford D. Horwitt, *Let Them Call Me Rebel: Saul Alinsky—His Life and Legacy* (New York: Alfred A. Knopf, 1989), 401.

13. Aristide Zolberg quoted from Zolberg, "Moments of Madness," *Politics and Society* 2, no. 2 (Winter 1972): 183. In a related vein, sociologist Sidney Tarrow has studied "cycles of contention," such as the Revolutions of 1848, the student-led uprisings of 1968, and the democratic upheavals that brought about the fall of the Soviet bloc starting in 1989; according to Tarrow, these are periods in which heightened social conflict have reached their fullest expression and widest geographical diffusion. See Sidney Tarrow, "From 'Moments of Madness' to Waves of Contention," in *Strangers at the Gates: Movements and States in Contentious Politics* (New York: Cambridge University Press, 2012); and Sidney Tarrow, *Power in Movement: Social Movements and Contentious Politics* (Cambridge: Cambridge University Press, 1998), 91–105.

14. A notable exception to Cloward and Piven's typical focus is their essay "Disruptive Dissensus: People and Power in the Industrial Age," in which they consider the use of disruption as a "mobilizing model, as contrasted to an organizing model." See Richard A. Cloward and Frances Fox Piven, "Disruptive Dissensus: People and Power in the Industrial Age," in *Reflections on Community Organization*, ed. Jack Rothman (Itasca, IL: F. E. Peacock Publishers, 1999), 176.

15. See Bill Moyer with JoAnn McAllister, Mary Lou Finley, and Steven Soifer, *Doing Democracy: The MAP Model for Organizing Social Movements* (Gabriola Island, BC, Canada: New Society Publishers, 2001), 186. Additionally, a memorial statement prepared after Moyer's death noted a variety of biographical details from his early life. This document is available at http://web.archive.org/web/20120204070517/http://www .sfquakers.org/arch/mem/bill_moyer_memorial.pdf.

16. Moyer, *Doing Democracy*, 186.

17. Bill Moyer, "The Movement Action Plan: A Strategic Framework Describing the Eight Stages of Successful Social Movements," Spring 1987, 3, https://www.indybay.org/olduploads/movement_action_plan.pdf.

18. Moyer quoted from Moyer, *Doing Democracy*, 4. For an example of a popular training manual in the Alinskyite lineage, see Kim Bobo, Jackie Kendall, and Steve Max, *Organizing for Social Change: Midwest Academy Manual for Activists* (Orange County, CA: Forum Press, 2010).

19. Circulation numbers for the MAP as cited in Moyer, "The Movement Action Plan."

20. Moyer, *Doing Democracy*, 54.

21. Ibid.

22. On February 15, 2003, the day of action, see Phyllis Bennis, "February 15, 2003. The Day the World Said No to War," Institute for Policy Studies, February 15, 2013, http://www.ips-dc.org/february_15_2003_the_day_the_world_said_no_to_war/. On protests in San Francisco, see "Protest Creates Gridlock on SF Streets," SFGate, March 20, 2003, http://www.sfgate.com/news/article/Protest-creates-gridlock-on-SF-streets-2627975.php; and Tim Gee, *Counterpower: Making Change Happen* (Oxford: New Internationalist Publications, 2011), 170.

23. See "Immigrant Rights Protests Rock the Country: Up to 2 Million Take to the Streets in the Largest Wave of Demonstrations in U.S. History," *Democracy Now!*, April 11, 2006, http://www.democracynow.org/2006/4/11/immigrant_rights_protests_rock_the_country.

24. Moyer, *Doing Democracy*, 54.

25. Colvin as quoted in Margot Adler, "Before Rosa Parks, There Was Claudette Colvin," NPR, March 15, 2009, http://www.npr.org/templates/story/story.php?storyId=101719889. See also David J. Garrow, *Bearing the Cross: Martin Luther King, Jr., and the Southern Christian Leadership Conference* (New York: Random House, 1986), 15.

26. On Yacoub Ould Dahoud, see "Man Dies After Setting Himself on Fire in Saudi Arabia," BBC, January 23, 2011, http://www.bbc.com/news/world-middle-east-12260465. On Charles Moore, see Lindsey Bever, "A Texas Minister Set Himself on Fire and Died to 'Inspire' Justice," *Washington Post*, July 16, 2014, http://www.washingtonpost.com/news/morning-mix/wp/2014/07/16/79-year-old-retired-reverend-set-himself-on-fire-to-inspire-social-justice/.

27. See Hardy Merriman, "The Trifecta of Civil Resistance: Unity, Planning, Discipline," openDemocracy, November 19, 2010, https://www.opendemocracy.net/hardy-merriman/trifecta-of-civil-resistance-unity-planning-discipline.

28. Merriman, "Trifecta of Civil Resistance."

29. See Moyer, *Doing Democracy*, 138.

30. King quoted from Martin Luther King Jr., "Where Do We Go from Here: Chaos or Community?" Chapter 5, as printed in *A Testament of Hope: The Essential Writings and Speeches of Martin Luther King, Jr.*, ed. James M. Washington (New York: Harper-Collins, 1986), 167–168.

31. James Farmer as quoted in Adam Fairclough, *To Redeem the Soul of America: The Southern Christian Leadership Conference and Martin Luther King, Jr.* (Athens: University of Georgia Press, 1987), 135. "The surge of nonviolent protest . . . " quoted from

Fairclough, *To Redeem the Soul of America*, 141. Regarding arrest statistics, Fairclough cites the figures of "about 1000 demonstrations involving more than 20,000 arrests" by the end of the summer (135). Using a slightly more confined time frame, Taylor Branch cites "758 racial demonstrations and 14,733 arrests in 186 American cities" in the ten-week period after the Birmingham settlement: Taylor Branch, *Parting the Waters: America in the King Years 1954–63* (New York: Simon & Schuster, 1988), 825.

32. Krishnalal Shridharani, *War Without Violence: A Study of Gandhi's Method and Its Accomplishments* (New York: Harcourt Brace, 1939), 278.

33. Shridharani, *War Without Violence*, 279.

34. Regarding other living wage and antisweatshop sit-ins, see Aaron Kreider, "Sit In! A Tactical Analysis," January 19, 2005, http://www.bhopal.net/old_studentsforbhopal _org/Assets/sit-in-tactical-analysis.pdf; Rosanna Kim, "John Hopkins University Community Demand a Living Wage for Campus and Health System Employees, 1996–2000," Global Nonviolent Action Database, September 16, 2012, http://nvdatabase .swarthmore.edu/content/johns-hopkins-university-community-demand-living-wage -campus-and-health-system-employees-199; and Guido Girgenti, "Wesleyan Student-Labor Coalition Wins Living Wages and Unionization for Campus Janitors, 1999–2000," Global Nonviolent Action Database, February 2, 2014, http://nvdatabase .swarthmore.edu/content/wesleyan-student-labor-coalition-wins-living-wages-and -unionization-campus-janitors-1999-200.

35. Tina Rosenberg, *Join the Club: How Peer Pressure Can Transform the World* (New York: W. W. Norton, 2011), 265.

36. Edward T. Chambers, *Roots for Radicals: Organizing for Power, Action, and Justice* (New York: Bloomsbury Academic, 2003), 80–81. "Sending busloads of inner-city residents to picket . . . " and "filling the lobby of City Hall . . . " reference tactics described by Saul Alinsky himself. See Saul Alinsky, *Rules for Radicals: A Pragmatic Primer for Realistic Radicals* (New York: Vintage Books, 1989), 144 and 160.

37. Bill Moyer quoted from Moyer, *Doing Democracy*, 57.

38. Patrick Reinsborough and Doyle Canning, *Re:Imagining Change: How to Use Story-Based Strategy to Win Campaigns, Build Movements, and Change the World* (Oakland, CA: PM Press, 2010), 105. Piven and Cloward concur. "Disruptive protests have communicative power, the capacity—through the drama of defiant actions and the conflicts they provoke—to project a vision of the world different from that in ruling-class propaganda, and to politicize millions of voters," they write; Cloward and Piven, "Disruptive Dissensus," 173–174.

39. Zolberg, "Moments of Madness," 206. This passage is also quoted in Tarrow, "From 'Moments of Madness' to Waves of Contention," 144.

40. Moyer, *Doing Democracy*, 57–58.

41. Alinsky, *Rules for Radicals*, xx; and Cloward and Piven, "Disruptive Dissensus," 186.

42. Moyer, "Movement Action Plan," 2.

43. Ibid.

44. Moyer, *Doing Democracy*, 60, 5.

45. See Nathan Schneider, "Breaking Up with Occupy," *The Nation*, September 11, 2013, http://www.thenation.com/article/176142/breaking-occupy?page=0,0; and "Glenn, Pat and Stu Run Through the 8 Steps of a Successful Movement," Glenn Live!,

June 26, 2014, http://www.glennbeck.com/2014/06/26/where-does-the-tea-party
-fall-on-the-movement-action-plan/.

46. Moyer, *Doing Democracy*, 85.

47. Amy Offner quoted from Offner, "The Harvard Living Wage Campaign," 141.
Economics Professor Caroline Hoxby as quoted in "Airing Out the Living Wage," *Harvard Magazine*, January–February 2002, http://harvardmagazine.com/2002/01/airing
-out-the-living-wa.html.

48. McKean, "At Harvard, Living Wage Meets the Ivy League." See also Brad S. Epps,
Tom Jehn, and Timothy Patrick McCarthy, "Why Hoxby Is Wrong," *The Harvard Crimson*, October 25, 2001, http://www.thecrimson.com/article/2001/10/25/why-hoxby
-is-wrong-when-professor/.

49. Bill Moyer quoted from Moyer, *Doing Democracy*, 16.

CHAPTER EIGHT: THE DIVIDERS

1. See Lawrence K. Altman, "Rare Cancer Seen in 41 Homosexuals," *New York Times*,
July 3, 1981, http://www.nytimes.com/1981/07/03/us/rare-cancer-seen-in-41-homo
sexuals.html; Joe Wright, "Remembering the Early Days of 'Gay Cancer,'" NPR, May 8,
2006, http://www.npr.org/templates/story/story.php?storyId=5391495; and Elizabeth
Landau, "HIV in the '80s: 'People Didn't Want to Kiss You on the Cheek,'" CNN, May
25, 2011, http://www.cnn.com/2011/HEALTH/05/25/edmund.white.hiv.aids/.

2. As quoted in Landau, "HIV in the '80s."

3. Falwell as quoted in Hans Johnson and William Eskridge, "The Legacy of Falwell's
Bully Pulpit," *Washington Post*, May 19, 2007, http://www.washingtonpost.com
/wp-dyn/content/article/2007/05/18/AR2007051801392.html. On Reagan and AIDS,
see "History of HIV and AIDS in the U.S.A.," AVERT, http://www.avert.org/history
-hiv-aids-usa.htm.

4. *Los Angeles Times* poll as cited in Emma Mustich, "A History of AIDS Hysteria,"
Salon, June 5, 2011, http://www.salon.com/2011/06/05/aids_hysteria/. On Ryan White,
see Dirk Johnson, "Ryan White Dies of AIDS at 18; His Struggle Helped Pierce Myths,"
New York Times, April 9, 1990, http://www.nytimes.com/1990/04/09/obituaries/ryan
-white-dies-of-aids-at-18-his-struggle-helped-pierce-myths.html, as cited in Mustich.
See also Evan Thomas, "The New Untouchables," *Time*, September 23, 1985, http://
content.time.com/time/magazine/article/0,9171,959944,00.html#ixzz1ODE14wsi, as
cited in Mustich.

5. Deborah Gould quoted from Gould, *Moving Politics: Emotion and ACT UP's Fight
Against AIDS* (Chicago: University of Chicago Press, 2009), 50.

6. See "Massive Demonstration by ACT UP: Hundreds of Protesters Paralyze Wall
Street," ACT UP, http://www.actupny.org/%2010thanniversary/10th%20repor.html;
and "Larry Kramer on the 20th Anniversary of ACT UP, the Government's Failure to
Prevent the AIDS Crisis and the State of Gay Activism Today," *Democracy Now!*, March
29, 2007, http://www.democracynow.org/2007/3/29/larry_kramer_on_the_20th
_anniversary.

7. See Michael Specter, "Public Nuisance," *The New Yorker*, May 13, 2002, http://
www.newyorker.com/magazine/2002/05/13/public-nuisance.

8. "Interview with Larry Kramer," ACT UP Oral History Project, November 15, 2003, http://www.actuporalhistory.org/interviews/images/kramer.pdf.

9. See Janos Marton, "Today in NYC History: ACT UP Fights Back Against AIDS Crisis," Janos.nyc, March 10, 2015, http://janos.nyc/2015/03/10/today-in-nyc-history -act-up-fights-back-against-aids-crisis-1987/; and Abigail Halcli, "AIDS, Anger, and Activism: ACT UP as a Social Movement Organization," in *Waves of Protest: Social Movements Since the Sixties*, ed. Jo Freeman and Victoria Johnson (Lanham, MD: Rowman & Littlefield, 1999), 139–140.

10. Specter, "Public Nuisance."

11. See Douglas Crimp, "Before Occupy: How AIDS Activists Seized Control of the FDA in 1988," *The Atlantic*, December 6, 2011, http://www.theatlantic.com/health /archive/2011/12/before-occupy-how-aids-activists-seized-control-of-the-fda-in-1988 /249302/; and "Transcript: Acting Up," Sound Portraits, June 15, 2001, http://sound portraits.org/on-air/acting_up/transcript.php.

12. On the Jesse Helms action, see Mark Allen, "I Wrapped a Giant Condom Over Jesse Helms' House," WFMU, January 18, 2006, http://blog.wfmu.org /freeform/2006/01/i_wrapped_a_gia.html.

13. See David Handelman, "Act Up in Anger," *Rolling Stone*, March 8, 1990, http:// www.rollingstone.com/culture/features/act-up-in-anger-19900308; and Jason DeParle, "Rude, Rash, Effective, Act-Up Shifts AIDS Policy," *New York Times*, January 3, 1990, http://www.nytimes.com/1990/01/03/nyregion/rude-rash-effective-act-up-shifts-aids -policy.html.

14. Quote on Kramer from Jose Antonio Vargas, "The Pessivist," *Washington Post*, May 9, 2005, http://www.washingtonpost.com/wp-dyn/content/article/2005/05/08 /AR2005050800988.html. See also Josh Getlin, "Kramer vs. Kramer: Activism: Even Friends Say that Incendiary AIDS Activist Larry Kramer Is Sometimes a Man at War with Himself," *Los Angeles Times*, June 20, 1990, http://articles.latimes.com/1990-06 -20/news/vw-179_1_larry-kramer; and Michael Shnayerson, "Kramer vs. Kramer," *Vanity Fair*, October 1992, http://www.vanityfair.com/news/1992/10/larry-kramer.

15. "Interview: Larry Kramer," PBS, May 30, 2006, http://www.pbs.org/wgbh/pages /frontline/aids/interviews/kramer.html. Others in ACT UP group offered a subtler take: "The key to a good demo of this sort is to break the rules enough so people can't help but pay attention to what you're doing," activist Mark Allen would later write, "but not break them to the point where people hate you once they start paying attention to you." See Allen, "I Wrapped a Giant Condom Over Jesse Helms' House."

16. Petrelis as quoted in Handelman, "Act Up in Anger."

17. See "History of HIV and AIDS in the U.S.A." Randy Shaw quoted from Shaw, *The Activist's Handbook: Winning Social Change in the 21st Century*, 2nd ed. (Berkeley: University of California Press, 2013), 201.

18. See Joel Roberts, "Helms Sorry on AIDS, Not Race," CBS, June 9, 2005, http:// www.cbsnews.com/news/helms-sorry-on-aids-not-race/.

19. Jose Antonio Vargas quoted from Vargas, "The Pessivist."

20. See Steven Heller, "How AIDS Was Branded: Looking Back at ACT UP Design," *The Atlantic*, January 12, 2012, http://www.theatlantic.com/entertainment/archive /2012/01/how-aids-was-branded-looking-back-at-act-up-design/251267/; and Handelman, "Act Up in Anger."

21. As quoted in Specter, "Public Nuisance."

22. Specter, "Public Nuisance."

23. DeParle, "Rude, Rash, Effective, Act-Up."

24. See Andrew Tangel, "Occupy Movement Turns 1 Year Old, Its Effect Still Hard to Define," *Los Angeles Times*, September 15, 2012, http://articles.latimes.com/2012 /sep/15/business/la-fi-occupy-anniversary-20120915; and Tom Jacobs, "Study: Everyone Hates Environmentalists and Feminists," Salon, September 26, 2013, http://www. salon.com/2013/09/26/study_everyone_hates_environmentalists_and_feminists _partner/.

25. Frederick Douglass, "The Significance of Emancipation in the West Indies" speech, Canandaigua, New York, August 3, 1857; collected in pamphlet by author. As printed in *The Frederick Douglass Papers, Series One: Speeches, Debates, and Interviews—Volume 3: 1855–63*, ed. John Blassingame (New Haven, CT: Yale University Press, 1985), 204.

26. Gene Sharp, *The Politics of Nonviolent Action: Part Three—the Dynamics of Nonviolent Action* (Boston: Porter Sargent Publishers, 1973), 523.

27. Ibid., 524.

28. Ibid., 523–525.

29. Gene Sharp quoted from Sharp, *Politics of Nonviolent Action: Part Three*, 525–526.

30. Richard A. Cloward and Frances Fox Piven, "Disruptive Dissensus: People and Power in the Industrial Age," in ed. Jack Rothman, *Reflections on Community Organization* (Itasca, IL: F. E. Peacock Publishers, 1999), 173–174.

31. Francis Fox Piven, *Challenging Authority* (Plymouth, United Kingdom: Rowman & Littlefield, 2006), 104.

32. See Martin Luther King Jr., "Letter from a Birmingham Jail," as printed in *A Testament of Hope: The Essential Writings and Speeches of Martin Luther King, Jr.*, ed. James M. Washington (New York: HarperCollins, 1986), 289.

33. "White Clergyman Urge Local Negroes to Withdraw Support for Demonstrations," *Birmingham News*, April 13, 1963. The open letter is also posted at: http:// mlk-kpp01.stanford.edu/kingweb/popular_requests/frequentdocs/clergy.pdf.

34. King, "Letter from a Birmingham Jail," 291.

35. Ibid.

36. Ibid., 295.

37. See Andrew B. Lewis, "The Sit-Ins That Changed America," *Los Angeles Times*, January 31, 2010, http://articles.latimes.com/2010/jan/31/opinion/la-oe-lewis31 -2010jan31; and Richard K. Scher, *Politics in the New South: Republicanism, Race, and Leadership in the Twentieth Century* (Armonk, NY: M. E. Sharpe, 1997), 238.

38. See "Show Transcript: Interview on 'Meet the Press,'" The Martin Luther King, Jr. Papers Project, April 17, 1960, http://mlk-kpp01.stanford.edu/primarydocuments /Vol5/17Apr1960_InterviewonMeetthePress.pdf; and "'Meet the Press' with Martin Luther King, Jr.," March 28, 1965, http://www.c-span.org/video/?324749-1/reel-america -meet-press-martin-luther-king-jr-1965.

39. Numan V. Bartley, *The Rise of Massive Resistance: Race and Politics in the South During the 1950's* (1969; repr., Baton Rouge: Louisiana State University Press, 1999), 90.

Gayle as quoted in "White Citizens' Council," The Martin Luther King, Jr. Research and Education Institute, http://mlk-kpp01.stanford.edu/index.php/encyclopedia/encyclo pedia/enc_white_citizens_councils_wcc/.

40. Political scientist Joseph Luders writes, "In addition to the Council, the Klan in Mississippi revived in the early 1960s with the escalation of civil rights protests." As a result, "organized segregationists wielded considerable clout in Jackson, and Mississippi more generally, until the mid-1960s." See Joseph E. Luders, "Civil Rights Success and the Politics of Racial Violence," *Polity* 37, no. 1 (January 2005): 122–123.

41. "I will never be out-niggered again," as quoted in "Wallace Quotes," PBS, http:// www.pbs.org/wgbh/amex/wallace/sfeature/quotes.html.

42. Nick Kotz, as quoted by Katrina vanden Heuvel in "Film 'Selma' Is About More Than 'Dreamers,'" *Washington Post*, January 6, 2015, http://www.washingtonpost.com /opinions/katrina-vanden-heuvel-film-selma-portrays-more-than-dreamers/2015 /01/05/257d00be-950f-11e4-aabd-d0b93ff613d5_story.html.

43. Donie Jones, as quoted in *Voices of Freedom: An Oral History of the Civil Rights Movement from the 1950s Through the 1980s*, Henry Hampton and Steve Fayer, (New York: Random House, 2011), 24.

44. Aldon Morris, *The Origins of the Civil Rights Movement: Black Communities Organizing for Change* (New York: The Free Press, 1984), 213.

45. Kirkpatrick Sale, *SDS: The Rise and Development of the Students for a Democratic Society* (New York: Random House, 1973), 23, as quoted in Morris, *Origins of the Civil Rights Movement*, 221.

46. George H. Gallup, *The Gallup Poll: Public Opinion, 1935–1971* (New York: Random House, 1972), 1894, as cited in Joseph E. Luders, "Civil Rights Success," 125. Michael Kazin quoted from Kazin, "Stop Looking for the Next JFK," *Dissent*, November 21, 2013, http://www.dissentmagazine.org/blog/stop-looking-for-the-next-jfk.

47. Luders, "Civil Rights Success," 126.

48. As quoted in Keith M. Finley, "Southern Opposition to Civil Rights in the United States Senate: A Tactical and Ideological Analysis, 1938–1965" (doctoral dissertation, Louisiana State University, August 2003), 333–334, http://etd.lsu.edu/docs/available /etd-0702103-151627/unrestricted/Finley_dis.pdf.

49. Howell Raines, "George Wallace, Segregation Symbol, Dies at 79," *New York Times*, September 14, 1998, http://www.nytimes.com/1998/09/14/us/george-wallace -segregation-symbol-dies-at-79.html.

50. See "S. 2454 (109th): Securing America's Borders Act," GovTrack, https://www .govtrack.us/congress/bills/109/s2454; and "S. 2611 (109th): Comprehensive Immigration Reform Act of 2006," GovTrack, https://www.govtrack.us/congress/bills/109 /s2611.

51. See "Rallies Across U.S. Call for Illegal Immigrant Rights," CNN, April 10, 2006, http://www.cnn.com/2006/POLITICS/04/10/immigration/; and "Immigrant Rights Protests Rock the Country: Up to 2 Million Take to the Streets in the Largest Wave of Demonstrations in U.S. History," *Democracy Now!*, April 11, 2006, http://www.democ racynow.org/2006/4/11/immigrant_rights_protests_rock_the_country.

52. See Rachel L. Swarns, "Immigrants Rally in Scores of Cities for Legal Status," *New York Times*, April 11, 2006, http://www.nytimes.com/2006/04/11/us/11immig

.html?pagewanted=all; Tara Bahrampour and Maria Glod, "Students Walk Out in 2nd Day of Immigration Rights Protest," *Washington Post*, March 29, 2006, http://www .washingtonpost.com/wp-dyn/content/article/2006/03/28/AR2006032800982.html; Joel Roberts, "Thousands Rally for Immigrants' Rights," CBS, March 24, 2006, http:// www.cbsnews.com/news/thousands-rally-for-immigrants-rights/; and Joel Roberts, "Student Immigration Protests Continue," CBS, March 28, 2006, http://www.cbsnews .com/news/student-immigration-protests-continue/.

53. As quoted in Bahrampour and Glod, "Students Walk Out."

54. Shaw, *Activist's Handbook*, 217.

55. Elizabeth G. Olson, "Where Will Occupy Wall Street Take Us?" *Fortune*, October 14, 2011, http://fortune.com/2011/10/14/where-will-occupy-wall-street-take-us/.

56. See Liz Goodwin, "The End of the Minutemen: Tea Party Absorbs the Border-Watching Movement," Huffington Post, April 16, 2012, http://news.yahoo.com /blogs/lookout/end-minutemen-tea-party-absorbs-border-watching-movement -173424401.html; and Lourdes Medrano, "What Happened to Minuteman Project? It's Still Roiling Immigration Reform," *Christian Science Monitor*, April 30, 2014, http:// www.csmonitor.com/USA/2014/0430/What-happened-to-Minuteman-Project -It-s-still-roiling-immigration-reform.

57. David Holthouse, "Minutemen, Other Anti-Immigrant Militia Groups Stake Out Arizona Border," Southern Poverty Law Center, Summer 2005, http://www.splcenter .org/get-informed/intelligence-report/browse-all-issues/2005/summer/arizona -showdown.

58. See "CNN: Lou Dobbs or Latinos in America?" video, October 13, 2009, https:// www.youtube.com/watch?v=IqKvSxmUoVQ.

59. "State and Local Immigration Laws," ACLU, https://www.aclu.org/issues /immigrants-rights/state-and-local-immigration-laws?redirect=immigrants-rights /state-anti-immigrant-laws.

60. On the "Today we march. Tomorrow we vote!" slogan, see, as one example, Swarns, "Immigrants Rally in Scores of Cities."

61. In the end, We Are America was not able to raise as much money or register as many voters as it had wanted to. Nevertheless, as the *Los Angeles Times* reported, "Angelica Salas, executive director of the Coalition for Humane Immigrant Rights of Los Angeles . . . and others said the pro-immigrant marches and rallies this year had energized record numbers of immigrants into volunteering for voter outreach and education programs." Teresa Watanabe and Nicole Gaouette, "Latinos Throw More Support to Democrats," *Los Angeles Times*, November 10, 2006, http://articles.latimes.com/2006 /nov/10/nation/na-latino10.

62. Andres Oppenheimer, "The Oppenheimer Report: Immigration Issue May Have Doomed GOP in Midterm Vote," *Orange County Register*, August 21, 2013, http:// www.ocregister.com/articles/immigration-197273-percent-republican.html.

63. As cited in Oppenheimer, "Oppenheimer Report: Immigration Issue." See also Michelle Mittelstadt, "Economy, War Cited for Hispanics Deserting GOP," *Houston Chronicle*, November 28, 2006, http://www.chron.com/news/nation-world/article /Economy-war-cited-for-Hispanics-deserting-GOP-1858192.php.

64. Karl Rove as quoted in Amy Clark, "'Today We March, Tomorrow We Vote,'" CBS, July 15, 2006, http://www.cbsnews.com/stories/2006/07/15/eveningnews /main1807172.shtml; and in Joshua Hoyt, "Full Throttle on Wrong Track," *Chicago Tribune*, December 5, 2008, http://articles.chicagotribune.com/2008-12-05 /news/0812040798_1_hispanic-vote-immigration-reform-sen-john-mccain.

65. On the 2012 election, see Elise Foley, "Latino Voters in Election 2012 Help Sweep Obama to Reelection," Huffington Post, November 7, 2012, http://www.huffingtonpost .com/2012/11/07/latino-voters-election-2012_n_2085922.html.

66. See Dara Lind, "The Massive Prisoner's Dilemma the GOP Faces on Immigration," *Vox*, January 5, 2012, http://www.vox.com/2015/1/5/7494179/immigration -republican-president.

67. As quoted in Kelsey Whipple, "Update: Undocumented Immigrant Activists Call Off Hunger Strike, Sit-In," *Westword*, June 11, 2012, http://www.westword.com/news /update-undocumented-immigrant-activists-call-off-hunger-strike-sit-in-5884616.

68. Statistic on undocumented immigrant population cited in Jens Manuel Krogstad and Jeffrey S. Passel, "5 Facts About Illegal Immigration in the U.S.," Pew Research Center, November 18, 2014, http://www.pewresearch.org/fact-tank/2015/07/24/5 -facts-about-illegal-immigration-in-the-u-s/.

69. See Julia Preston and Helene Cooper, "After Chorus of Protest, New Tune on Deportations," *New York Times*, June 17, 2012, http://www.nytimes.com/2012/06/18 /us/politics/deportation-policy-change-came-after-protests.html; "DREAM Act Protesters Who Staged Sit-In at Obama's Denver Campaign Office, Call Off Hunger Strike, Vow More Actions to Come," Huffington Post, June 13, 2012, http://www.huffington post.com/2012/06/13/dream-act-protesters-who-_n_1593739.html; and "National Immigrant Youth Alliance Responds to Obama Administration's New Policy Toward Immigrant Youth," National Immigrant Youth Alliance, June 15, 2011, https://solidari ty-us.org/node/3630.

70. Preston and Cooper, "After Chorus of Protest."

71. See "Trail of DREAMs Walkers Arrive in Washington, D.C. to Deliver Message to President Obama," Trail of DREAMs, http://www.trail2010.org/press/obama/; Bertrand M. Gutierrez, "Young Immigrants Arrested During Charlotte Protest," *Winston -Salem Journal*, September 6, 2011, http://www.journalnow.com/news/local /young-immigrants-arrested-during-charlotte-protest/article_139bc926-665f-5159 -a64f-71ba3a4f2e94.html; Julianne Hing, "Six Undocumented Students Arrested for Protesting Georgia's HB 87," Colorlines, June 28, 2011, http://www.colorlines.com /articles/six-undocumented-students-arrested-protesting-georgias-hb-87; and "Rep. Luis Gutierrez Arrested Outside White House Protesting Record Deportations Under Obama's Watch," *Democracy Now!*, July 29, 2011, http://www.democracynow. org/2011/7/29/rep_luis_gutierrez_arrested_outside_white.

72. As quoted in Andrea Long Chavez, "DREAM Act Student-Activists Ramp Up Tactics, Risk Deportation for Cause," Huffington Post, December 16, 2011, http://www .huffingtonpost.com/2011/12/16/dream-act-students-risk-deportation_n_1152874 .html.

73. See Julia Preston, "Young Immigrants Say It's Obama's Time to Act," *New York Times*, November 30, 2012, http://www.nytimes.com/2012/12/01/us/dream-act-gives -young-immigrants-a-political-voice.html.

74. DREAMer as quoted in Julia Preston and John H. Cushman Jr., "Obama to Permit Young Migrants to Remain in U.S.," *New York Times*, June 15, 2012, http://www .nytimes.com/2012/06/16/us/us-to-stop-deporting-some-illegal-immigrants.html; see also Elise Foley, "Obama Moves to Protect Millions from Deportation," Huffington Post, November 20, 2014, http://www.huffingtonpost.com/2014/11/20/obama-immi gration-plan_n_6178774.html.

75. See "CBS News Poll," July 29–August 2, 2005, available at: http://www.polling report.com/immigration4.htm.

76. See "CBS News/*New York Times* Poll," April 22–26, 2009, available at: http:// www.pollingreport.com/immigration3.htm; and "CBS News/*New York Times* Poll," April 30–May 3, 2015, available at: http://www.pollingreport.com/immigration.htm.

77. David Noriega, "Alabama's Draconian Anti-Immigrant Law Dies with a Whimper," BuzzFeed, October 13, 2014, http://www.buzzfeed.com/davidnoriega/alabamas -draconian-anti-immigrant-law-dies-with-a-whimper#.rkj67qyR1. Mark Potok as quoted in Lourdes Medrano, "What Happened to Minuteman Project?"

78. "President Obama's Unilateral Action on Immigration Has No Precedent," *Washington Post*, December 3, 2014, http://www.washingtonpost.com/opinions/presi dent-obamas-unilateral-action-on-immigration-has-no-precedent/2014/12 /03/3fd78650-79a3-11e4-9a27-6fdbc612bff8_story.html. See also Michael D. Shear, "Obama, Daring Congress, Acts to Overhaul Immigration," *New York Times*, November 20, 2014, http://www.nytimes.com/2014/11/21/us/obama-immigration-speech .html?gwh=41DCD9819D6FEE8BD439BC01D3BC72F7&gwt=pay&assetType=nyt _now. Given the sweeping nature of the president's action, opponents have promised a legal battle; their challenges are now winding their way through the courts.

CHAPTER NINE: THE DISCIPLINE

1. As quoted in Judi Bari, *Timber Wars* (Monroe, ME: Common Courage Press, 1994), 267.

2. See Zachary Fryer-Briggs and Malcolm Cecil-Cockwell, "The Radicals: How Extreme Environmentalists Are Made," *The Atlantic*, February 8, 2012, http://www.the atlantic.com/national/archive/2012/02/the-radicals-how-extreme-environmentalists -are-made/252768/; and Mickey Z., "From Earth First! to Climate Ground Zero, Mike Roselle Is a Radical Lifer," Truthout, October 8, 2010, http://truth-out.org/archive /component/k2/item/92225:from-earth-first-to-climate-ground-zero-mike-roselle -is-a-radical-lifer.

3. Dean Kuipers quoted from Kuipers, *Operation Bite Back: Rod Coronado's War to Save American Wilderness* (New York: Bloomsbury USA, 2009), 48.

4. As quoted in Bari, *Timber Wars*, 274.

5. See Bari, *Timber Wars*, 269; and Mike Roselle with Josh Mahan, *Tree Spiker: From Earth First! to Lowbagging: My Struggles in Radical Environmental Action* (New York: St. Martin's Press, 2009), 125.

6. Press statements as quoted in Bari, *Timber Wars*, 267. See also Dean Miller, "Environmentalist Sabotage Threatens Loggers. Idaho Senator Wants to Make Tree-Spiking a Federal Offense," *Christian Science Monitor*, August 11, 1987, http://www.csmonitor.com/1987/0811/aspike.html.

7. Roselle, *Tree Spiker*, 126.

8. Ibid., 124.

9. See Jesse McKinley, "Judi Bari, 47, Leader of Earth First Protest on Redwoods in 1990," *New York Times*, March 4, 1997, http://www.nytimes.com/1997/03/04/us/judi-bari-47-leader-of-earth-first-protest-on-redwoods-in-1990.html; and Nicholas Wilson, "Judi Bari (1949–1997)," *Albion Monitor*, March 1997, http://www.iww.org/history/biography/JudiBari/1.

10. As quoted in Wilson, "Judi Bari."

11. Environmental activist Betty Ball reflected that Bari "innately understood the importance of community-based organizing, as opposed to the nomadic style that Earth First! had before that." As quoted in Wilson, "Judi Bari."

12. Bari, *Timber Wars*, 221.

13. See Douglas Bevington, *The Rebirth of Environmentalism: Grassroots Activism from the Spotted Owl to the Polar Bear* (Washington, DC: Island Press, 2009), 44; and Bari, *Timber Wars*, 14–15, 85.

14. Foreman as quoted in Bari, *Timber Wars*, 268. Alexander as quoted in *Timber Wars*, 267, 270.

15. Bari, *Timber Wars*, 219.

16. Ibid., 281.

17. Ibid., 222, 282.

18. Steve Ongerth, "The Secret History of Tree Spiking, Part 3," Earth First! Newswire, April 23, 2015, http://earthfirstjournal.org/newswire/2015/04/23/the-secret-history-of-tree-spiking-part-3/.

19. Bari, *Timber Wars*, 57–58.

20. See Bevington, *Rebirth of Environmentalism*, 41; and Bari, *Timber Wars*, 70.

21. See Bevington, *Rebirth of Environmentalism*, 45.

22. See Bari, *Timber Wars*, 127.

23. See Bevington, *Rebirth of Environmentalism*, 98.

24. Bevington, *Rebirth of Environmentalism*, 103–104. See also Bari, *Timber Wars*, 73.

25. See Bevington, *Rebirth of Environmentalism*, 46; Bari, *Timber Wars*, 72–78; and Roselle, *Tree Spiker*, 133.

26. Roselle, *Tree Spiker*, 135.

27. See Bevington, *Rebirth of Environmentalism*, 98.

28. As cited in Bevington, *Rebirth of Environmentalism*, 149.

29. Roselle, *Tree Spiker*, 209.

30. Michael Albert, *The Trajectory of Change* (Brooklyn, NY: South End Press, 2002), 26, as quoted in Matt Dineen, "Violence vs. Nonviolence," Indybay, August 15, 2002, https://www.indybay.org/newsitems/2002/08/15/1409331.php.

31. Gene Sharp quoted from Sharp, *The Politics of Nonviolent Action: Part Two—the Methods of Nonviolent Action* (Boston: Porter Sargent Publishers, 1973), 112–113; and

Sharp, *The Politics of Nonviolent Action: Part Three—the Dynamics of Nonviolent Action* (Boston: Porter Sargent Publishers, 1973), 601.

32. "Bring to the surface the hidden tension that is already alive" quoted from Martin Luther King Jr., "Letter from a Birmingham Jail," as printed in *A Testament of Hope: The Essential Writings and Speeches of Martin Luther King, Jr.*, ed. James M. Washington (New York: HarperCollins, 1986), 295.

33. King, *Autobiography of Martin Luther King, Jr.*, 329.

34. See Bari, *Timber Wars*, 50, 285.

35. Bari, *Timber Wars*, 284.

36. See "Little or No Change in Attitudes on Abortion; Clinic Bombings Are Universally Condemned," *Family Planning Perspectives* 17, no. 2 (March–April 1985): 76–78, http://digitalcollections.library.cmu.edu/awweb/awarchive?type=file&item=417631; and Laurie Goodstein and Pierre Thomas, "Clinic Killings Follow Years of Antiabortion Violence," *Washington Post*, January 17, 1995, http://www.washingtonpost.com/wp-srv/national/longterm/abortviolence/stories/salvi3.htm.

37. Boots Riley, "The use of the blac bloc tactic in all situations is not useful," Boots Riley's Facebook page, October 8, 2012, https://www.facebook.com/boots.riley/posts/10151186157408664.

38. As quoted in Gene Sharp, *The Politics of Nonviolent Action: Part Three*, 594.

39. See Seth Rosenfeld, "Man Who Armed Black Panthers Was FBI Informant, Records Show," The Center for Investigative Reporting, August 20, 2012, http://cironline.org/reports/man-who-armed-black-panthers-was-fbi-informant-records-show-3753; and Rosenfeld, "New FBI Files Show Wide Range of Black Panther Informant's Activities," Reveal (The Center for Investigative Reporting), June 9, 2015, https://www.reveal news.org/article/new-fbi-files-show-wide-range-of-black-panther-informants-activities/.

40. See Michael Linfield, *Freedom Under Fire: U.S. Civil Liberties in Times of War* (Brooklyn, NY: South End Press, 1990), 140; Todd Gitlin, "The Wonderful American World of Informers and Agents Provocateurs," *The Nation*, June 27, 2013, http://www.thenation.com/article/175005/wonderful-american-world-informers-and-agents-provocateurs; "Materials on the Tommy the Traveler Incident, 1970–1975," Hobart and William Smith Colleges Archives and Special Collections, https://library.hws.edu/archives/findingaids/findingaid.cfm?name=tommy; William Morrissey, "Who's Tommy the Traveler?" *New Orleans States-Item*, July 13, 1970, http://jfk.hood.edu/Collection/White%20%20Files/Informers%20And%20Provocateurs/Info-Prov%20012.pdf; and Jeremy Varon, *Bringing the War Home: The Weather Underground, the Red Army Faction, and Revolutionary Violence in the Sixties and Seventies* (Berkeley: University of California Press, 2004), 171–172.

41. See Rory Carroll, et al., "Men in Black Behind Chaos," *The Guardian*, July 22, 2001, http://www.theguardian.com/world/2001/jul/23/globalisation.davidpallister. Regarding activist accusations, see "Blackbloc FAQ," Infoshop, January 31, 2004, http://www.infoshop.org/Blackbloc-Faq.

42. See Michael M. Phillips and Yaroslav Trofimov, "Police Infiltrate Radical Protest Groups to Stop Antiglobalization Demonstrations," *Wall Street Journal*, September 11, 2001, http://www.wsj.com/articles/SB1000154442745453472; and "Genoa Police 'Ad-

mit Fabrication,'" BBC News, January 7, 2003, http://news.bbc.co.uk/2/hi/europe /2636647.stm.

43. Jeffrey S. Juris, *Networking Futures: The Movement Against Corporate Globalization* (Durham, NC: Duke University Press, 2008), 195–196.

44. See Rick Perlstein, "How FBI Entrapment Is Inventing 'Terrorists'–and Letting Bad Guys Off the Hook," *Rolling Stone*, May 15, 2012, http://www.rollingstone.com /politics/news/how-fbi-entrapment-is-inventing-terrorists-and-letting-bad-guys-off -the-hook-20120515; Jake Olzen, "Entrapment of Cleveland 5 and NATO 3 Is Nothing New," Waging Nonviolence, May 20, 2012, http://wagingnonviolence.org/feature /entrapment-of-cleveland-5-and-the-nato-3-is-nothing-new/; and Ryan J. Reilly, "Occupy Cleveland Distances Itself from May Day Bridge Bomb Plot," Talking Points Memo, http://talkingpointsmemo.com/muckraker/occupy-cleveland-distances-itself -from-may-day-bridge-bomb-plot?ref=fpblg.

45. Todd Gitlin, *The Whole World Is Watching: Mass Media in the Making and Unmaking of the New Left* (Berkeley: University of California Press, 1980), 189.

46. As quoted in Varon, *Bringing the War Home*, 81.

47. Mark Rudd quoted from Rudd, *Underground: My Life with SDS and the Weathermen* (New York: HarperCollins, 2009), 156. Dohrn as quoted in Rudd, *Underground*, 189; and Varon, *Bringing the War Home*, 160.

48. SDS membership estimates as cited in Max Elbaum, *Revolution in the Air: Sixties Radicals Turn to Lenin, Mao and Che* (Brooklyn, NY: Verso, 2002), 69. FBI report as quoted in Rudd, *Underground*, 190.

49. Rudd, *Underground*, 190.

50. Ibid., ix.

51. See Rudd, *Underground*, 161, 191; and Varon, *Bringing the War Home*, 171.

52. Rudd, *Underground*, 156.

53. See "Insurrectionary Anarchy," *Do or Die*, no. 10 (2003), http://www.eco-action .org/dod/no10/anarchy.htm; and Peter Gelderloos, "Insurrection vs. Organization," 2007, http://theanarchistlibrary.org/library/peter-gelderloos-insurrection-vs-organization.

54. Rebecca Solnit quoted from Solnit, "Throwing Out the Master's Tools and Building a Better House: Thoughts on the Importance of Nonviolence in the Occupy Revolution," Common Dreams, November 14, 2011, http://www.commondreams.org/ views/2011/11/14/throwing-out-masters-tools-and-building-better-house-thoughts -importance.

55. Roselle, *Tree Spiker*, 205.

56. Gene Sharp, *Politics of Nonviolent Action: Part Three*, 606.

57. "Deadwood Bummer" and "leading lambs to the slaughter" quoted from Kuipers, *Operation Bite Back*, 64.

58. As quoted in Kuipers, *Operation Bite Back*, 272.

59. Kurt Schock, *Unarmed Insurrections: People Power Movements in Nondemocracies* (Minneapolis: University of Minnesota Press, 2005), 47.

60. See Erica Chenoweth, "Nonviolent Discipline and Violent Flanks" (conference presentation, Fletcher Summer Institute for the Advanced Study of Nonviolent Conflict, Medford, MA, June 10, 2015), https://www.youtube.com/watch?v=2VlVsRW F9y8.

CHAPTER TEN: THE ECOLOGY OF CHANGE

1. Ahmed Salah, interview with the authors, January 31, 2014.

2. See Simon Tisdall, "Hosni Mubarak: Egyptian 'Pharaoh' Dethroned Amid Gunfire and Blood," *The Guardian*, February 11, 2011, http://www.theguardian.com /world/2011/feb/11/hosni-mubarak-resigns-analysis. Salah as quoted in Ahmed Salah and Alex Mayyasi, "The Spark: Starting the Revolution," Huffington Post, July 29, 2013, http://www.huffingtonpost.com/ahmed-salah/egypt-january-25-revolution_b_367 1877.html.

3. Ahmed Salah, interview with the authors, January 31, 2014.

4. "Ahmed Salah" interview, International Center on Nonviolent Conflict, http:// www.nonviolent-conflict.org/index.php/learning-and-resources/on-the-ground /1547-ahmed-salah.

5. David D. Kirkpatrick, "Egypt Erupts in Jubilation as Mubarak Steps Down," *New York Times*, February 11, 2011, http://www.nytimes.com/2011/02/12/world/middleeast /12egypt.html.

6. As quoted in Tom Perry, "Egyptian Liberal Finds Enemies on All Sides," Aswat Masriya, January 26, 2014, http://en.aswatmasriya.com/analysis/view.aspx?id=04634519 -6119-413a-a06a-911c4aa9812c.

7. Hassiba Hadj Sahraoui, "Bitter Anniversary for Egyptian Women," Amnesty International, January 24, 2015, https://www.amnesty.org/en/latest/campaigns/2015/01 /bitter-anniversary-for-egyptian-women/.

8. See Robert Dreyfuss, "What Is the Muslim Brotherhood, and Will It Take Over Egypt?" *Mother Jones*, February 11, 2011, http://www.motherjones.com/politics /2011/02/what-is-the-muslim-brotherhood; Nadine Farag, "Between Piety and Politics: Social Services and the Muslim Brotherhood," Frontline, February 22, 2011, http:// www.pbs.org/wgbh/pages/frontline/revolution-in-cairo/inside-muslim-brotherhood /piety-and-politics.html; and Salah and Mayyasi, "The Spark."

9. David Wolman, "How the January 25 Egyptian Revolution Was Organized," *The Atlantic*, May 4, 2011, http://www.theatlantic.com/technology/archive/2011/05 /how-the-january-25-egyptian-revolution-was-organized/238336/.

10. See Fatma Naib, "Women of the Revolution," Al Jazeera, February 19, 2011, http://www.aljazeera.com/indepth/features/2011/02/2011217134411934738.html.

11. Salah and Mayyasi, "The Spark."

12. Ahmed Salah quoted from interview with the authors, January 31, 2014. For an overview of the structural and institutional forces activated by the growing uprising, see Paul Amar, "Mubarak's Phantom Presidency," Al Jazeera English, February 3, 2011, http://www.aljazeera.com/indepth/opinion/2011/02/20112310511432916.html.

13. See Dreyfuss, "What Is the Muslim Brotherhood?"

14. For examples of the use of "breaking the fear barrier," see "Egypt's Revolution Two Years On: 'The Fear Is Gone,'" *The Guardian*, February 1, 2013, http://www .theguardian.com/commentisfree/video/2013/feb/01/egypt-revolution-fear-video; and Naib, "Women of the Revolution."

15. *The Square*, Noujaim Films, 2013, documentary film.

16. Abdul-Fatah Madi, "Where Are the Youth of the Egyptian Revolution?" *Middle East Monitor*, November 23, 2013, https://www.middleeastmonitor.com/articles/africa/8467-where-are-the-youth-of-the-egyptian-revolution-.

17. See "Egypt Three Years On, Wide-Scale Repression Continues Unabated," Amnesty International, January 23, 2014, https://www.amnesty.org/en/latest/news/2014/01/egypt-three-years-wide-scale-repression-continues-unabated/.

18. See David D. Kirkpatrick, "Revolt Leaders Cite Failure to Uproot Old Order in Egypt," *New York Times*, June 14, 2012, http://www.nytimes.com/2012/06/15/world/middleeast/egyptian-revolts-leaders-count-their-mistakes.html.

19. Ahmed Salah, interview with the authors, January 31, 2014.

20. Gene Sharp, *From Dictatorship to Democracy: A Conceptual Framework for Liberation* (Boston: Albert Einstein Institute, 2008), 73.

21. See Adrian Karatnycky and Peter Ackerman, "How Freedom Is Won: From Civil Resistance to Durable Democracy," *International Journal of Not-for-Profit Law* 7, no. 3 (June 2005), http://www.icnl.org/research/journal/vol7iss3/special_3.htm.

22. Matthew Collin, *The Time of the Rebels: Youth Resistance Movements and 21st Century Revolutions* (London: Profile Books, 2007), 183.

23. See "The 1936–37 Flint, Michigan Sit-Down Strike," BBC, January 28, 2002, http://www.bbc.co.uk/dna/place-london/A672310.

24. Regarding the forces that organized the strike, most conventional narratives credit the UAW and the larger CIO; as an example, see "Sit-Down Strike Begins in Flint," History, http://www.history.com/this-day-in-history/sit-down-strike-begins-in-flint. However, Jeremy Brecher's history *Strike!* as well as Piven and Cloward's *Poor People's Movements* dispute this standard account. See: Jeremy Brecher, *Strike! Revised, Expanded, and Updated* (Oakland, CA: PM Press, 2014), 169–207; and Frances Fox Piven and Richard A. Cloward, *Poor People's Movements: Why They Succeed, How They Fail* (New York: Vintage Books, 1979), 96–180.

25. See Brecher, *Strike!*, 191.

26. See Brecher, *Strike!*, 191, 204; and Piven and Cloward, *Poor People's Movements*, 141.

27. As quoted in *Sit Down and Fight: Walter Reuther and Rise of the Auto Workers Union* (American Experience Films), documentary film, https://www.youtube.com/watch?v=l0bXOOjR_Uw.

28. The CIO later changed its name from the Committee for Industrial Organization to the Congress of Industrial Organizations. Regarding the efforts of John L. Lewis to capitalize on the sit-down strikes, see Piven and Cloward, *Poor People's Movements*, 151–153; and "John L. Lewis (1880–1969)," AFL-CIO, http://www.aflcio.org/About/Our-History/Key-People-in-Labor-History/John-L.-Lewis-1880-1969. Union membership numbers from *Sit Down and Fight*.

29. Piven and Cloward, *Poor People's Movements*, 157.

30. Moyer quoted from Bill Moyer with JoAnn McAllister, Mary Lou Finley, and Steven Soifer, *Doing Democracy: The MAP Model for Organizing Social Movements* (Gabriola Island, BC, Canada: New Society Publishers, 2001), 56.

31. Piven quoted from interview with the authors, March 5, 2015. Richard A. Cloward and Frances Fox Piven quoted from "Disruptive Dissensus: People and Power in

the Industrial Age," in *Reflections on Community Organization*, ed. Jack Rothman (Itasca, IL: F. E. Peacock Publishers, 1999), 176, 179.

32. See Piven and Cloward, *Poor People's Movements*, xvi.

33. As quoted in Sanford D. Horwitt, *Let Them Call Me Rebel: Saul Alinsky—His Life and Legacy* (New York: Alfred A. Knopf, 1989), 401.

34. Cloward and Piven, "Disruptive Dissensus," 178.

35. Rinku Sen, *Stir It Up: Lessons in Community Organizing and Advocacy* (San Francisco: Jossey-Bass, 2003), 21.

36. Ibid., 23.

37. Martin Luther King Jr., *Where Do We Go from Here: Chaos or Community?* (1967; repr., Boston: Beacon Press, 2010), 167. Page references are to the 2010 edition.

38. King, *Where Do We Go from Here*, 167–168.

39. Martin Luther King Jr., "Nonviolence: The Only Road to Freedom," as printed in *A Testament of Hope: The Essential Writings and Speeches of Martin Luther King, Jr.*, ed. James M. Washington (New York: HarperCollins, 1986), 60–61.

40. See Martin Luther King Jr., "The Trumpet of Conscience," as printed in *A Testament of Hope: The Essential Writings and Speeches of Martin Luther King, Jr.*, ed. James M. Washington (New York: HarperCollins, 1986), 651.

41. Steven Greenhouse, "Nike Shoe Plant in Vietnam Is Called Unsafe for Workers," *New York Times*, November 8, 1997, http://www.nytimes.com/1997/11/08/business /nike-shoe-plant-in-vietnam-is-called-unsafe-for-workers.html.

42. "Frequently Asked Questions (FAQ)," Workers Rights Consortium, http://www .workersrights.org/faq.asp.

43. Ibid.

44. See Randy Shaw, *The Activist's Handbook: Winning Social Change in the 21st Century*, 2nd ed. (Berkeley: University of California Press, 2013), 201.

45. See Tom Hayden, *The Long Sixties: From 1960 to Barack Obama* (Boulder, CO: Paradigm Publishers, 2009), 9–11.

46. See Luke Yates, "Rethinking Prefiguration: Alternatives, Micropolitics and Goals in Movements," *Social Movement Studies* 14, no. 1 (2015), http://www.tandfonline.com /doi/abs/10.1080/14742837.2013.870883#.VdKhBJf1_gA.

47. Wini Breines, "Community and Organization: The New Left and Michels' 'Iron Law,'" *Social Problems* 27, no. 4 (April 1980): 421.

48. See Jonathan Matthew Smucker, Joshua Kahn Russell, and Zack Malitz, "Theory: Expressive and Instrumental Actions," *Beautiful Trouble: A Toolbox for Revolution*, ed. Andrew Boyd and Dave Oswald Mitchell (New York: OR Books, 2012), 232–233.

49. Saul Alinsky, *Rules for Radicals: A Pragmatic Primer for Realistic Radicals* (New York: Vintage Books, 1989), xix.

50. Jonathan Matthew Smucker, "Theory: Political Identity Paradox," in *Beautiful Trouble: A Toolbox for Revolution*, ed. Andrew Boyd and Dave Oswald Mitchell (New York: OR Books, 2012), 254.

51. *Berkeley in the Sixties* (Kitchell Films, 1990), documentary film.

52. Cheryl Greenberg quoted from Greenberg, "Hands on the Freedom Plow: Personal Accounts by Women in SNCC (review)," *Kentucky Historical Society* 109, no. 1

(Winter 2011), http://muse.jhu.edu/journals/register_of_the_kentucky_historical
_society/summary/v109/109.1.greenberg.html.

53. Ori Brafman and Rod A. Beckstrom, *The Starfish and the Spider* (New York: Penguin Group, 2006), 96.

54. Claudine Ferrell as quoted in Ralph Dannheisser, "Quakers Played Major Role in Ending Slavery in United States," IPP Digital, November 12, 2008, http://iipdigital .usembassy.gov/st/english/article/2008/11/20081112170035abretnuh3.838748e-02 .html#ixzz3dS1KoPyt.

55. As quoted in Mary Lou Finley and Steven Soifer, "Social Movement Theories and MAP: Beginnings of a Dialogue," in *Doing Democracy: The MAP Model for Organizing Social Movements* (Gabriola Island, BC, Canada: New Society Publishers, 2001), 110.

56. Hayden, *Long Sixties*, 16.

CONCLUSION

1. For details about the Dorchester center, see David J. Garrow, *Bearing the Cross: Martin Luther King, Jr., and the Southern Christian Leadership Conference* (New York: Random House, 1986), 151, 161; and Andrew Young, *An Easy Burden: The Civil Rights Movement and the Transformation of America* (Waco, TX: Baylor University Press, 2008), 134, 144.

2. See "Minutes of Staff Conference Held at Dorchester," September 5–7, 1963, box 153, file 21, Southern Christian Leadership Conference Papers, Martin Luther King Center, Atlanta.

3. Saul Alinsky quoted from Alinsky, *Rules for Radicals: A Pragmatic Primer for Realistic Radicals* (New York: Vintage Books, 1989), xviii.

INDEX

Mark Engler, a writer based in Philadelphia, is an editorial board member at *Dissent*, a contributing editor at *Yes! Magazine*, and a senior analyst with Foreign Policy In Focus. He is the author of *How to Rule the World: The Coming Battle over the Global Economy*. He can be reached via the website www.democracyuprising.com.

Paul Engler is founding director of the Center for the Working Poor, based in Los Angeles. He worked for more than a decade as an organizer in the immigrant rights, global justice, and labor movements. Paul is one of the founders of the Momentum Training, which educates hundreds of activists each year in the principles of momentum-driven mobilization. For more information about the trainings, visit www .momentumcommunity.org.

The Nation Institute

**NATION BOOKS**

Founded in 2000, **Nation Books** has become a leading voice in American independent publishing. The inspiration for the imprint came from the *Nation* magazine, the oldest independent and continuously published weekly magazine of politics and culture in the United States.

The imprint's mission is to produce authoritative books that break new ground and shed light on current social and political issues. We publish established authors who are leaders in their area of expertise, and endeavor to cultivate a new generation of emerging and talented writers. With each of our books we aim to positively affect cultural and political discourse.

Nation Books is a project of The Nation Institute, a nonprofit media center dedicated to strengthening the independent press and advancing social justice and civil rights. The Nation Institute is home to a dynamic range of programs: the award-winning Investigative Fund, which supports ground-breaking investigative journalism; the widely read and syndicated website TomDispatch; the Victor S. Navasky Internship Program in conjunction with the *Nation* magazine; and Journalism Fellowships that support up to 25 high-profile reporters every year.

For more information on Nation Books, The Nation Institute, and the *Nation* magazine, please visit:

www.nationbooks.org

www.nationinstitute.org

www.thenation.com

www.facebook.com/nationbooks.ny

Twitter: @nationbooks